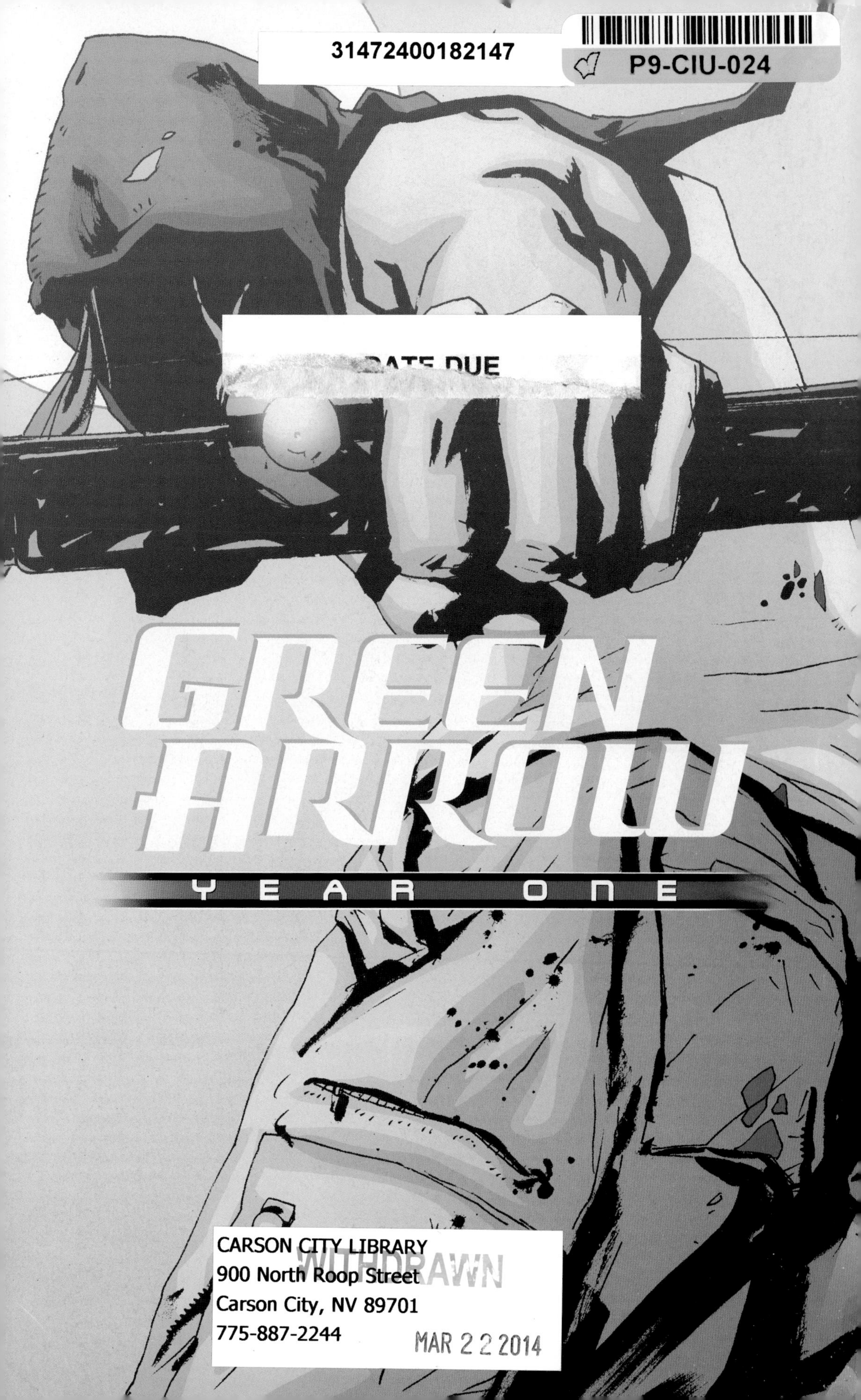
GREEN
ARROW
YEAR ONE

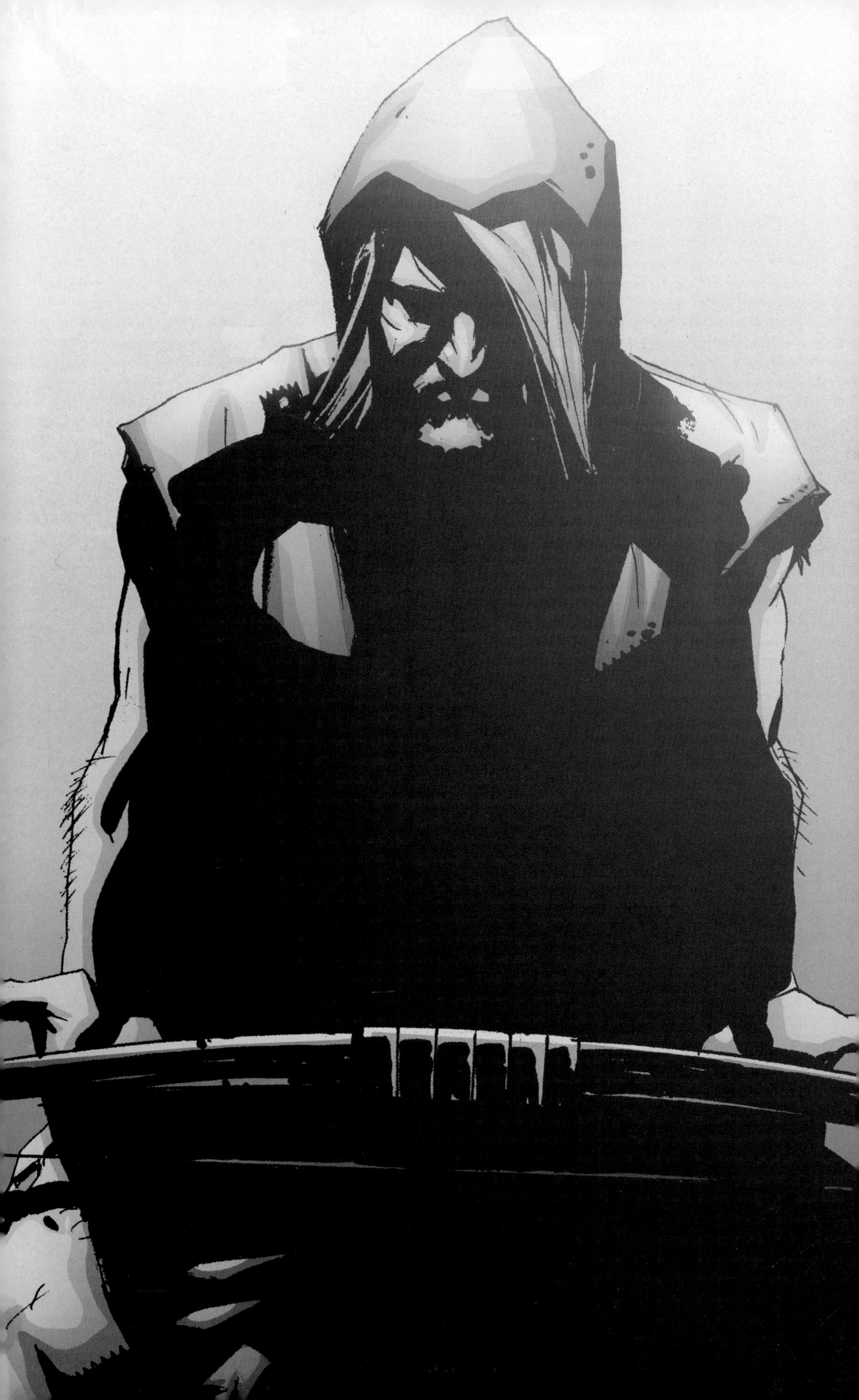

GREEN ARROW

YEAR ONE

Andy Diggle Writer

Jock Artist

David Baron Colorist

Jared K. Fletcher Letterer

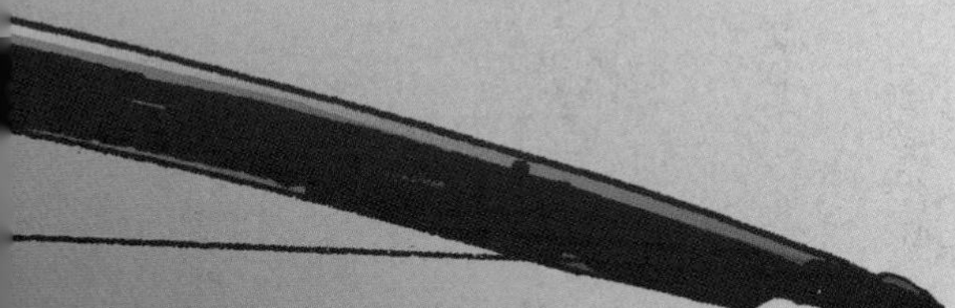

For Jake Oliver Diggle
ANDY DIGGLE

Dedicated to my Mum, Elizabeth Simpson,
who passed away unexpectedly while I was drawing this
JOCK

Mike Carlin
Editor – original series

Tom Palmer, Jr.
Associate Editor – original series

Anton Kawasaki
Editor

Robbin Brosterman
Design Director – Books

Bob Harras
Senior VP – Editor-in-Chief, DC Comics

Diane Nelson
President

Dan DiDio and Jim Lee
Co-Publishers

Geoff Johns
Chief Creative Officer

John Rood
Executive VP – Sales, Marketing &
Business Development

Amy Genkins
Senior VP – Business & Legal Affairs

Nairi Gardiner
Senior VP – Finance

Jeff Boison
VP – Publishing Planning

Mark Chiarello
VP – Art Direction & Design

John Cunningham
VP – Marketing

Terri Cunningham
VP – Editorial Administration

Alison Gill
Senior VP – Manufacturing &
Operations

Hank Kanalz
Senior VP – Vertigo &
Integrated Publishing

Jay Kogan
VP – Business & Legal Affairs,
Publishing

Jack Mahan
VP – Business Affairs, Talent

Nick Napolitano
VP – Manufacturing Administration

Sue Pohja
VP – Book Sales

Courtney Simmons
Senior VP – Publicity

Bob Wayne
Senior VP – Sales

Cover by Jock

GREEN ARROW: YEAR ONE

Published by DC Comics.
Cover, introduction and compilation
Copyright © 2008 DC Comics.
All Rights Reserved.

Originally published in single
magazine form in GREEN ARROW:
YEAR ONE #1-6. Copyright © 2007
DC Comics. All Rights Reserved. All
characters, their distinctive likenesses
and related elements featured in this
publication are trademarks of DC
Comics. The stories, characters and
incidents featured in this publication
are entirely fictional. DC Comics
does not read or accept unsolicited
submissions of ideas, stories or artwork.

DC Comics, 1700 Broadway,
New York, NY 10019
A Warner Bros. Entertainment
Company. Printed by RR Donnelley,
Salem, VA, USA. 2/7/14.
Fourth Printing.

ISBN: 978-1-4012-1743-3

Library of Congress
Cataloging-in-Publication Data

Diggle, Andy.
 Green Arrow : year one / Andy
Diggle, Jock.
 p. cm.
 "Originally published in single mag-
azine form in Green Arrow: Year One
1-6."
 ISBN 9781401217433
 1. Graphic novels. I. Diggle, Andy. II.
Jock. III. Title.
PN6728.G725 D55 2008
 741.5'973–dc23
                    2008295668

SUSTAINABLE
FORESTRY
INITIATIVE

Certified Chain of Custody
At Least 20% Certified Forest Content
www.sfiprogram.org
SFI-01042
APPLIES TO TEXT STOCK ONLY

Introduction by Brian K. Vaughan

These days, you only get one page.

A few years ago, readers would give you maybe five or six issues to decide whether or not they were going to follow a particular comic. But as our hobby grew more expensive and as countless new entertainment options cropped up to compete with poor ol' funny books, that window grew smaller and smaller. Today, we creators would be lucky to find a fan willing to give us the benefit of an entire issue. No, you have to wow 'em with that very first page or you fail the in-store "flip test," and back onto the rack go all of your stupid hopes and dreams.

The guys behind GREEN ARROW: YEAR ONE get this, completely, as evidenced by their perfect opener to this story, a clever, economic and insanely visual prologue that instantly establishes the themes, characters, and action-packed narrative about to unfold.

I would expect no less from Andy Diggle and Jock, two of my favorite creators making comics today. These two have both done excellent work with other collaborators, but they also make up one of those rare writer/artist duos that consistently bring out the best in each other. They're even greater than the sum of their exemplary parts, much like — wait for it — the proverbial bow and arrow. (I'll let them fight over who gets to be what.)

Calling any streamlined re-imagining of a character's origin "Year One" is a pretty ballsy move, since it invites comparisons to Frank Miller and David Mazzucchelli's decidedly incomparable Batman tale, but the story you hold in your hands actually wears that mantle pretty well. It's got all the fun of the boxing-glove-arrow-era from way back when the character was created by Mort Weisinger and George Papp, the slam-bang social relevance of Dennis O'Neil's groundbreaking Green Arrow/Green Lantern team-ups, and the bloodstained realism of Mike Grell's THE LONGBOW HUNTERS (a beautiful piece of storytelling from the unfairly maligned "grim and gritty" era that holds up surprisingly well).

Anyway, great as Diggle and Jock are at breathing new life into an old fave, this whole adventure wouldn't have worked nearly as well without the colors of David Baron, who helps turns China White (love that name!) into a genuinely frightening new villain. Special credit also to letterer Jared K. Fletcher, who makes even my off-key dialogue sing over in the pages of EX MACHINA every month.

So if you're still trying to decide whether or not to pick up this collection, quit reading my pointless rambling already and flip ahead to the real first page.

Because if you think that's cool, wait until you see Page Two…

Brian K. Vaughan
January 2008

Along with being a writer-producer on the television series Lost, *Vaughan is the co-creator of* Y: THE LAST MAN *and* PRIDE OF BAGHDAD. *His parents never let him have an archery kit, no matter how much he begged.*

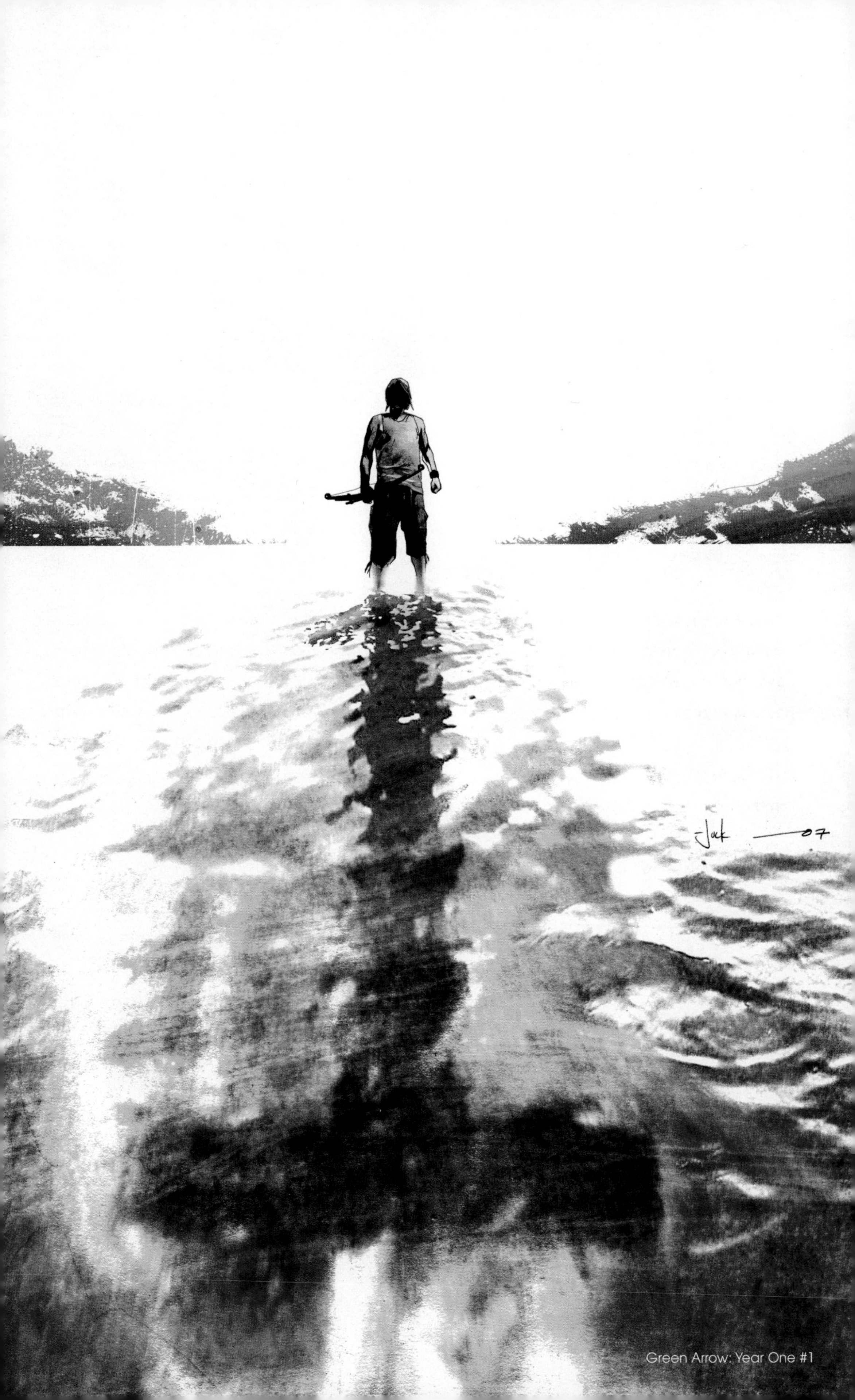

Green Arrow: Year One #1

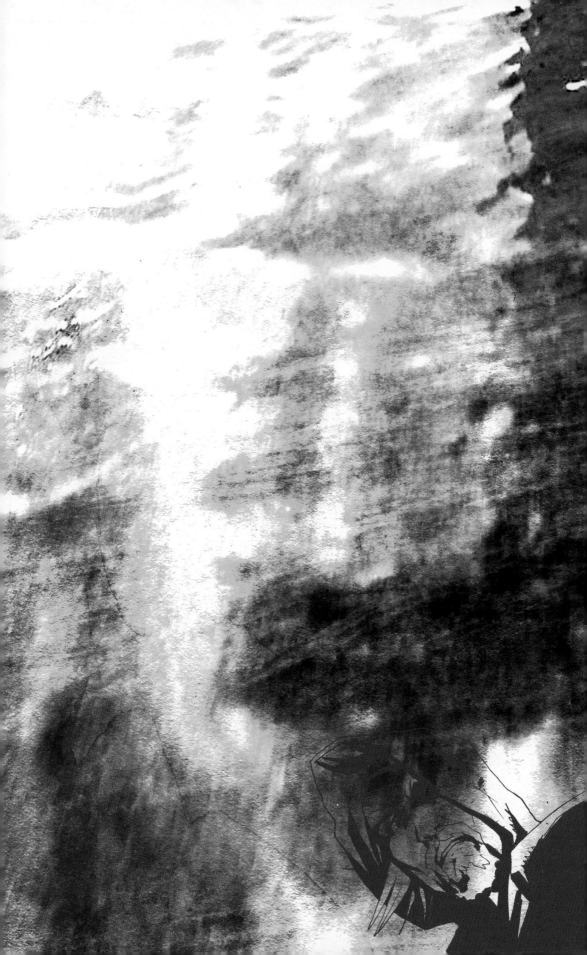

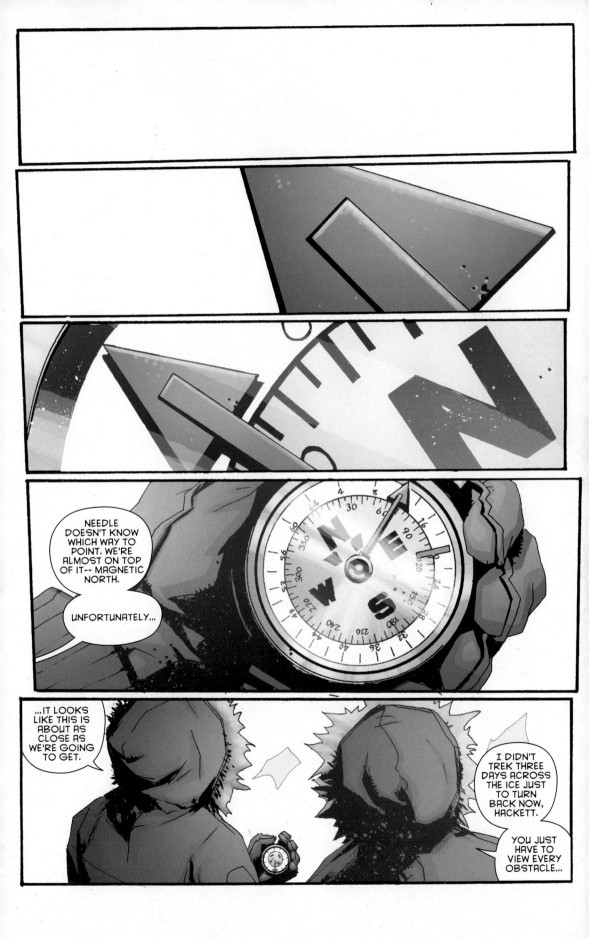

NEEDLE DOESN'T KNOW WHICH WAY TO POINT. WE'RE ALMOST ON TOP OF IT-- MAGNETIC NORTH.

UNFORTUNATELY...

...IT LOOKS LIKE THIS IS ABOUT AS CLOSE AS WE'RE GOING TO GET.

I DIDN'T TREK THREE DAYS ACROSS THE ICE JUST TO TURN BACK NOW, HACKETT.

YOU JUST HAVE TO VIEW EVERY OBSTACLE...

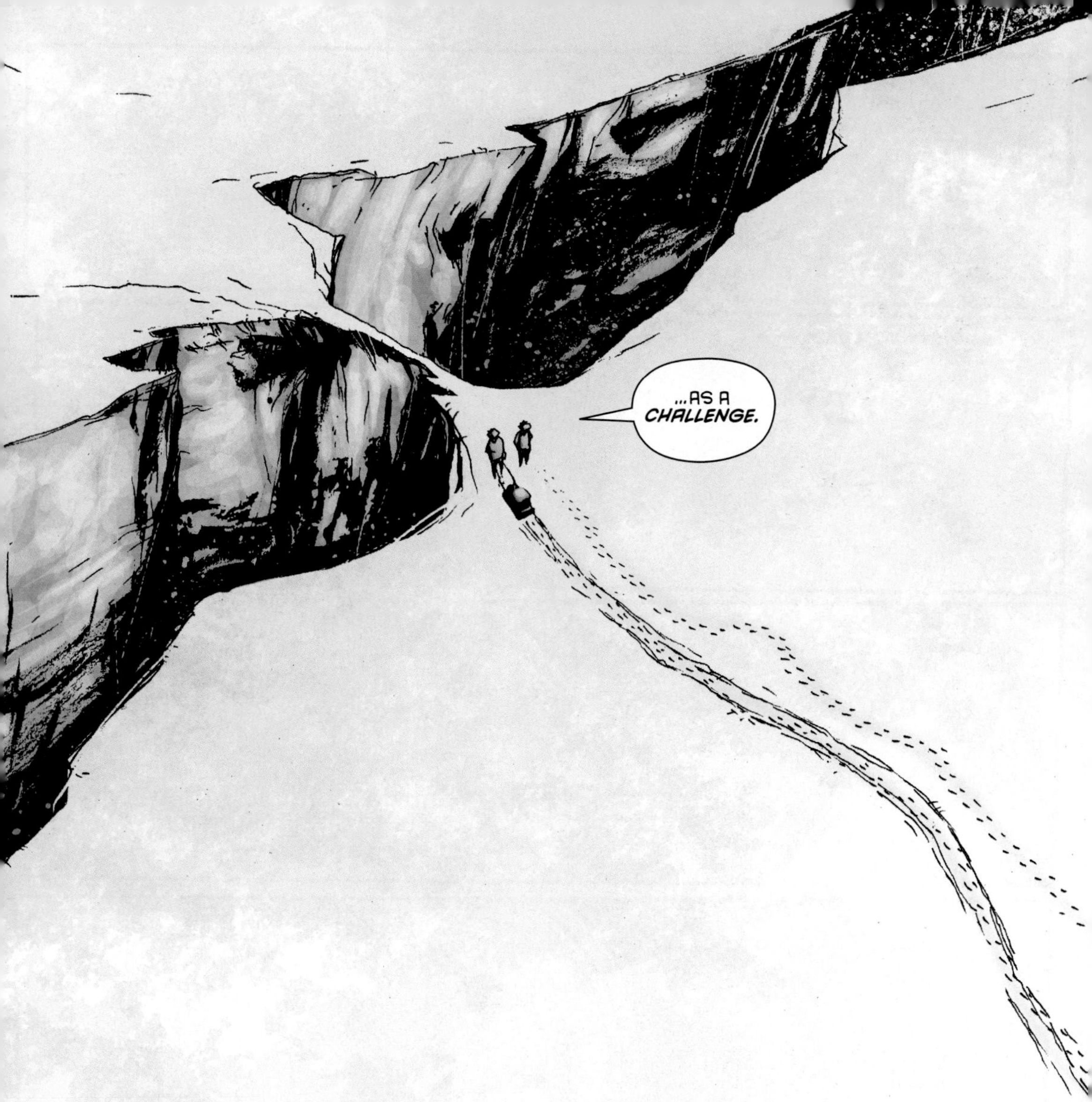
...AS A CHALLENGE.

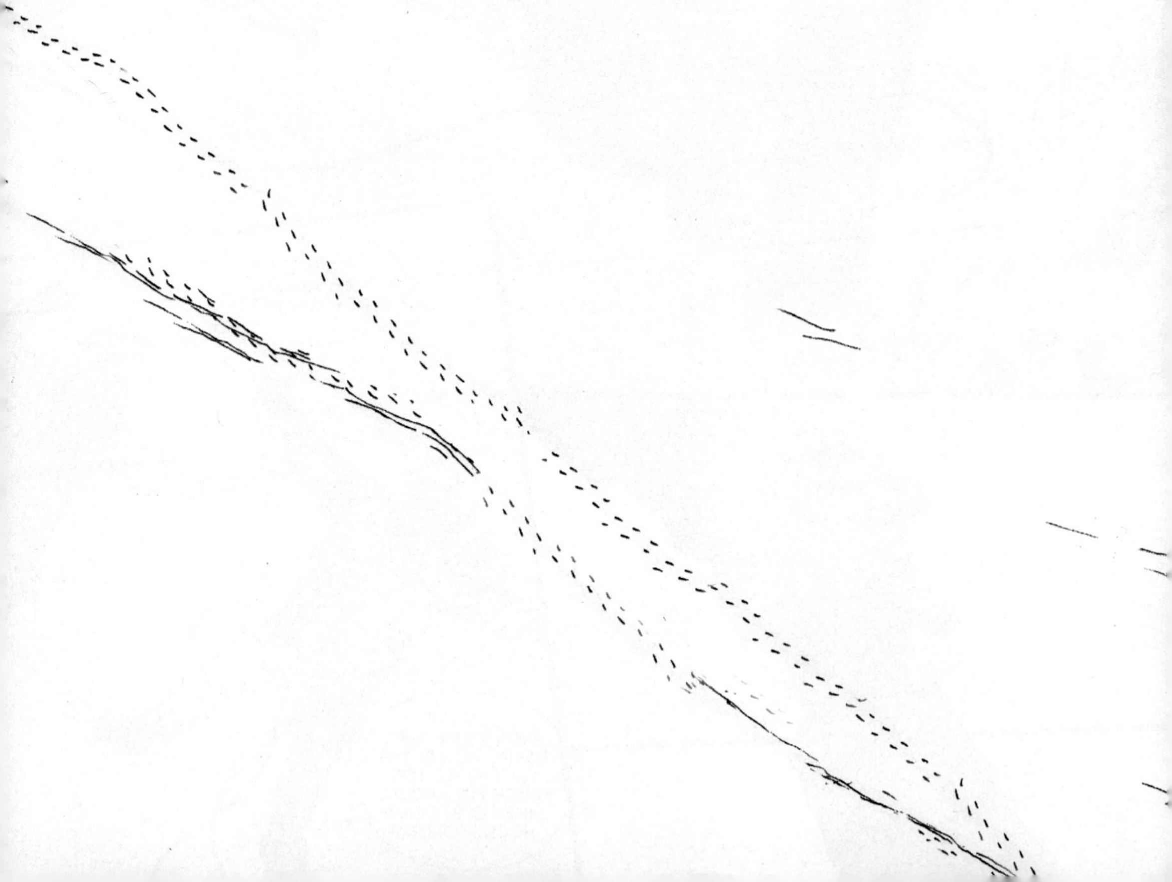

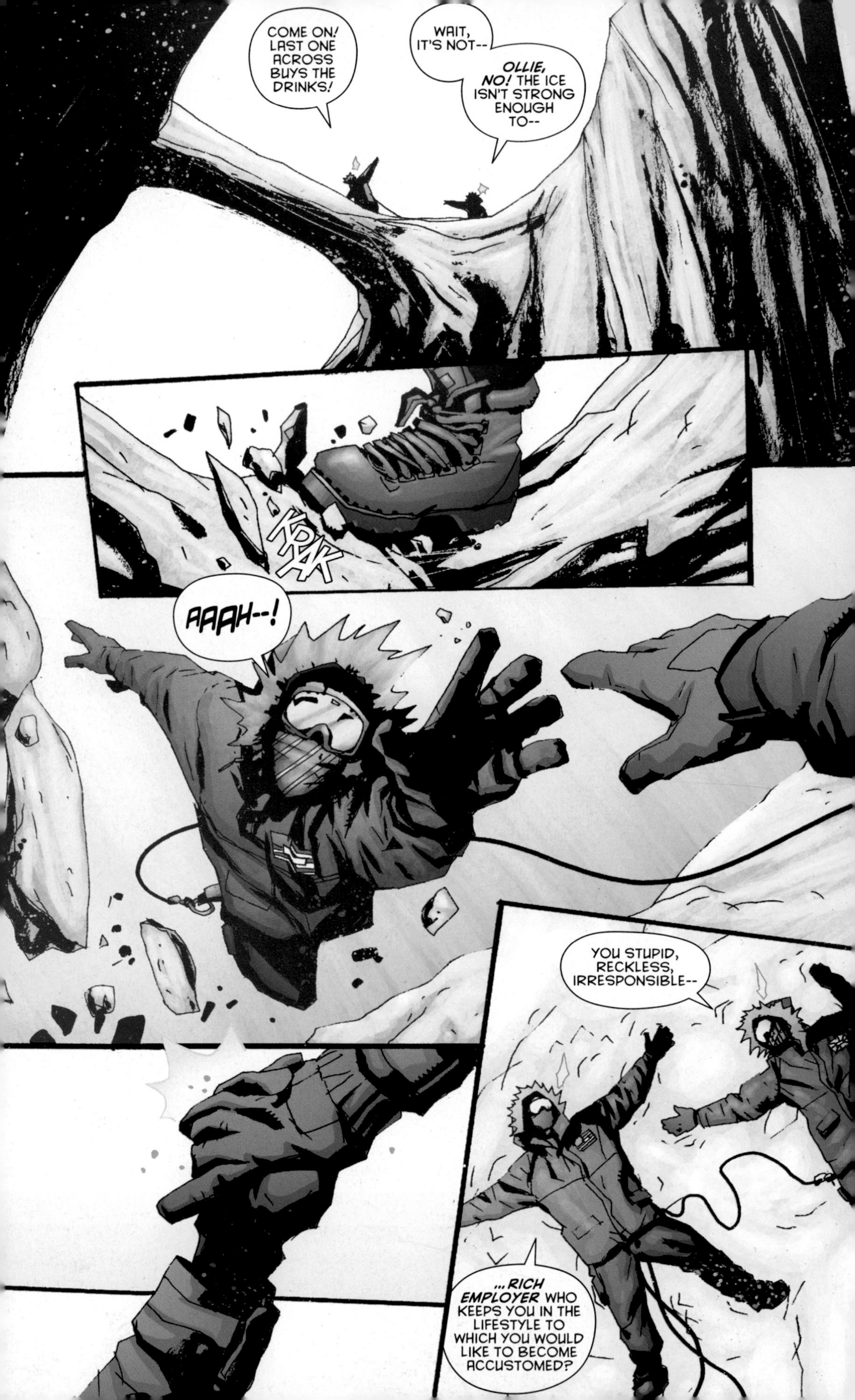

COME ON! LAST ONE ACROSS BUYS THE DRINKS!
WAIT, IT'S NOT--
OLLIE, NO! THE ICE ISN'T STRONG ENOUGH TO--
KRAK
AAAH--!
YOU STUPID, RECKLESS, IRRESPONSIBLE--
...RICH EMPLOYER WHO KEEPS YOU IN THE LIFESTYLE TO WHICH YOU WOULD LIKE TO BECOME ACCUSTOMED?

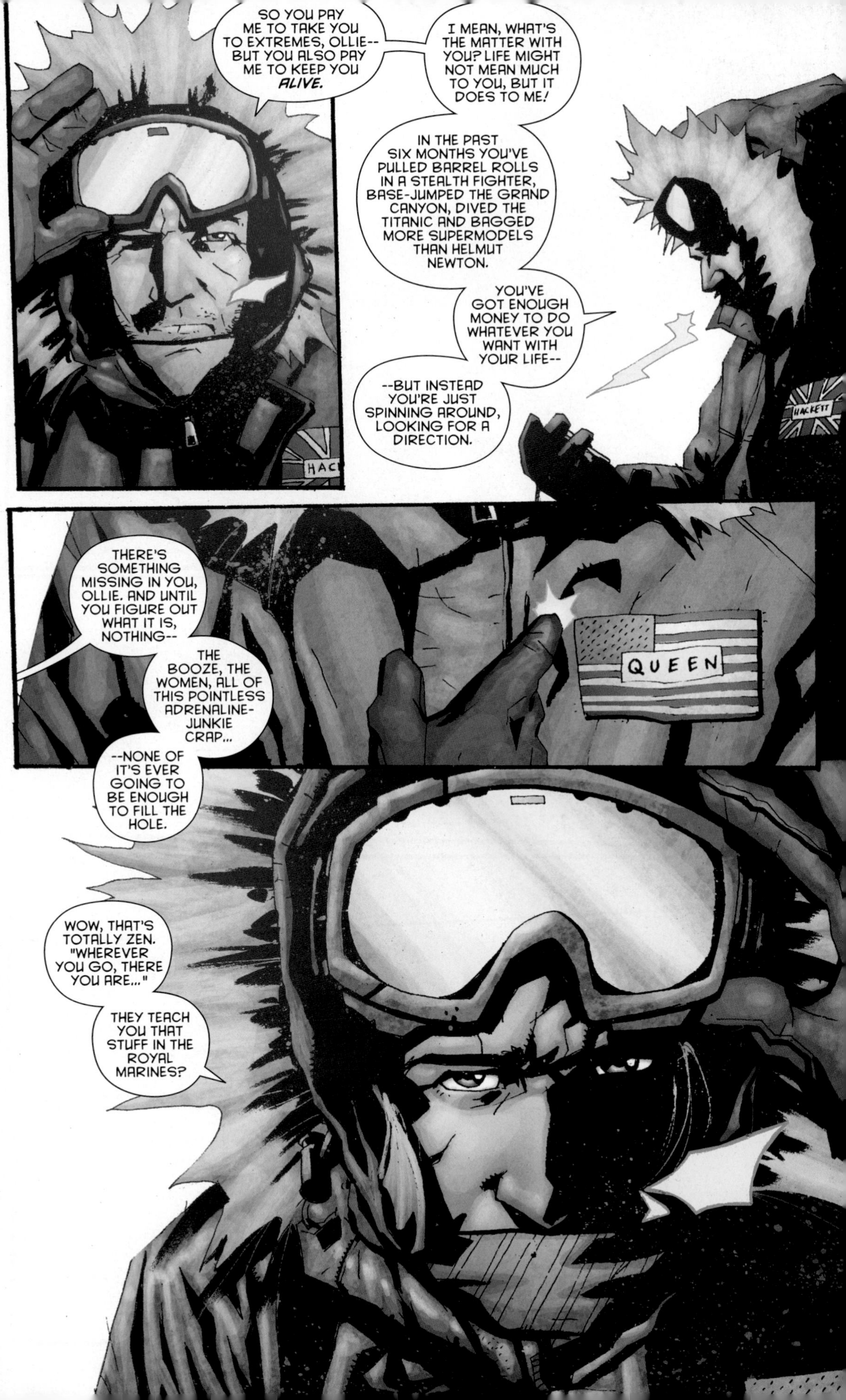
SO YOU PAY ME TO TAKE YOU TO EXTREMES, OLLIE-- BUT YOU ALSO PAY ME TO KEEP YOU ALIVE.
I MEAN, WHAT'S THE MATTER WITH YOU? LIFE MIGHT NOT MEAN MUCH TO YOU, BUT IT DOES TO ME!
IN THE PAST SIX MONTHS YOU'VE PULLED BARREL ROLLS IN A STEALTH FIGHTER, BASE-JUMPED THE GRAND CANYON, DIVED THE TITANIC AND BAGGED MORE SUPERMODELS THAN HELMUT NEWTON.
YOU'VE GOT ENOUGH MONEY TO DO WHATEVER YOU WANT WITH YOUR LIFE--
--BUT INSTEAD YOU'RE JUST SPINNING AROUND, LOOKING FOR A DIRECTION.
HACKETT
THERE'S SOMETHING MISSING IN YOU, OLLIE. AND UNTIL YOU FIGURE OUT WHAT IT IS, NOTHING--
THE BOOZE, THE WOMEN, ALL OF THIS POINTLESS ADRENALINE-JUNKIE CRAP...
QUEEN
--NONE OF IT'S EVER GOING TO BE ENOUGH TO FILL THE HOLE.
WOW, THAT'S TOTALLY ZEN. "WHEREVER YOU GO, THERE YOU ARE..."
THEY TEACH YOU THAT STUFF IN THE ROYAL MARINES?

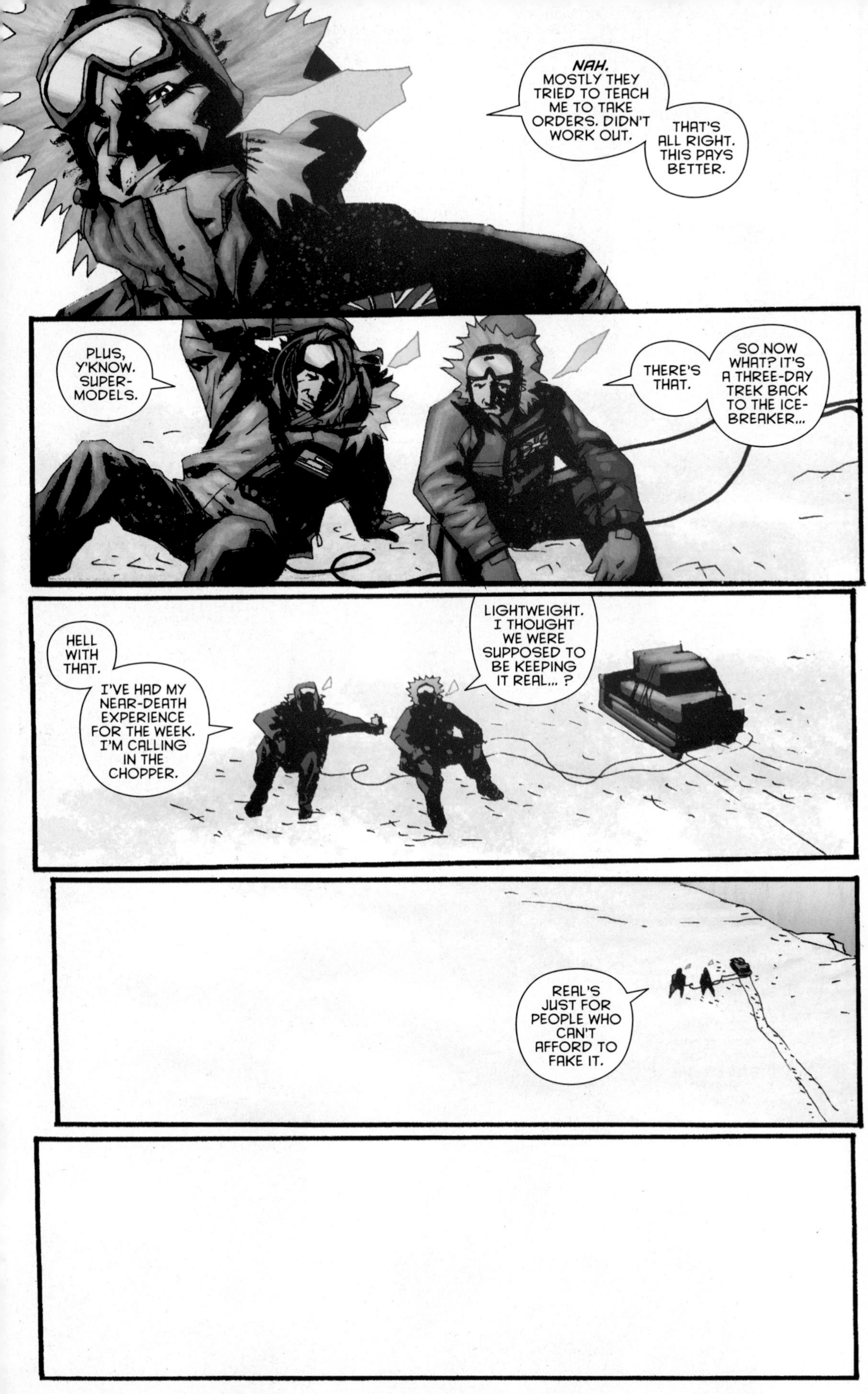
NAH.
MOSTLY THEY TRIED TO TEACH ME TO TAKE ORDERS. DIDN'T WORK OUT.
THAT'S ALL RIGHT. THIS PAYS BETTER.
PLUS, Y'KNOW. SUPER-MODELS.
THERE'S THAT.
SO NOW WHAT? IT'S A THREE-DAY TREK BACK TO THE ICE-BREAKER...
HELL WITH THAT.
I'VE HAD MY NEAR-DEATH EXPERIENCE FOR THE WEEK. I'M CALLING IN THE CHOPPER.
LIGHTWEIGHT. I THOUGHT WE WERE SUPPOSED TO BE KEEPING IT REAL... ?
REAL'S JUST FOR PEOPLE WHO CAN'T AFFORD TO FAKE IT.

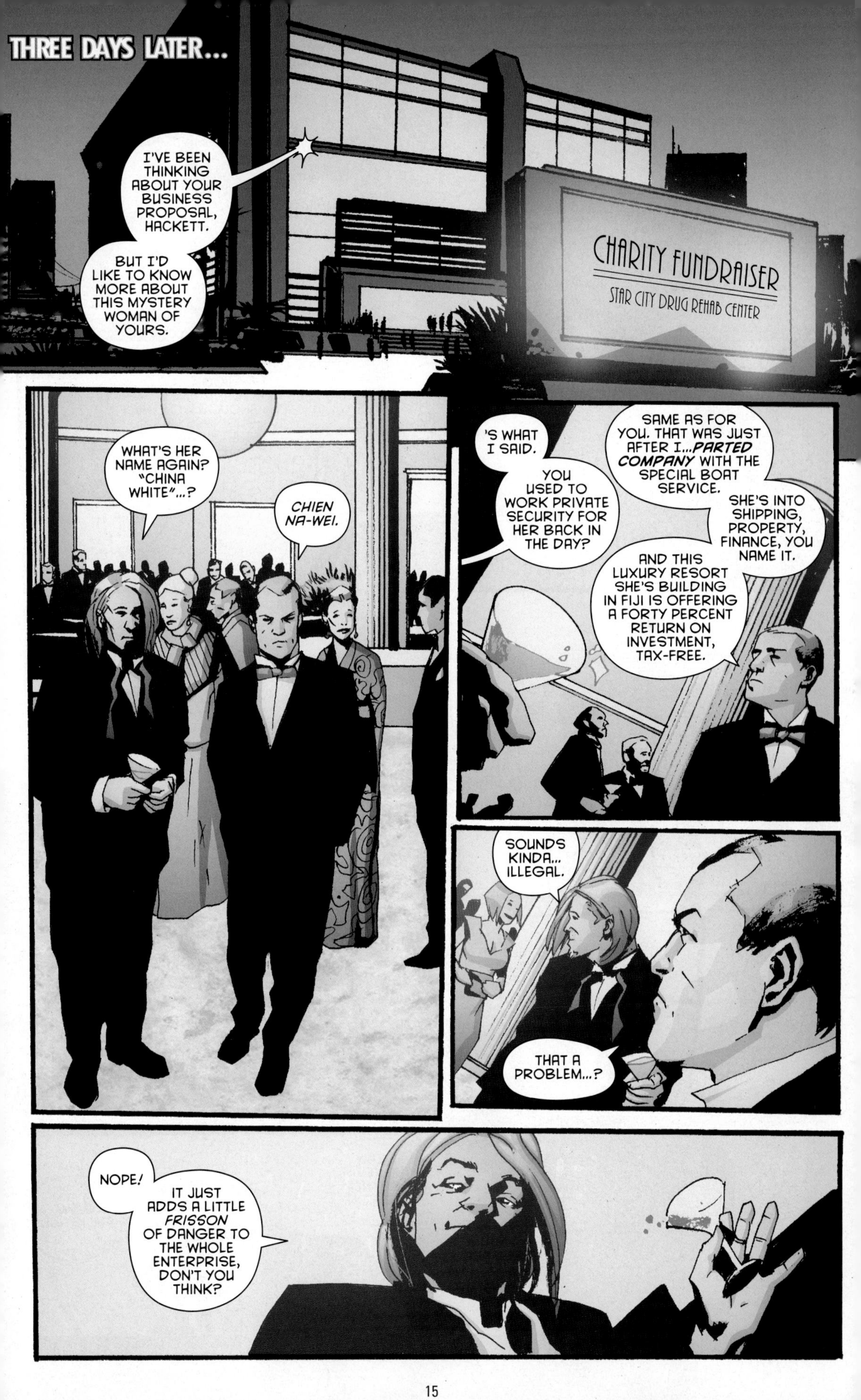
THREE DAYS LATER...
I'VE BEEN THINKING ABOUT YOUR BUSINESS PROPOSAL, HACKETT.
BUT I'D LIKE TO KNOW MORE ABOUT THIS MYSTERY WOMAN OF YOURS.
CHARITY FUNDRAISER
STAR CITY DRUG REHAB CENTER
WHAT'S HER NAME AGAIN? "CHINA WHITE"...?
CHIEN NA-WEI.
'S WHAT I SAID.
YOU USED TO WORK PRIVATE SECURITY FOR HER BACK IN THE DAY?
SAME AS FOR YOU. THAT WAS JUST AFTER I...PARTED COMPANY WITH THE SPECIAL BOAT SERVICE.
SHE'S INTO SHIPPING, PROPERTY, FINANCE, YOU NAME IT.
AND THIS LUXURY RESORT SHE'S BUILDING IN FIJI IS OFFERING A FORTY PERCENT RETURN ON INVESTMENT, TAX-FREE.
SOUNDS KINDA... ILLEGAL.
THAT A PROBLEM...?
NOPE!
IT JUST ADDS A LITTLE FRISSON OF DANGER TO THE WHOLE ENTERPRISE, DON'T YOU THINK?

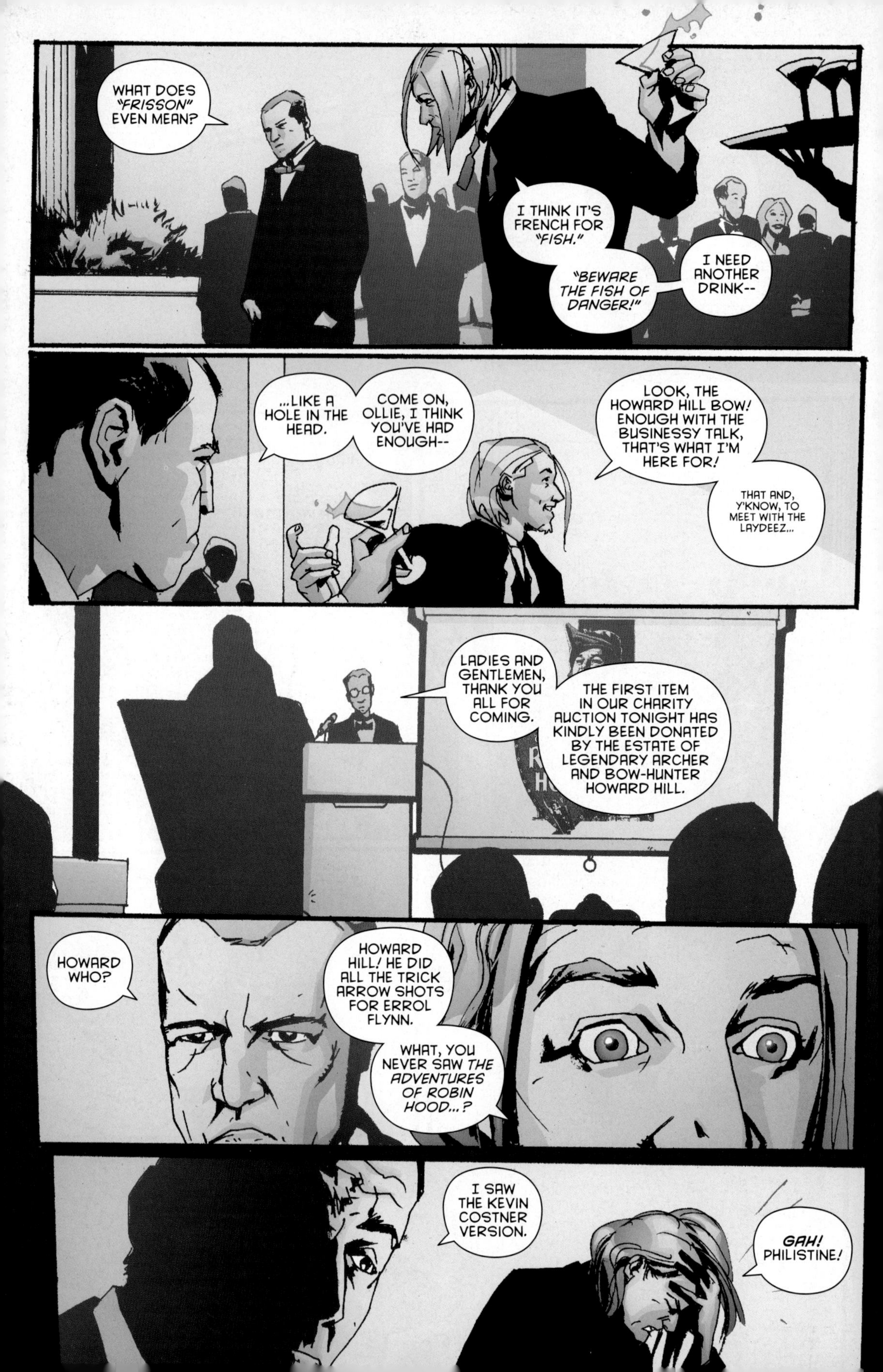
WHAT DOES "FRISSON" EVEN MEAN?
I THINK IT'S FRENCH FOR "FISH."
"BEWARE THE FISH OF DANGER!"
I NEED ANOTHER DRINK--
...LIKE A HOLE IN THE HEAD.
COME ON, OLLIE, I THINK YOU'VE HAD ENOUGH--
LOOK, THE HOWARD HILL BOW! ENOUGH WITH THE BUSINESSY TALK, THAT'S WHAT I'M HERE FOR!
THAT AND, Y'KNOW, TO MEET WITH THE LAYDEEZ...
LADIES AND GENTLEMEN, THANK YOU ALL FOR COMING.
THE FIRST ITEM IN OUR CHARITY AUCTION TONIGHT HAS KINDLY BEEN DONATED BY THE ESTATE OF LEGENDARY ARCHER AND BOW-HUNTER HOWARD HILL.
HOWARD WHO?
HOWARD HILL! HE DID ALL THE TRICK ARROW SHOTS FOR ERROL FLYNN.
WHAT, YOU NEVER SAW *THE ADVENTURES OF ROBIN HOOD*...?
I SAW THE KEVIN COSTNER VERSION.
GAH! PHILISTINE!

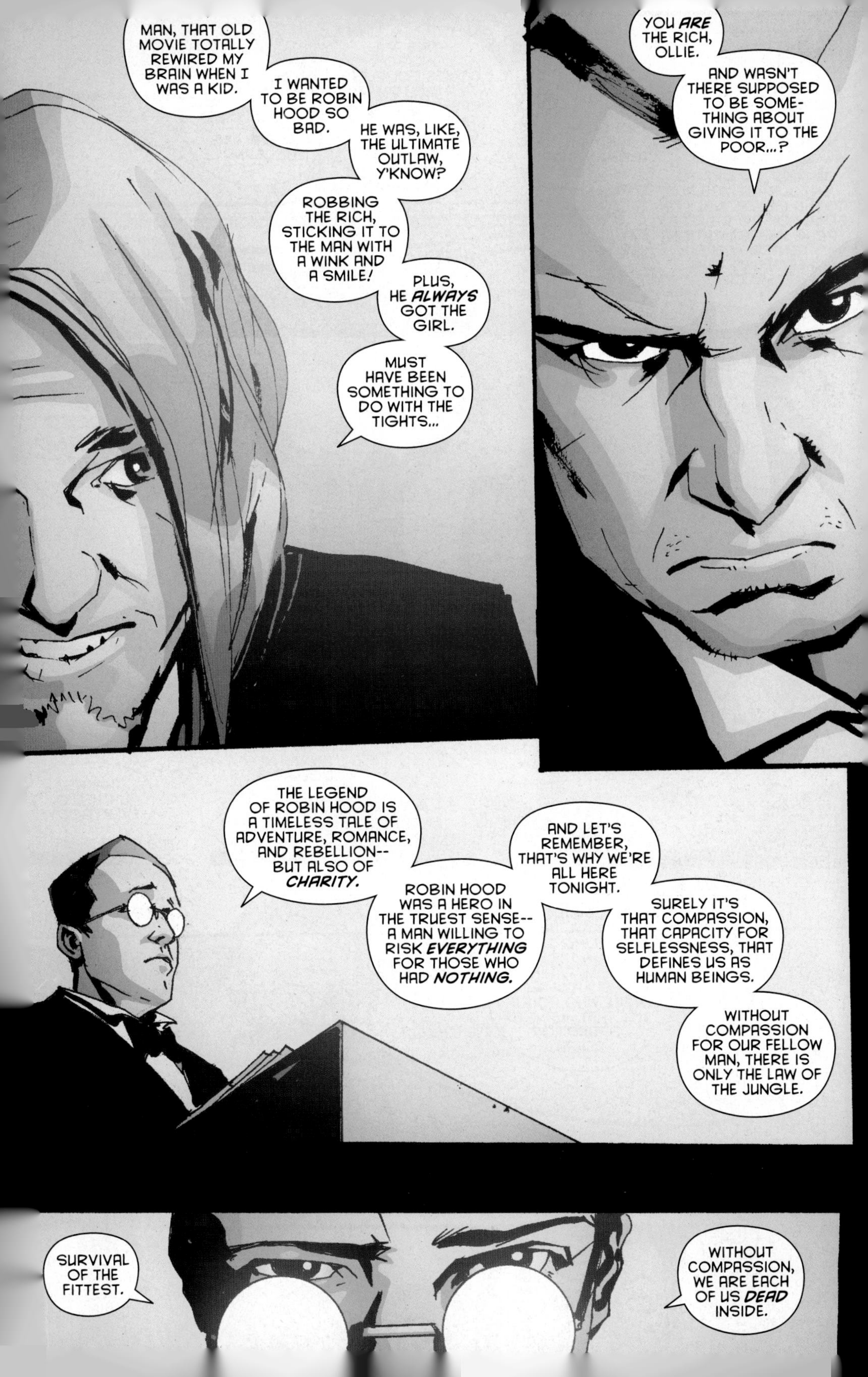
MAN, THAT OLD MOVIE TOTALLY REWIRED MY BRAIN WHEN I WAS A KID.
I WANTED TO BE ROBIN HOOD SO BAD.
HE WAS, LIKE, THE ULTIMATE OUTLAW, Y'KNOW?
ROBBING THE RICH, STICKING IT TO THE MAN WITH A WINK AND A SMILE!
PLUS, HE *ALWAYS* GOT THE GIRL.
MUST HAVE BEEN SOMETHING TO DO WITH THE TIGHTS...
YOU *ARE* THE RICH, OLLIE.
AND WASN'T THERE SUPPOSED TO BE SOME-THING ABOUT GIVING IT TO THE POOR...?
THE LEGEND OF ROBIN HOOD IS A TIMELESS TALE OF ADVENTURE, ROMANCE, AND REBELLION-- BUT ALSO OF *CHARITY.*
ROBIN HOOD WAS A HERO IN THE TRUEST SENSE-- A MAN WILLING TO RISK *EVERYTHING* FOR THOSE WHO HAD *NOTHING.*
AND LET'S REMEMBER, THAT'S WHY WE'RE ALL HERE TONIGHT.
SURELY IT'S THAT COMPASSION, THAT CAPACITY FOR SELFLESSNESS, THAT DEFINES US AS HUMAN BEINGS.
WITHOUT COMPASSION FOR OUR FELLOW MAN, THERE IS ONLY THE LAW OF THE JUNGLE.
SURVIVAL OF THE FITTEST.
WITHOUT COMPASSION, WE ARE EACH OF US *DEAD* INSIDE.

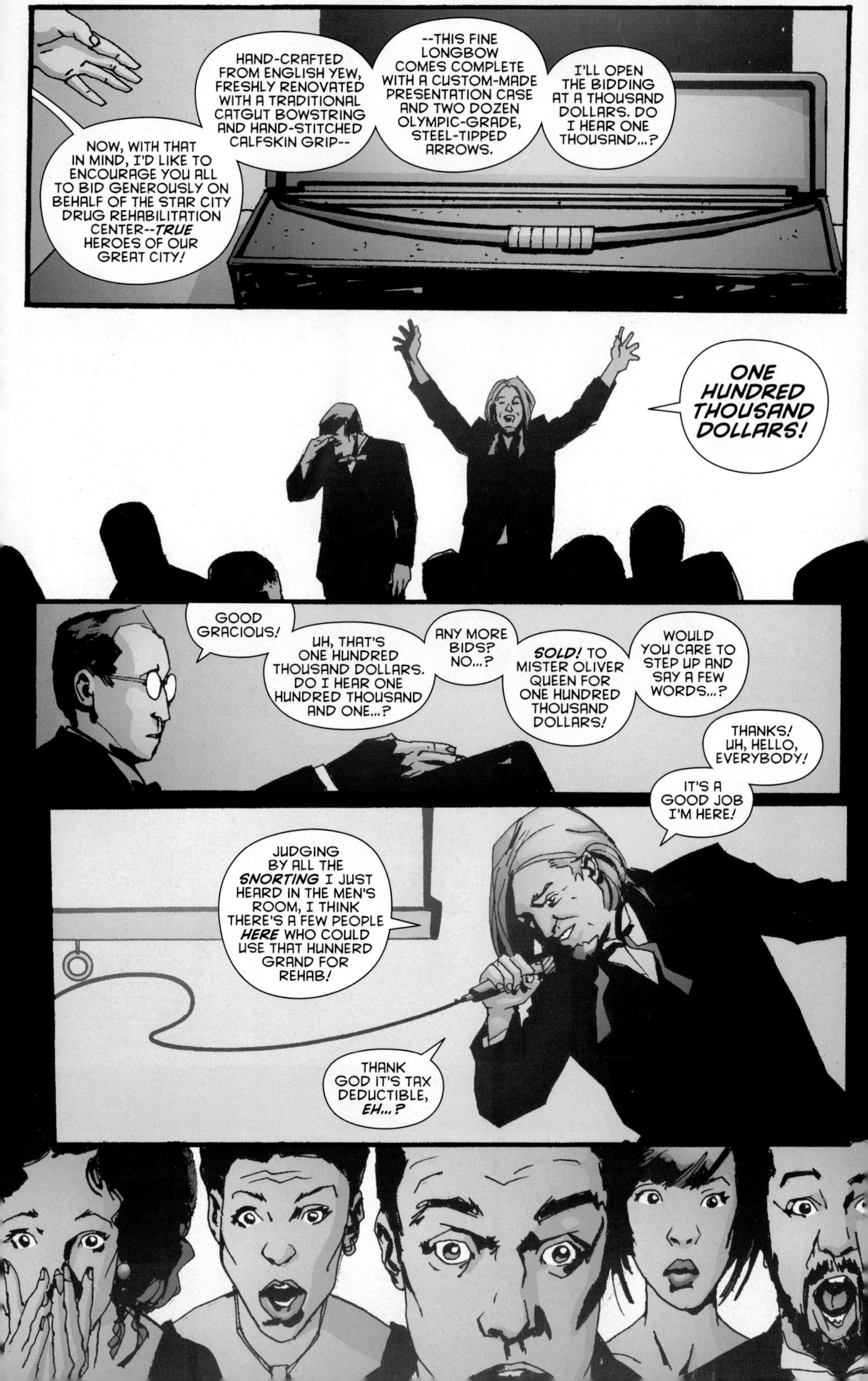
NOW, WITH THAT IN MIND, I'D LIKE TO ENCOURAGE YOU ALL TO BID GENEROUSLY ON BEHALF OF THE STAR CITY DRUG REHABILITATION CENTER--*TRUE* HEROES OF OUR GREAT CITY!
HAND-CRAFTED FROM ENGLISH YEW, FRESHLY RENOVATED WITH A TRADITIONAL CATGUT BOWSTRING AND HAND-STITCHED CALFSKIN GRIP--
--THIS FINE LONGBOW COMES COMPLETE WITH A CUSTOM-MADE PRESENTATION CASE AND TWO DOZEN OLYMPIC-GRADE, STEEL-TIPPED ARROWS.
I'LL OPEN THE BIDDING AT A THOUSAND DOLLARS. DO I HEAR ONE THOUSAND...?
ONE HUNDRED THOUSAND DOLLARS!
GOOD GRACIOUS!
UH, THAT'S ONE HUNDRED THOUSAND DOLLARS. DO I HEAR ONE HUNDRED THOUSAND AND ONE...?
ANY MORE BIDS? NO...?
SOLD! TO MISTER OLIVER QUEEN FOR ONE HUNDRED THOUSAND DOLLARS!
WOULD YOU CARE TO STEP UP AND SAY A FEW WORDS...?
THANKS! UH, HELLO, EVERYBODY!
IT'S A GOOD JOB I'M HERE!
JUDGING BY ALL THE *SNORTING* I JUST HEARD IN THE MEN'S ROOM, I THINK THERE'S A FEW PEOPLE *HERE* WHO COULD USE THAT HUNNERD GRAND FOR REHAB!
THANK GOD IT'S TAX DEDUCTIBLE, *EH...?*

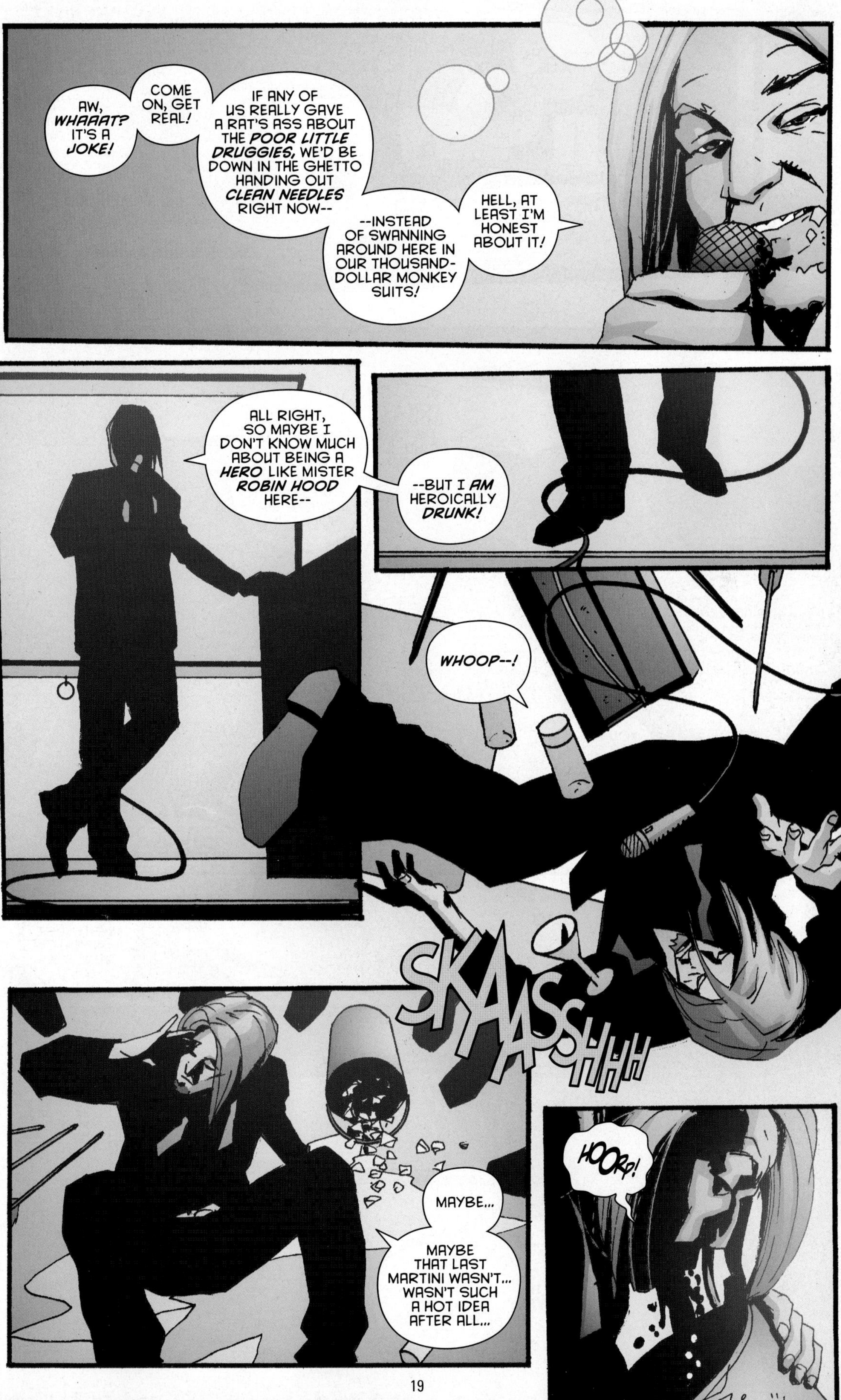

AW, WHAAAT? IT'S A JOKE!
COME ON, GET REAL!
IF ANY OF US REALLY GAVE A RAT'S ASS ABOUT THE POOR LITTLE DRUGGIES, WE'D BE DOWN IN THE GHETTO HANDING OUT CLEAN NEEDLES RIGHT NOW--
--INSTEAD OF SWANNING AROUND HERE IN OUR THOUSAND-DOLLAR MONKEY SUITS!
HELL, AT LEAST I'M HONEST ABOUT IT!
ALL RIGHT, SO MAYBE I DON'T KNOW MUCH ABOUT BEING A HERO LIKE MISTER ROBIN HOOD HERE--
--BUT I AM HEROICALLY DRUNK!
WHOOP--!
SKAASSHHH
MAYBE...
MAYBE THAT LAST MARTINI WASN'T... WASN'T SUCH A HOT IDEA AFTER ALL...
HOORP!

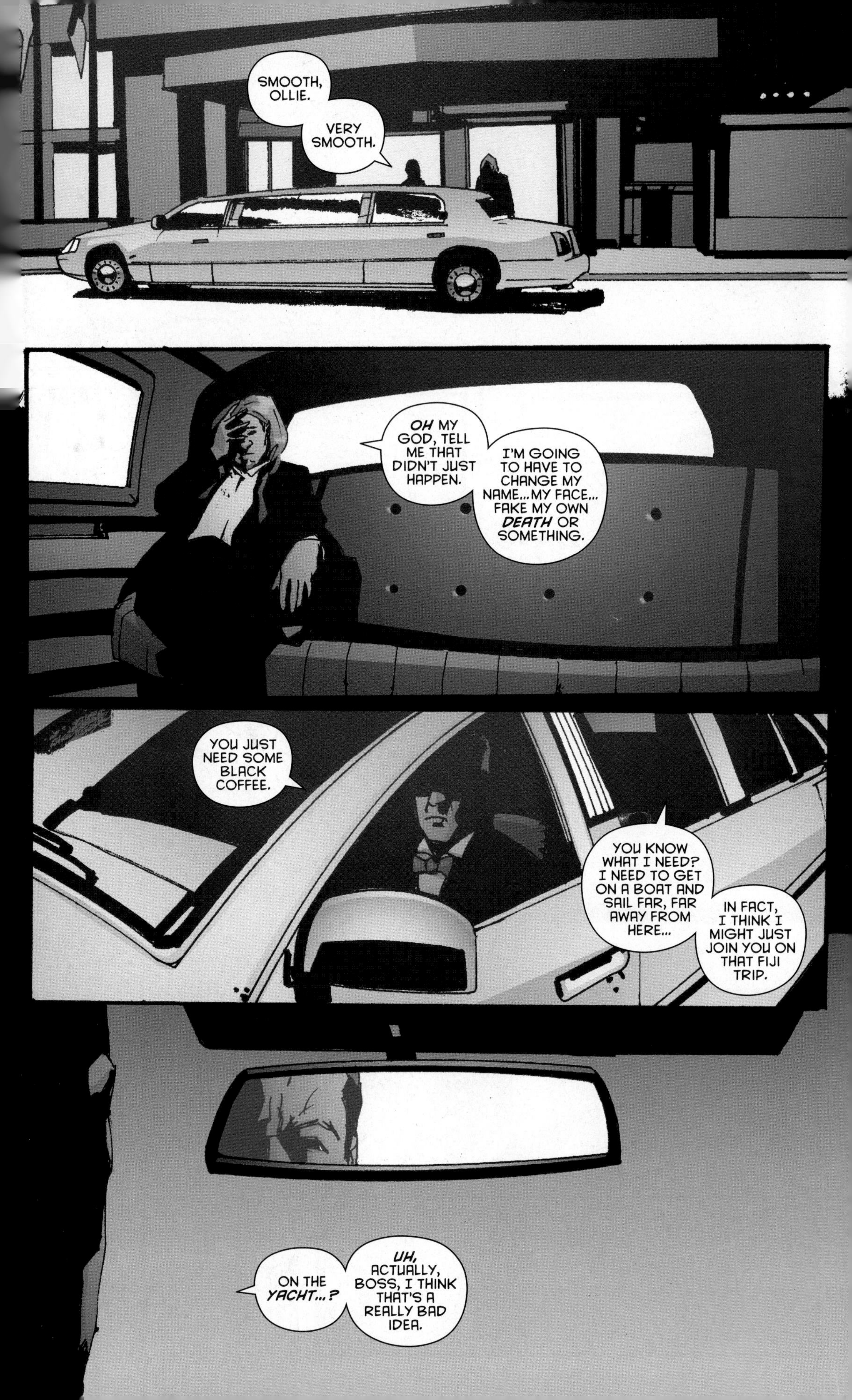
SMOOTH, OLLIE.
VERY SMOOTH.
OH MY GOD, TELL ME THAT DIDN'T JUST HAPPEN.
I'M GOING TO HAVE TO CHANGE MY NAME...MY FACE... FAKE MY OWN DEATH OR SOMETHING.
YOU JUST NEED SOME BLACK COFFEE.
YOU KNOW WHAT I NEED? I NEED TO GET ON A BOAT AND SAIL FAR, FAR AWAY FROM HERE...
IN FACT, I THINK I MIGHT JUST JOIN YOU ON THAT FIJI TRIP.
ON THE YACHT...?
UH, ACTUALLY, BOSS, I THINK THAT'S A REALLY BAD IDEA.

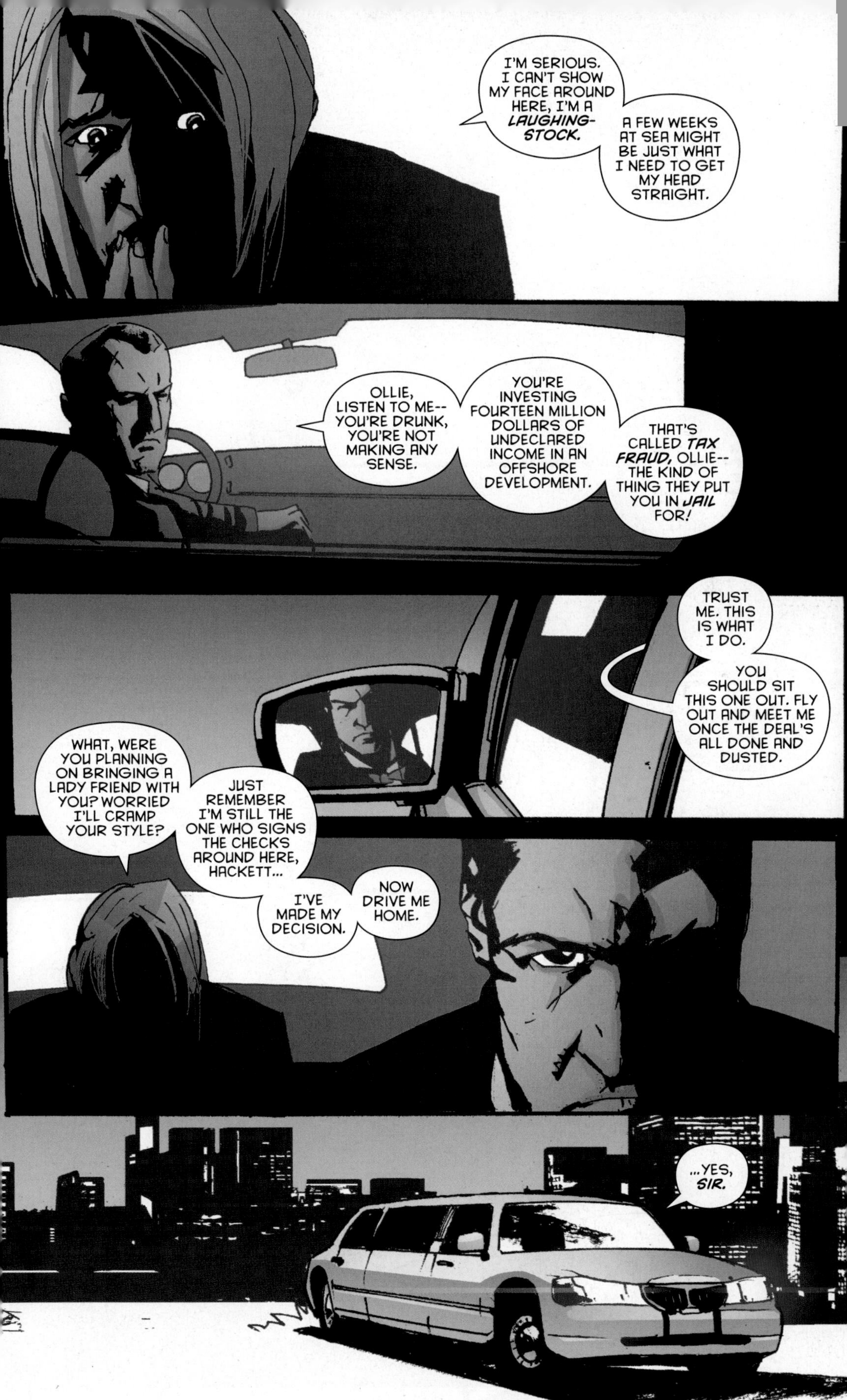
I'M SERIOUS. I CAN'T SHOW MY FACE AROUND HERE, I'M A *LAUGHING-STOCK.*
A FEW WEEKS AT SEA MIGHT BE JUST WHAT I NEED TO GET MY HEAD STRAIGHT.
OLLIE, LISTEN TO ME-- YOU'RE DRUNK, YOU'RE NOT MAKING ANY SENSE.
YOU'RE INVESTING FOURTEEN MILLION DOLLARS OF UNDECLARED INCOME IN AN OFFSHORE DEVELOPMENT.
THAT'S CALLED *TAX FRAUD,* OLLIE-- THE KIND OF THING THEY PUT YOU IN *JAIL* FOR!
TRUST ME. THIS IS WHAT I DO.
YOU SHOULD SIT THIS ONE OUT. FLY OUT AND MEET ME ONCE THE DEAL'S ALL DONE AND DUSTED.
WHAT, WERE YOU PLANNING ON BRINGING A LADY FRIEND WITH YOU? WORRIED I'LL CRAMP YOUR STYLE?
JUST REMEMBER I'M STILL THE ONE WHO SIGNS THE CHECKS AROUND HERE, HACKETT...
I'VE MADE MY DECISION.
NOW DRIVE ME HOME.
...YES, *SIR.*

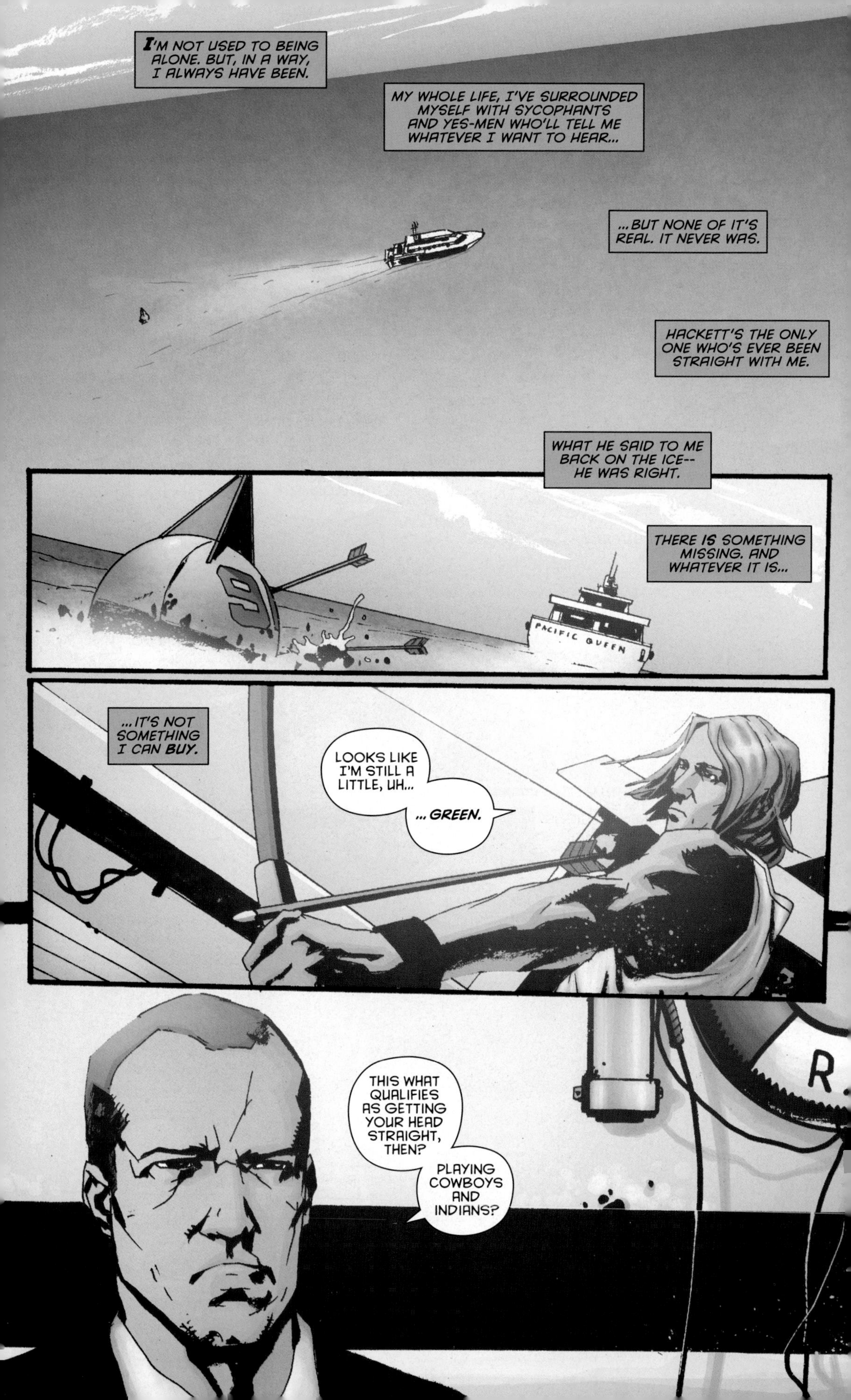
I'M NOT USED TO BEING ALONE. BUT, IN A WAY, I ALWAYS HAVE BEEN.
MY WHOLE LIFE, I'VE SURROUNDED MYSELF WITH SYCOPHANTS AND YES-MEN WHO'LL TELL ME WHATEVER I WANT TO HEAR...
...BUT NONE OF IT'S REAL. IT NEVER WAS.
HACKETT'S THE ONLY ONE WHO'S EVER BEEN STRAIGHT WITH ME.
WHAT HE SAID TO ME BACK ON THE ICE-- HE WAS RIGHT.
THERE IS SOMETHING MISSING. AND WHATEVER IT IS...
PACIFIC QUEEN
...IT'S NOT SOMETHING I CAN BUY.
LOOKS LIKE I'M STILL A LITTLE, UH...
...GREEN.
THIS WHAT QUALIFIES AS GETTING YOUR HEAD STRAIGHT, THEN?
PLAYING COWBOYS AND INDIANS?

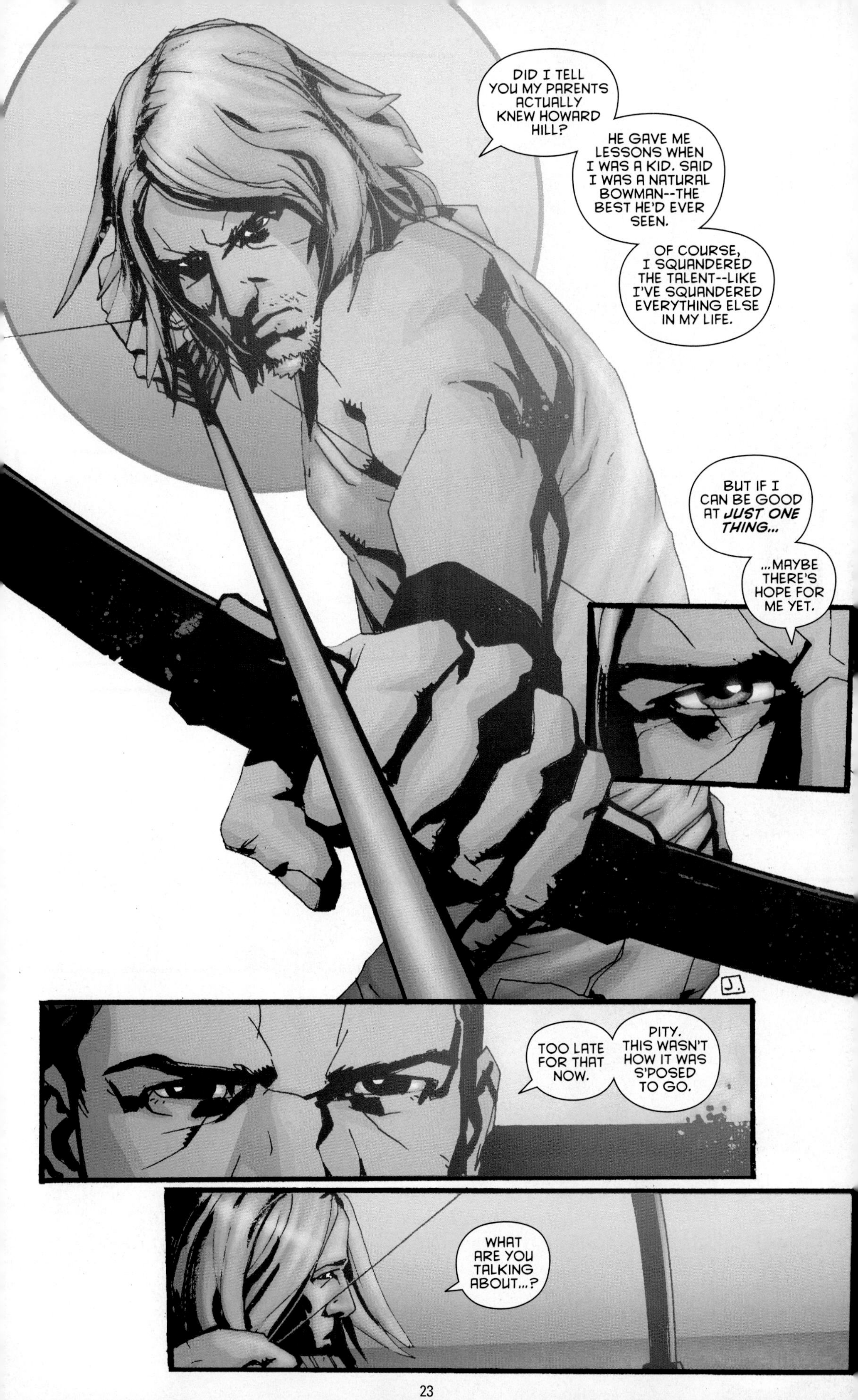
DID I TELL YOU MY PARENTS ACTUALLY KNEW HOWARD HILL?
HE GAVE ME LESSONS WHEN I WAS A KID. SAID I WAS A NATURAL BOWMAN--THE BEST HE'D EVER SEEN.
OF COURSE, I SQUANDERED THE TALENT--LIKE I'VE SQUANDERED EVERYTHING ELSE IN MY LIFE.
BUT IF I CAN BE GOOD AT *JUST ONE THING...*
...MAYBE THERE'S HOPE FOR ME YET.
J.
TOO LATE FOR THAT NOW.
PITY. THIS WASN'T HOW IT WAS S'POSED TO GO.
WHAT ARE YOU TALKING ABOUT...?

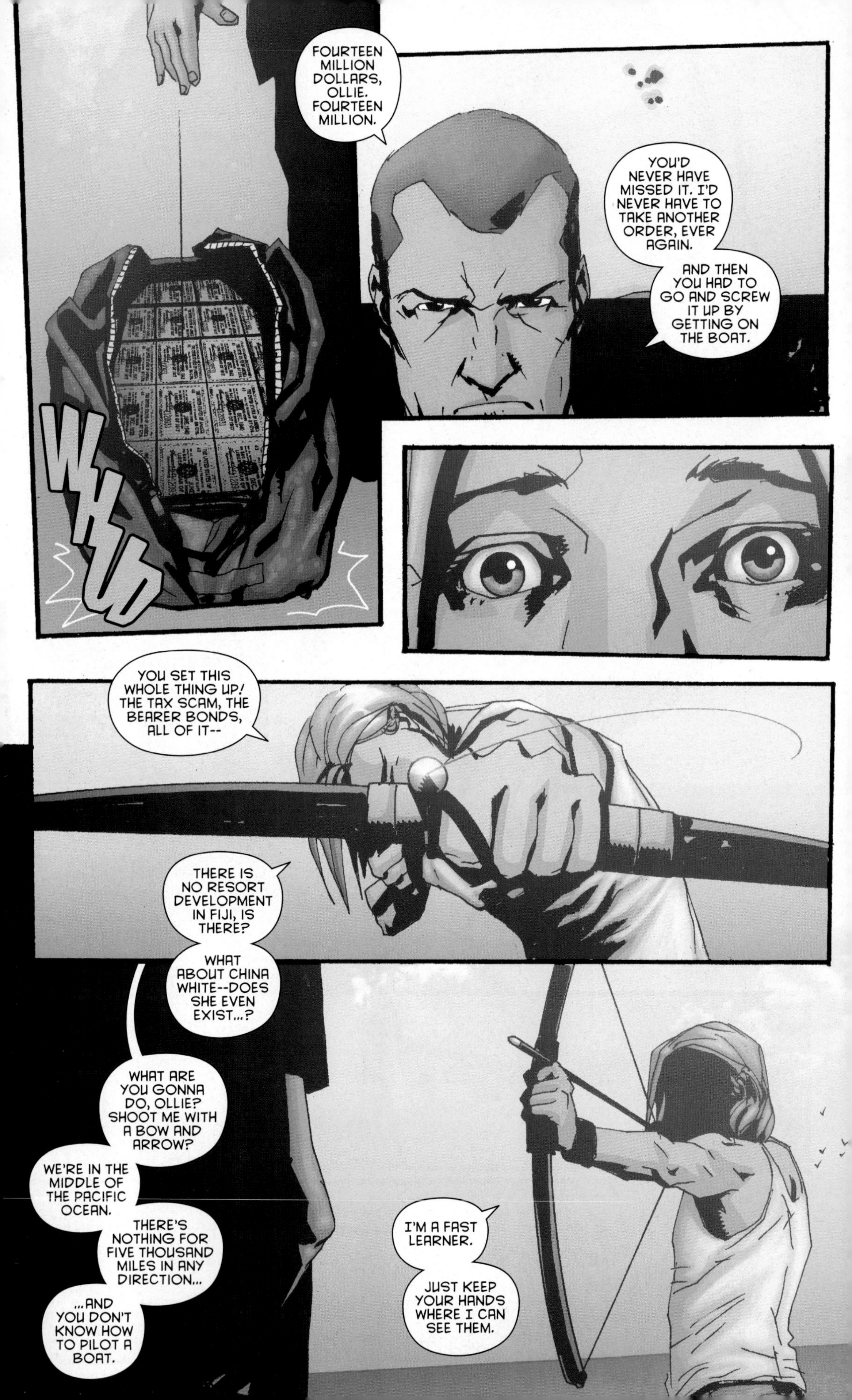

FOURTEEN MILLION DOLLARS, OLLIE. FOURTEEN MILLION.
YOU'D NEVER HAVE MISSED IT. I'D NEVER HAVE TO TAKE ANOTHER ORDER, EVER AGAIN.
AND THEN YOU HAD TO GO AND SCREW IT UP BY GETTING ON THE BOAT.
WHUD
YOU SET THIS WHOLE THING UP! THE TAX SCAM, THE BEARER BONDS, ALL OF IT--
THERE IS NO RESORT DEVELOPMENT IN FIJI, IS THERE?
WHAT ABOUT CHINA WHITE--DOES SHE EVEN EXIST...?
WHAT ARE YOU GONNA DO, OLLIE? SHOOT ME WITH A BOW AND ARROW?
WE'RE IN THE MIDDLE OF THE PACIFIC OCEAN.
THERE'S NOTHING FOR FIVE THOUSAND MILES IN ANY DIRECTION...
...AND YOU DON'T KNOW HOW TO PILOT A BOAT.
I'M A FAST LEARNER.
JUST KEEP YOUR HANDS WHERE I CAN SEE THEM.

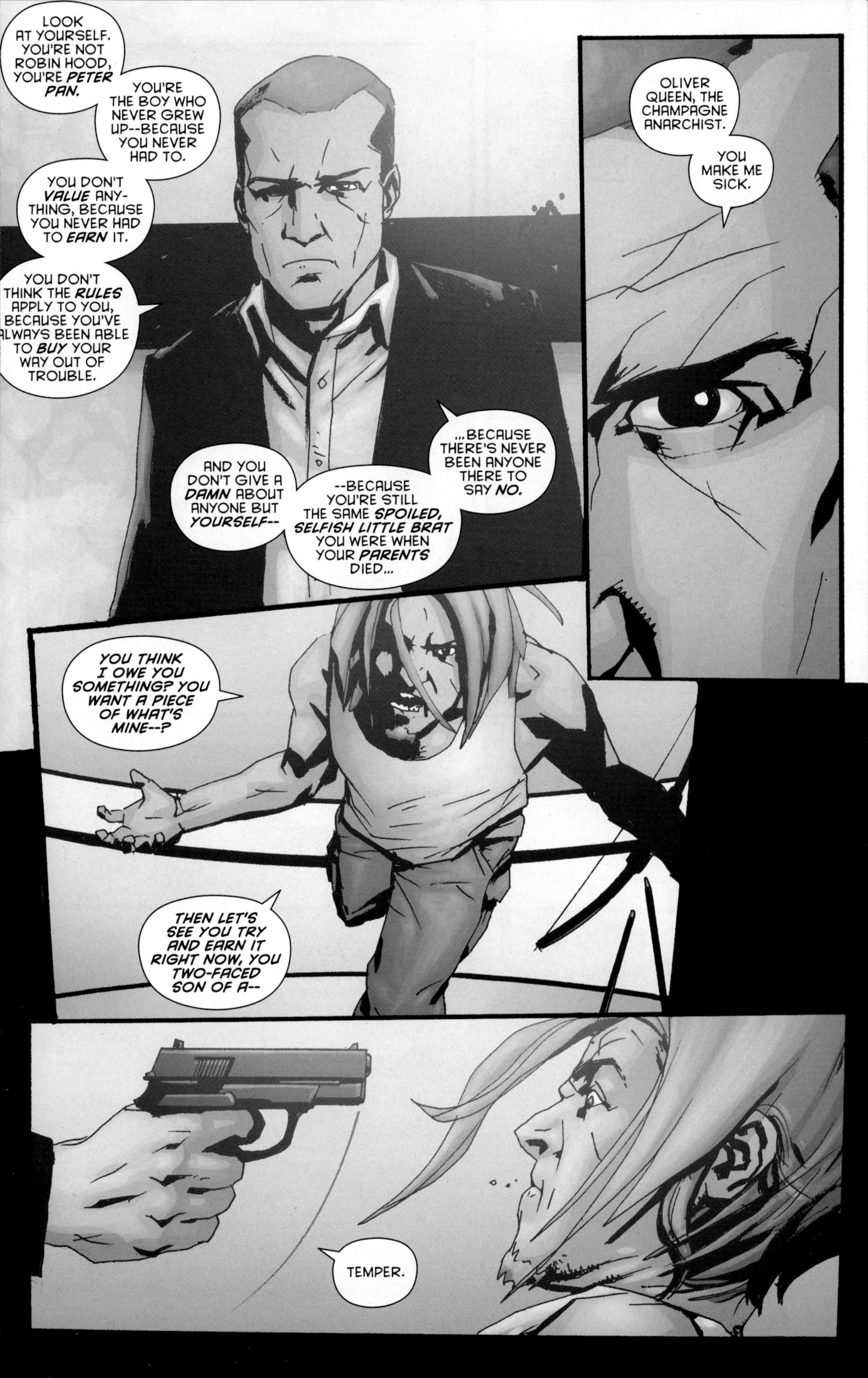
LOOK AT YOURSELF. YOU'RE NOT ROBIN HOOD, YOU'RE PETER PAN.
YOU'RE THE BOY WHO NEVER GREW UP--BECAUSE YOU NEVER HAD TO.
YOU DON'T VALUE ANYTHING, BECAUSE YOU NEVER HAD TO EARN IT.
YOU DON'T THINK THE RULES APPLY TO YOU, BECAUSE YOU'VE ALWAYS BEEN ABLE TO BUY YOUR WAY OUT OF TROUBLE.
OLIVER QUEEN, THE CHAMPAGNE ANARCHIST.
YOU MAKE ME SICK.
AND YOU DON'T GIVE A DAMN ABOUT ANYONE BUT YOURSELF--
--BECAUSE YOU'RE STILL THE SAME SPOILED, SELFISH LITTLE BRAT YOU WERE WHEN YOUR PARENTS DIED...
...BECAUSE THERE'S NEVER BEEN ANYONE THERE TO SAY NO.
YOU THINK I OWE YOU SOMETHING? YOU WANT A PIECE OF WHAT'S MINE--?
THEN LET'S SEE YOU TRY AND EARN IT RIGHT NOW, YOU TWO-FACED SON OF A--
TEMPER.

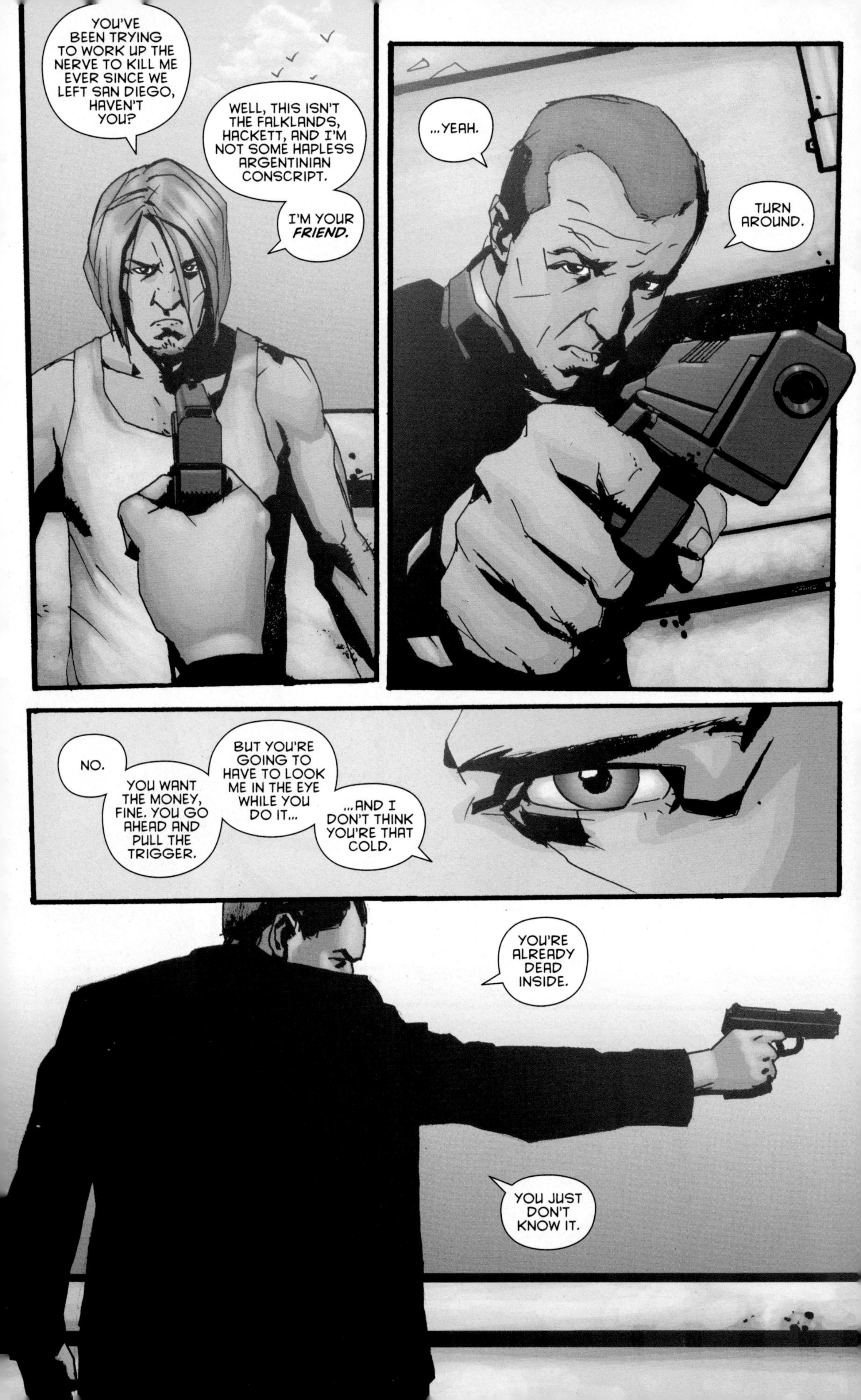
YOU'VE BEEN TRYING TO WORK UP THE NERVE TO KILL ME EVER SINCE WE LEFT SAN DIEGO, HAVEN'T YOU?
WELL, THIS ISN'T THE FALKLANDS, HACKETT, AND I'M NOT SOME HAPLESS ARGENTINIAN CONSCRIPT.
I'M YOUR *FRIEND.*
...YEAH.
TURN AROUND.
NO.
YOU WANT THE MONEY, FINE. YOU GO AHEAD AND PULL THE TRIGGER.
BUT YOU'RE GOING TO HAVE TO LOOK ME IN THE EYE WHILE YOU DO IT...
...AND I DON'T THINK YOU'RE THAT COLD.
YOU'RE ALREADY DEAD INSIDE.
YOU JUST DON'T KNOW IT.

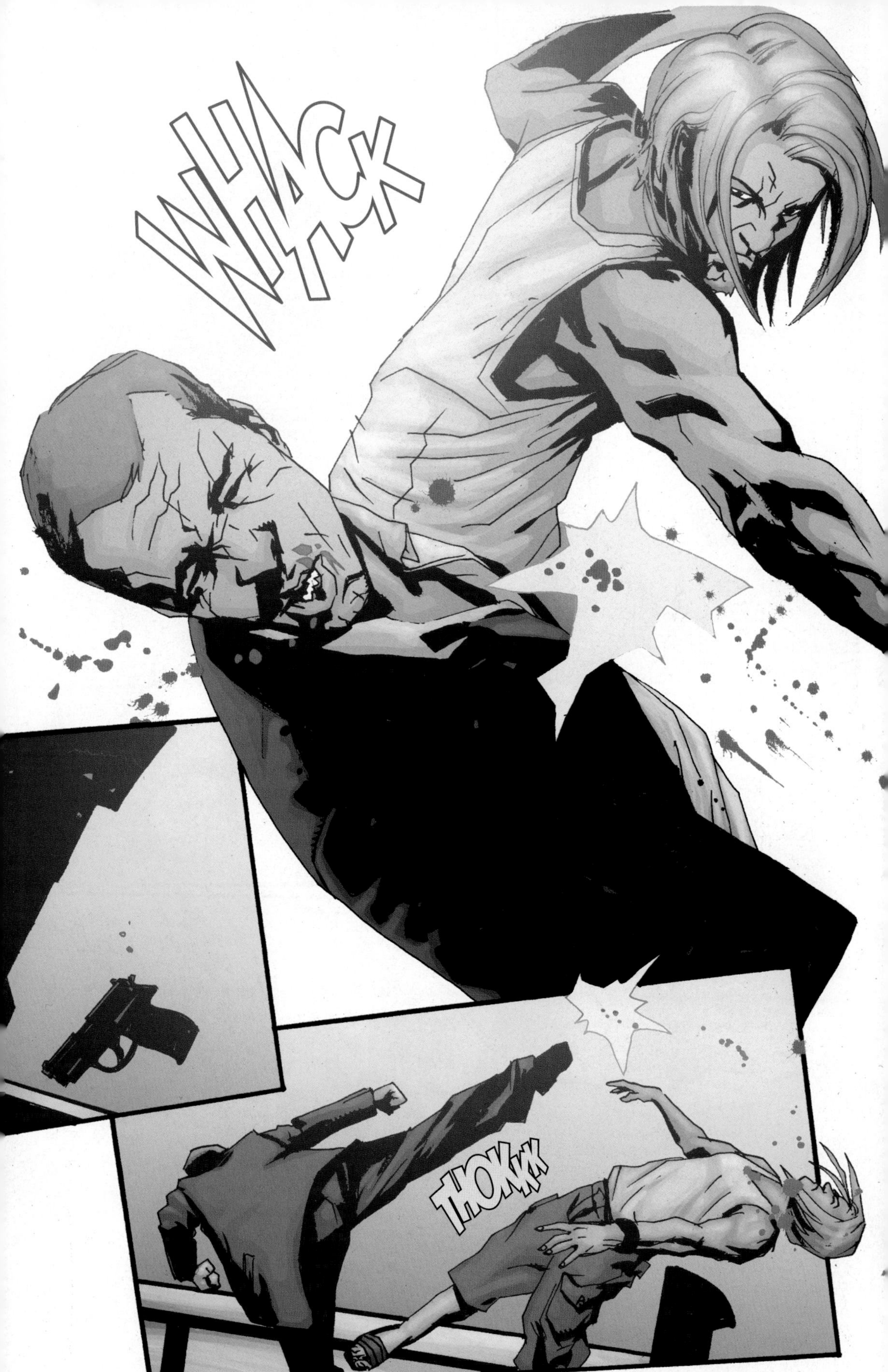
WHACK
THONKK

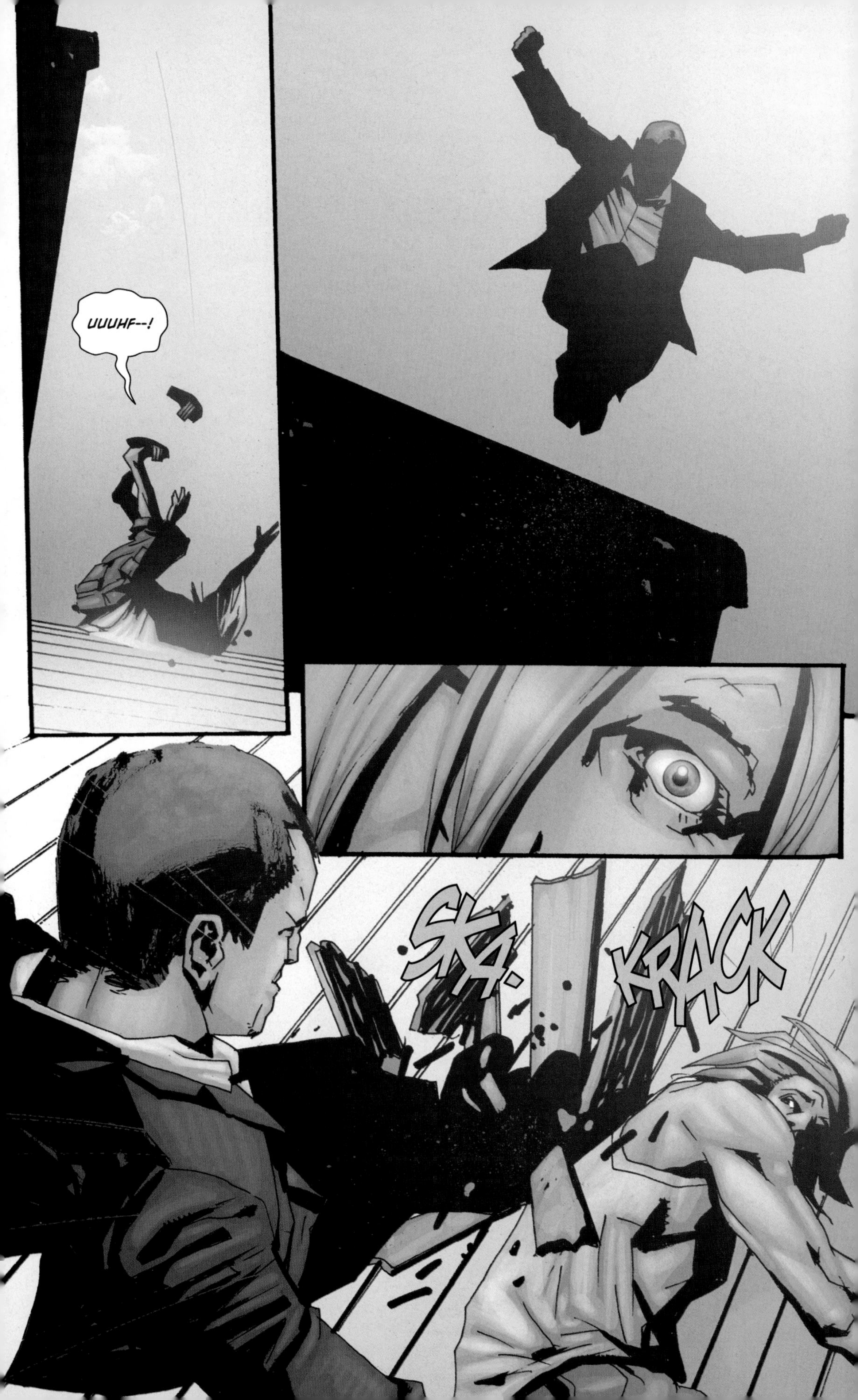
UUUHF--!
SKA-
KRACK

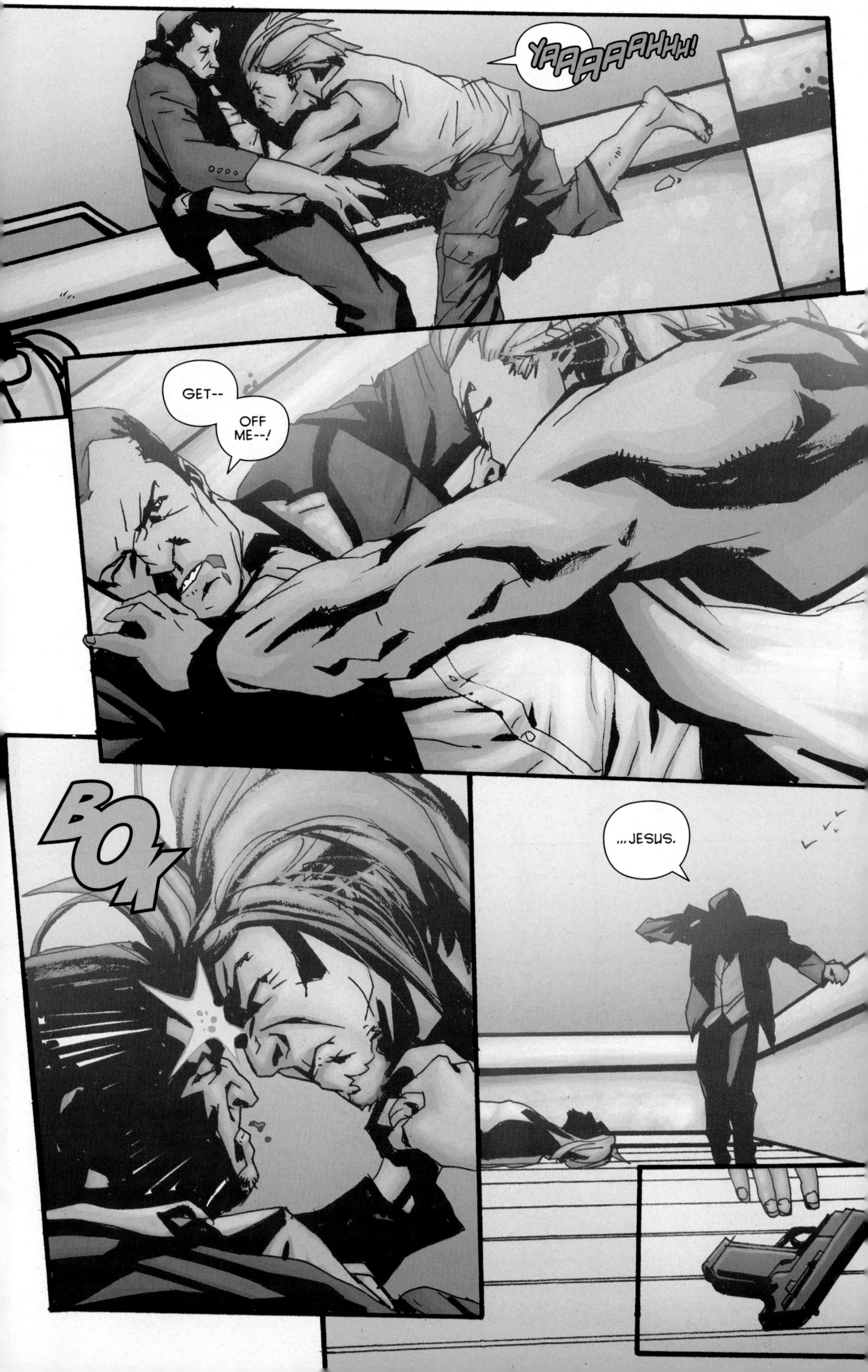
YAAAAAHHH!
GET--
OFF ME--!
BOK
...JESUS.

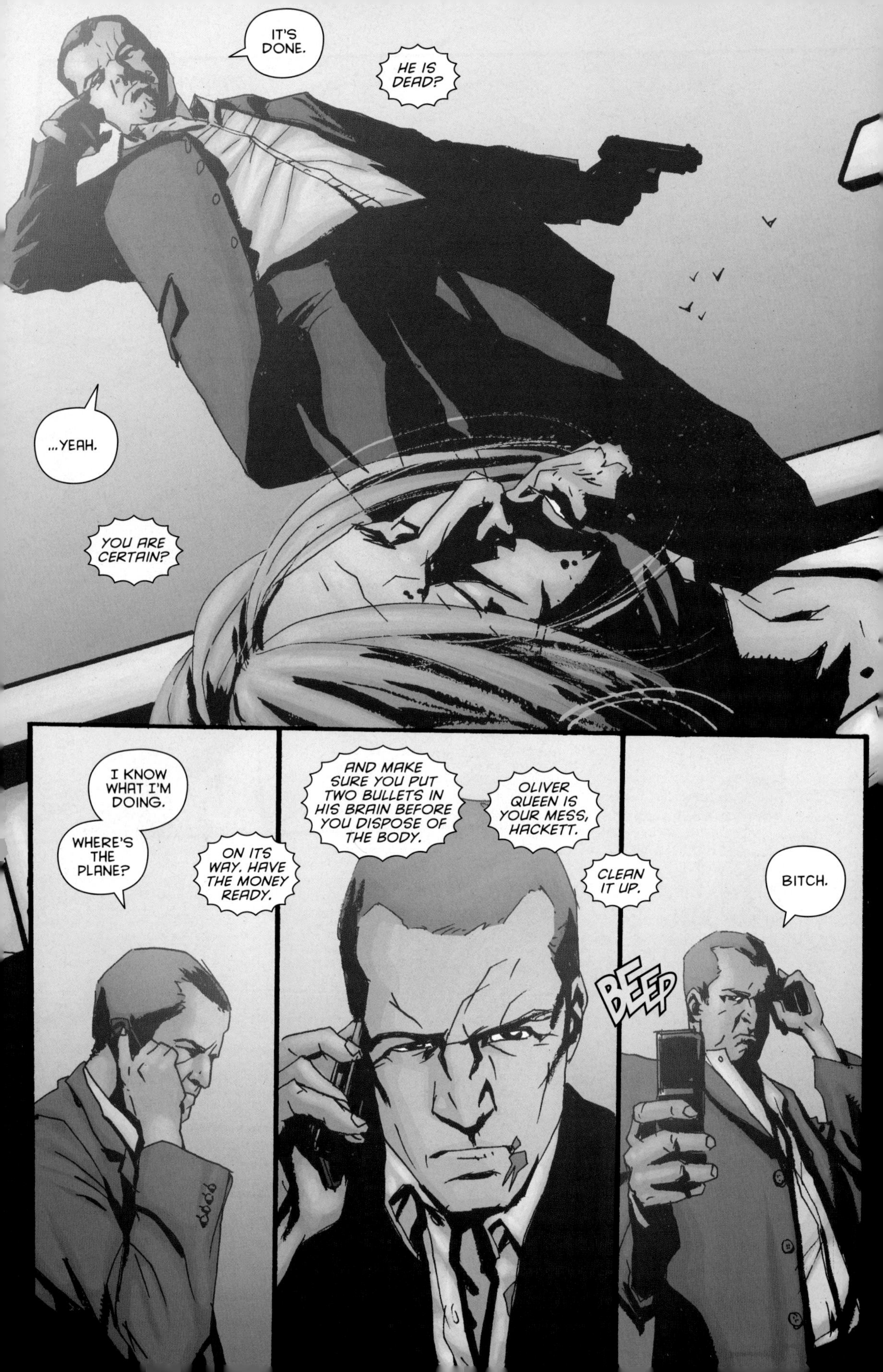
IT'S DONE.
HE IS DEAD?
...YEAH.
YOU ARE CERTAIN?
I KNOW WHAT I'M DOING.
WHERE'S THE PLANE?
ON ITS WAY. HAVE THE MONEY READY.
AND MAKE SURE YOU PUT TWO BULLETS IN HIS BRAIN BEFORE YOU DISPOSE OF THE BODY.
OLIVER QUEEN IS YOUR MESS, HACKETT.
CLEAN IT UP.
BEEP
BITCH.

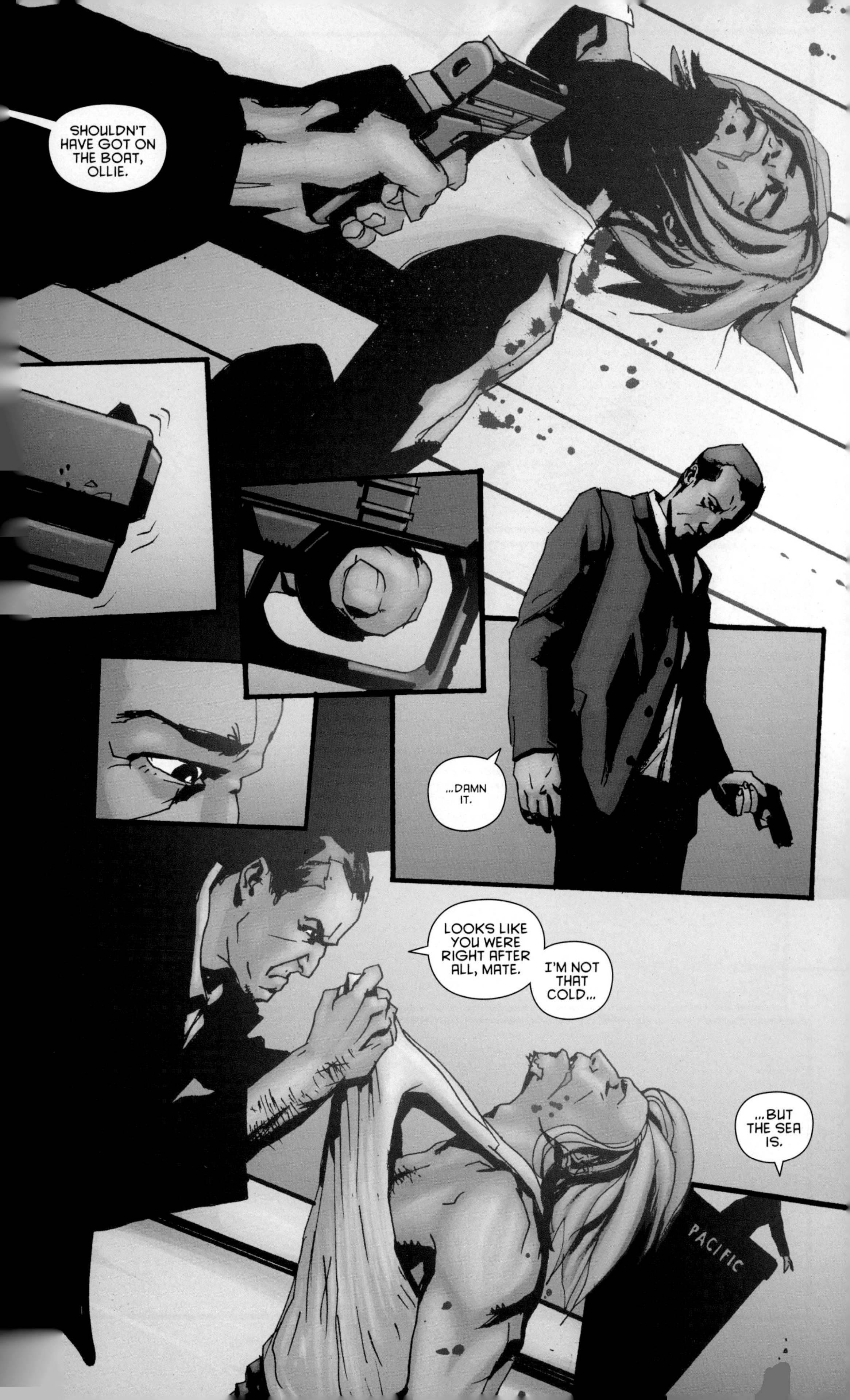
SHOULDN'T HAVE GOT ON THE BOAT, OLLIE.
...DAMN IT.
LOOKS LIKE YOU WERE RIGHT AFTER ALL, MATE.
I'M NOT THAT COLD...
...BUT THE SEA IS.
PACIFIC

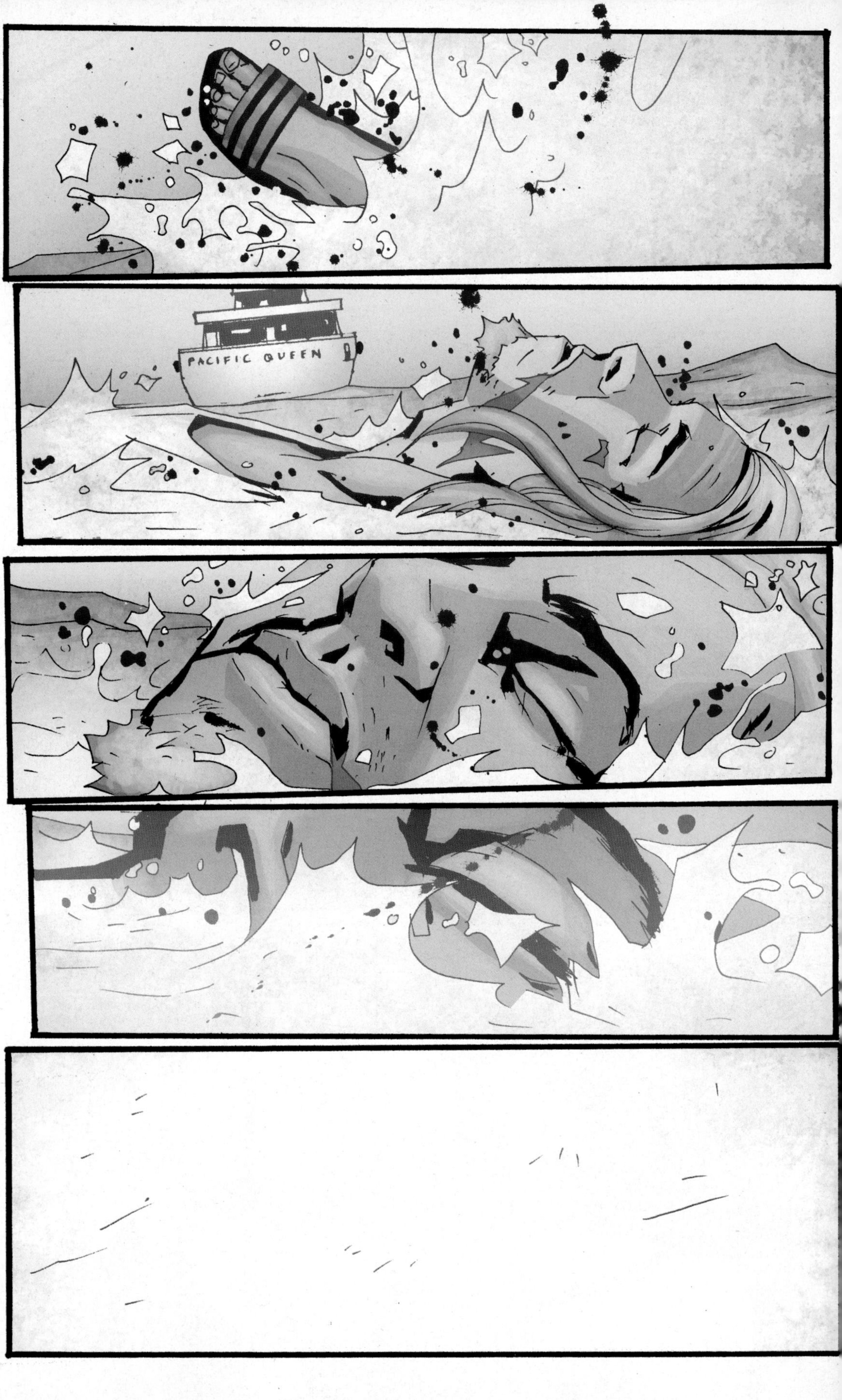
PACIFIC QUEEN

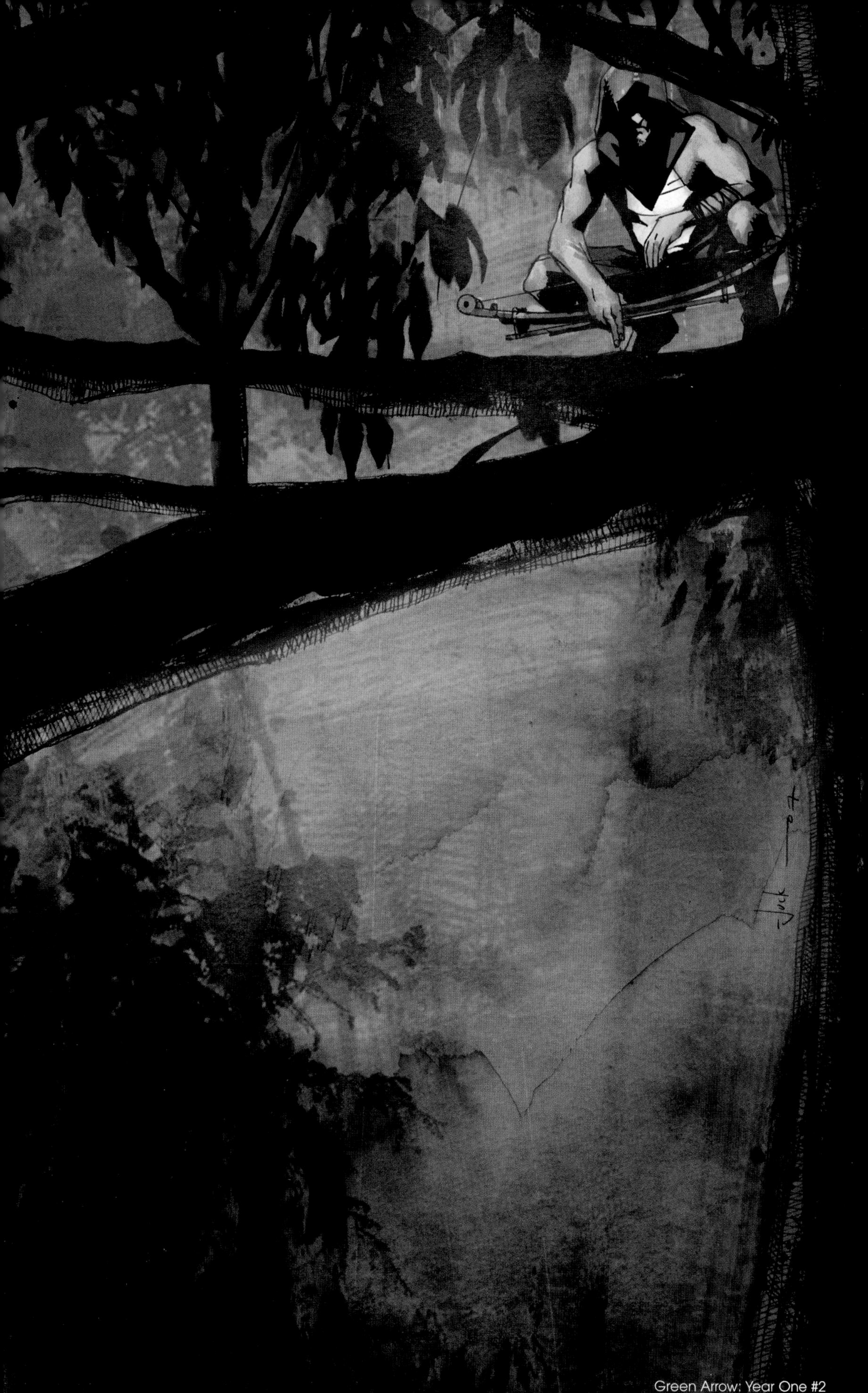

Green Arrow: Year One #2

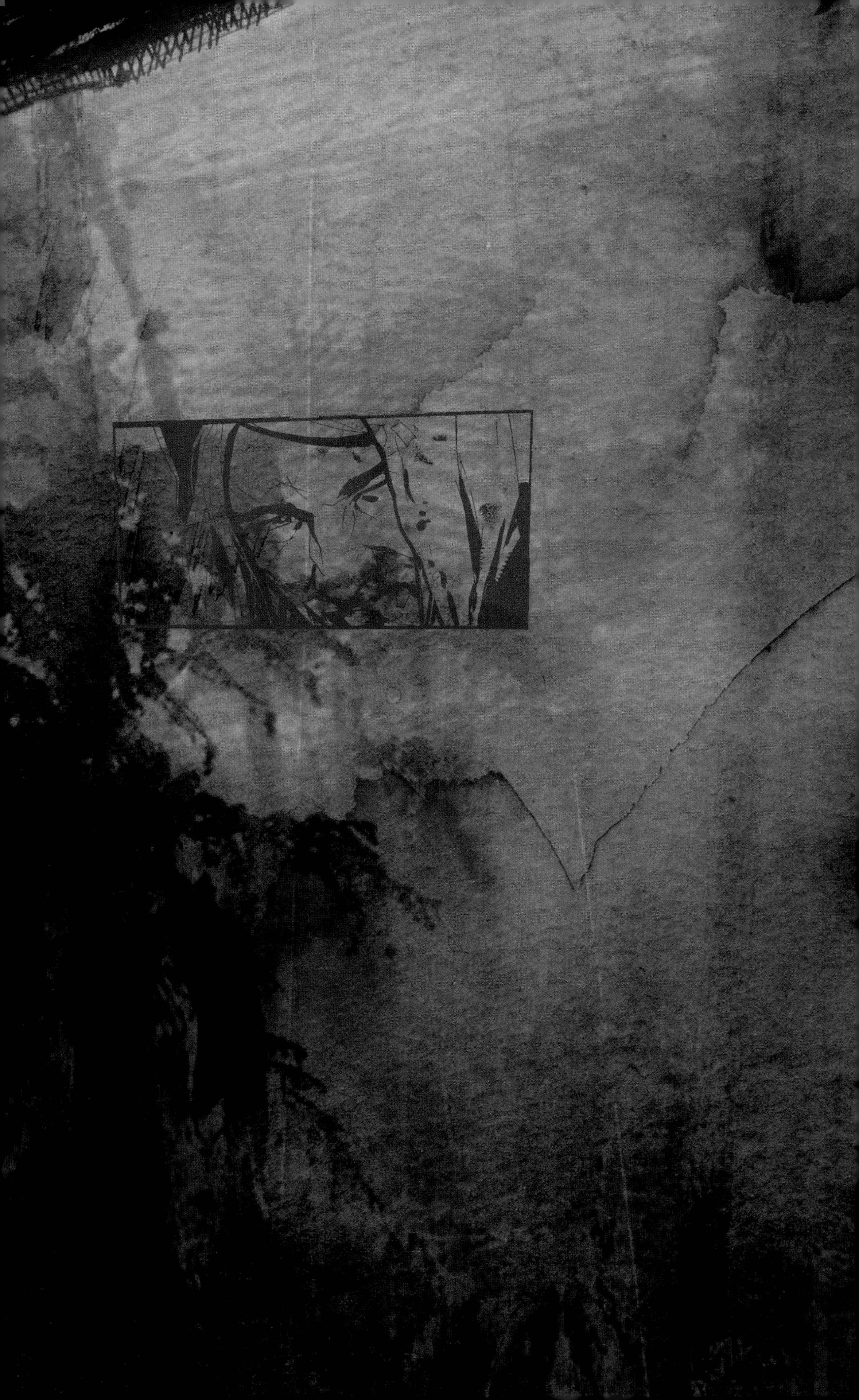

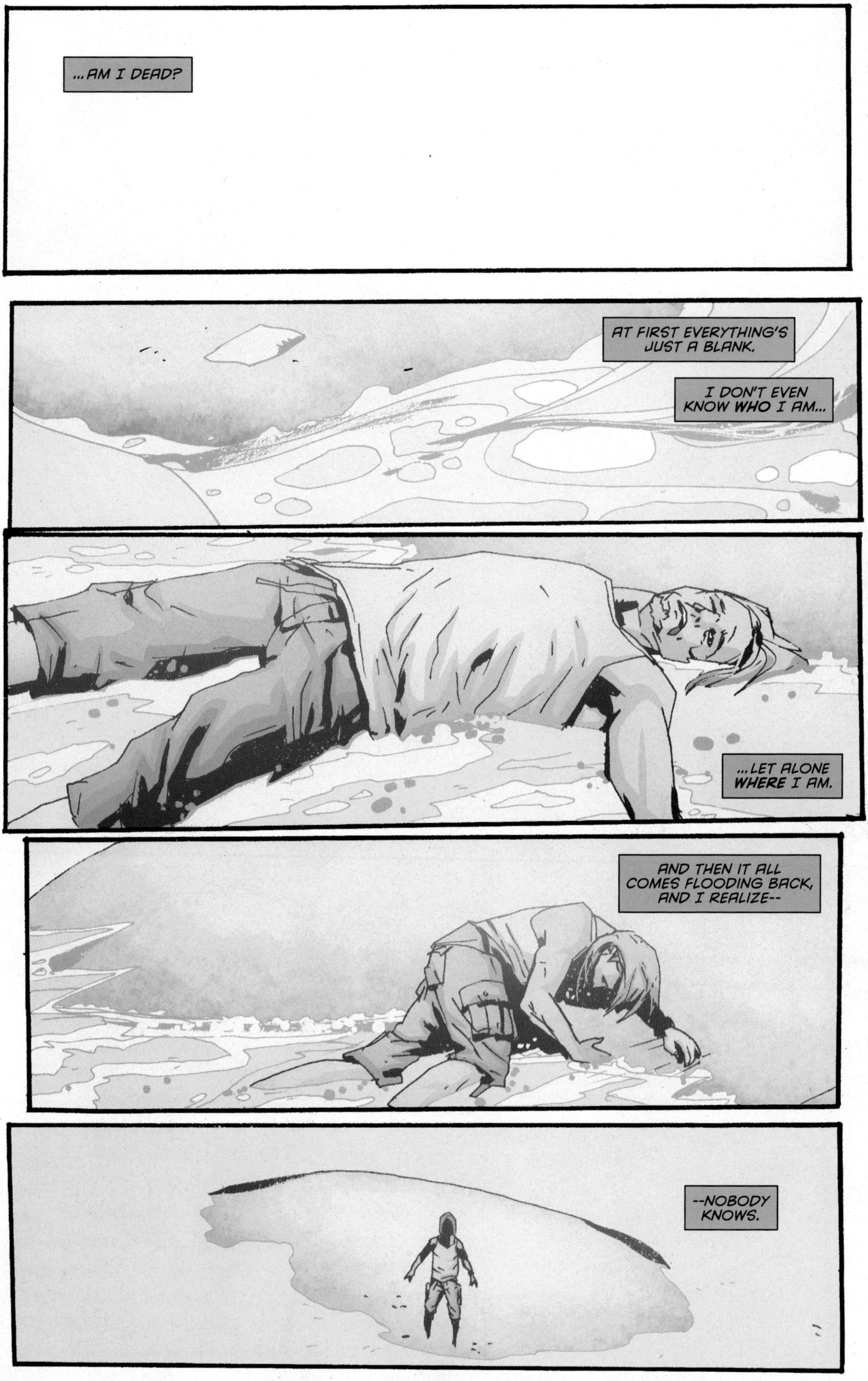
...AM I DEAD?
AT FIRST EVERYTHING'S JUST A BLANK.
I DON'T EVEN KNOW WHO I AM...
...LET ALONE WHERE I AM.
AND THEN IT ALL COMES FLOODING BACK, AND I REALIZE--
--NOBODY KNOWS.

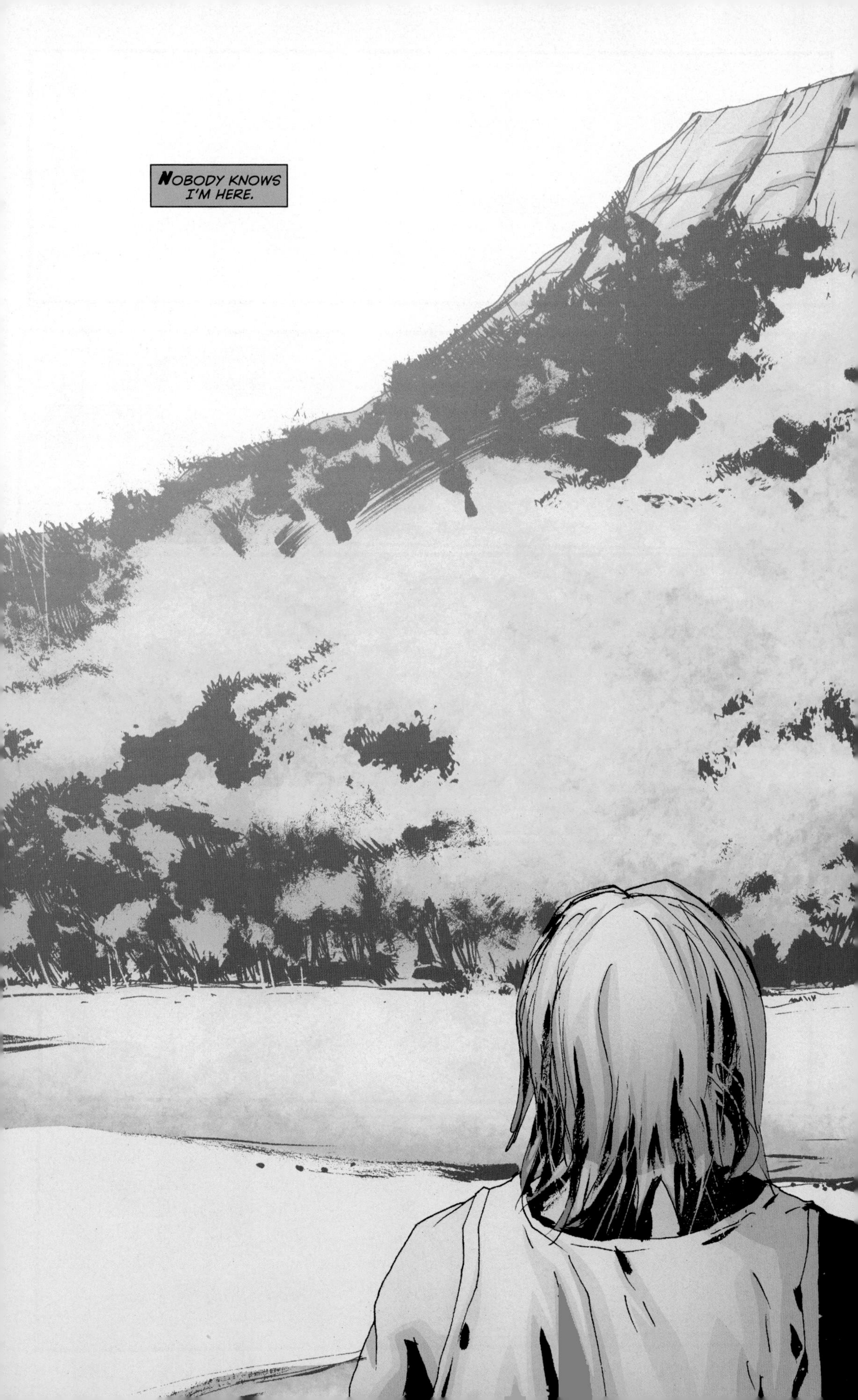
NOBODY KNOWS I'M HERE.

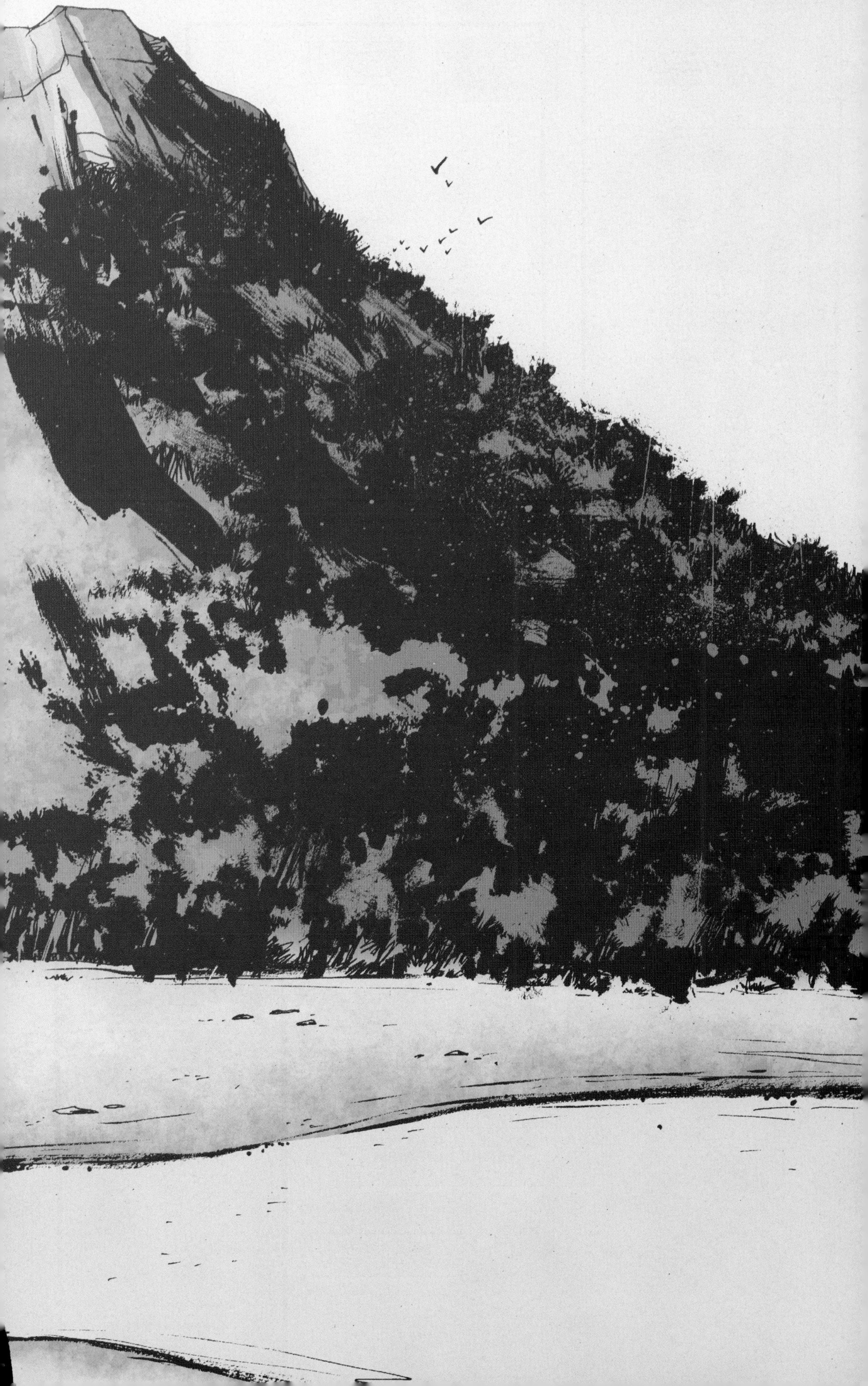

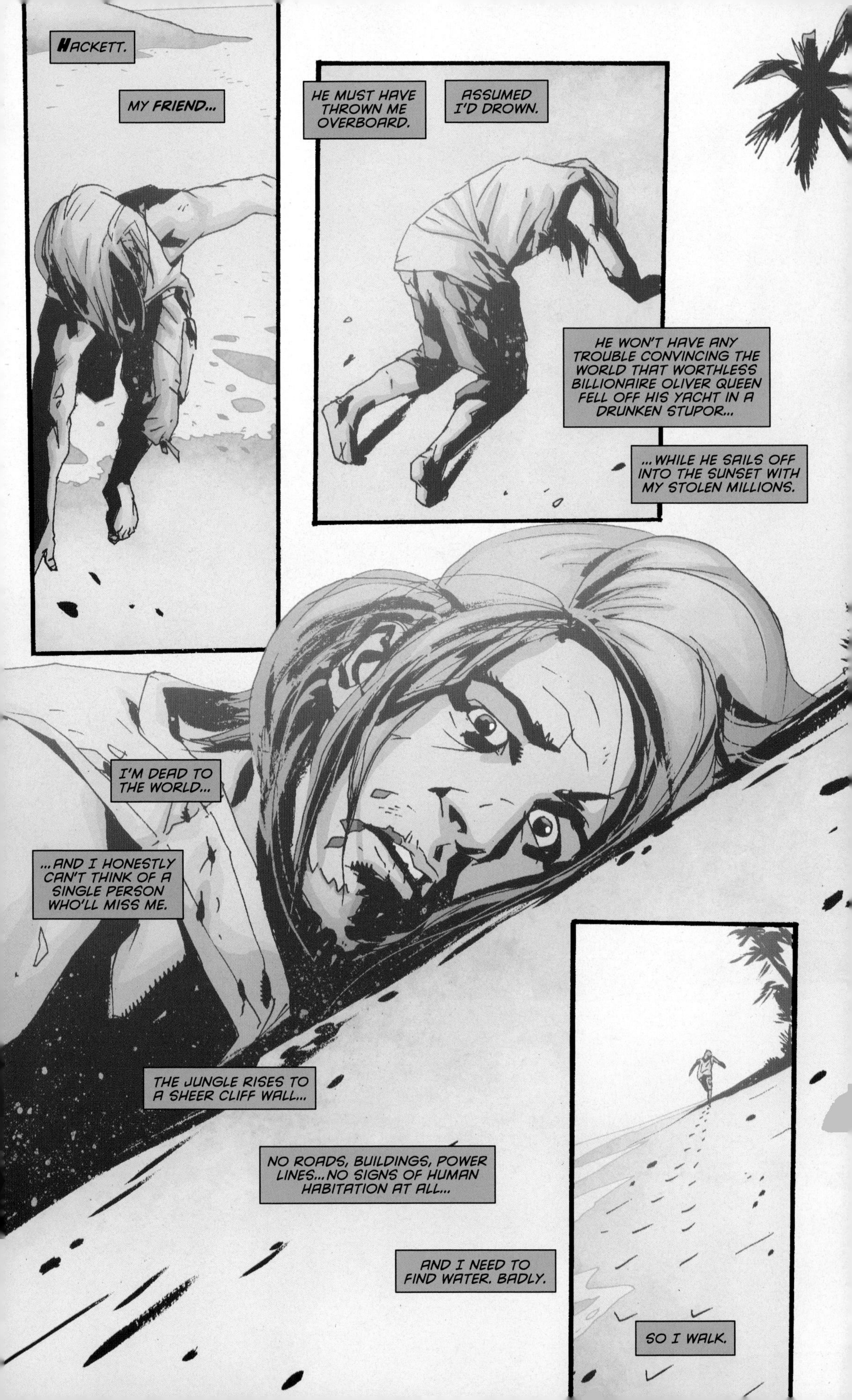
HACKETT.
MY FRIEND...
HE MUST HAVE THROWN ME OVERBOARD.
ASSUMED I'D DROWN.
HE WON'T HAVE ANY TROUBLE CONVINCING THE WORLD THAT WORTHLESS BILLIONAIRE OLIVER QUEEN FELL OFF HIS YACHT IN A DRUNKEN STUPOR...
...WHILE HE SAILS OFF INTO THE SUNSET WITH MY STOLEN MILLIONS.
I'M DEAD TO THE WORLD...
...AND I HONESTLY CAN'T THINK OF A SINGLE PERSON WHO'LL MISS ME.
THE JUNGLE RISES TO A SHEER CLIFF WALL...
NO ROADS, BUILDINGS, POWER LINES...NO SIGNS OF HUMAN HABITATION AT ALL...
AND I NEED TO FIND WATER. BADLY.
SO I WALK.

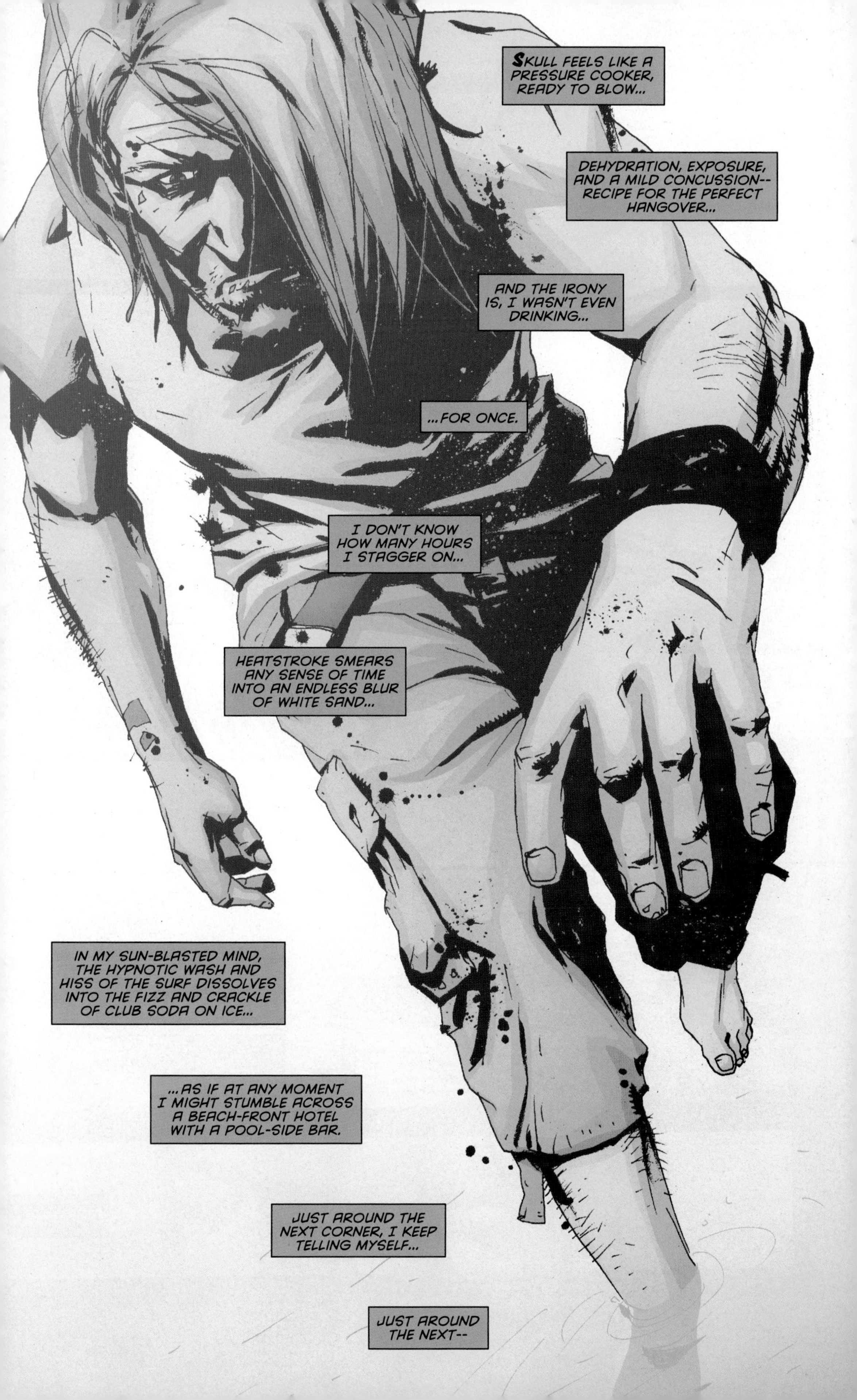
SKULL FEELS LIKE A PRESSURE COOKER, READY TO BLOW...
DEHYDRATION, EXPOSURE, AND A MILD CONCUSSION-- RECIPE FOR THE PERFECT HANGOVER...
AND THE IRONY IS, I WASN'T EVEN DRINKING...
...FOR ONCE.
I DON'T KNOW HOW MANY HOURS I STAGGER ON...
HEATSTROKE SMEARS ANY SENSE OF TIME INTO AN ENDLESS BLUR OF WHITE SAND...
IN MY SUN-BLASTED MIND, THE HYPNOTIC WASH AND HISS OF THE SURF DISSOLVES INTO THE FIZZ AND CRACKLE OF CLUB SODA ON ICE...
...AS IF AT ANY MOMENT I MIGHT STUMBLE ACROSS A BEACH-FRONT HOTEL WITH A POOL-SIDE BAR.
JUST AROUND THE NEXT CORNER, I KEEP TELLING MYSELF...
JUST AROUND THE NEXT--

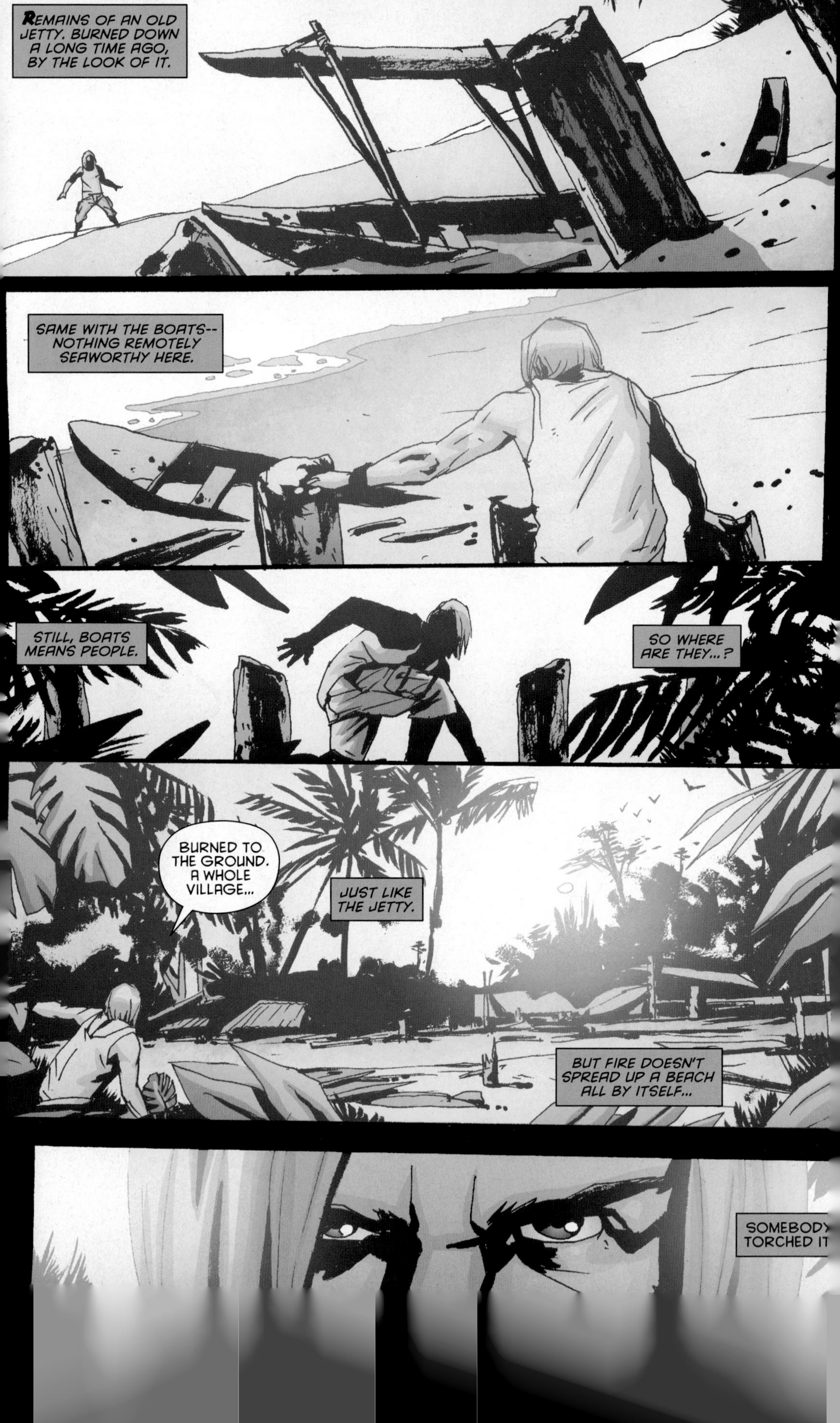
REMAINS OF AN OLD JETTY. BURNED DOWN A LONG TIME AGO, BY THE LOOK OF IT.
SAME WITH THE BOATS-- NOTHING REMOTELY SEAWORTHY HERE.
STILL, BOATS MEANS PEOPLE.
SO WHERE ARE THEY...?
BURNED TO THE GROUND. A WHOLE VILLAGE...
JUST LIKE THE JETTY.
BUT FIRE DOESN'T SPREAD UP A BEACH ALL BY ITSELF...
SOMEBODY TORCHED IT

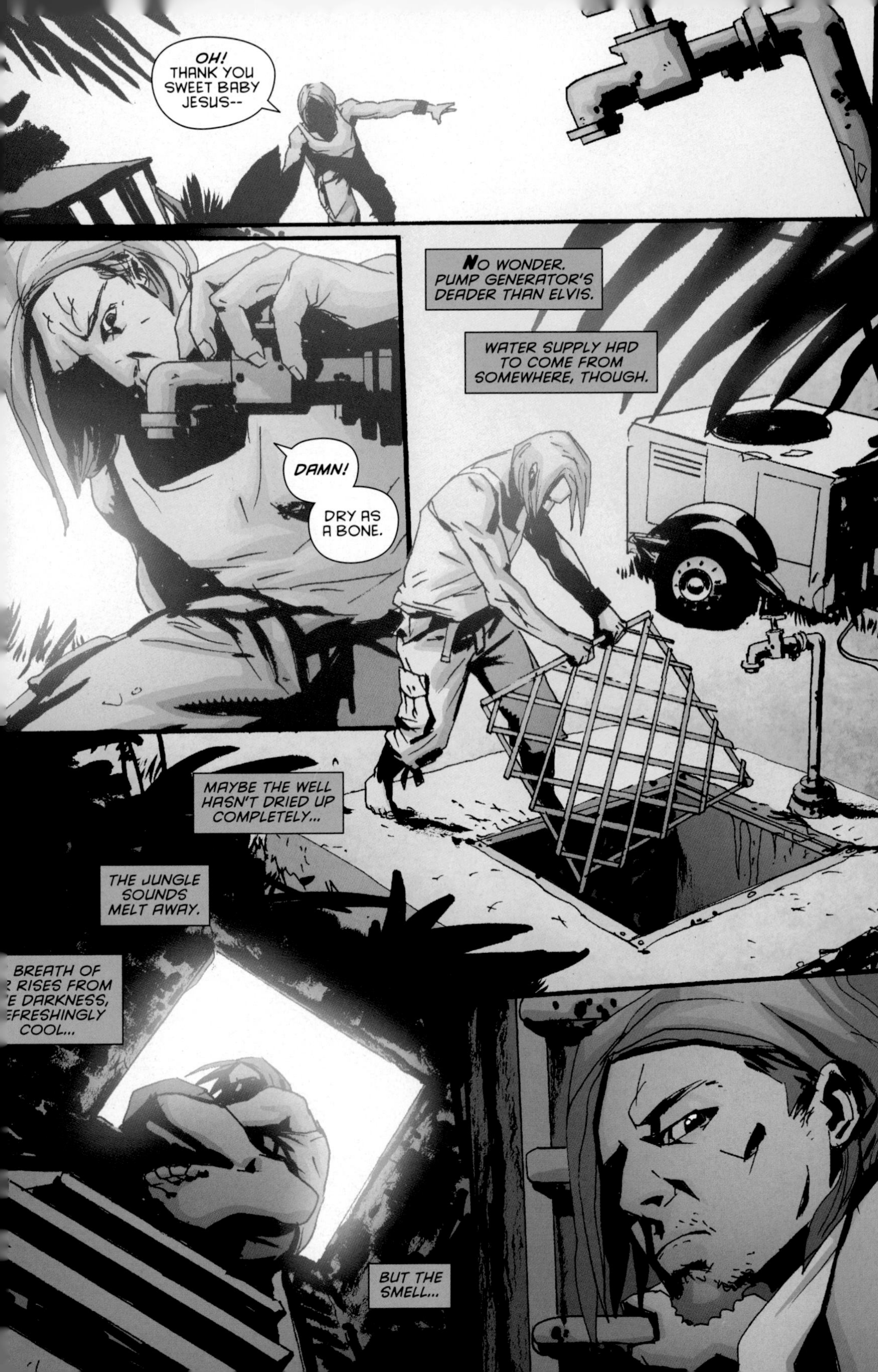
OH! THANK YOU SWEET BABY JESUS--
NO WONDER. PUMP GENERATOR'S DEADER THAN ELVIS.
WATER SUPPLY HAD TO COME FROM SOMEWHERE, THOUGH.
DAMN!
DRY AS A BONE.
MAYBE THE WELL HASN'T DRIED UP COMPLETELY...
THE JUNGLE SOUNDS MELT AWAY.
BREATH OF R RISES FROM E DARKNESS, EFRESHINGLY COOL...
BUT THE SMELL...

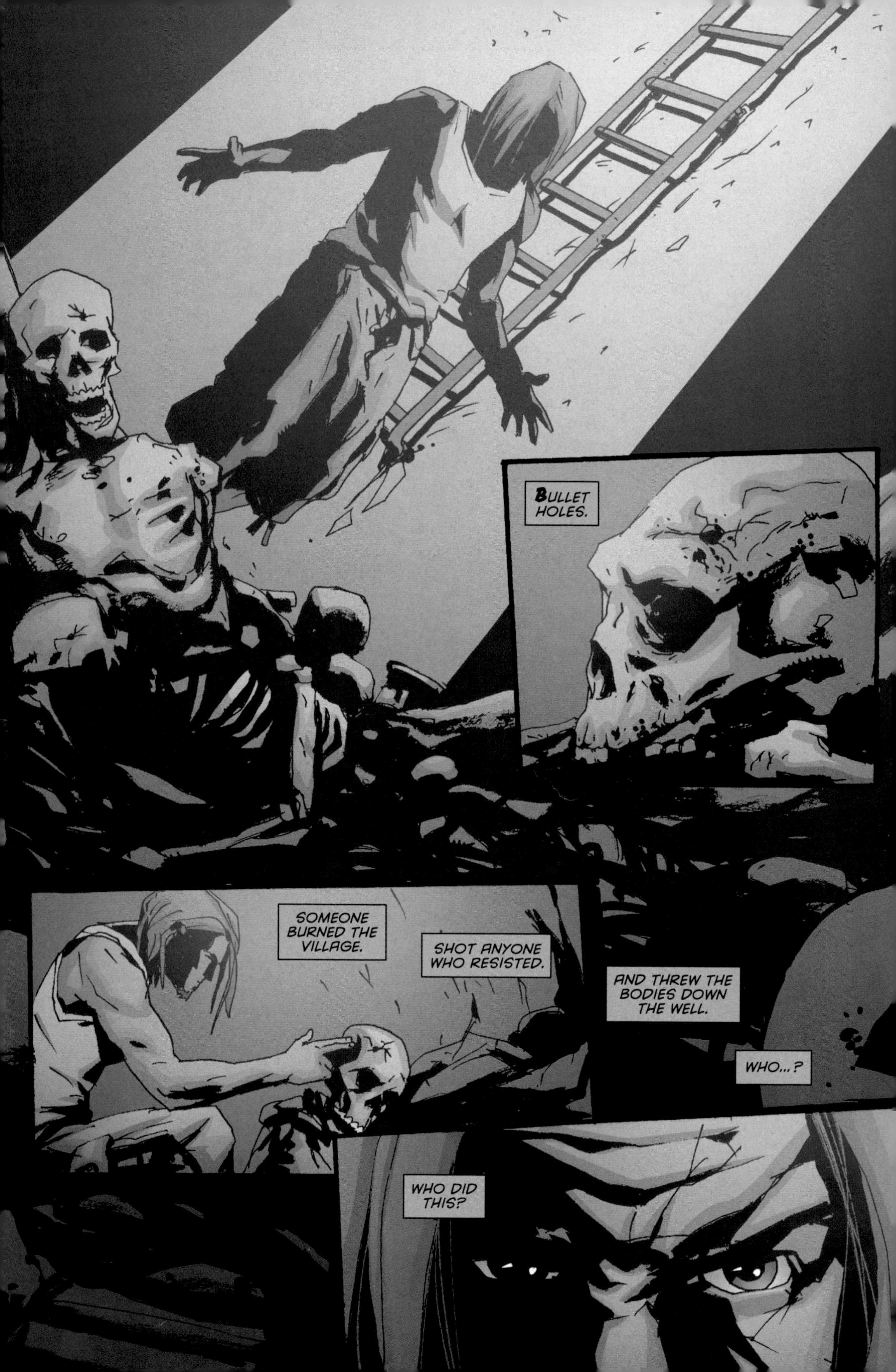
BULLET HOLES.
SOMEONE BURNED THE VILLAGE.
SHOT ANYONE WHO RESISTED.
AND THREW THE BODIES DOWN THE WELL.
WHO...?
WHO DID THIS?

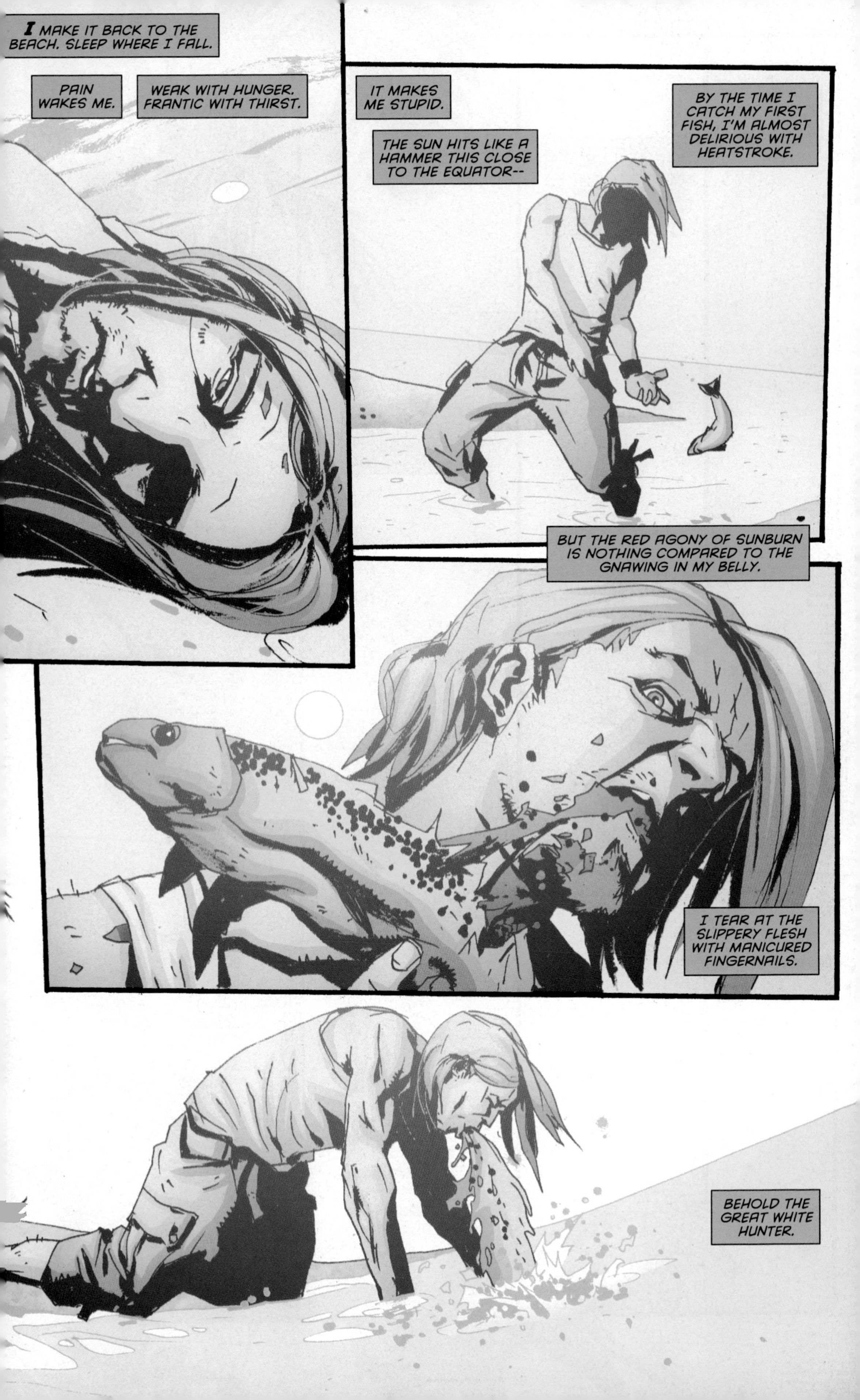
I MAKE IT BACK TO THE BEACH. SLEEP WHERE I FALL.
PAIN WAKES ME.
WEAK WITH HUNGER. FRANTIC WITH THIRST.
IT MAKES ME STUPID.
THE SUN HITS LIKE A HAMMER THIS CLOSE TO THE EQUATOR--
BY THE TIME I CATCH MY FIRST FISH, I'M ALMOST DELIRIOUS WITH HEATSTROKE.
BUT THE RED AGONY OF SUNBURN IS NOTHING COMPARED TO THE GNAWING IN MY BELLY.
I TEAR AT THE SLIPPERY FLESH WITH MANICURED FINGERNAILS.
BEHOLD THE GREAT WHITE HUNTER.

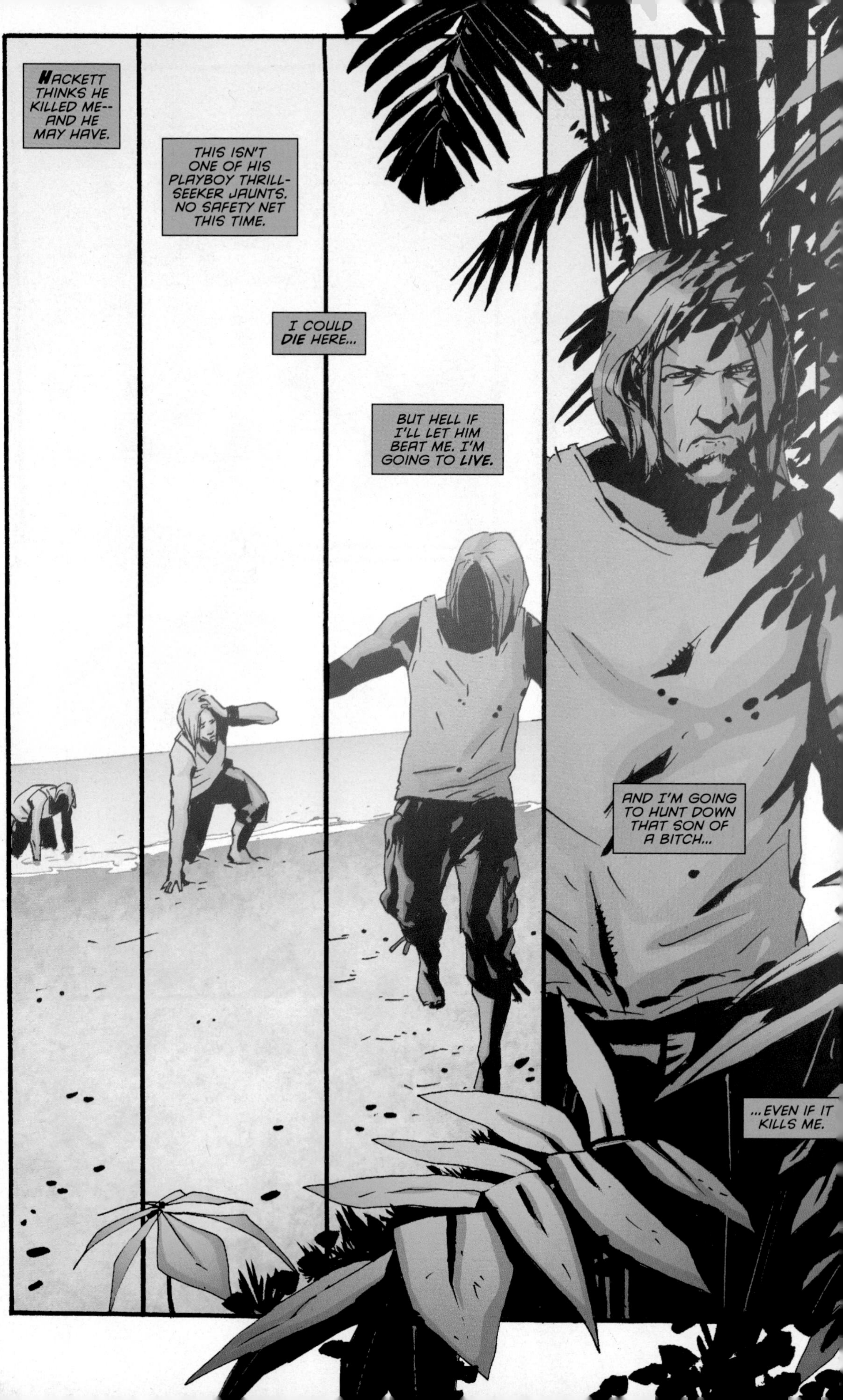
HACKETT THINKS HE KILLED ME-- AND HE MAY HAVE.
THIS ISN'T ONE OF HIS PLAYBOY THRILL-SEEKER JAUNTS. NO SAFETY NET THIS TIME.
I COULD DIE HERE...
BUT HELL IF I'LL LET HIM BEAT ME. I'M GOING TO LIVE.
AND I'M GOING TO HUNT DOWN THAT SON OF A BITCH...
...EVEN IF IT KILLS ME.

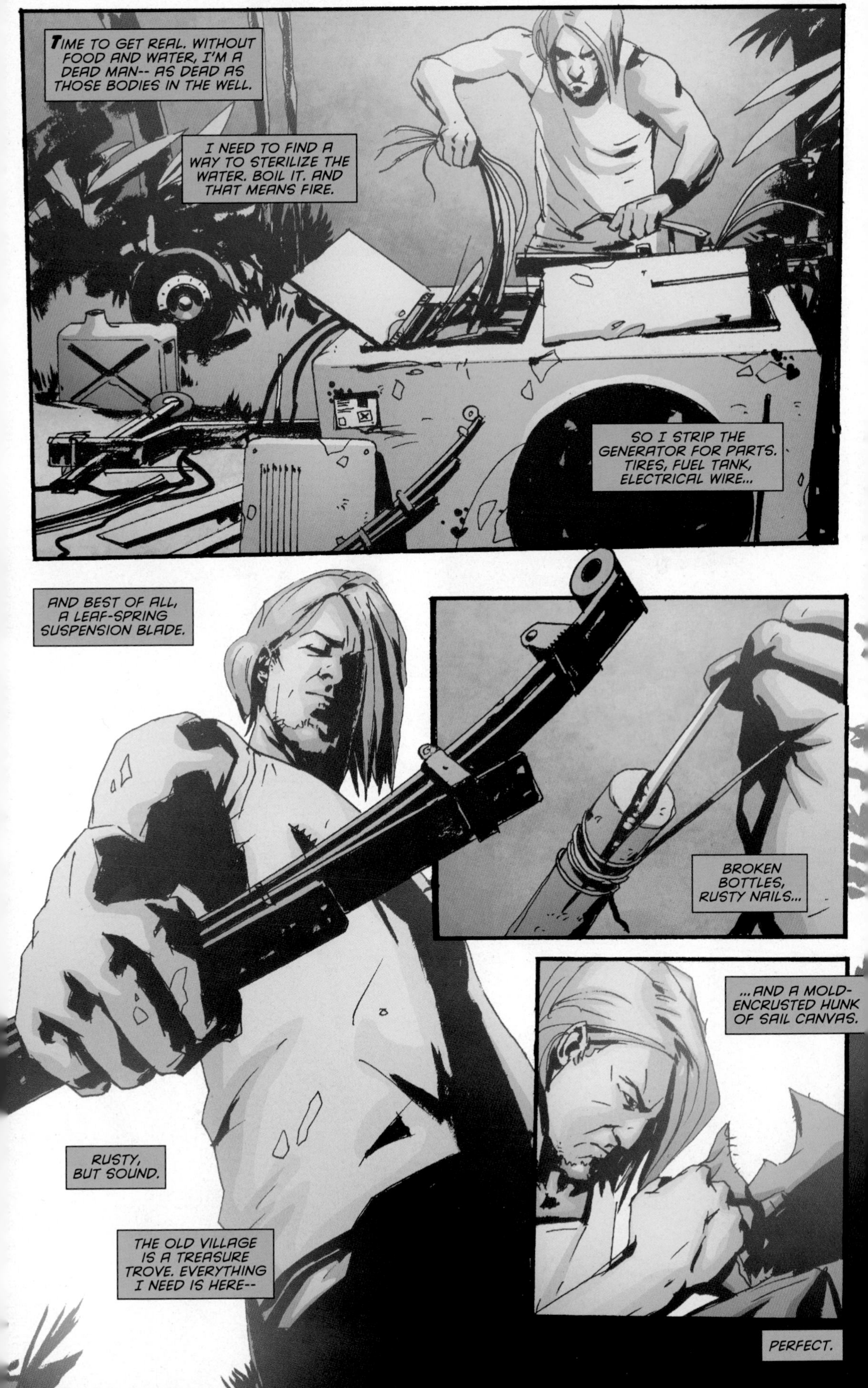
TIME TO GET REAL. WITHOUT FOOD AND WATER, I'M A DEAD MAN-- AS DEAD AS THOSE BODIES IN THE WELL.
I NEED TO FIND A WAY TO STERILIZE THE WATER. BOIL IT. AND THAT MEANS FIRE.
SO I STRIP THE GENERATOR FOR PARTS. TIRES, FUEL TANK, ELECTRICAL WIRE...
AND BEST OF ALL, A LEAF-SPRING SUSPENSION BLADE.
RUSTY, BUT SOUND.
THE OLD VILLAGE IS A TREASURE TROVE. EVERYTHING I NEED IS HERE--
BROKEN BOTTLES, RUSTY NAILS...
...AND A MOLD-ENCRUSTED HUNK OF SAIL CANVAS.
PERFECT.

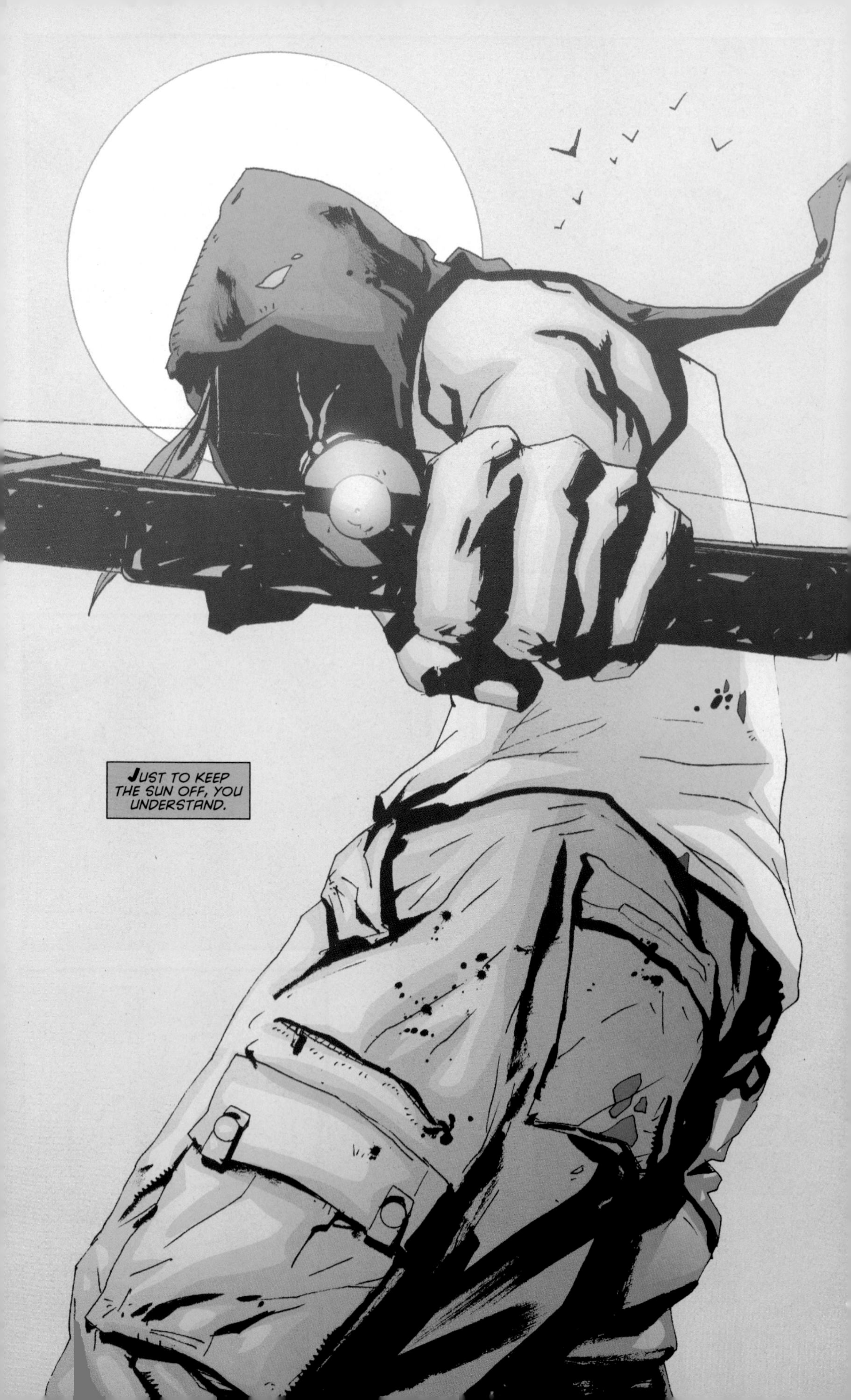
JUST TO KEEP THE SUN OFF, YOU UNDERSTAND.

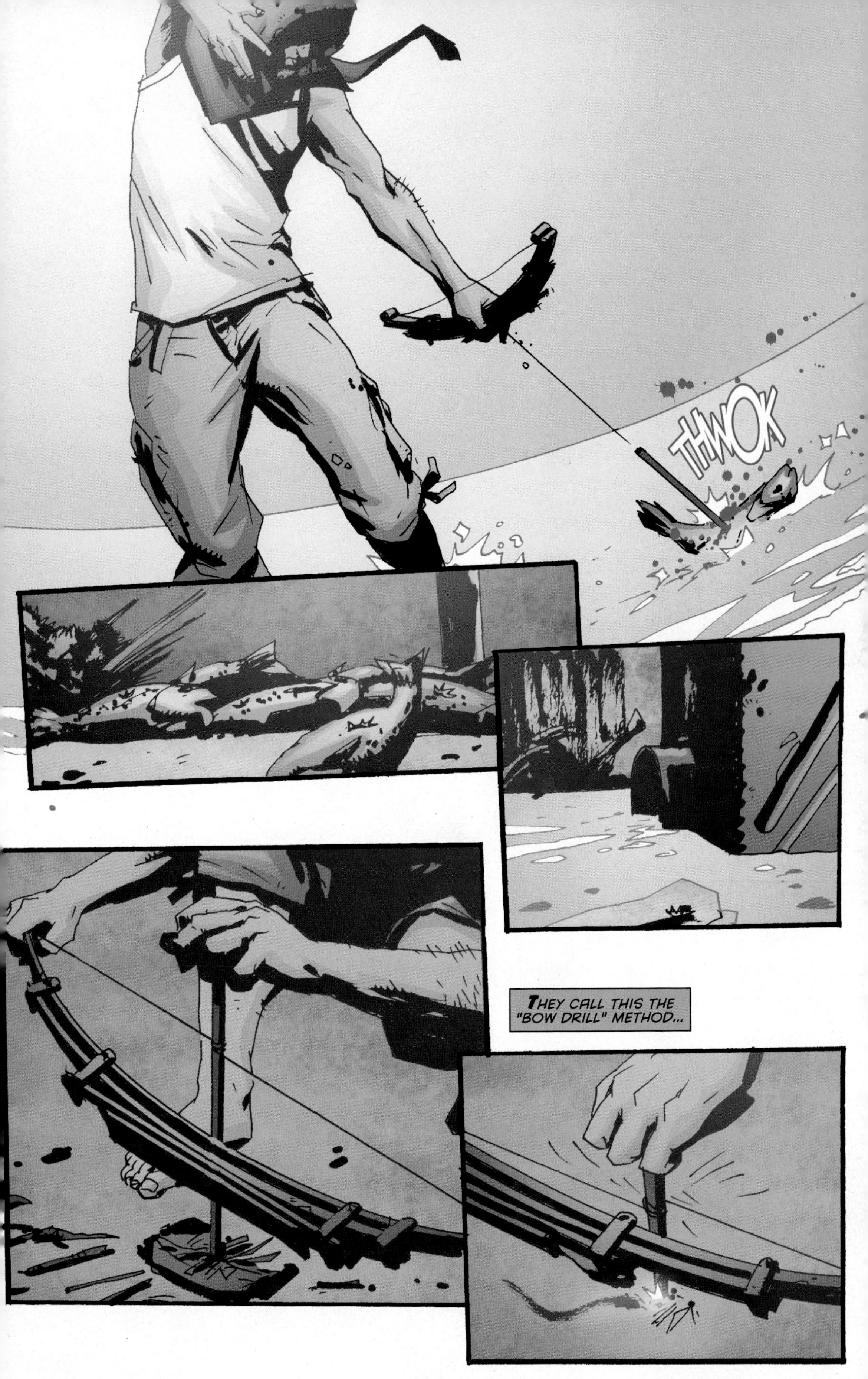
THWOK
THEY CALL THIS THE "BOW DRILL" METHOD...

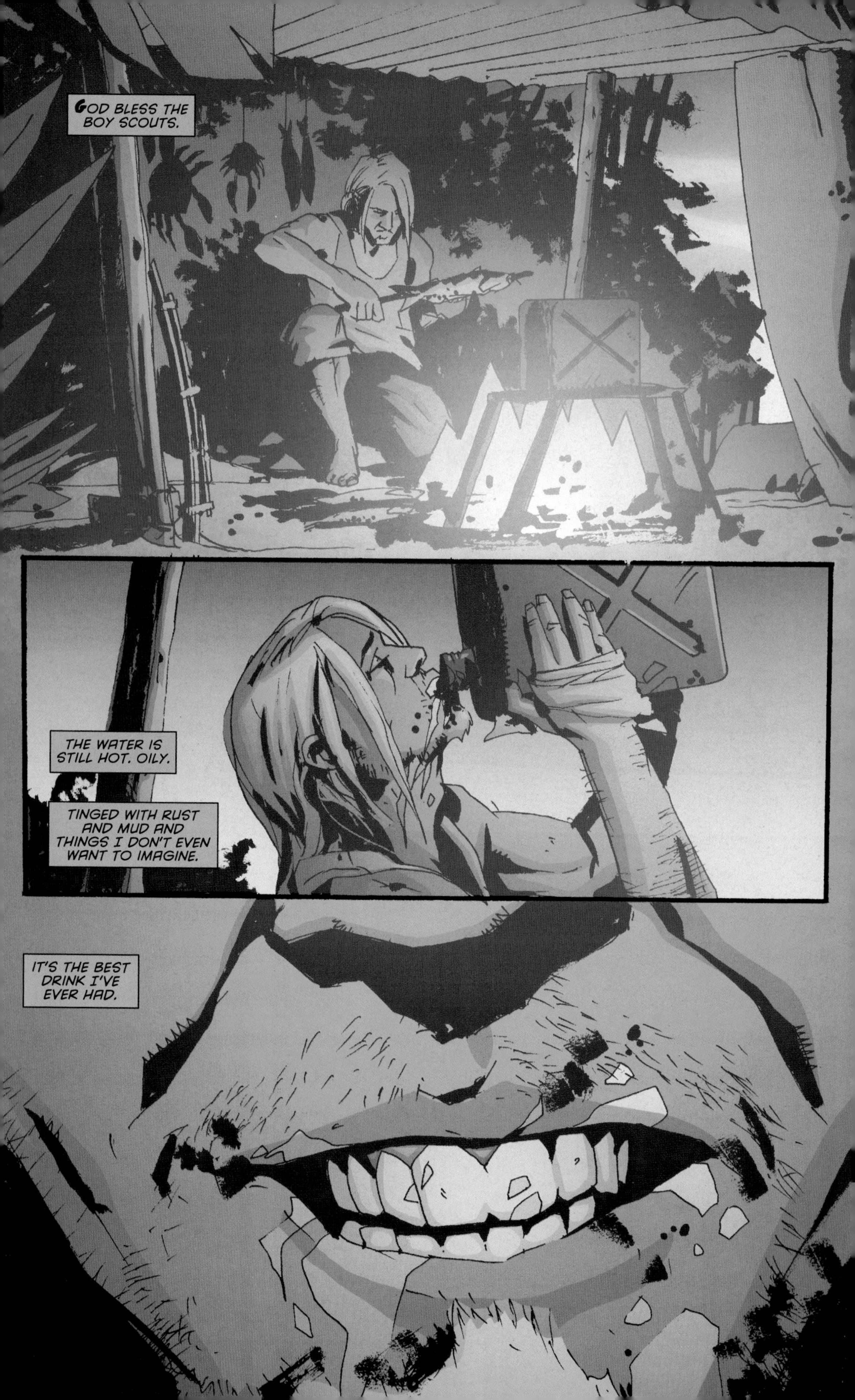
GOD BLESS THE BOY SCOUTS.
THE WATER IS STILL HOT. OILY.
TINGED WITH RUST AND MUD AND THINGS I DON'T EVEN WANT TO IMAGINE.
IT'S THE BEST DRINK I'VE EVER HAD.

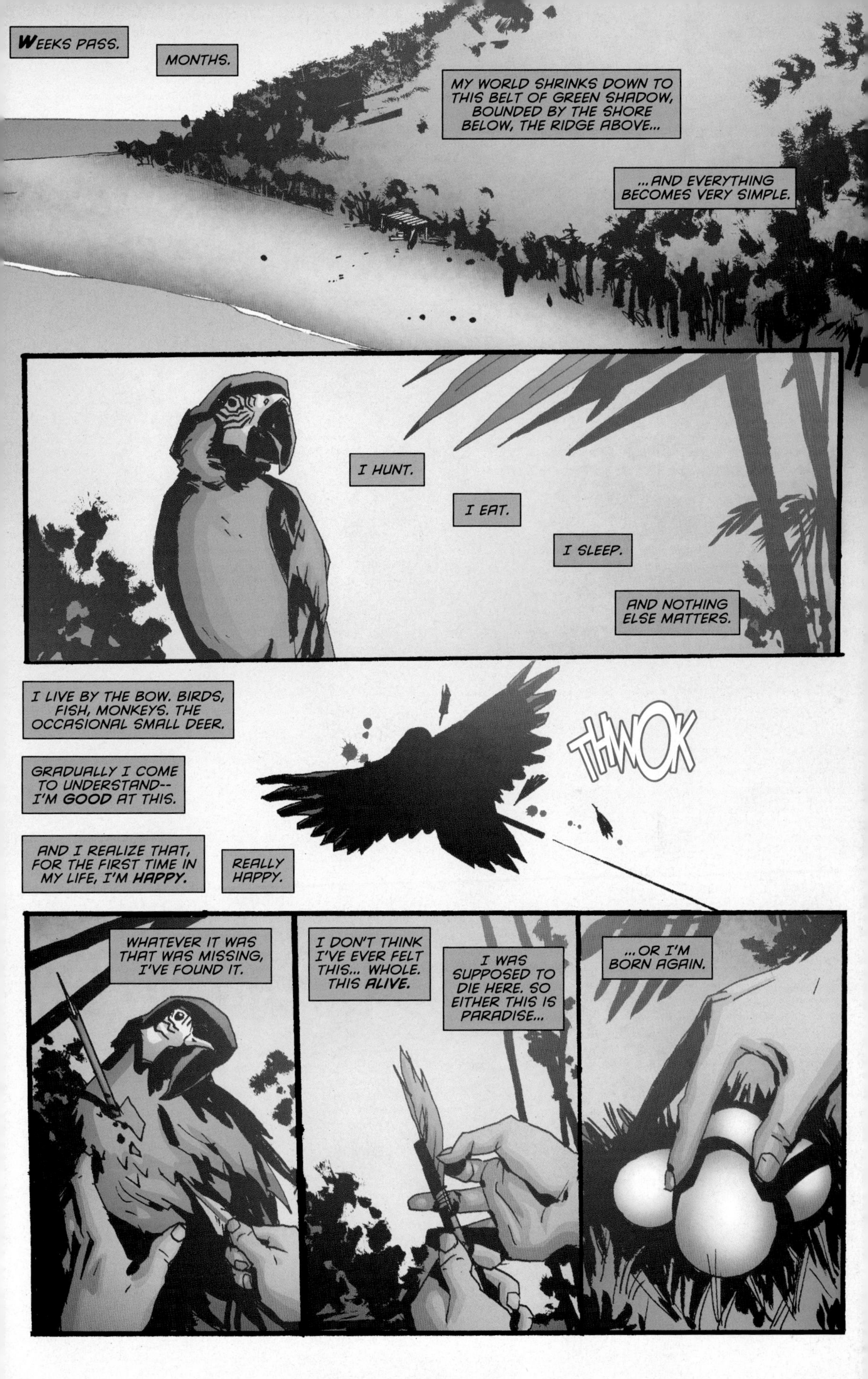
WEEKS PASS.
MONTHS.
MY WORLD SHRINKS DOWN TO THIS BELT OF GREEN SHADOW, BOUNDED BY THE SHORE BELOW, THE RIDGE ABOVE...
...AND EVERYTHING BECOMES VERY SIMPLE.
I HUNT.
I EAT.
I SLEEP.
AND NOTHING ELSE MATTERS.
I LIVE BY THE BOW. BIRDS, FISH, MONKEYS. THE OCCASIONAL SMALL DEER.
GRADUALLY I COME TO UNDERSTAND-- I'M GOOD AT THIS.
AND I REALIZE THAT, FOR THE FIRST TIME IN MY LIFE, I'M HAPPY.
REALLY HAPPY.
THWOK
WHATEVER IT WAS THAT WAS MISSING, I'VE FOUND IT.
I DON'T THINK I'VE EVER FELT THIS... WHOLE. THIS ALIVE.
I WAS SUPPOSED TO DIE HERE. SO EITHER THIS IS PARADISE...
...OR I'M BORN AGAIN.

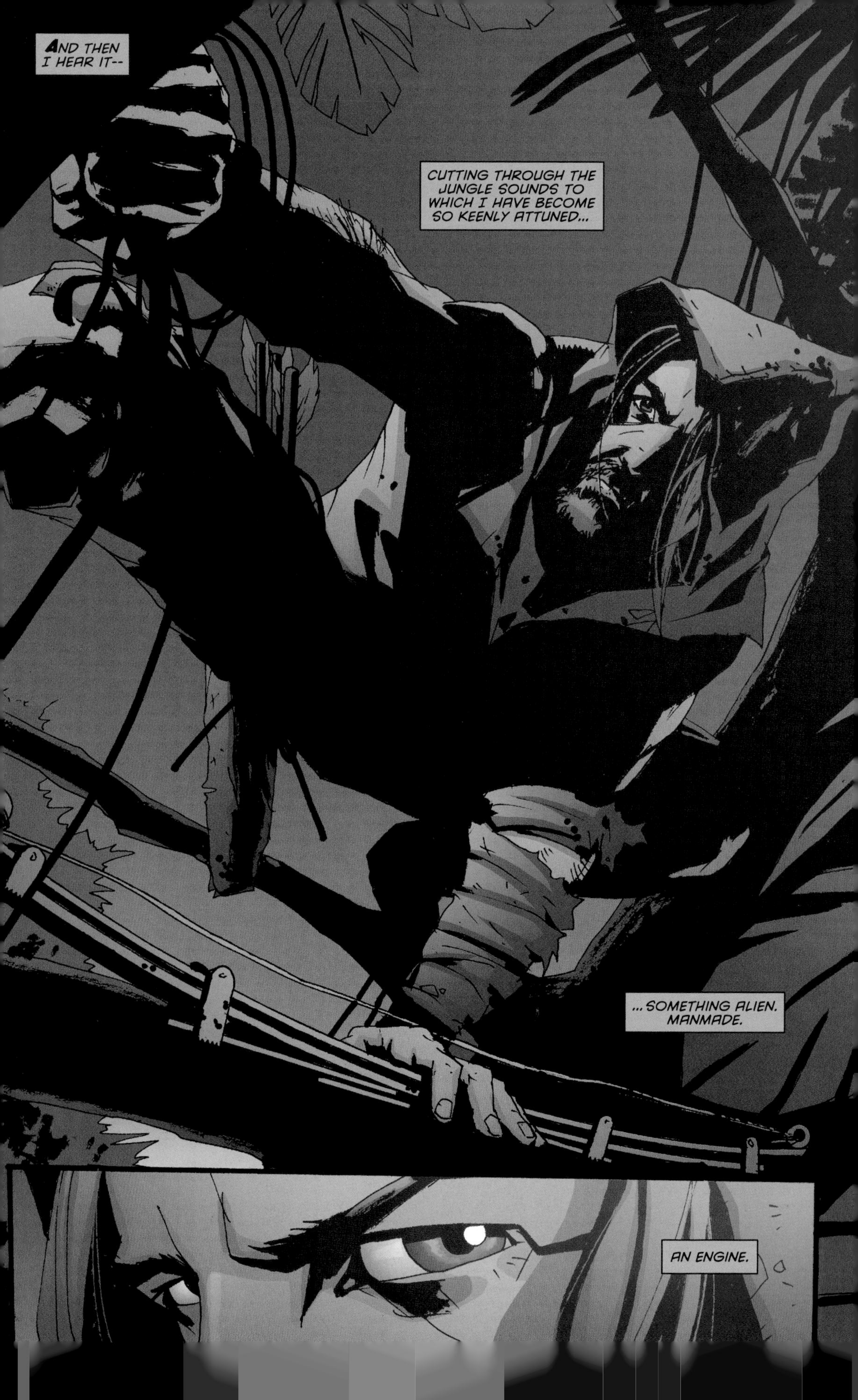
AND THEN I HEAR IT--
CUTTING THROUGH THE JUNGLE SOUNDS TO WHICH I HAVE BECOME SO KEENLY ATTUNED...
...SOMETHING ALIEN. MANMADE.
AN ENGINE.

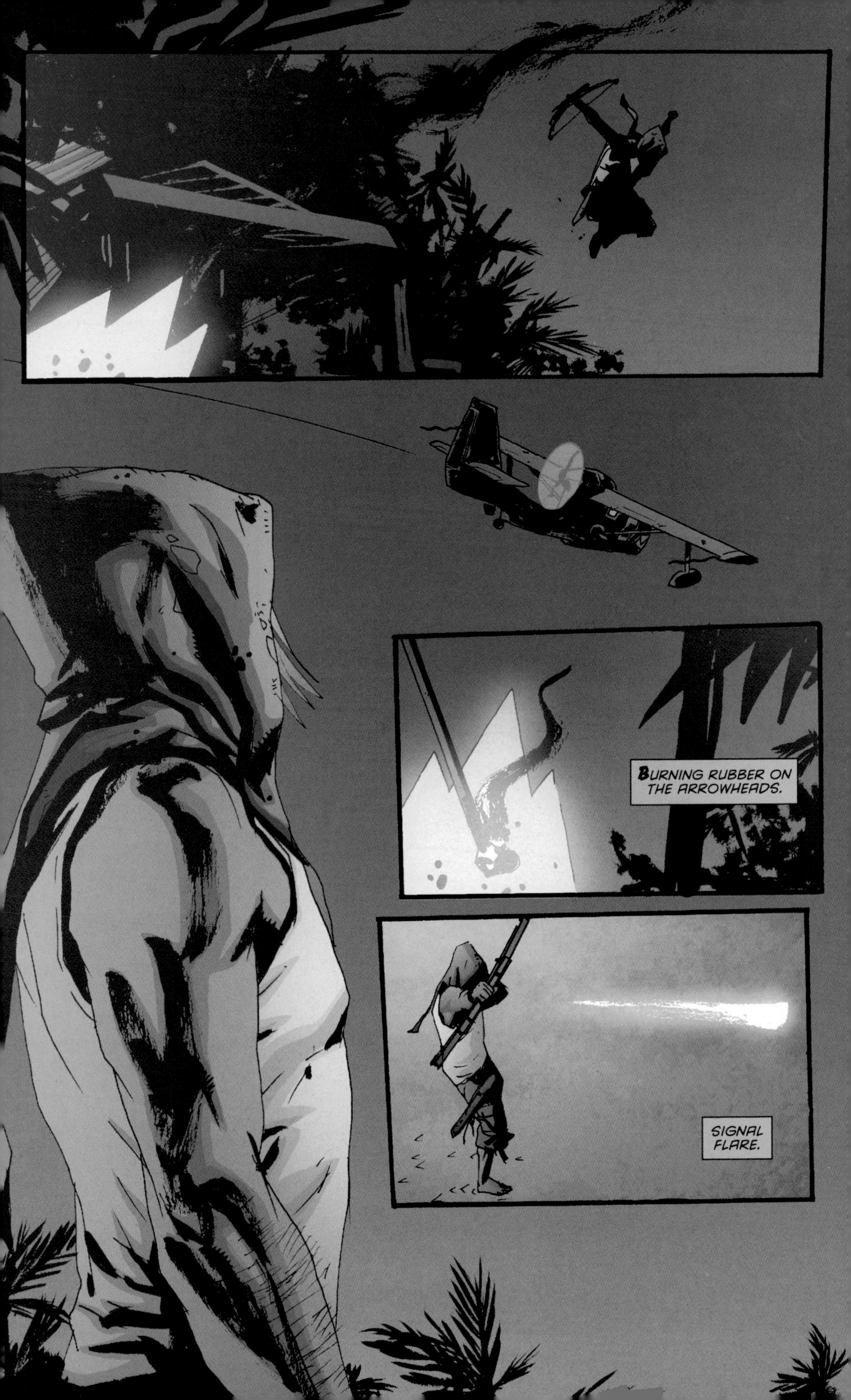
BURNING RUBBER ON THE ARROWHEADS.
SIGNAL FLARE.

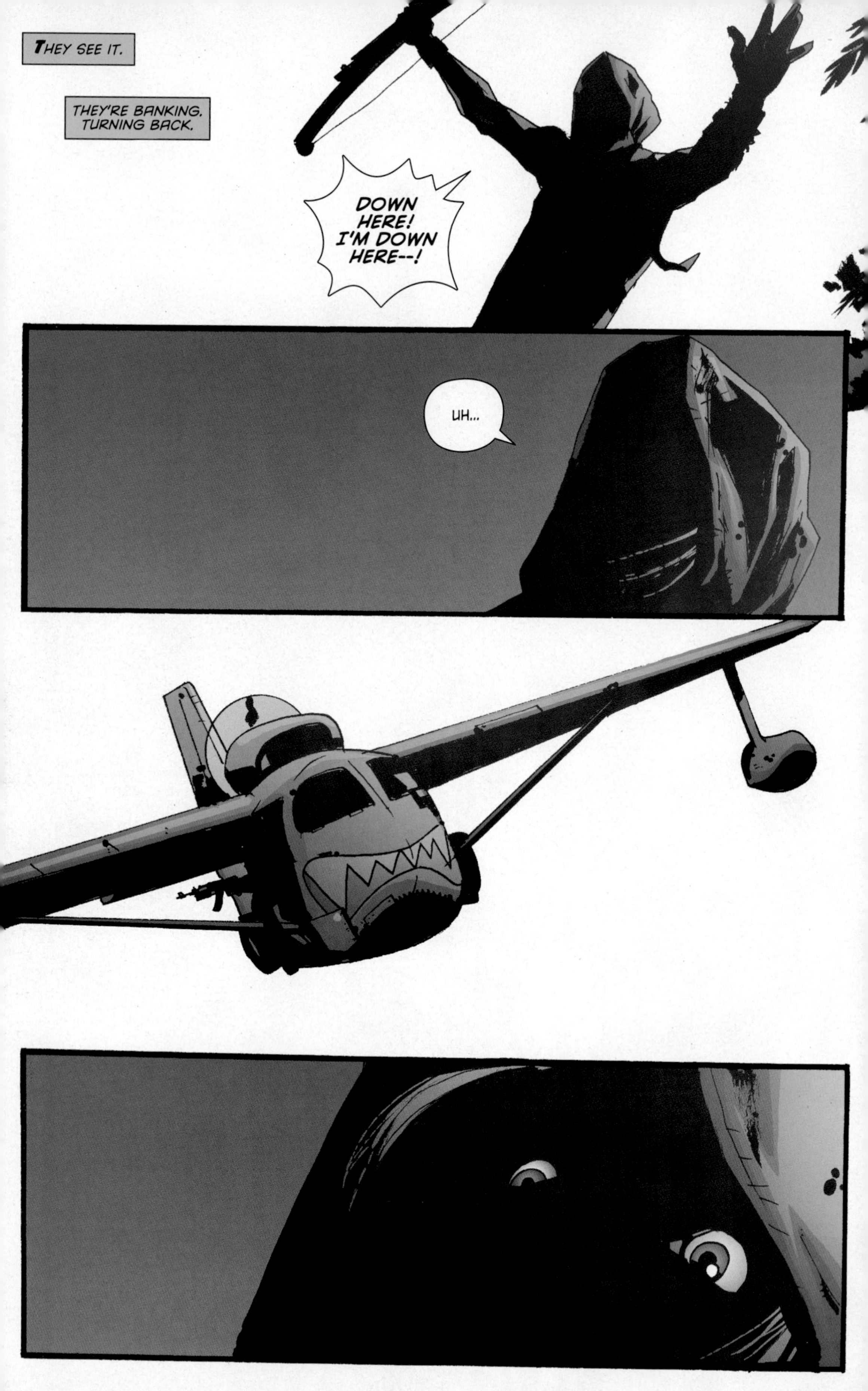
THEY SEE IT.
THEY'RE BANKING. TURNING BACK.
DOWN HERE! I'M DOWN HERE--!
UH...

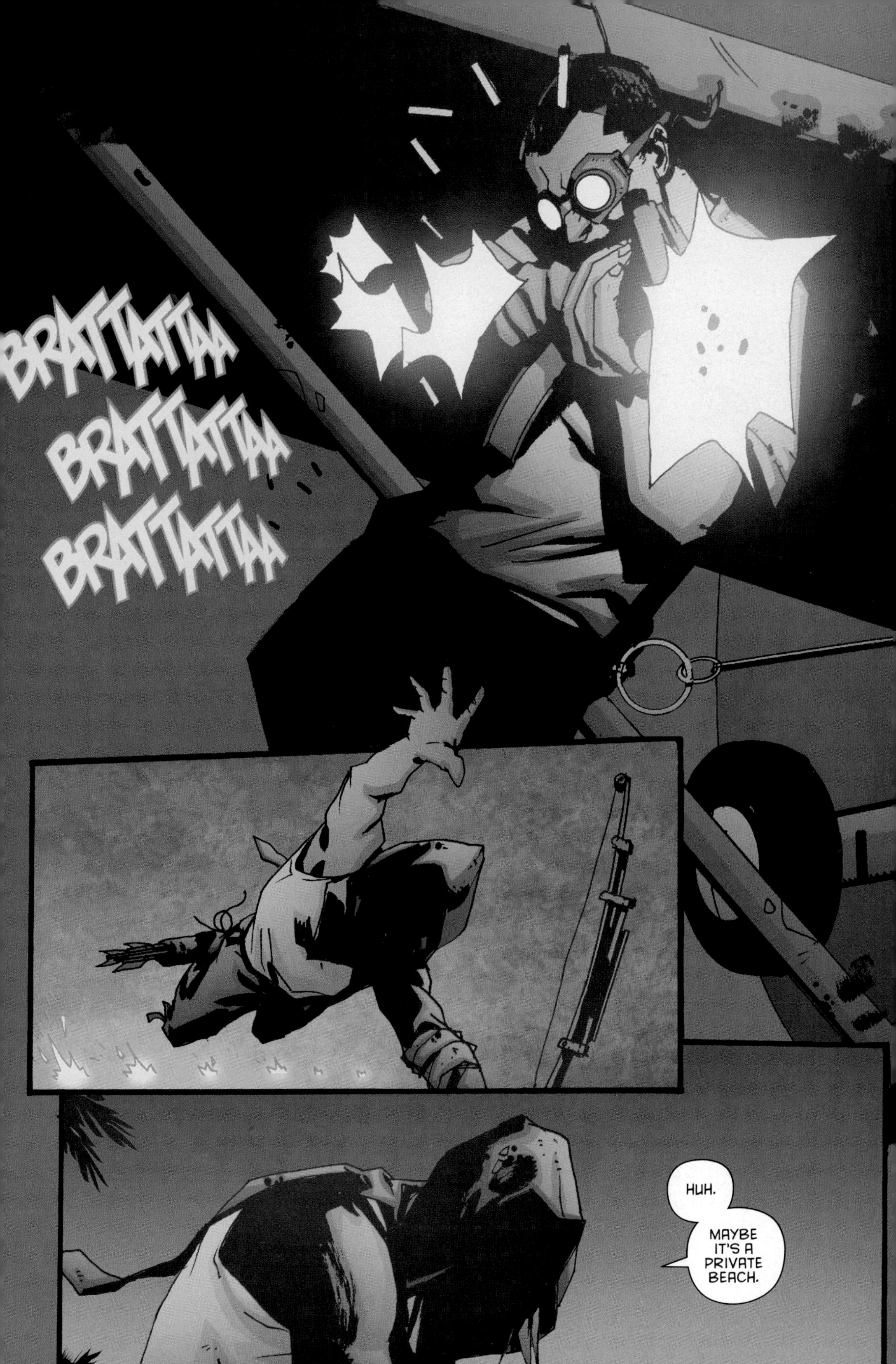
BRATTATTAA
BRATTATTAA
BRATTATTAA
HUH.
MAYBE IT'S A PRIVATE BEACH.

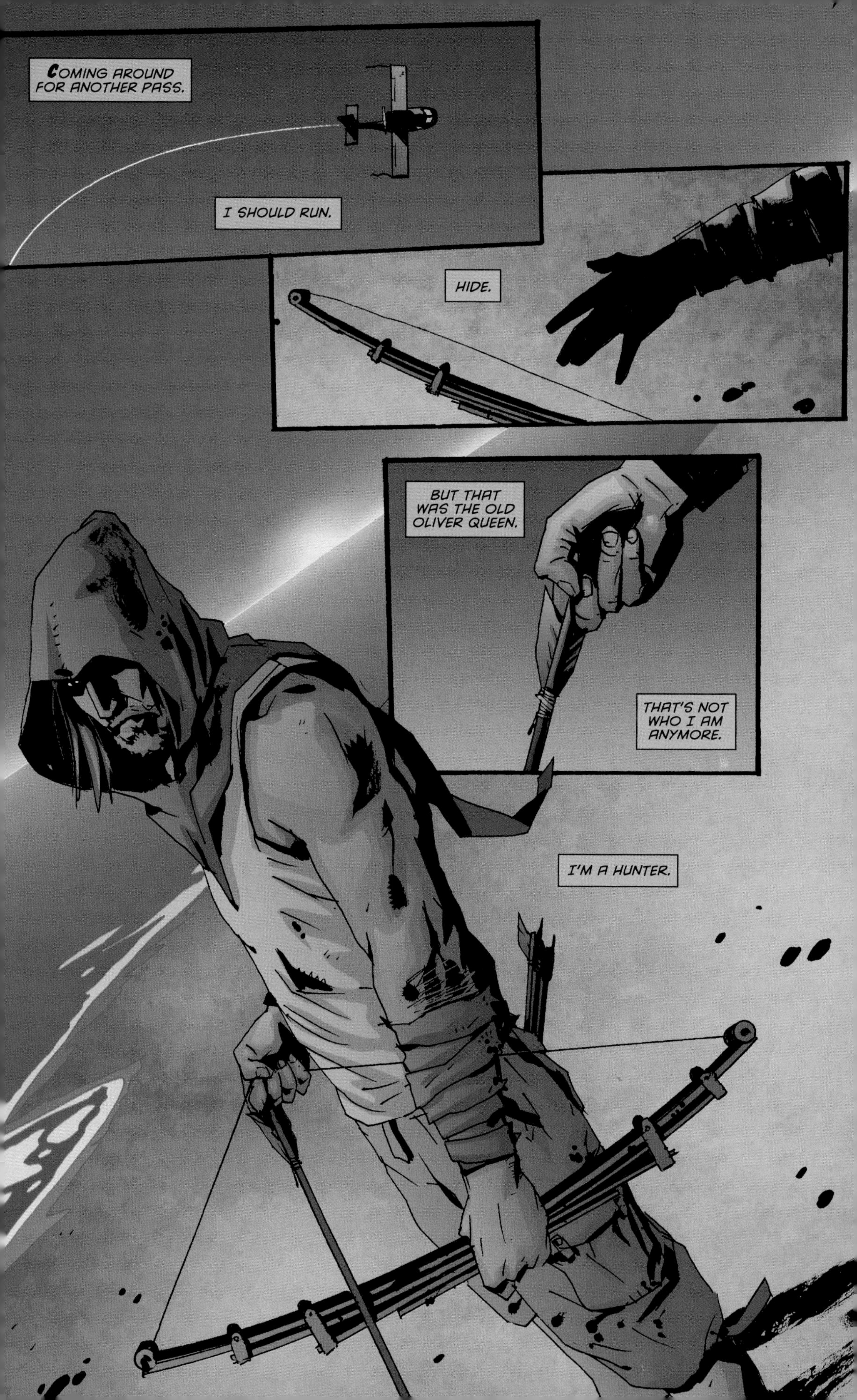
COMING AROUND FOR ANOTHER PASS.
I SHOULD RUN.
HIDE.
BUT THAT WAS THE OLD OLIVER QUEEN.
THAT'S NOT WHO I AM ANYMORE.
I'M A HUNTER.

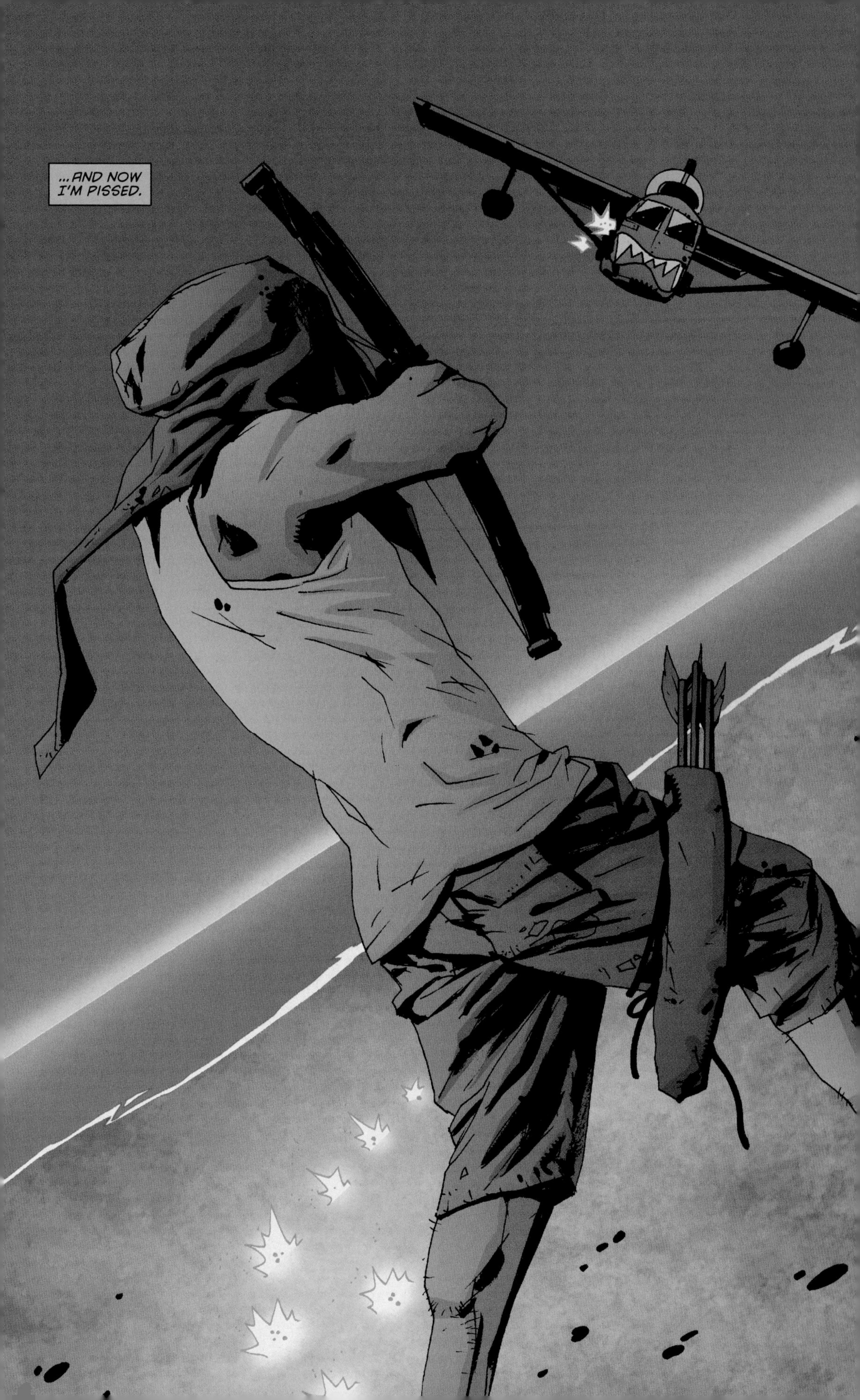
...AND NOW I'M PISSED.

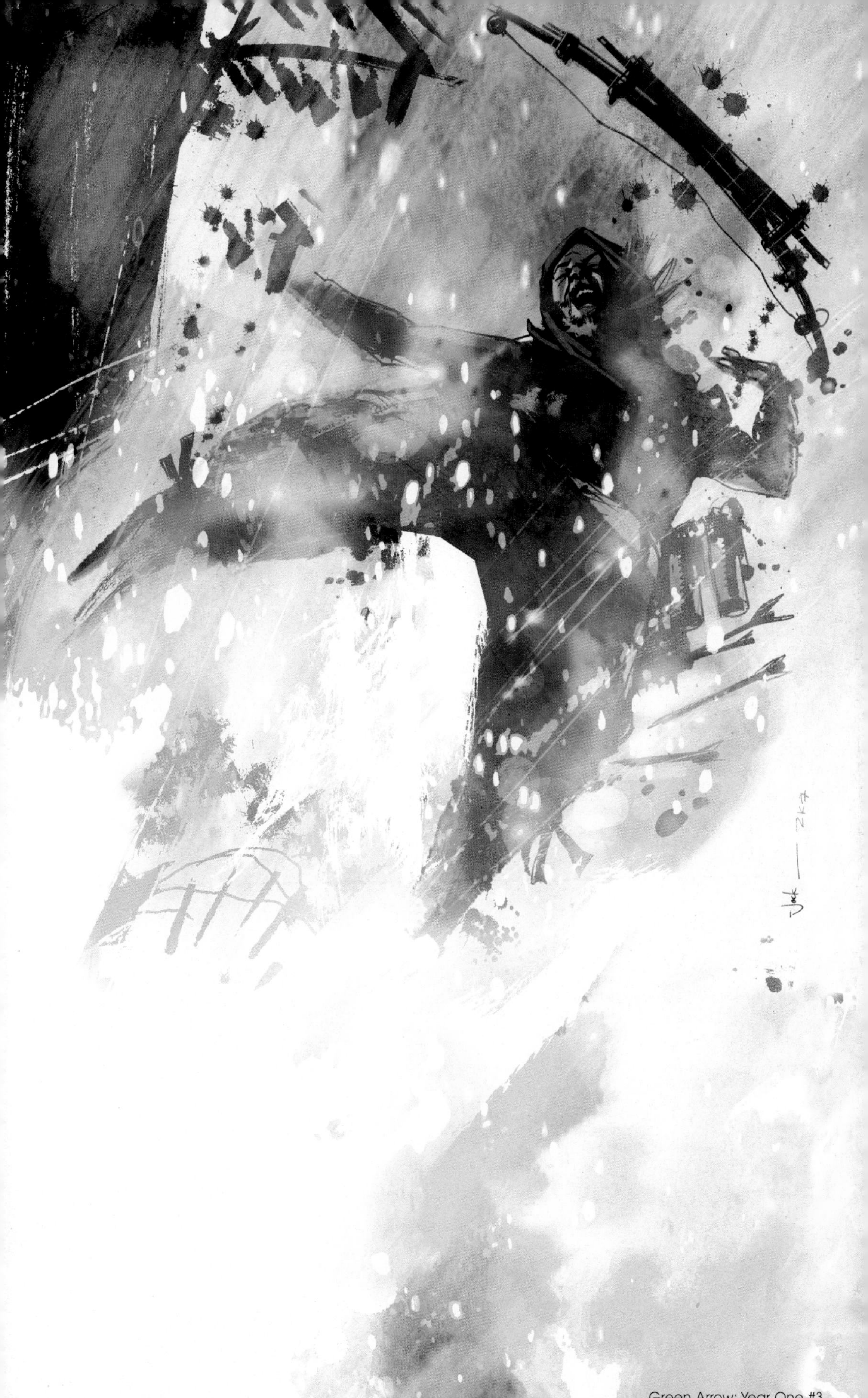

Green Arrow: Year One #3

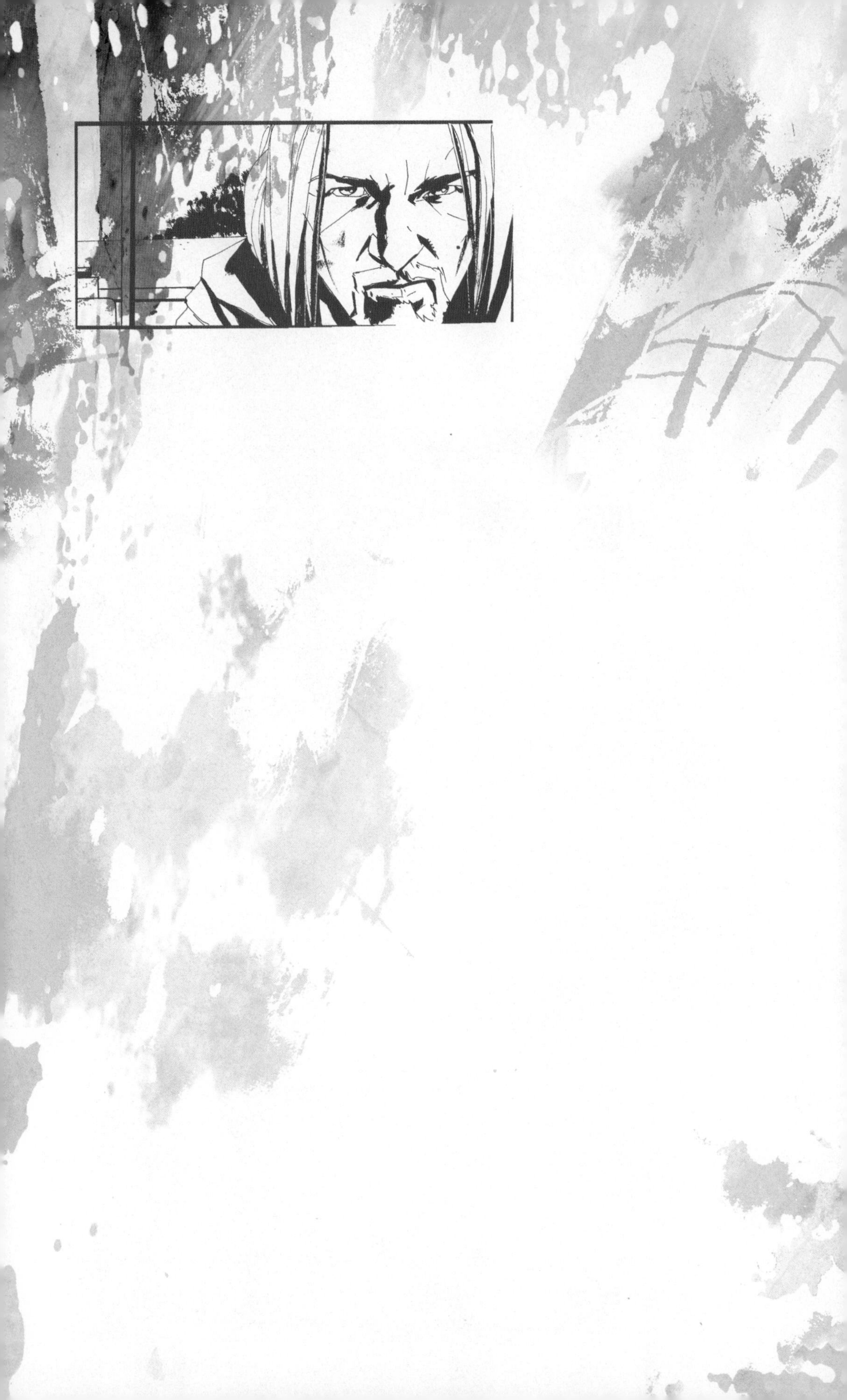

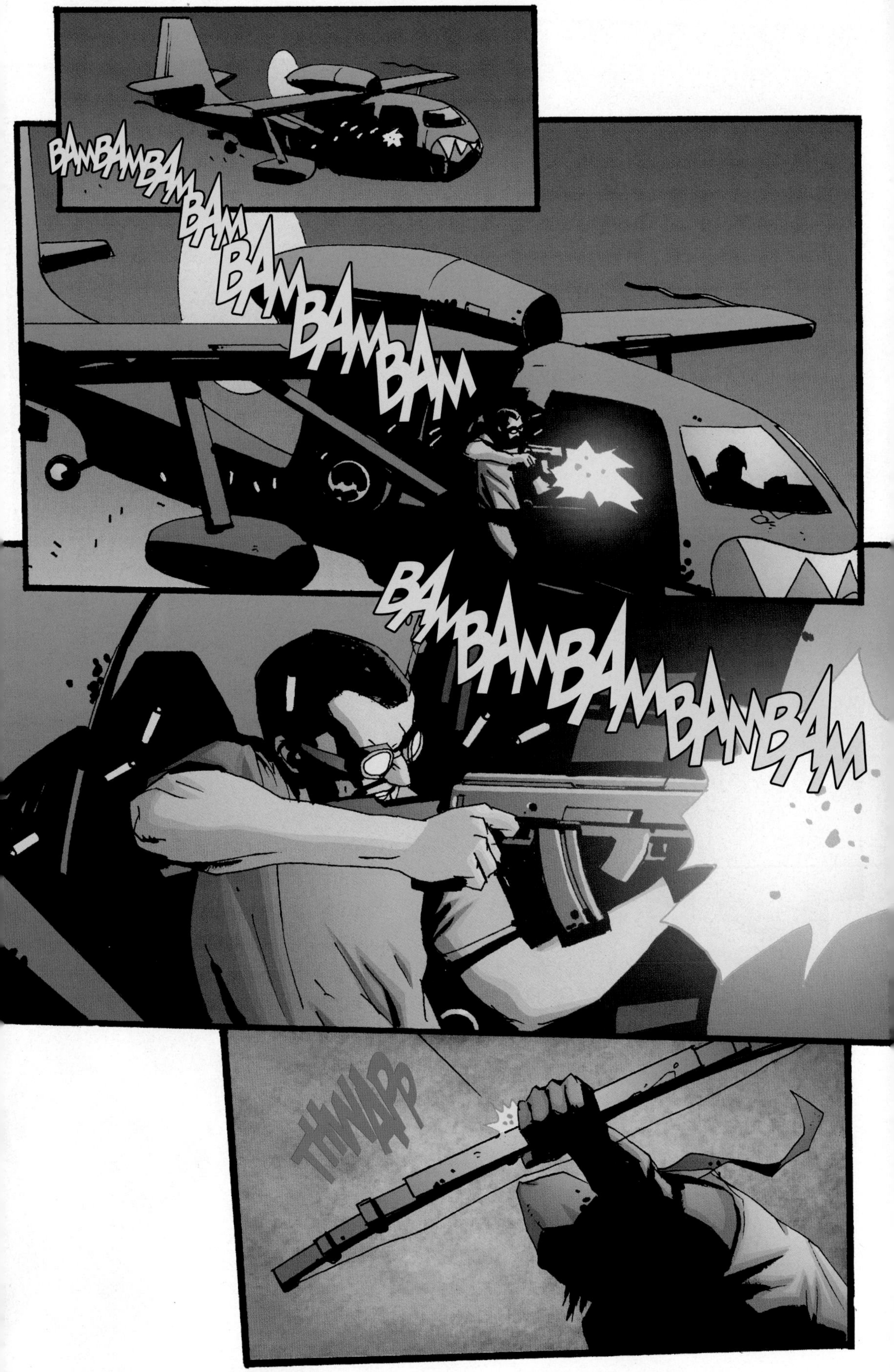
BAMBAMBAMBAM
BAMBAMBAM
BAMBAMBAMBAMBAMBAM
THWAPP

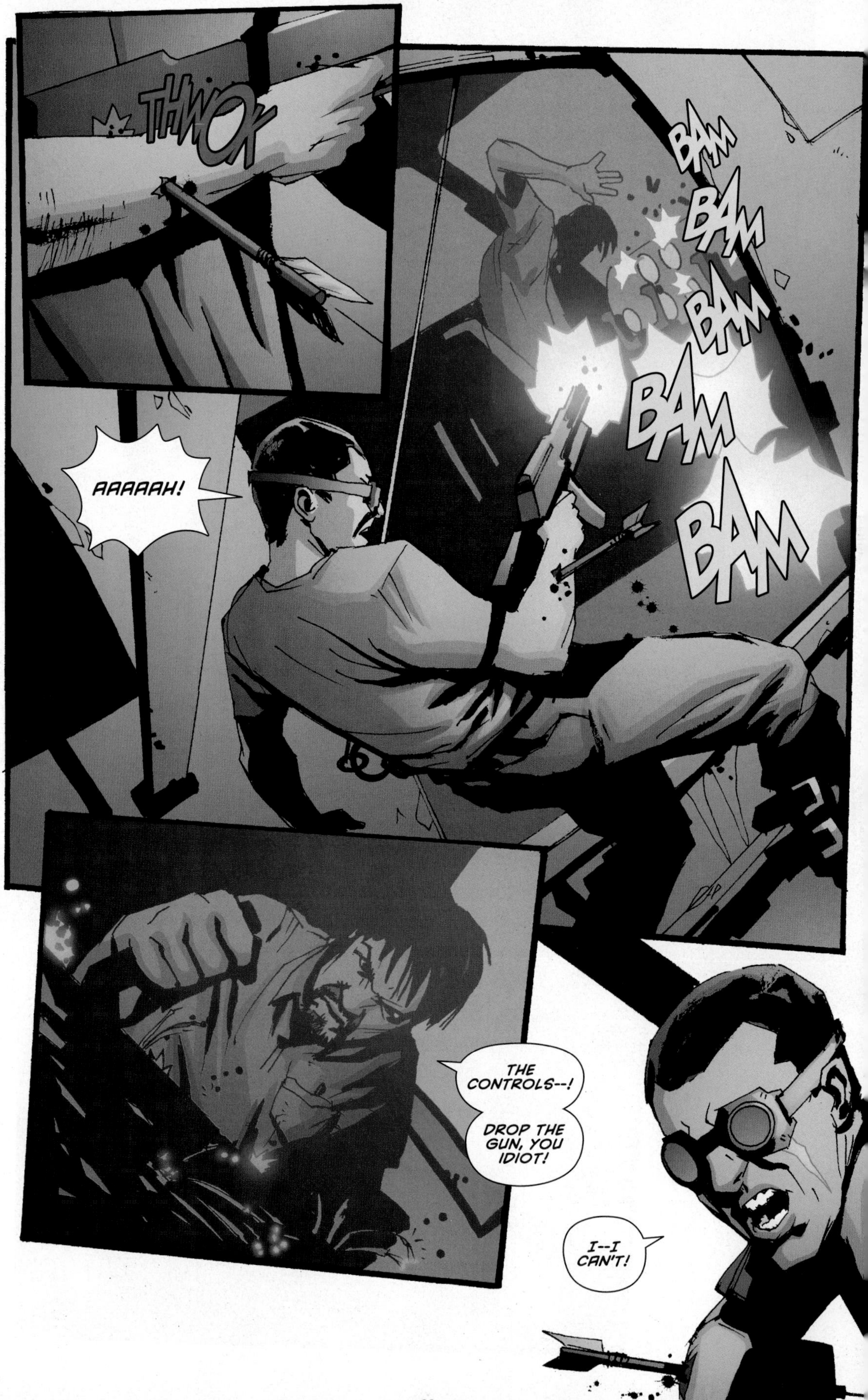
THWOK
BAM
BAM
BAM
BAM
BAM
AAAAAH!
THE CONTROLS--!
DROP THE GUN, YOU IDIOT!
I--I CAN'T!

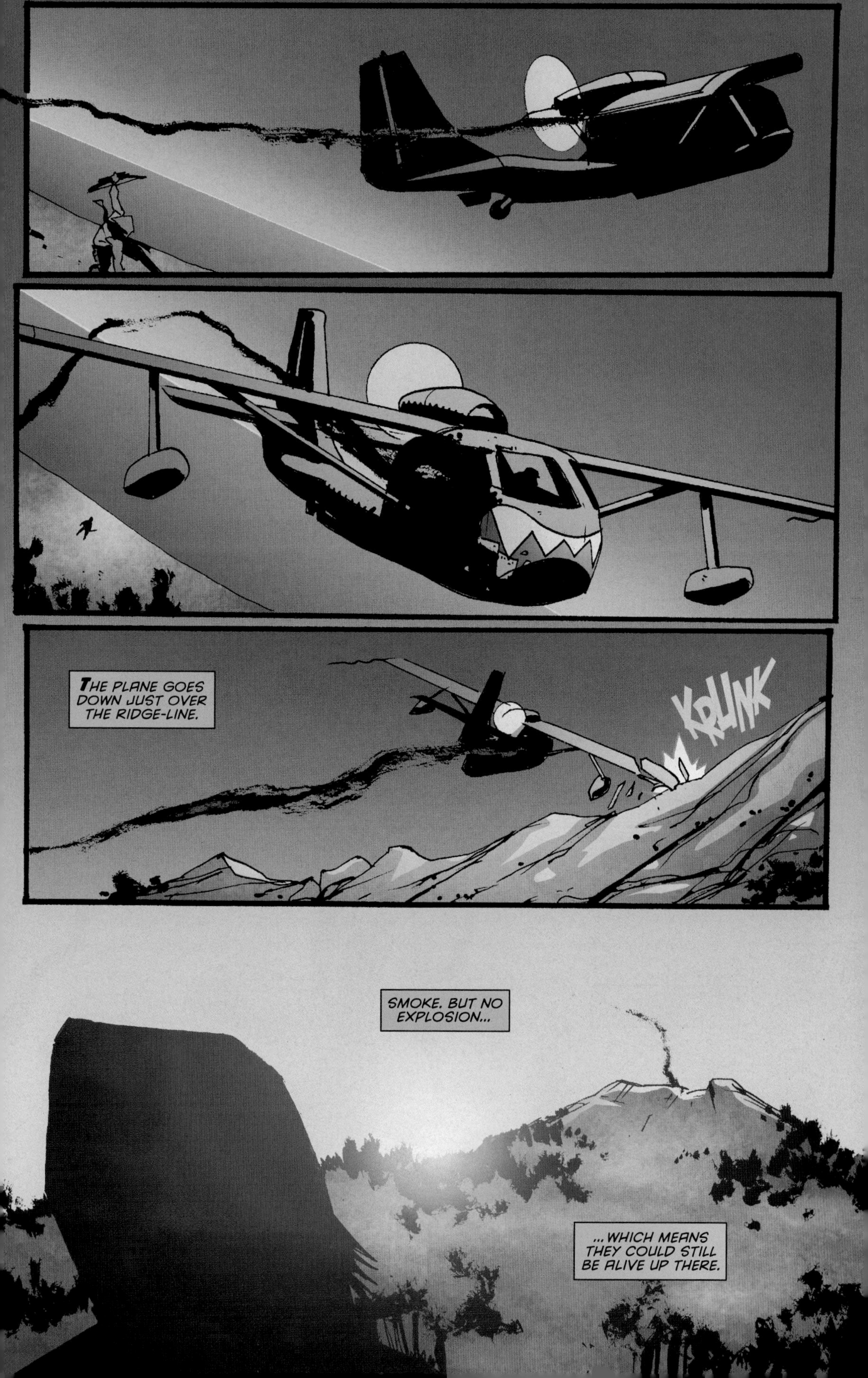
THE PLANE GOES DOWN JUST OVER THE RIDGE-LINE.
KRUNK
SMOKE. BUT NO EXPLOSION...
...WHICH MEANS THEY COULD STILL BE ALIVE UP THERE.

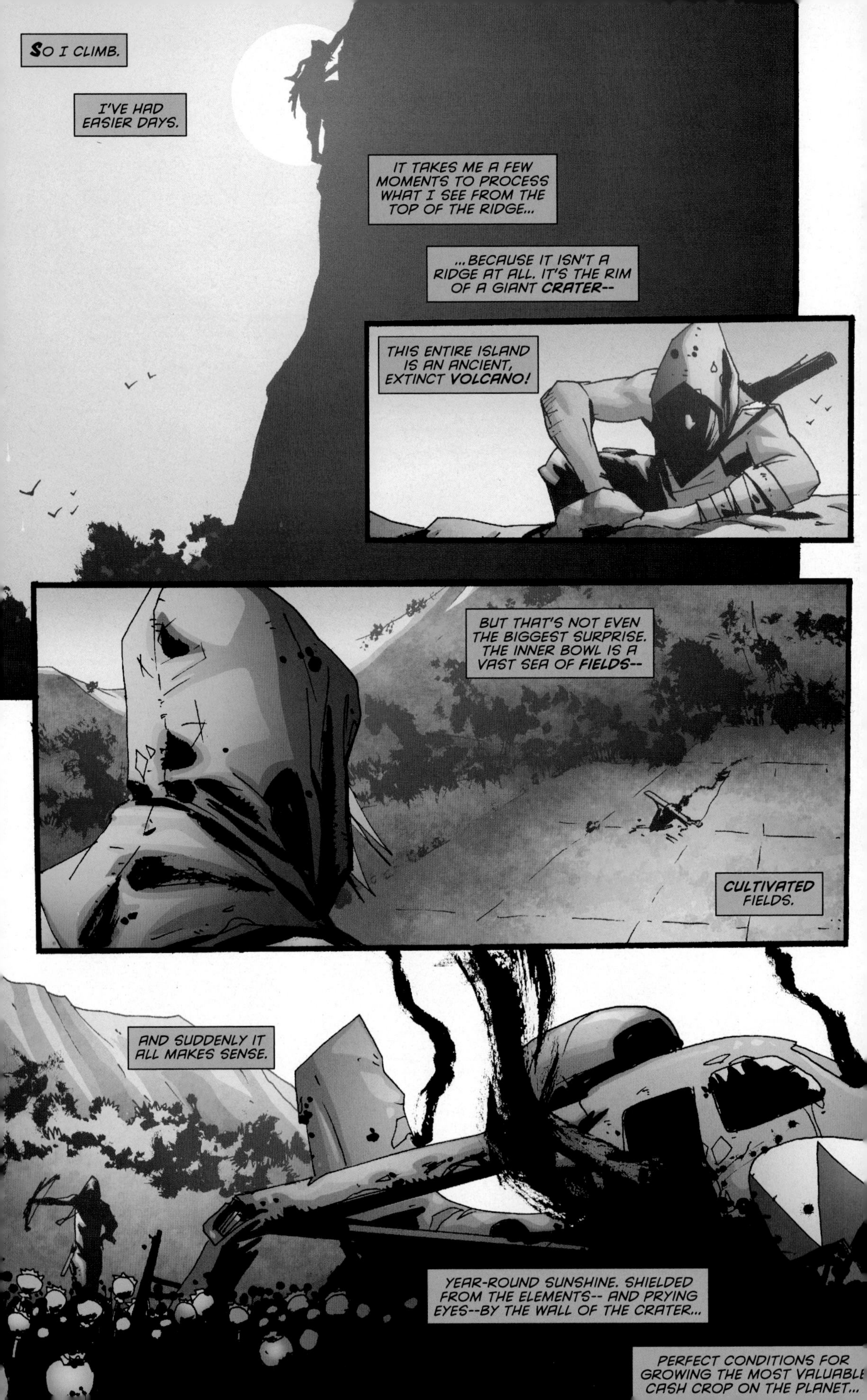
SO I CLIMB.
I'VE HAD EASIER DAYS.
IT TAKES ME A FEW MOMENTS TO PROCESS WHAT I SEE FROM THE TOP OF THE RIDGE...
...BECAUSE IT ISN'T A RIDGE AT ALL. IT'S THE RIM OF A GIANT CRATER--
THIS ENTIRE ISLAND IS AN ANCIENT, EXTINCT VOLCANO!
BUT THAT'S NOT EVEN THE BIGGEST SURPRISE. THE INNER BOWL IS A VAST SEA OF FIELDS--
CULTIVATED FIELDS.
AND SUDDENLY IT ALL MAKES SENSE.
YEAR-ROUND SUNSHINE. SHIELDED FROM THE ELEMENTS-- AND PRYING EYES--BY THE WALL OF THE CRATER...
PERFECT CONDITIONS FOR GROWING THE MOST VALUABLE CASH CROP ON THE PLANET...

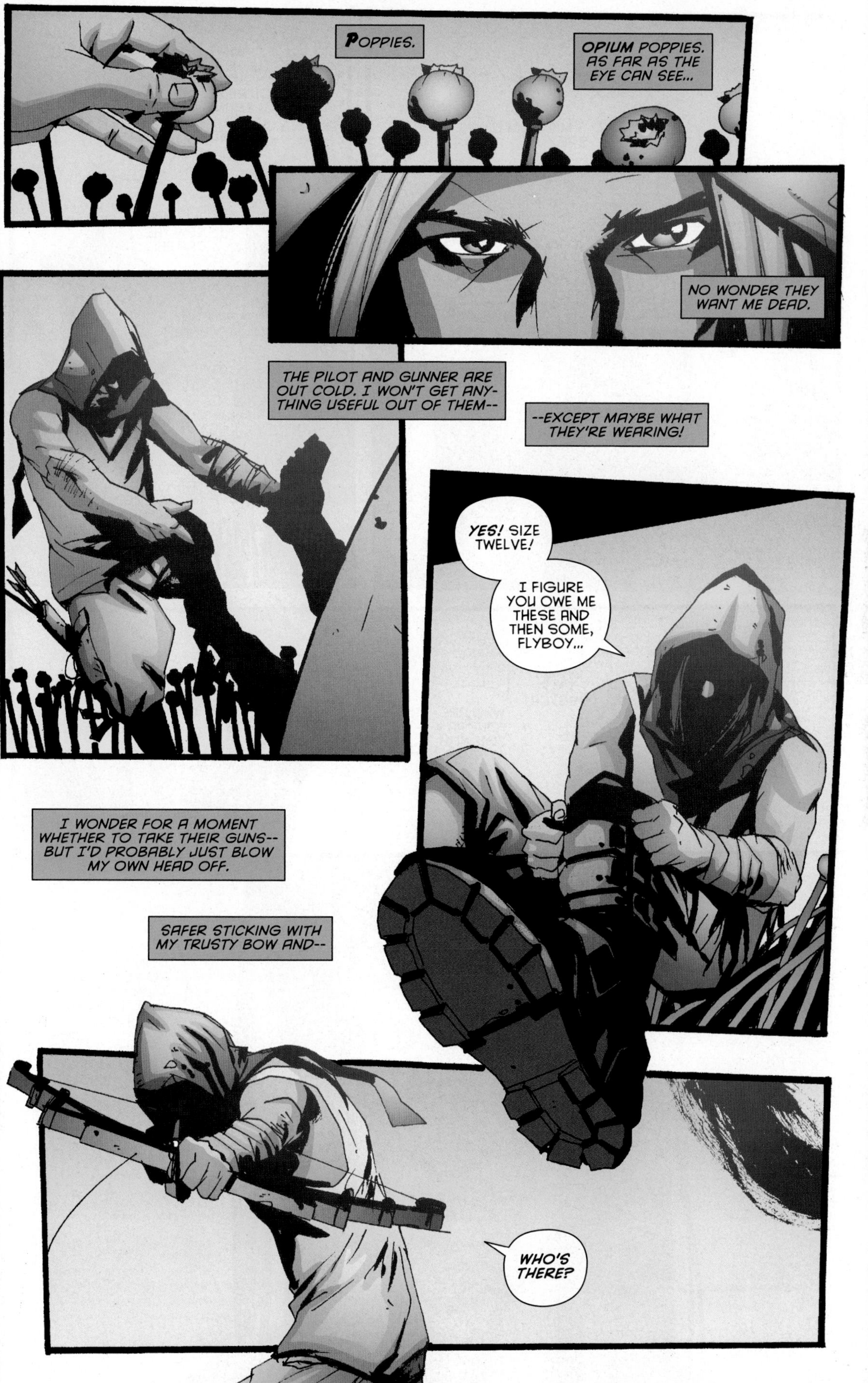
POPPIES.
OPIUM POPPIES. AS FAR AS THE EYE CAN SEE...
NO WONDER THEY WANT ME DEAD.
THE PILOT AND GUNNER ARE OUT COLD. I WON'T GET ANYTHING USEFUL OUT OF THEM--
--EXCEPT MAYBE WHAT THEY'RE WEARING!
YES! SIZE TWELVE!
I FIGURE YOU OWE ME THESE AND THEN SOME, FLYBOY...
I WONDER FOR A MOMENT WHETHER TO TAKE THEIR GUNS-- BUT I'D PROBABLY JUST BLOW MY OWN HEAD OFF.
SAFER STICKING WITH MY TRUSTY BOW AND--
WHO'S THERE?

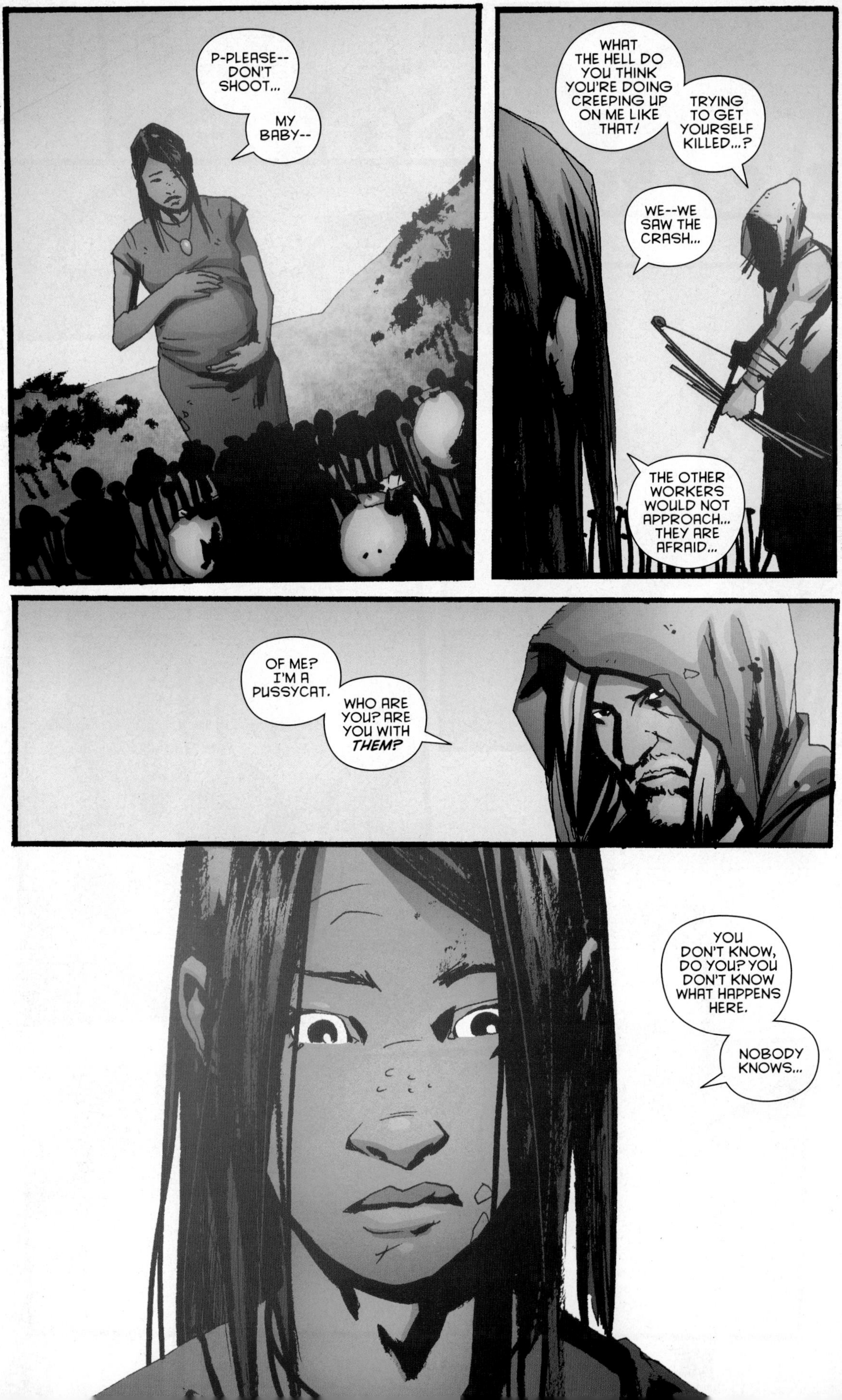
P-PLEASE--
DON'T
SHOOT...
MY
BABY--
WHAT
THE HELL DO
YOU THINK
YOU'RE DOING
CREEPING UP
ON ME LIKE
THAT!
TRYING
TO GET
YOURSELF
KILLED...?
WE--WE
SAW THE
CRASH...
THE OTHER
WORKERS
WOULD NOT
APPROACH...
THEY ARE
AFRAID...
OF ME?
I'M A
PUSSYCAT.
WHO ARE
YOU? ARE
YOU WITH
THEM?
YOU
DON'T KNOW,
DO YOU? YOU
DON'T KNOW
WHAT HAPPENS
HERE.
NOBODY
KNOWS...

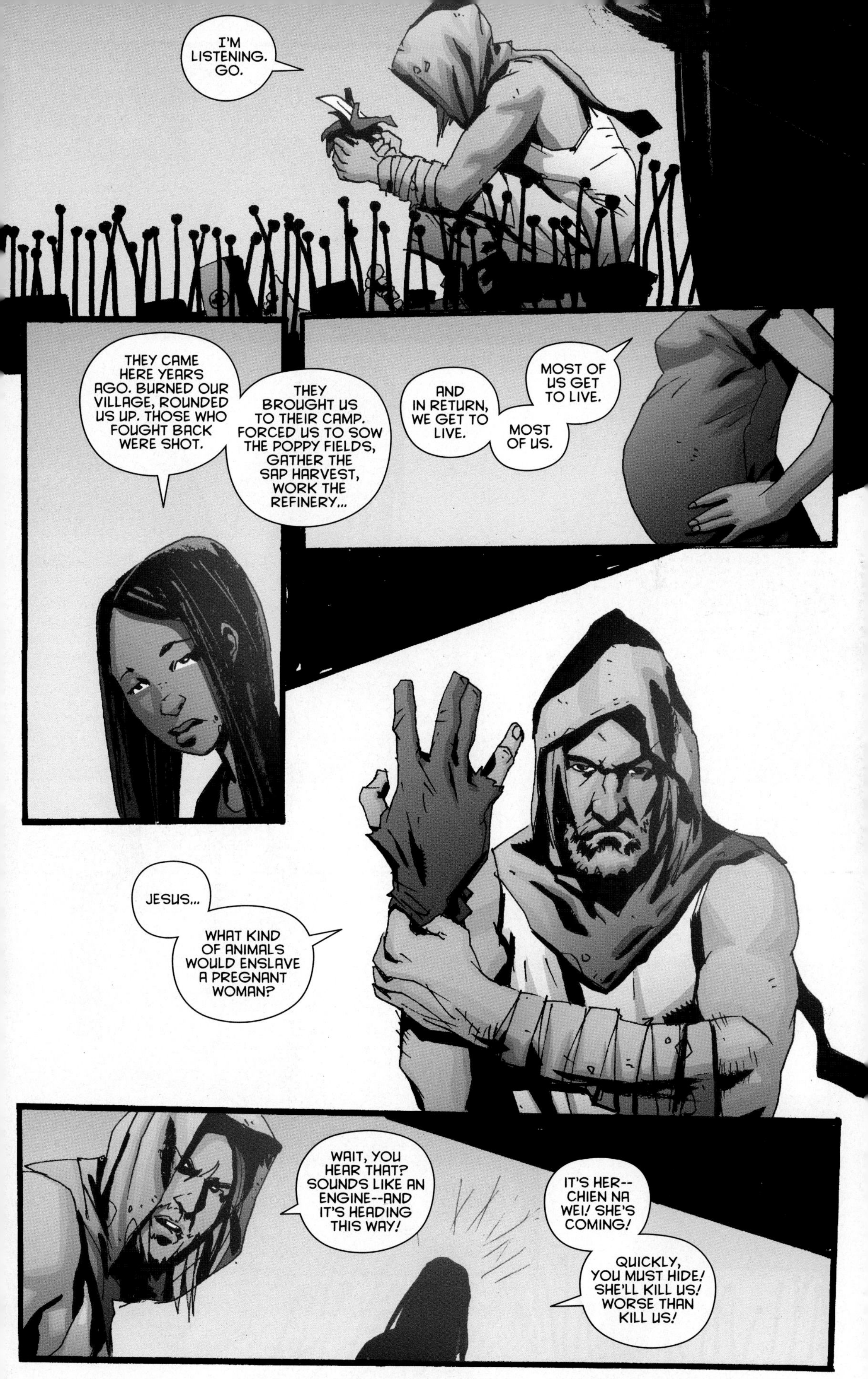

I'M LISTENING. GO.
THEY CAME HERE YEARS AGO. BURNED OUR VILLAGE, ROUNDED US UP. THOSE WHO FOUGHT BACK WERE SHOT.
THEY BROUGHT US TO THEIR CAMP. FORCED US TO SOW THE POPPY FIELDS, GATHER THE SAP HARVEST, WORK THE REFINERY...
AND IN RETURN, WE GET TO LIVE.
MOST OF US.
MOST OF US GET TO LIVE.
JESUS...
WHAT KIND OF ANIMALS WOULD ENSLAVE A PREGNANT WOMAN?
WAIT, YOU HEAR THAT? SOUNDS LIKE AN ENGINE--AND IT'S HEADING THIS WAY!
IT'S HER--CHIEN NA WEI! SHE'S COMING!
QUICKLY, YOU MUST HIDE! SHE'LL KILL US! WORSE THAN KILL US!

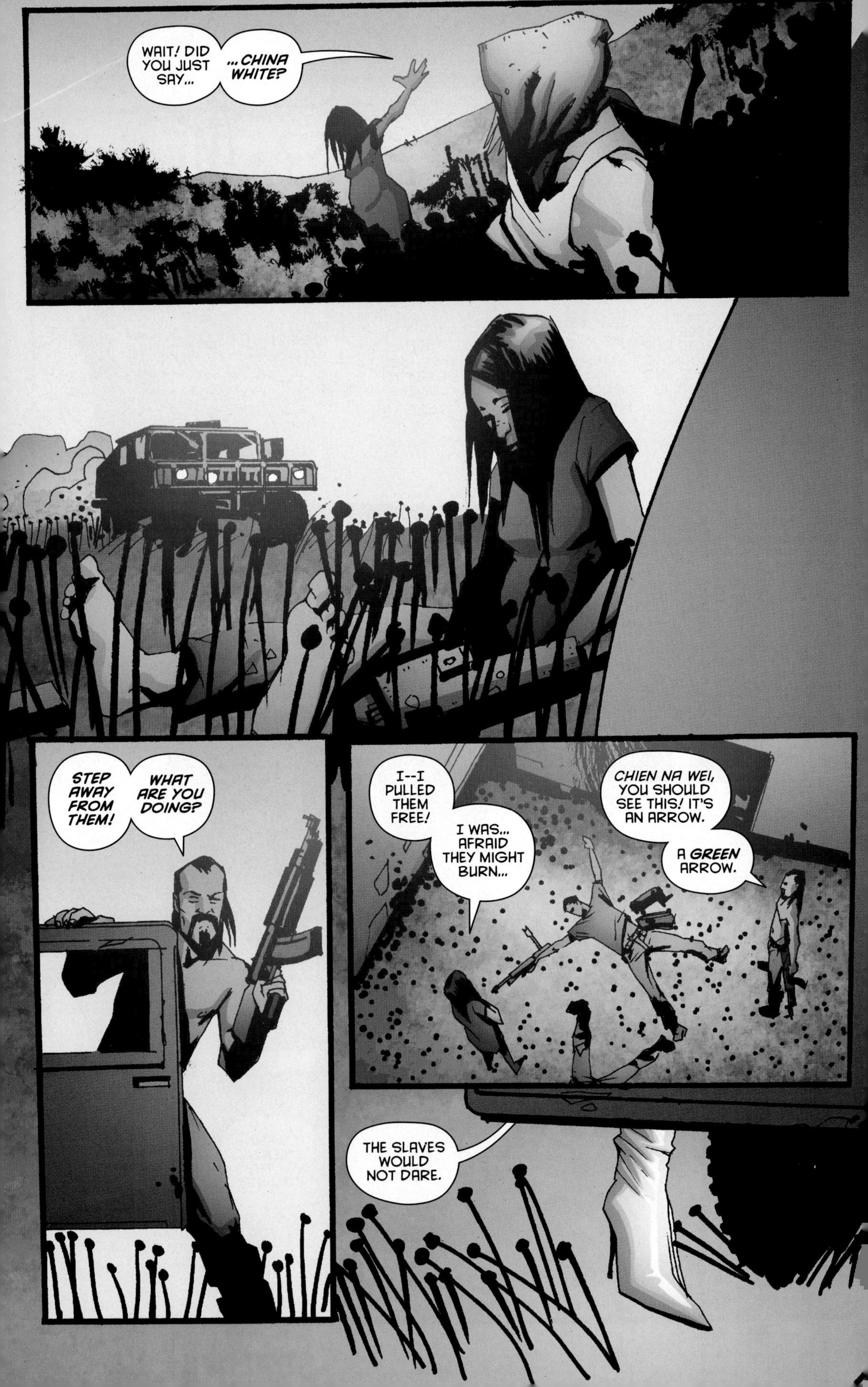
WAIT! DID YOU JUST SAY...
...CHINA WHITE?
STEP AWAY FROM THEM!
WHAT ARE YOU DOING?
I--I PULLED THEM FREE!
I WAS... AFRAID THEY MIGHT BURN...
CHIEN NA WEI, YOU SHOULD SEE THIS! IT'S AN ARROW.
A GREEN ARROW.
THE SLAVES WOULD NOT DARE.

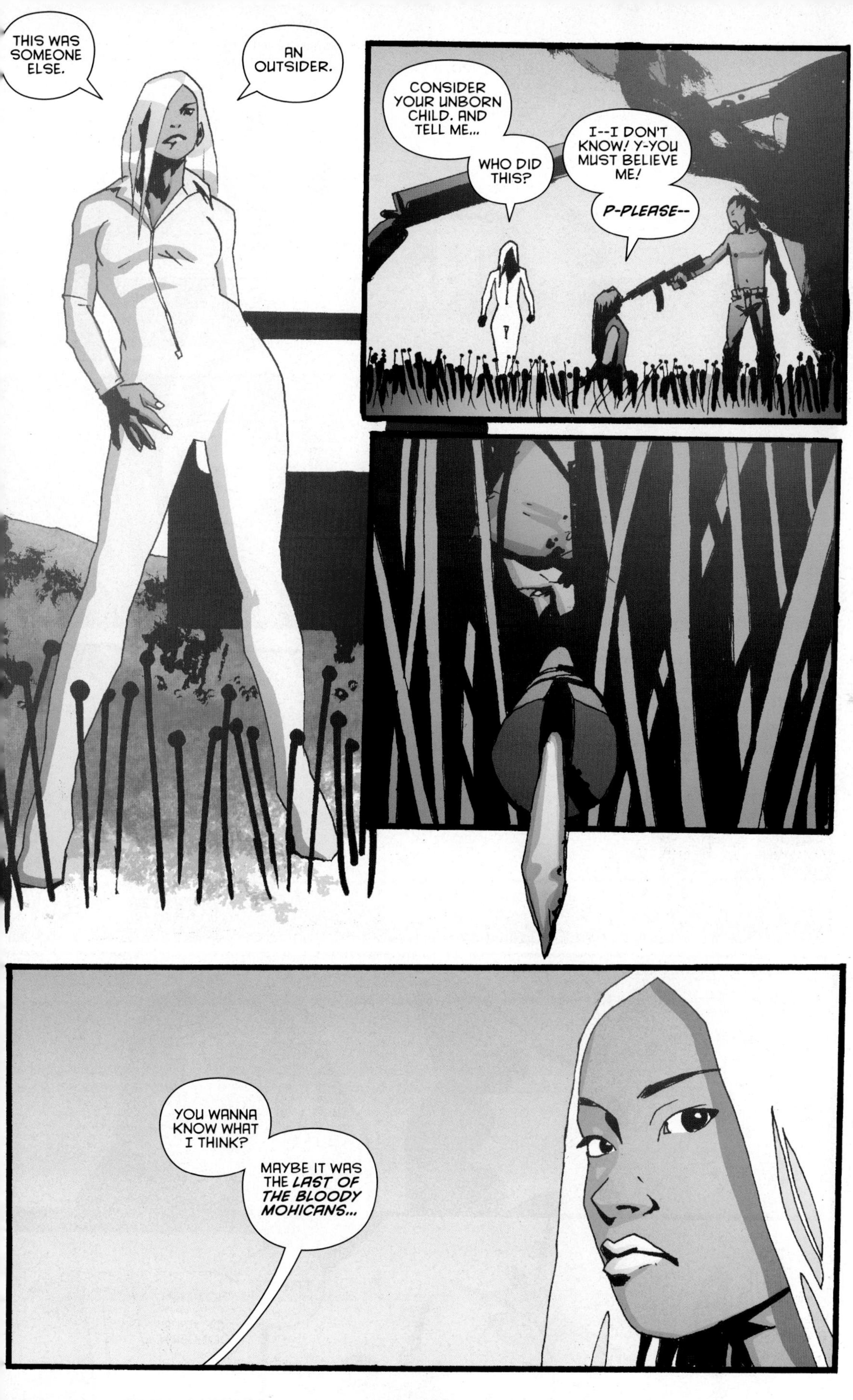
THIS WAS SOMEONE ELSE.
AN OUTSIDER.
CONSIDER YOUR UNBORN CHILD. AND TELL ME...
WHO DID THIS?
I--I DON'T KNOW! Y-YOU MUST BELIEVE ME!
P-PLEASE--
YOU WANNA KNOW WHAT I THINK?
MAYBE IT WAS THE *LAST OF THE BLOODY MOHICANS...*

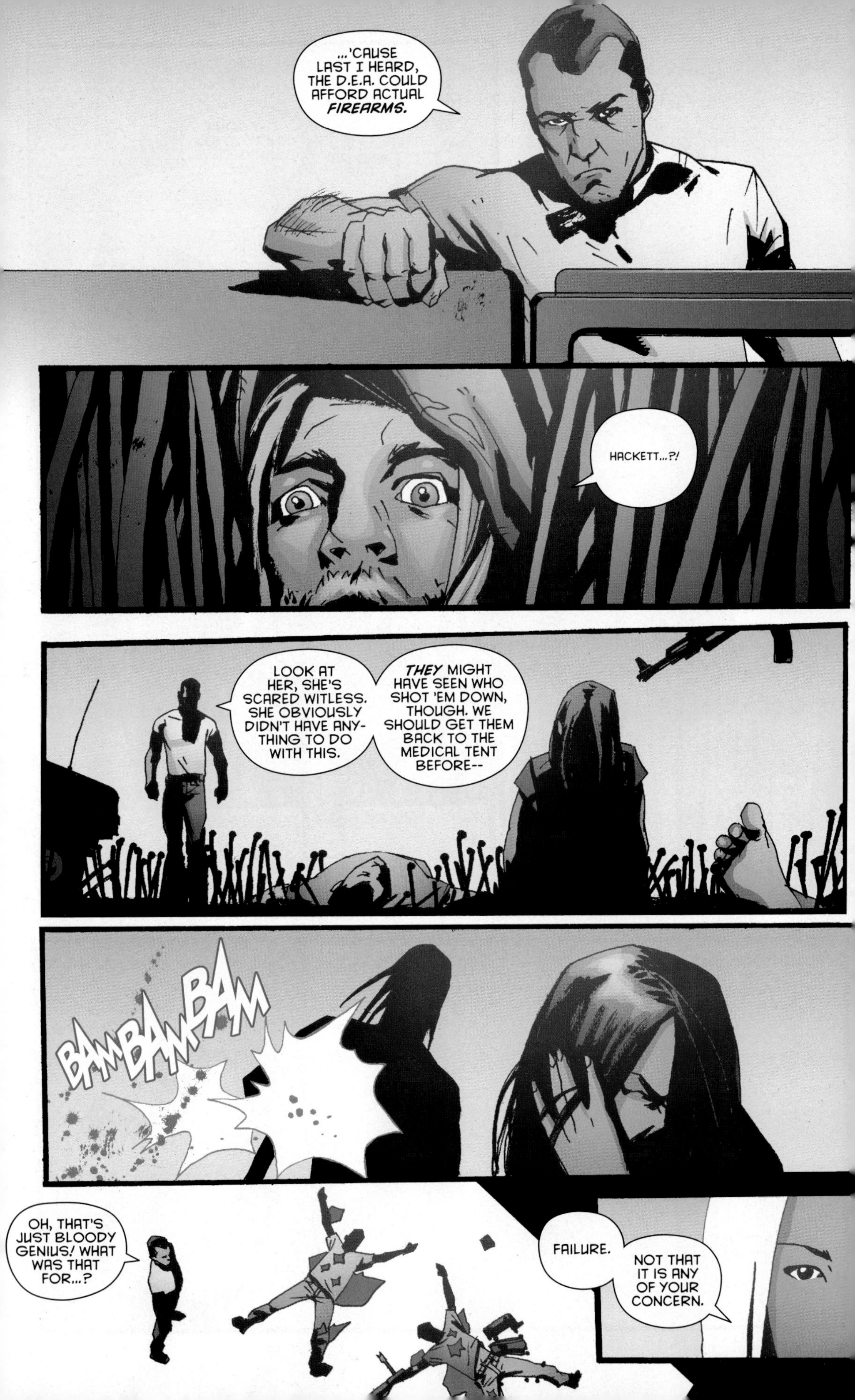
...'CAUSE LAST I HEARD, THE D.E.A. COULD AFFORD ACTUAL *FIREARMS.*
HACKETT...?!
LOOK AT HER, SHE'S SCARED WITLESS. SHE OBVIOUSLY DIDN'T HAVE ANY-THING TO DO WITH THIS.
THEY MIGHT HAVE SEEN WHO SHOT 'EM DOWN, THOUGH. WE SHOULD GET THEM BACK TO THE MEDICAL TENT BEFORE--
BAM BAM BAM
OH, THAT'S JUST BLOODY GENIUS! WHAT WAS THAT FOR...?
FAILURE.
NOT THAT IT IS ANY OF YOUR CONCERN.

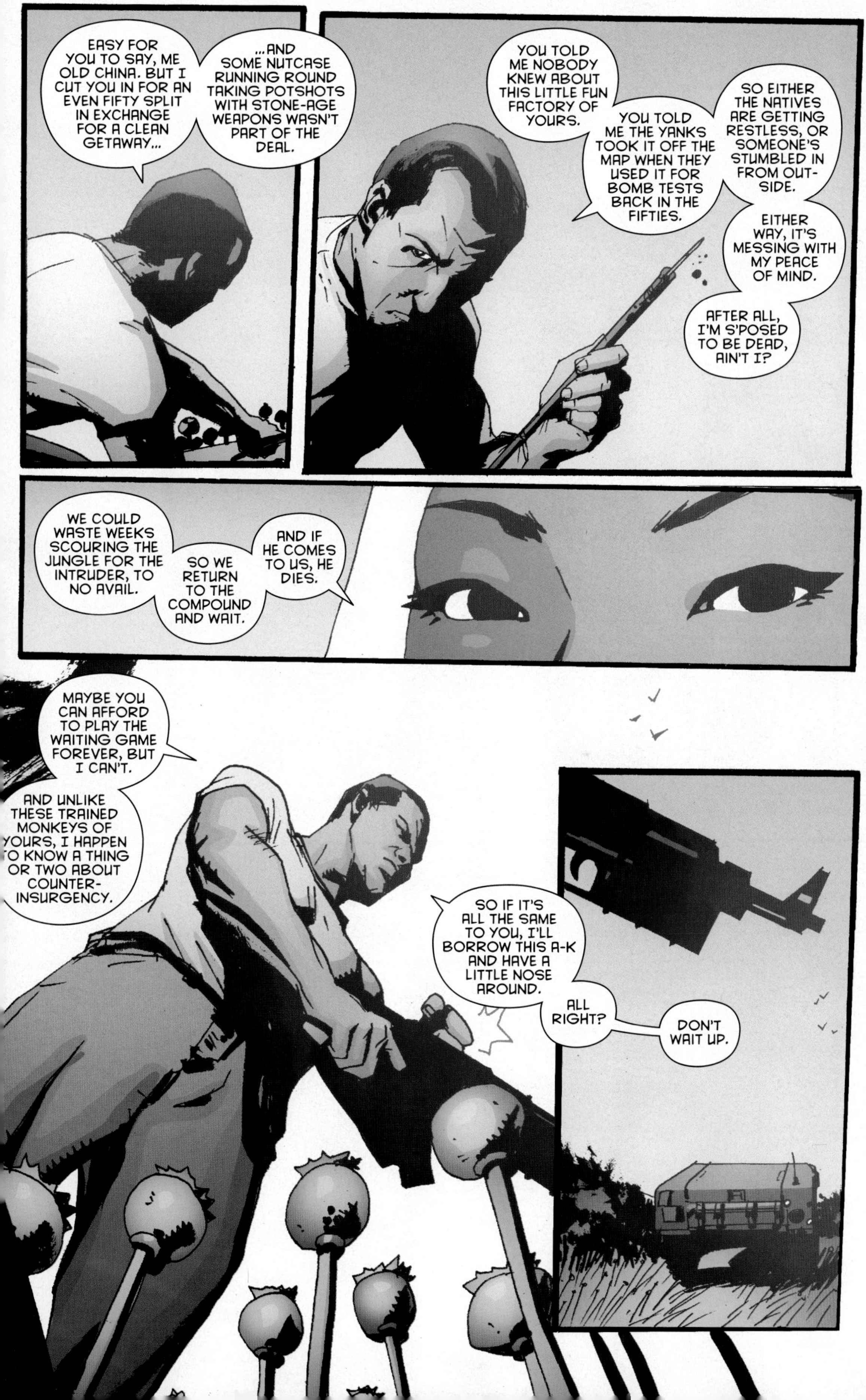
EASY FOR YOU TO SAY, ME OLD CHINA. BUT I CUT YOU IN FOR AN EVEN FIFTY SPLIT IN EXCHANGE FOR A CLEAN GETAWAY...
...AND SOME NUTCASE RUNNING ROUND TAKING POTSHOTS WITH STONE-AGE WEAPONS WASN'T PART OF THE DEAL.
YOU TOLD ME NOBODY KNEW ABOUT THIS LITTLE FUN FACTORY OF YOURS.
YOU TOLD ME THE YANKS TOOK IT OFF THE MAP WHEN THEY USED IT FOR BOMB TESTS BACK IN THE FIFTIES.
SO EITHER THE NATIVES ARE GETTING RESTLESS, OR SOMEONE'S STUMBLED IN FROM OUT-SIDE.
EITHER WAY, IT'S MESSING WITH MY PEACE OF MIND.
AFTER ALL, I'M S'POSED TO BE DEAD, AIN'T I?
WE COULD WASTE WEEKS SCOURING THE JUNGLE FOR THE INTRUDER, TO NO AVAIL.
SO WE RETURN TO THE COMPOUND AND WAIT.
AND IF HE COMES TO US, HE DIES.
MAYBE YOU CAN AFFORD TO PLAY THE WAITING GAME FOREVER, BUT I CAN'T.
AND UNLIKE THESE TRAINED MONKEYS OF YOURS, I HAPPEN TO KNOW A THING OR TWO ABOUT COUNTER-INSURGENCY.
SO IF IT'S ALL THE SAME TO YOU, I'LL BORROW THIS A-K AND HAVE A LITTLE NOSE AROUND.
ALL RIGHT?
DON'T WAIT UP.

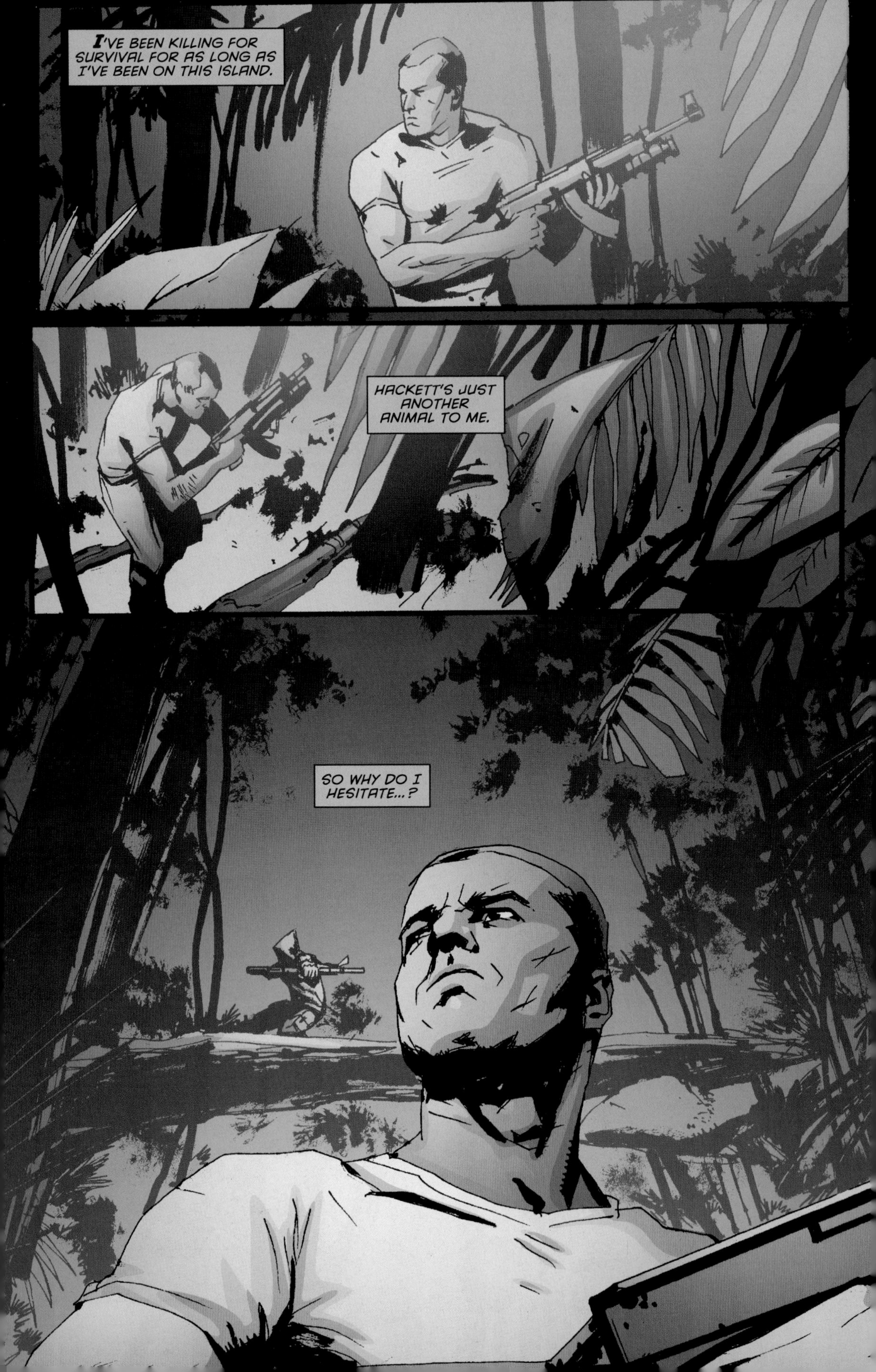
I'VE BEEN KILLING FOR SURVIVAL FOR AS LONG AS I'VE BEEN ON THIS ISLAND.
HACKETT'S JUST ANOTHER ANIMAL TO ME.
SO WHY DO I HESITATE...?

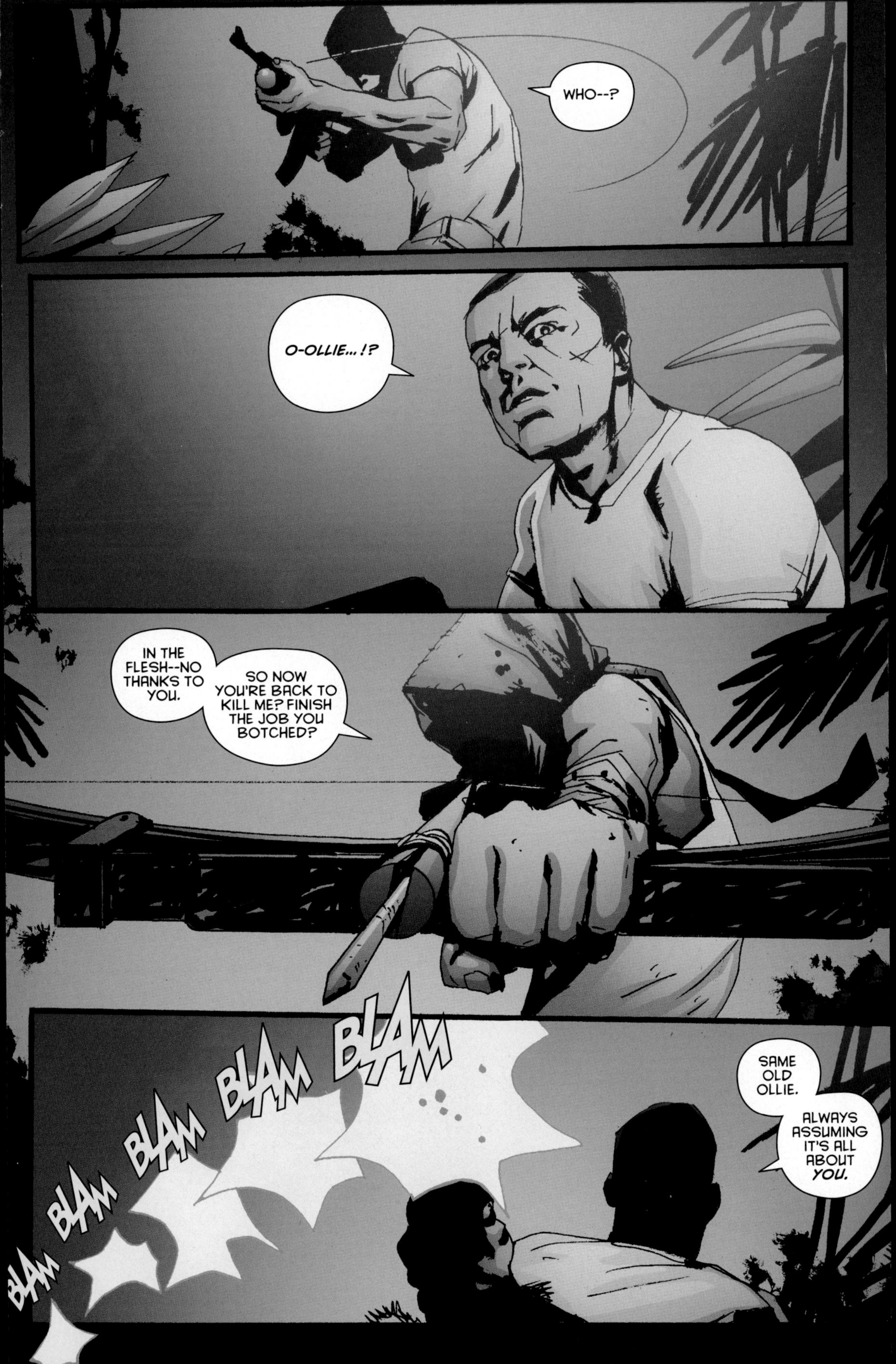
WHO--?
O-OLLIE...!?
IN THE FLESH--NO THANKS TO YOU.
SO NOW YOU'RE BACK TO KILL ME? FINISH THE JOB YOU BOTCHED?
BLAM BLAM BLAM BLAM BLAM BLAM
SAME OLD OLLIE.
ALWAYS ASSUMING IT'S ALL ABOUT *YOU.*

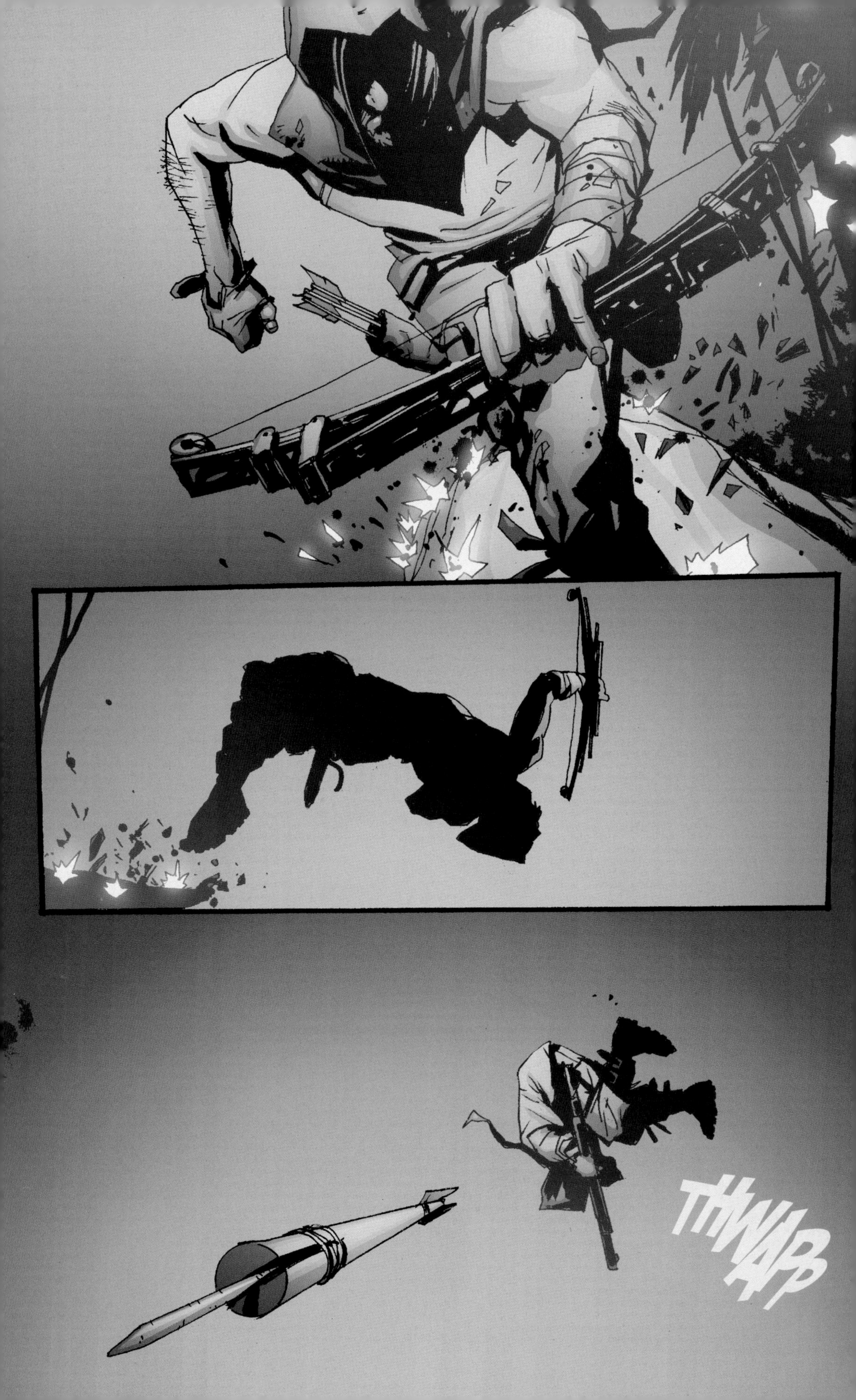
THWAPP

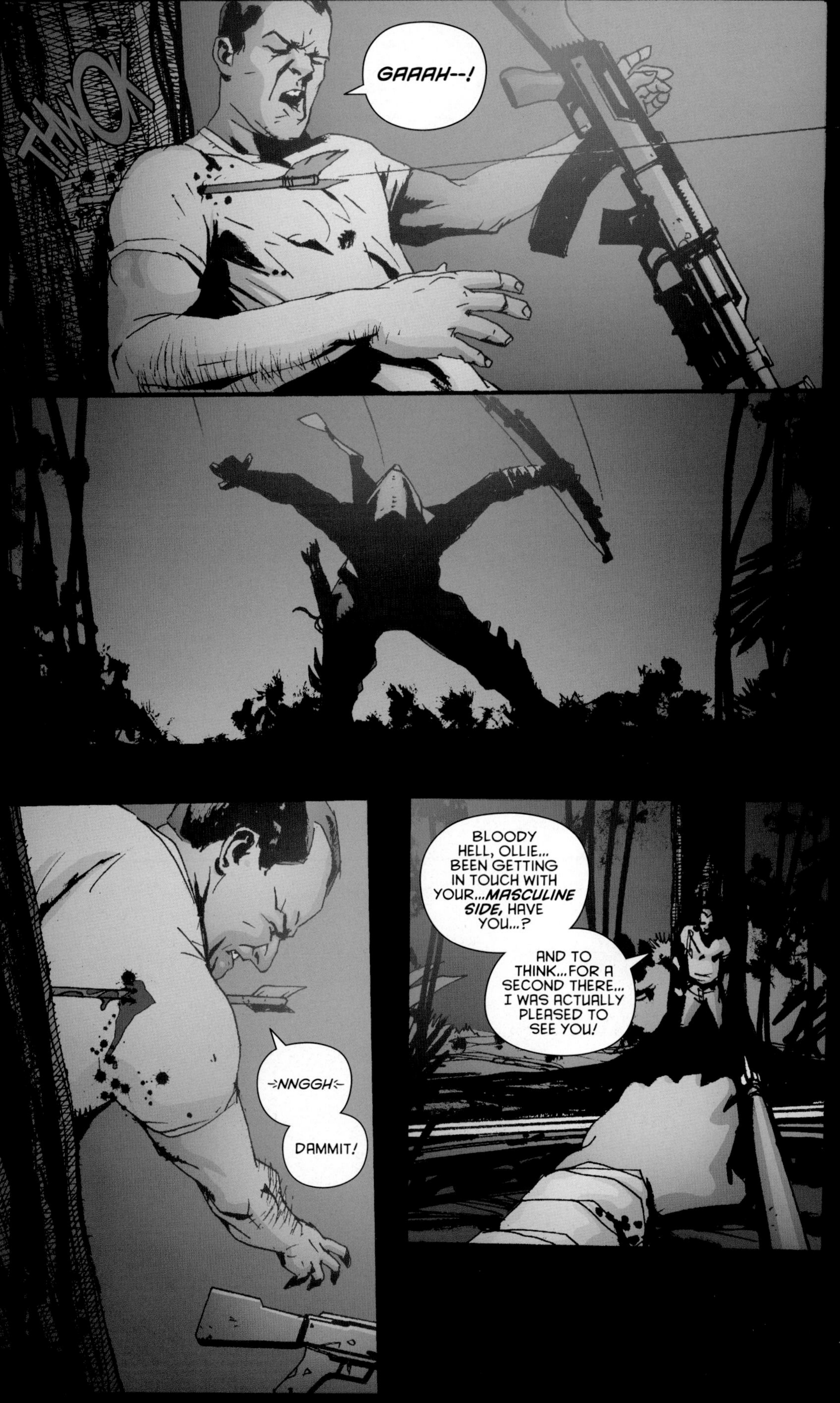
THWOCK
GAAAH--!
-NNGGH-
DAMMIT!
BLOODY HELL, OLLIE... BEEN GETTING IN TOUCH WITH YOUR...MASCULINE SIDE, HAVE YOU...?
AND TO THINK...FOR A SECOND THERE... I WAS ACTUALLY PLEASED TO SEE YOU!

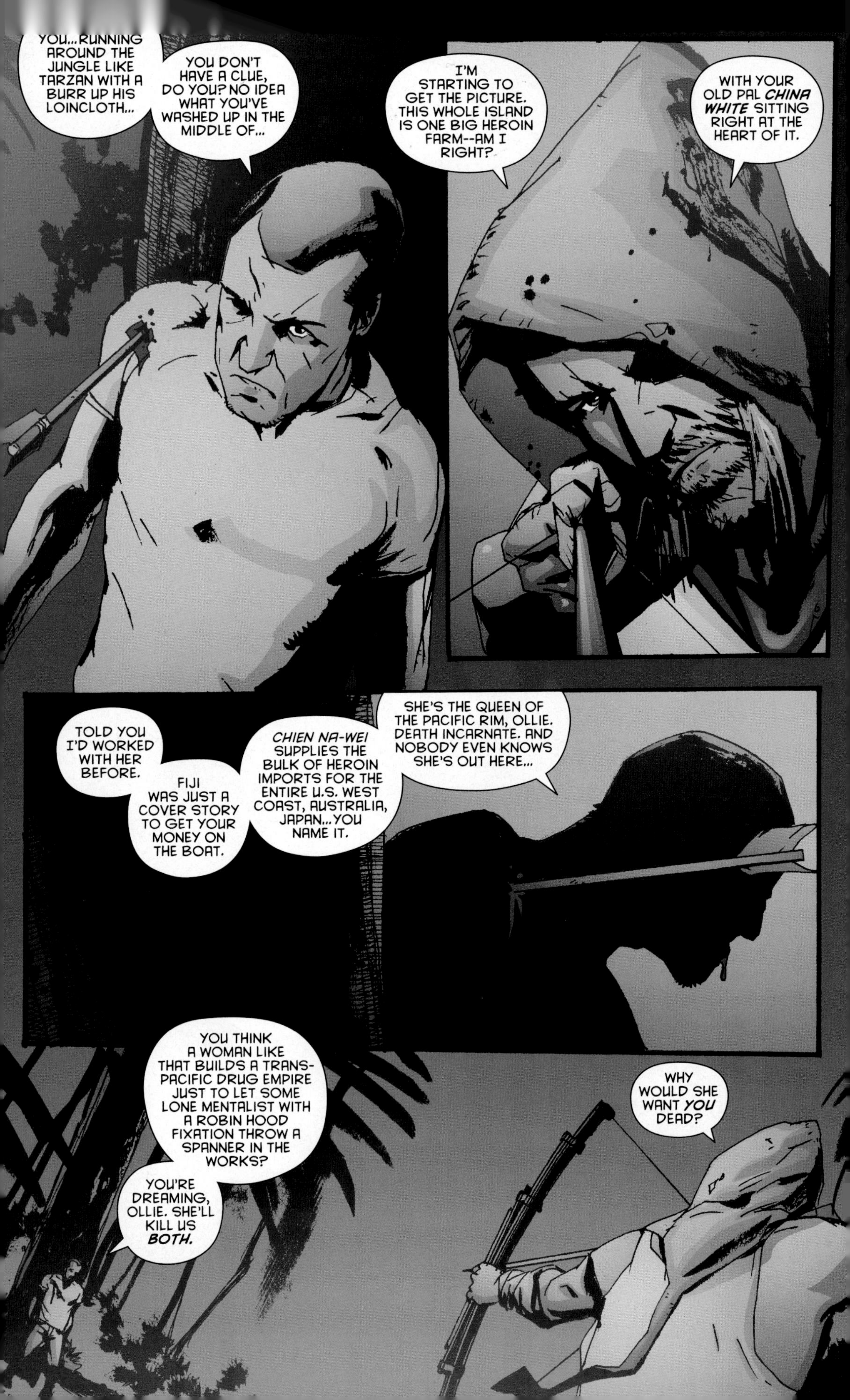
YOU...RUNNING AROUND THE JUNGLE LIKE TARZAN WITH A BURR UP HIS LOINCLOTH...
YOU DON'T HAVE A CLUE, DO YOU? NO IDEA WHAT YOU'VE WASHED UP IN THE MIDDLE OF...
I'M STARTING TO GET THE PICTURE. THIS WHOLE ISLAND IS ONE BIG HEROIN FARM--AM I RIGHT?
WITH YOUR OLD PAL *CHINA WHITE* SITTING RIGHT AT THE HEART OF IT.
TOLD YOU I'D WORKED WITH HER BEFORE.
FIJI WAS JUST A COVER STORY TO GET YOUR MONEY ON THE BOAT.
CHIEN NA-WEI SUPPLIES THE BULK OF HEROIN IMPORTS FOR THE ENTIRE U.S. WEST COAST, AUSTRALIA, JAPAN...YOU NAME IT.
SHE'S THE QUEEN OF THE PACIFIC RIM, OLLIE. DEATH INCARNATE. AND NOBODY EVEN KNOWS SHE'S OUT HERE...
YOU THINK A WOMAN LIKE THAT BUILDS A TRANS-PACIFIC DRUG EMPIRE JUST TO LET SOME LONE MENTALIST WITH A ROBIN HOOD FIXATION THROW A SPANNER IN THE WORKS?
YOU'RE DREAMING, OLLIE. SHE'LL KILL US ***BOTH.***
WHY WOULD SHE WANT *YOU* DEAD?

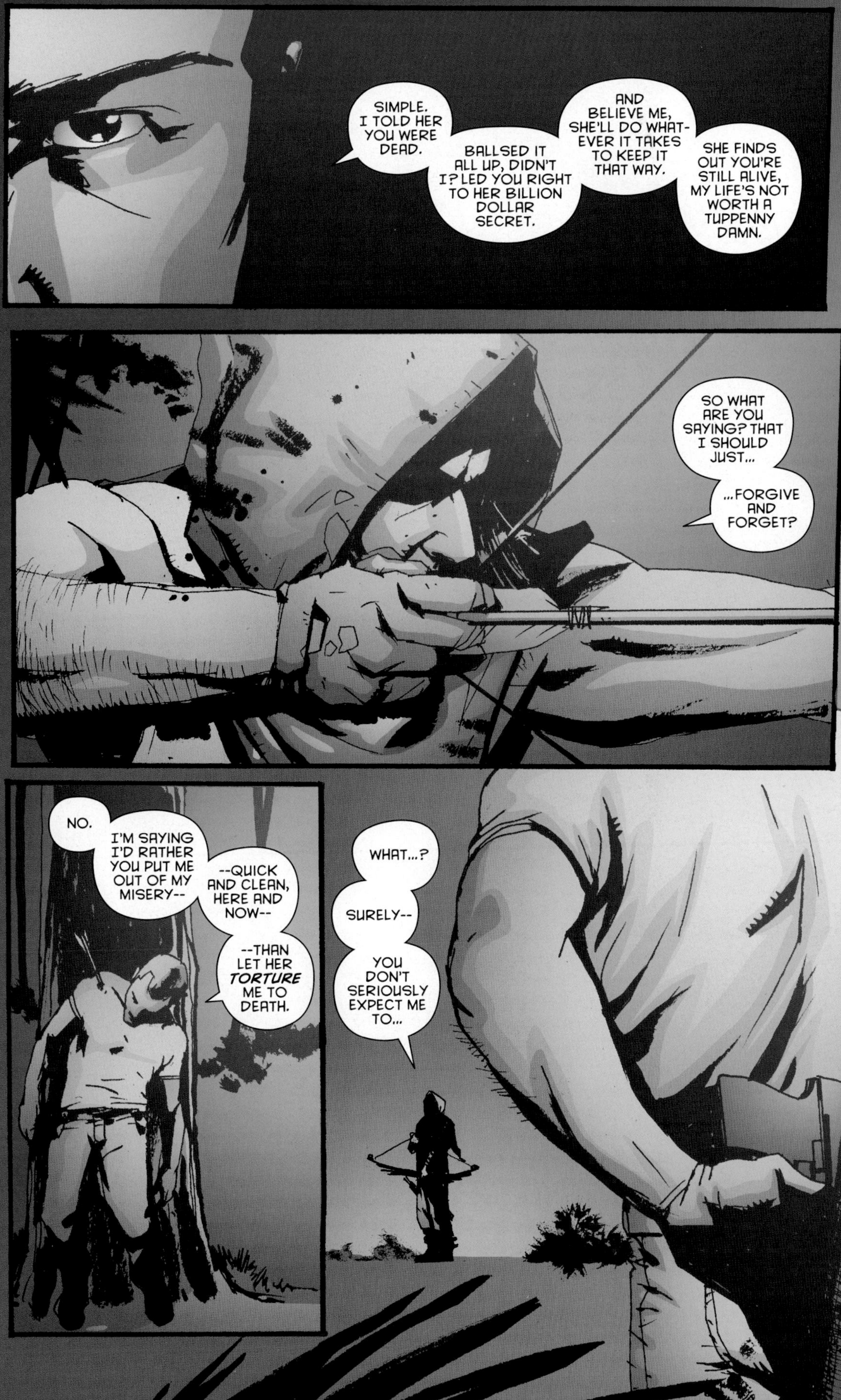
SIMPLE. I TOLD HER YOU WERE DEAD.
BALLSED IT ALL UP, DIDN'T I? LED YOU RIGHT TO HER BILLION DOLLAR SECRET.
AND BELIEVE ME, SHE'LL DO WHAT-EVER IT TAKES TO KEEP IT THAT WAY.
SHE FINDS OUT YOU'RE STILL ALIVE, MY LIFE'S NOT WORTH A TUPPENNY DAMN.
SO WHAT ARE YOU SAYING? THAT I SHOULD JUST...
...FORGIVE AND FORGET?
NO.
I'M SAYING I'D RATHER YOU PUT ME OUT OF MY MISERY--
--QUICK AND CLEAN, HERE AND NOW--
--THAN LET HER *TORTURE* ME TO DEATH.
WHAT...?
SURELY--
YOU DON'T SERIOUSLY EXPECT ME TO...

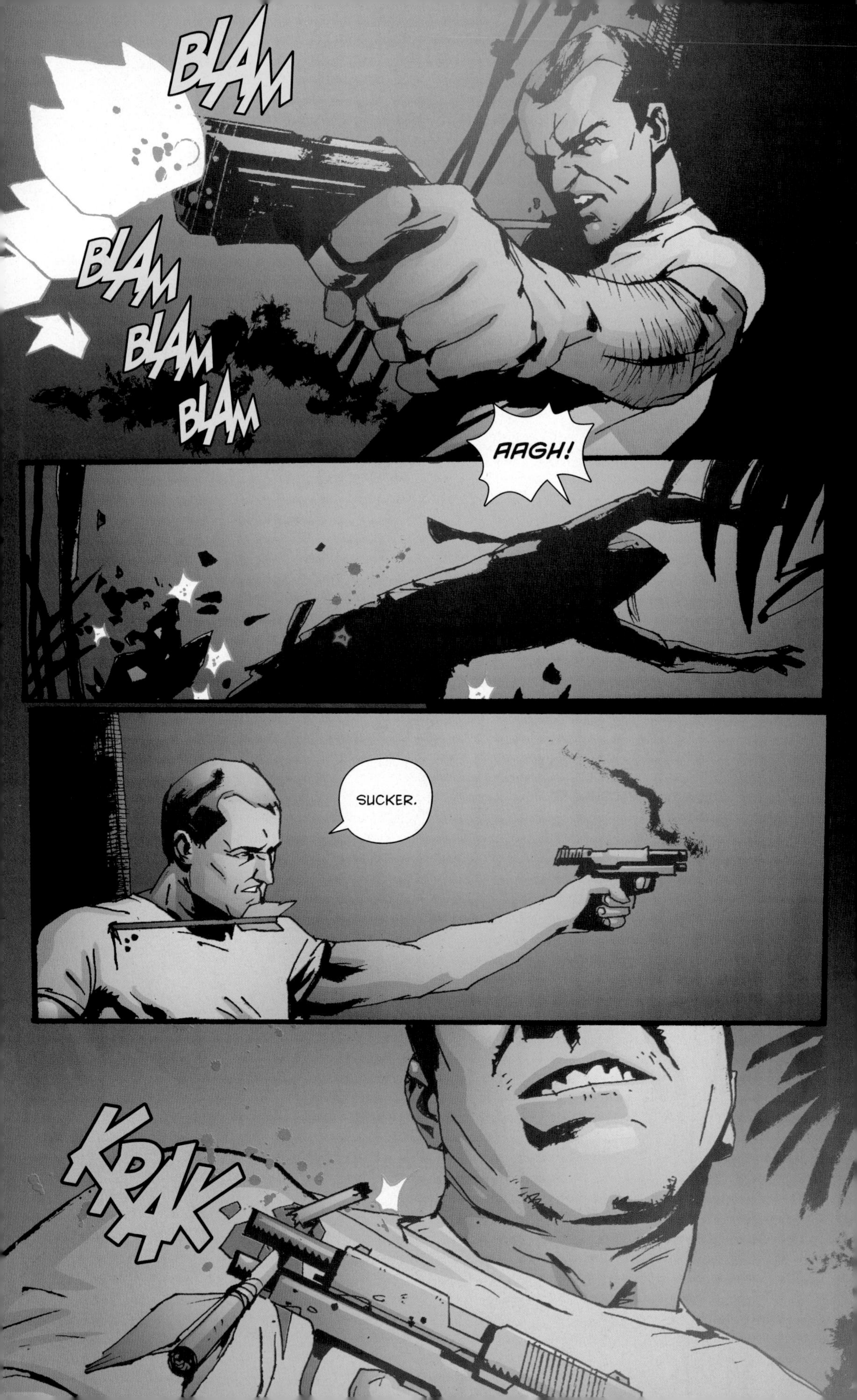
BLAM
BLAM
BLAM
BLAM
AAGH!
SUCKER.
KRAK

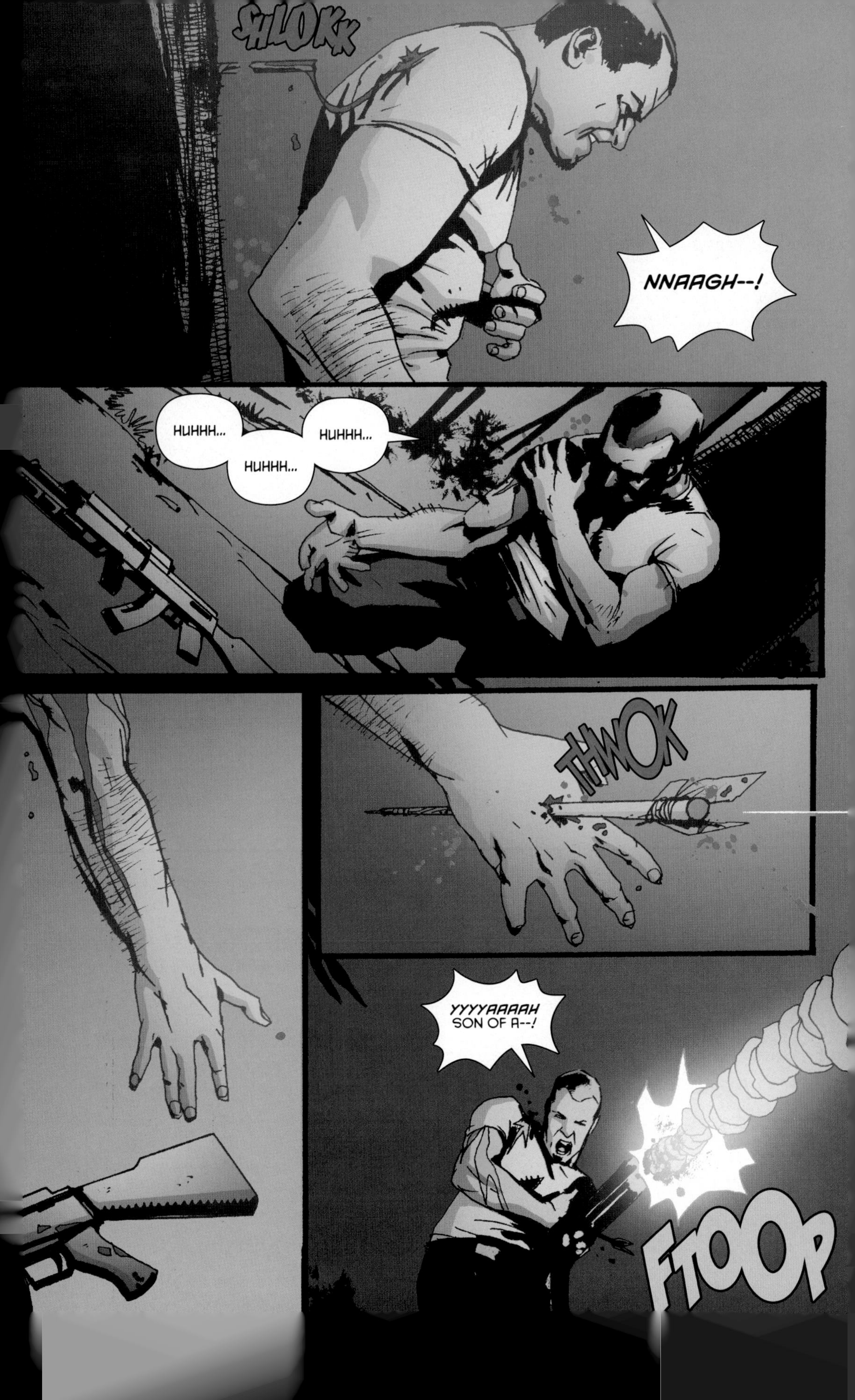
SHLOKK
NNAAGH--!
HUHHH...
HUHHH...
HUHHH...
THWOK
YYYYAAAAH
SON OF A--!
FTOOP

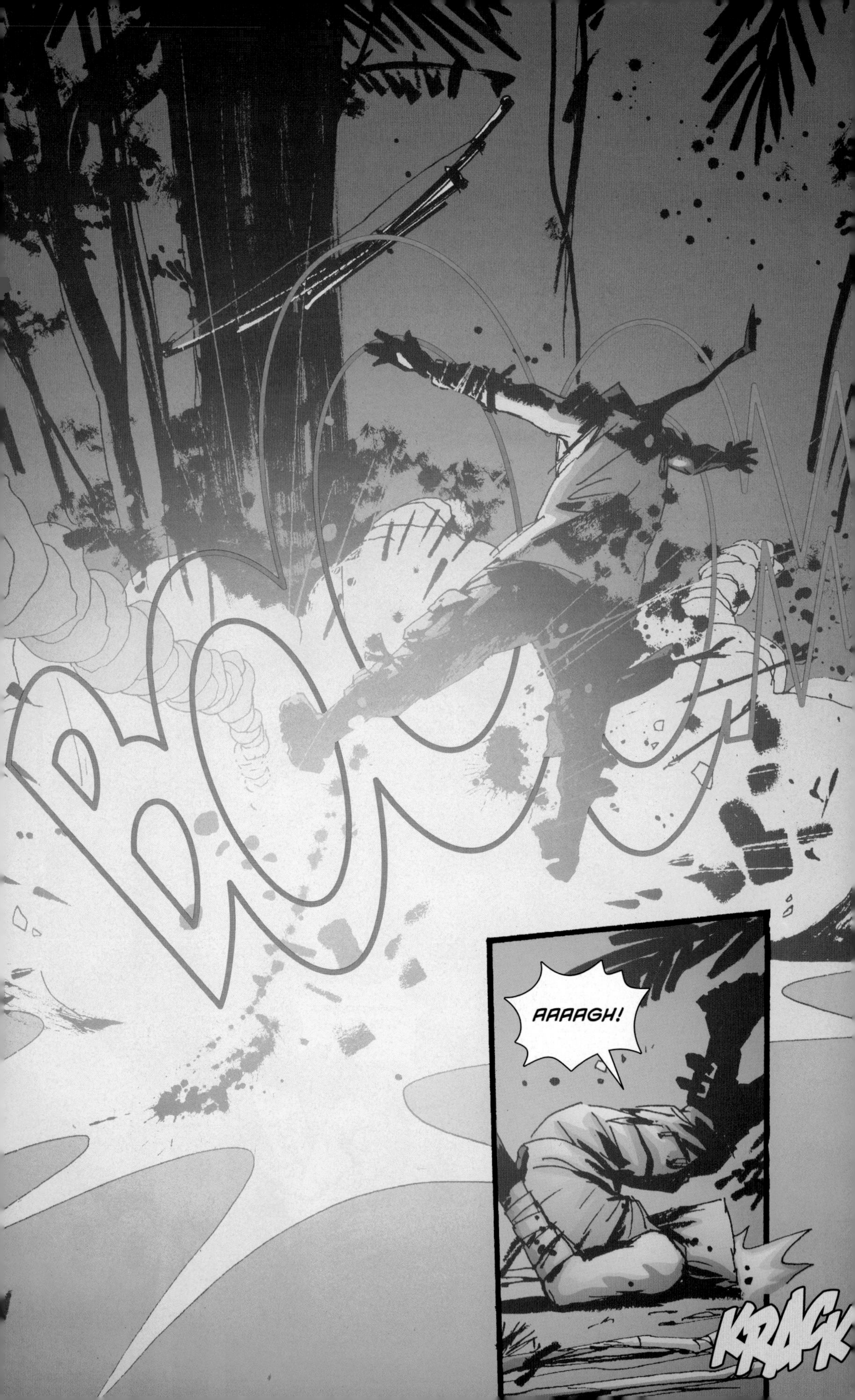
BOOM
AAAAGH!
KRACK

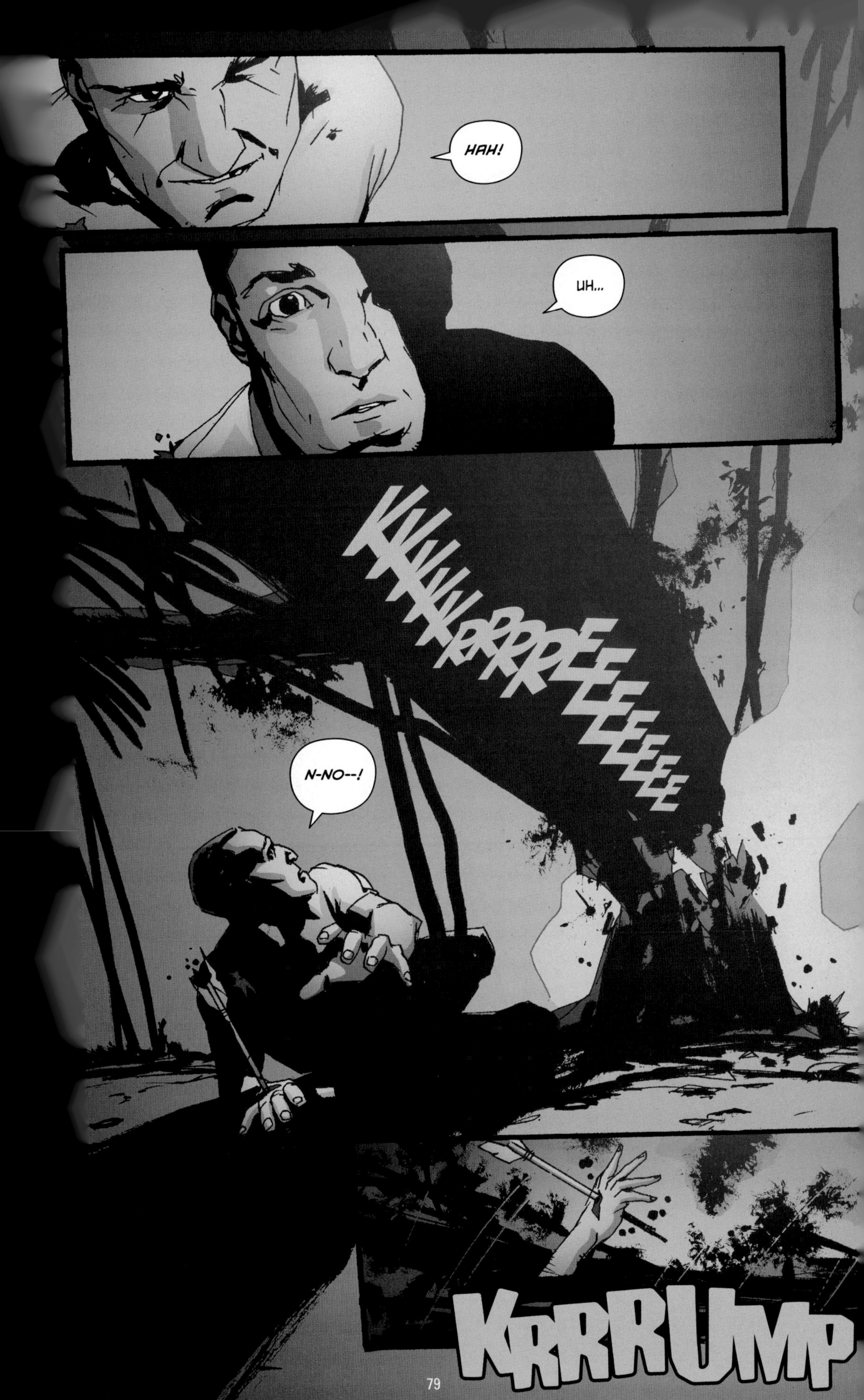
HAH!
UH...
KHHHRRRREEEEEEE
N-NO--!
KRRRUMP

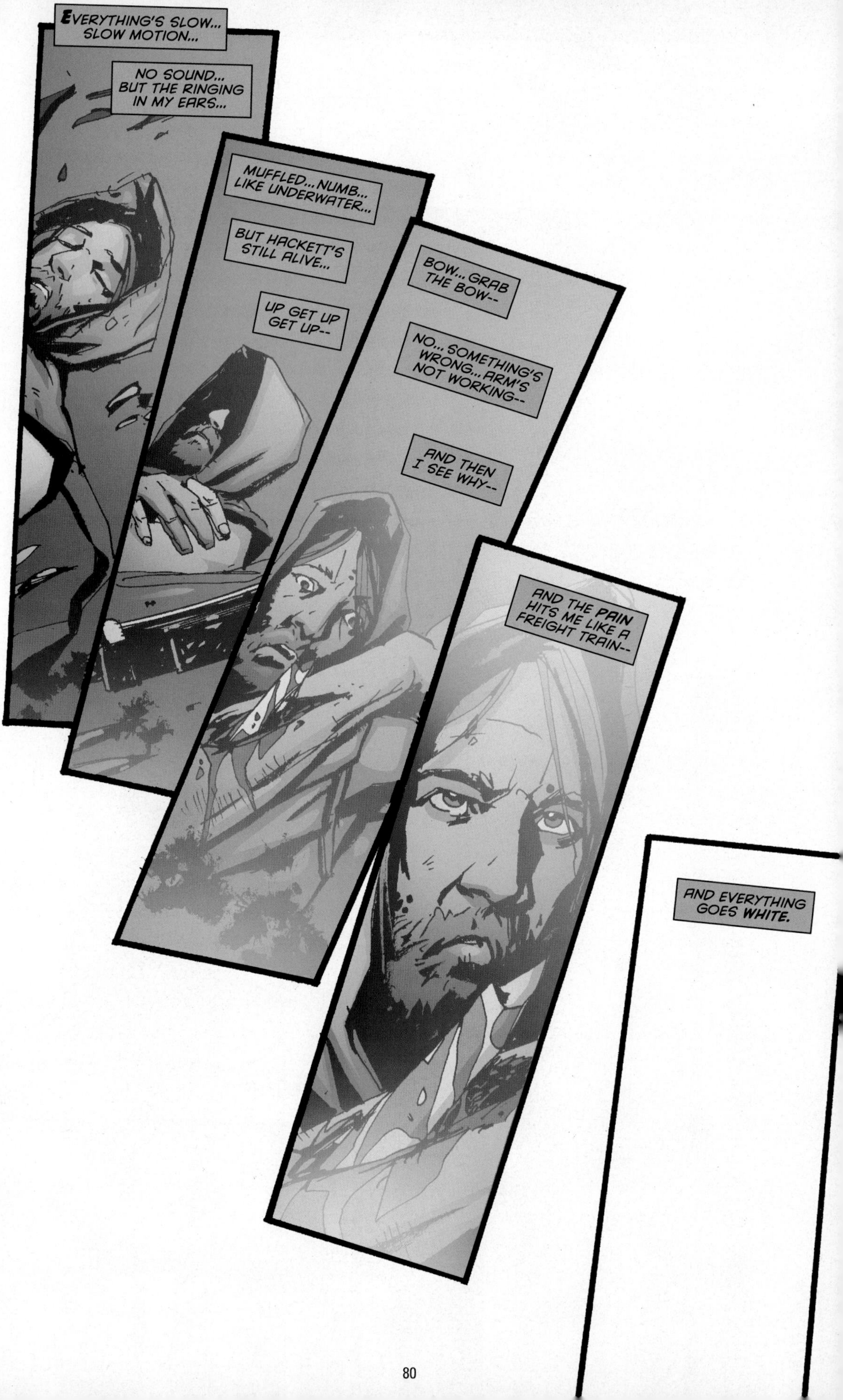
EVERYTHING'S SLOW... SLOW MOTION...
NO SOUND... BUT THE RINGING IN MY EARS...
MUFFLED...NUMB... LIKE UNDERWATER...
BUT HACKETT'S STILL ALIVE...
UP GET UP GET UP--
BOW...GRAB THE BOW--
NO... SOMETHING'S WRONG...ARM'S NOT WORKING--
AND THEN I SEE WHY--
AND THE PAIN HITS ME LIKE A FREIGHT TRAIN--
AND EVERYTHING GOES WHITE.

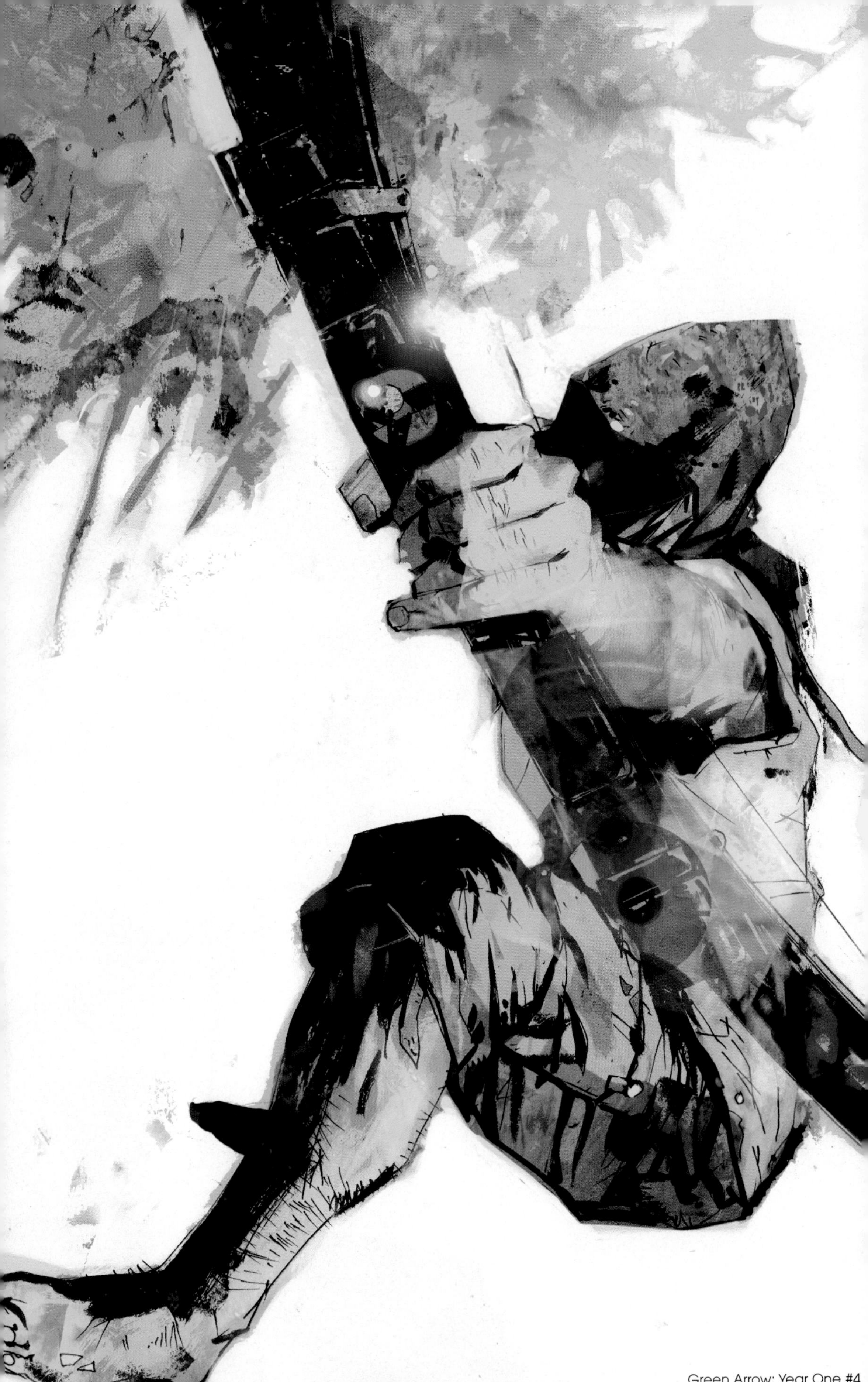

Green Arrow: Year One #4

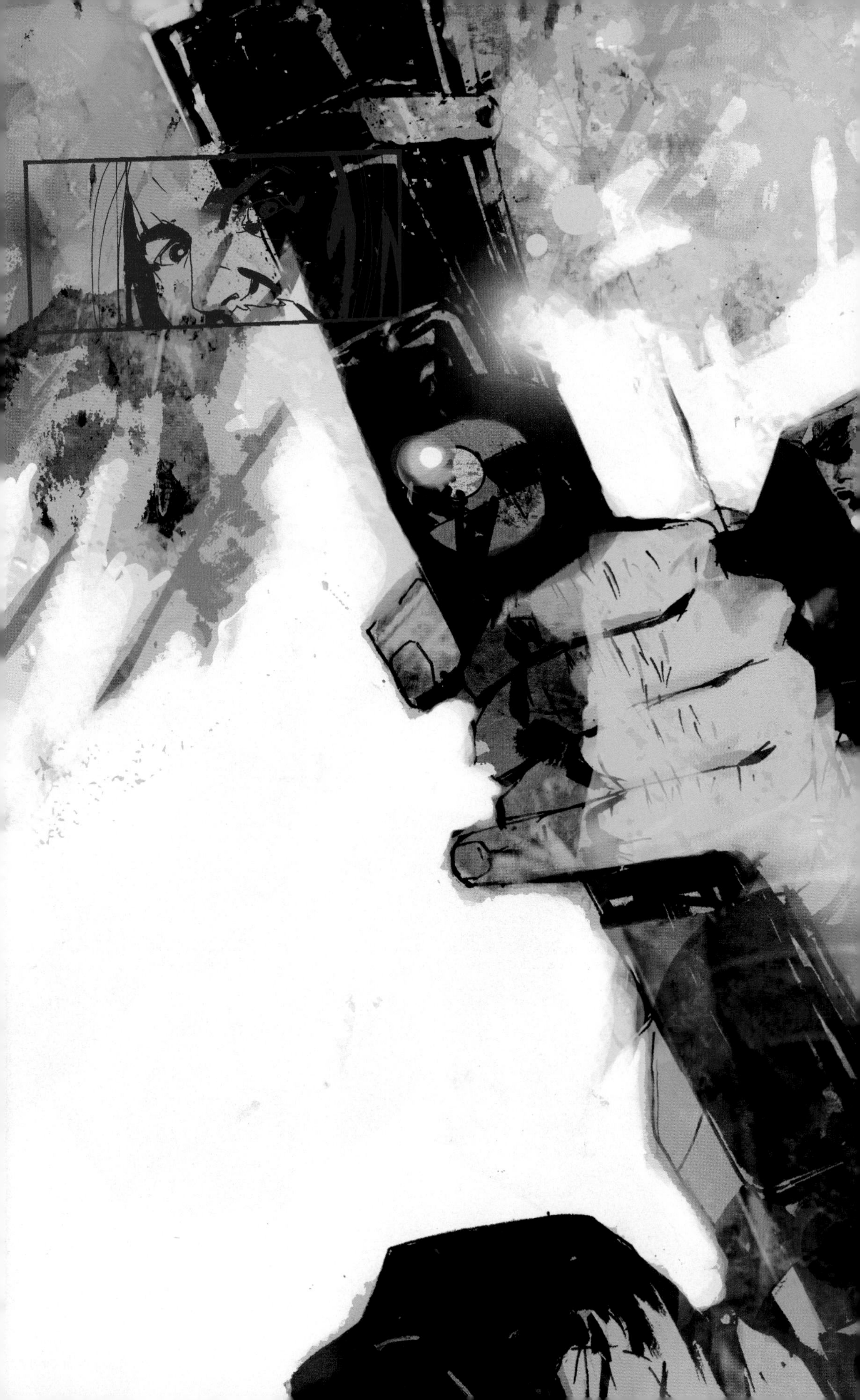

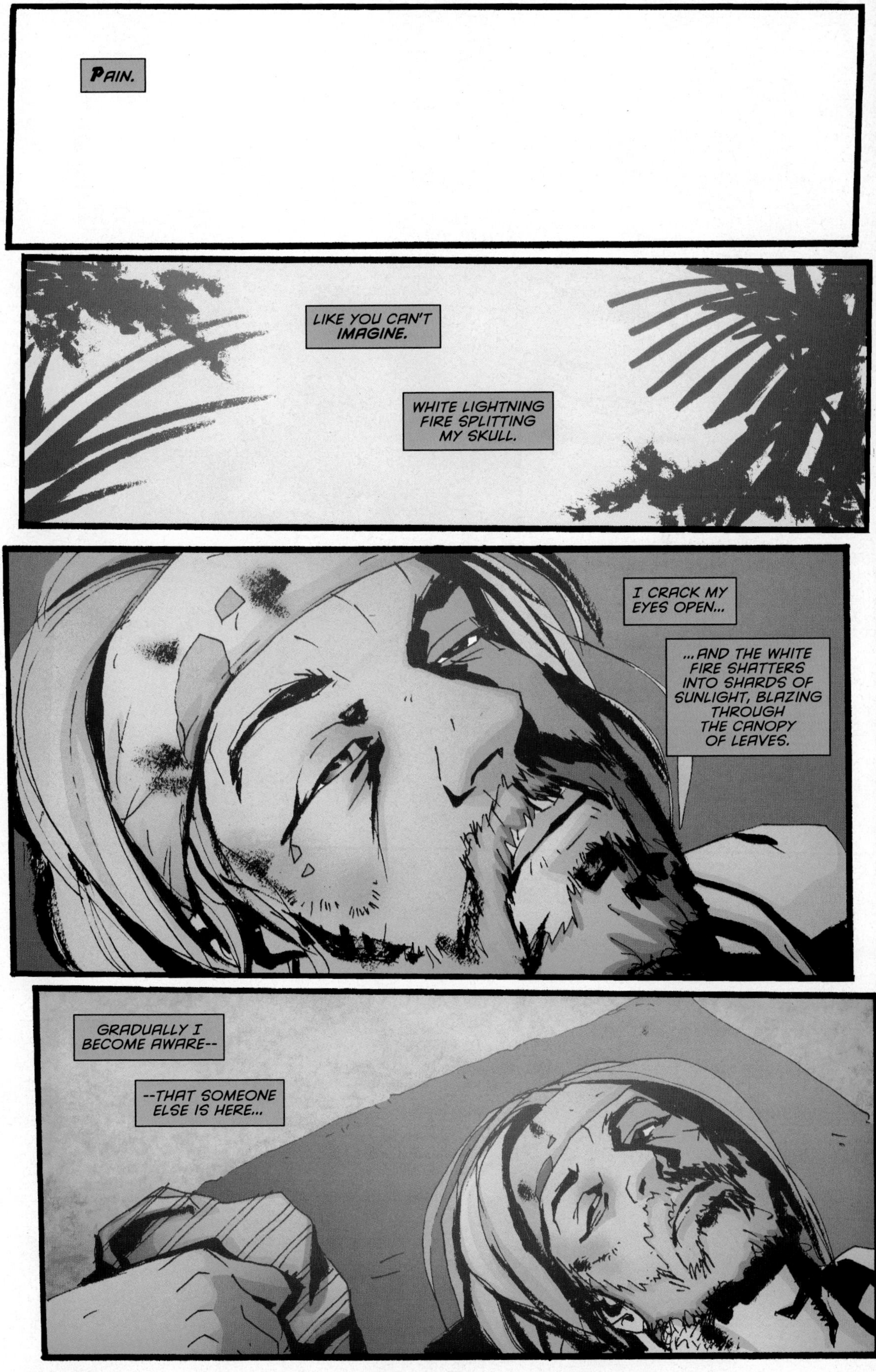
PAIN.
LIKE YOU CAN'T IMAGINE.
WHITE LIGHTNING FIRE SPLITTING MY SKULL.
I CRACK MY EYES OPEN...
...AND THE WHITE FIRE SHATTERS INTO SHARDS OF SUNLIGHT, BLAZING THROUGH THE CANOPY OF LEAVES.
GRADUALLY I BECOME AWARE--
--THAT SOMEONE ELSE IS HERE...

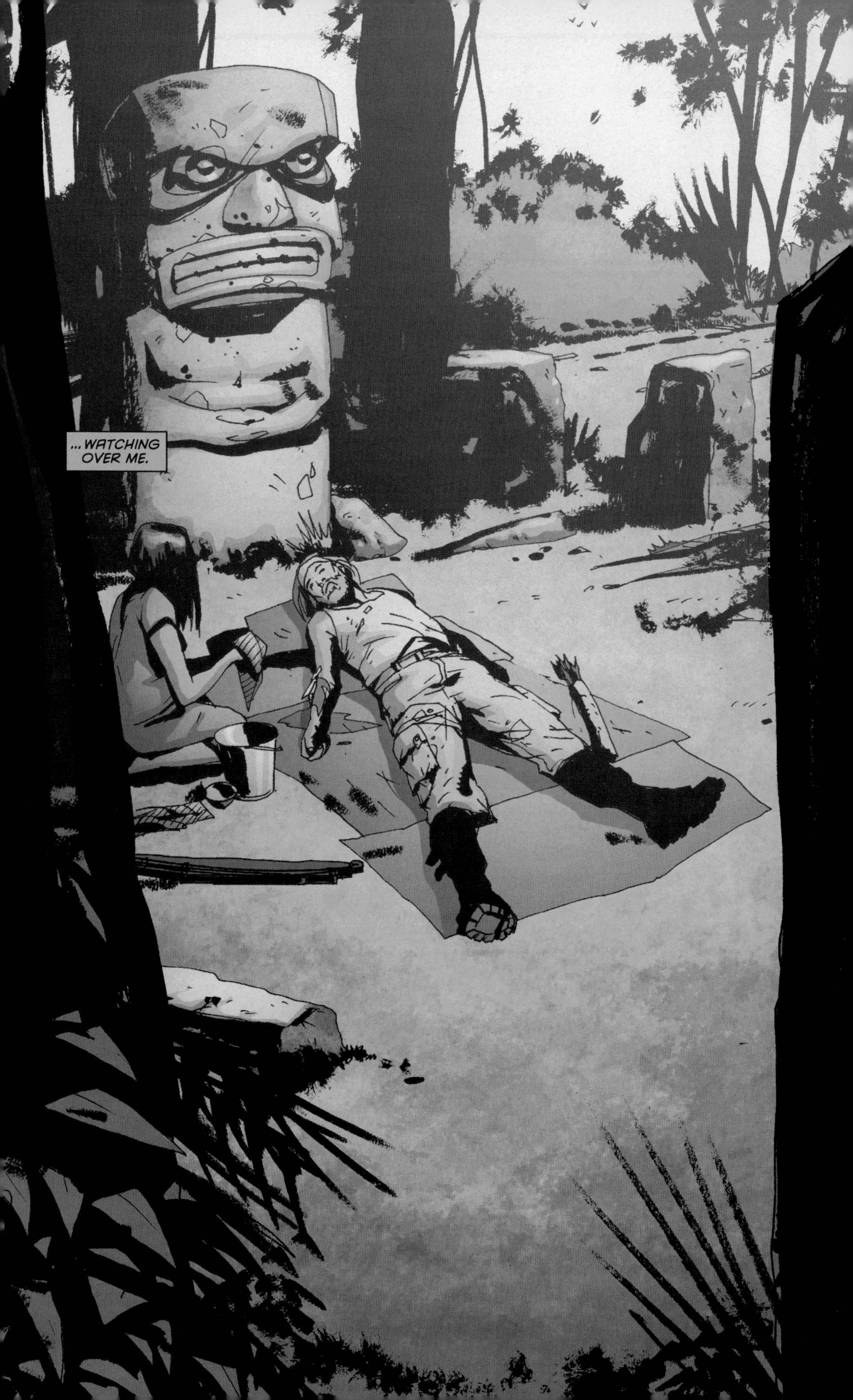
...WATCHING OVER ME.

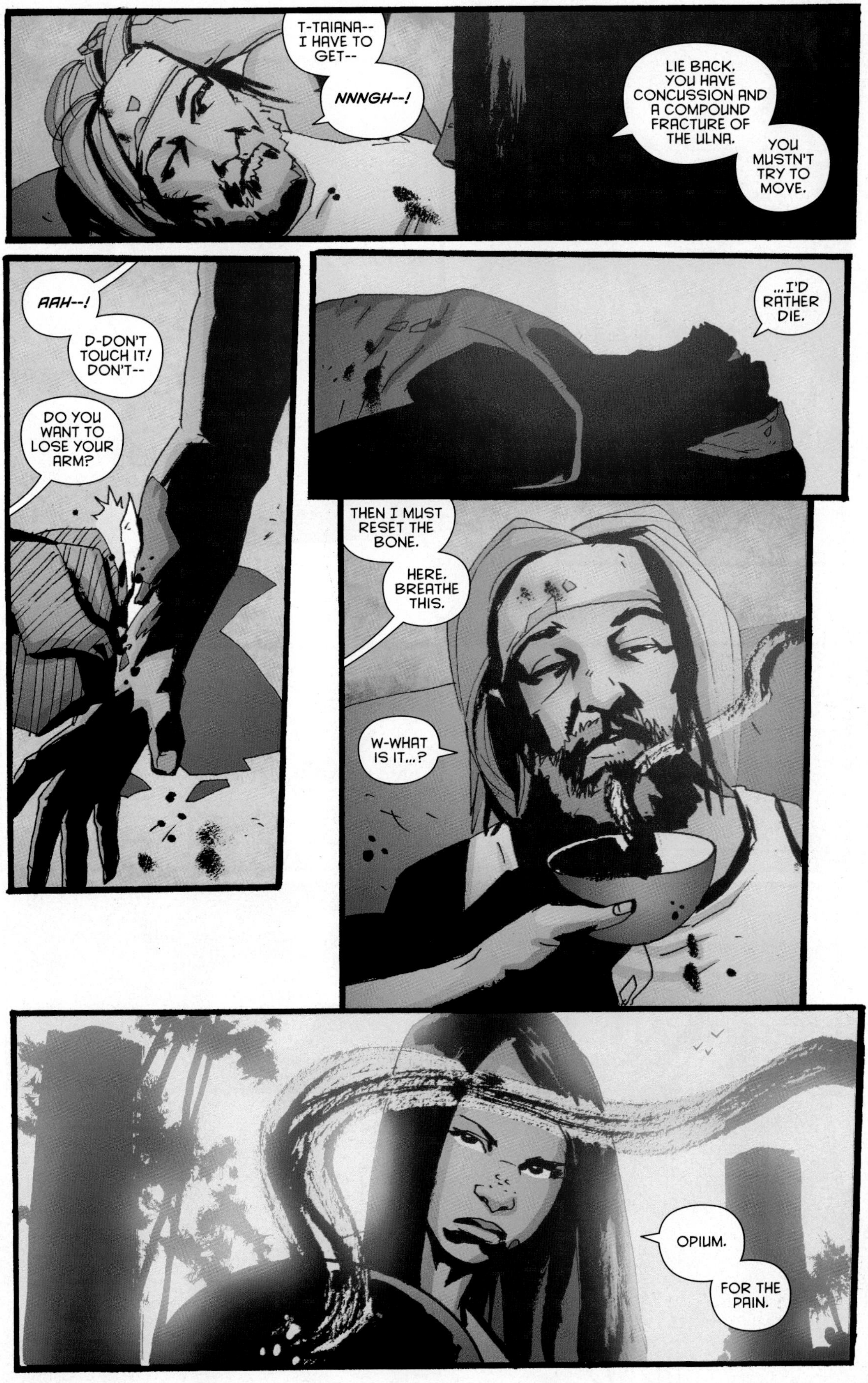
T-TAIANA-- I HAVE TO GET--
NNNGH--!
LIE BACK. YOU HAVE CONCUSSION AND A COMPOUND FRACTURE OF THE ULNA.
YOU MUSTN'T TRY TO MOVE.
AAH--!
D-DON'T TOUCH IT! DON'T--
DO YOU WANT TO LOSE YOUR ARM?
...I'D RATHER DIE.
THEN I MUST RESET THE BONE.
HERE. BREATHE THIS.
W-WHAT IS IT...?
OPIUM.
FOR THE PAIN.

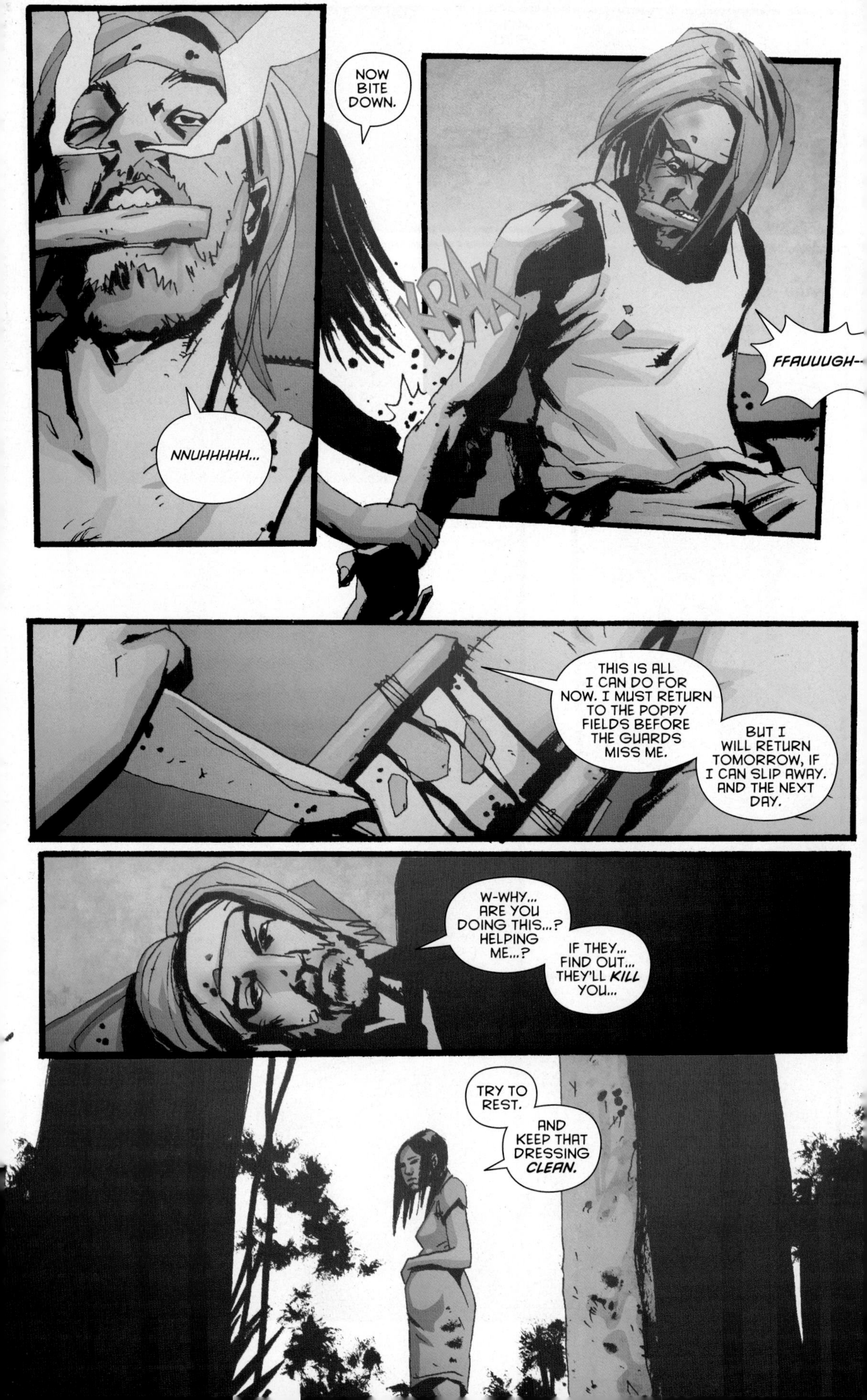
NOW BITE DOWN.
KRAK
NNUHHHHH...
FFAUUUGH--
THIS IS ALL I CAN DO FOR NOW. I MUST RETURN TO THE POPPY FIELDS BEFORE THE GUARDS MISS ME.
BUT I WILL RETURN TOMORROW, IF I CAN SLIP AWAY. AND THE NEXT DAY.
W-WHY... ARE YOU DOING THIS...? HELPING ME...?
IF THEY... FIND OUT... THEY'LL KILL YOU...
TRY TO REST.
AND KEEP THAT DRESSING CLEAN.

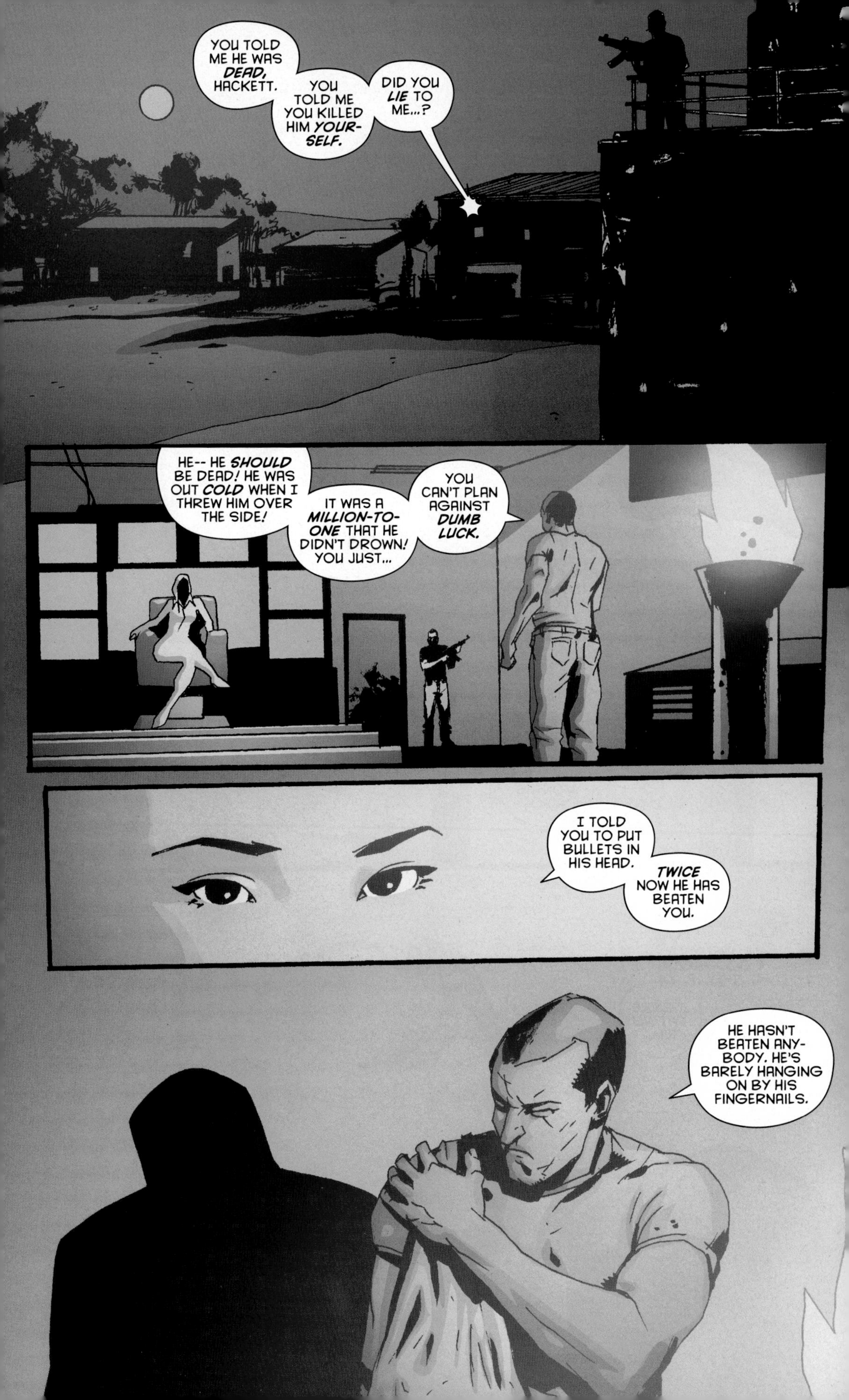
YOU TOLD ME HE WAS DEAD, HACKETT.
YOU TOLD ME YOU KILLED HIM YOURSELF.
DID YOU LIE TO ME...?
HE-- HE SHOULD BE DEAD! HE WAS OUT COLD WHEN I THREW HIM OVER THE SIDE!
IT WAS A MILLION-TO-ONE THAT HE DIDN'T DROWN! YOU JUST...
YOU CAN'T PLAN AGAINST DUMB LUCK.
I TOLD YOU TO PUT BULLETS IN HIS HEAD.
TWICE NOW HE HAS BEATEN YOU.
HE HASN'T BEATEN ANY-BODY. HE'S BARELY HANGING ON BY HIS FINGERNAILS.

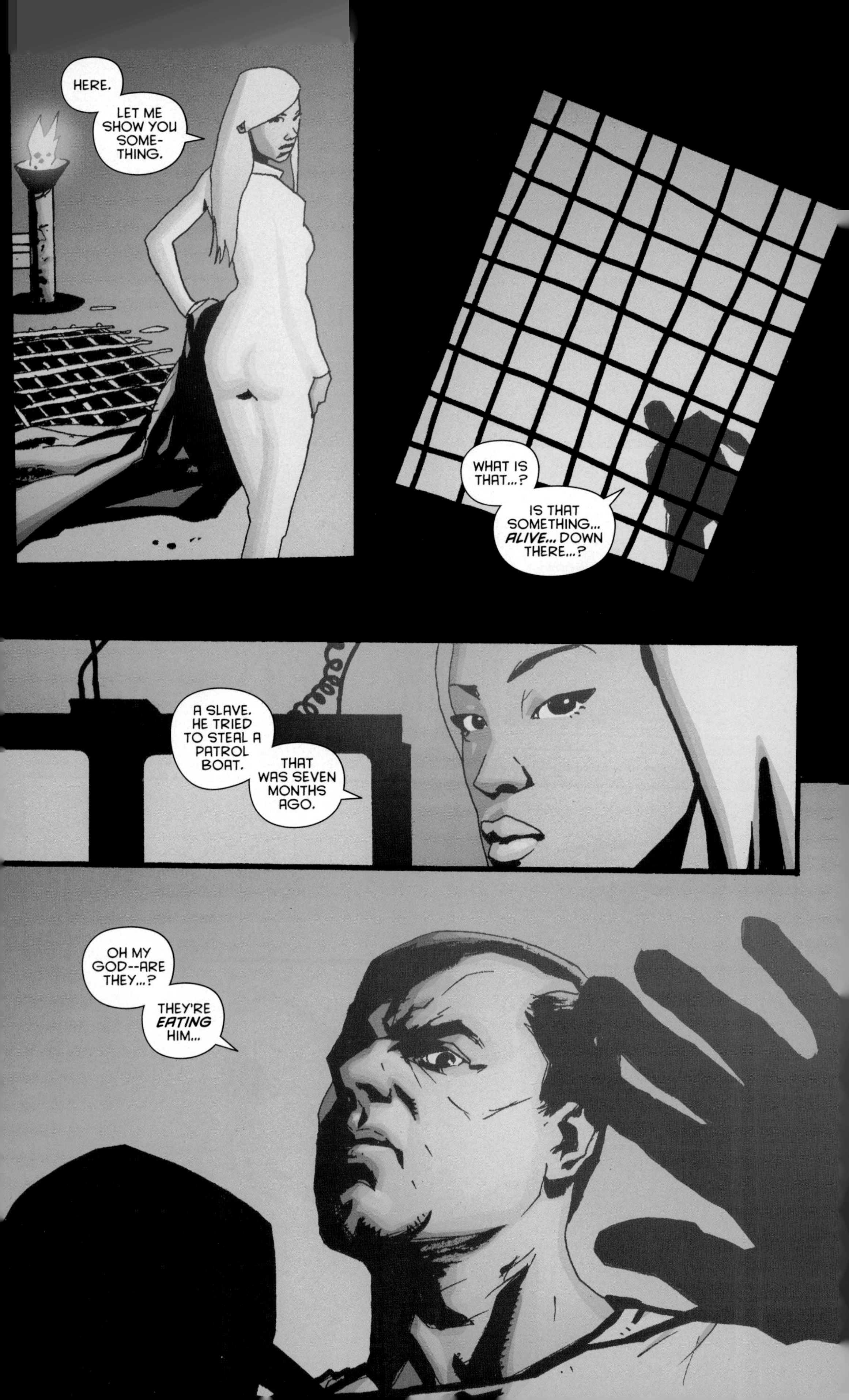
HERE.
LET ME SHOW YOU SOME-THING.
WHAT IS THAT...?
IS THAT SOMETHING... ALIVE... DOWN THERE...?
A SLAVE. HE TRIED TO STEAL A PATROL BOAT.
THAT WAS SEVEN MONTHS AGO.
OH MY GOD--ARE THEY...?
THEY'RE EATING HIM...

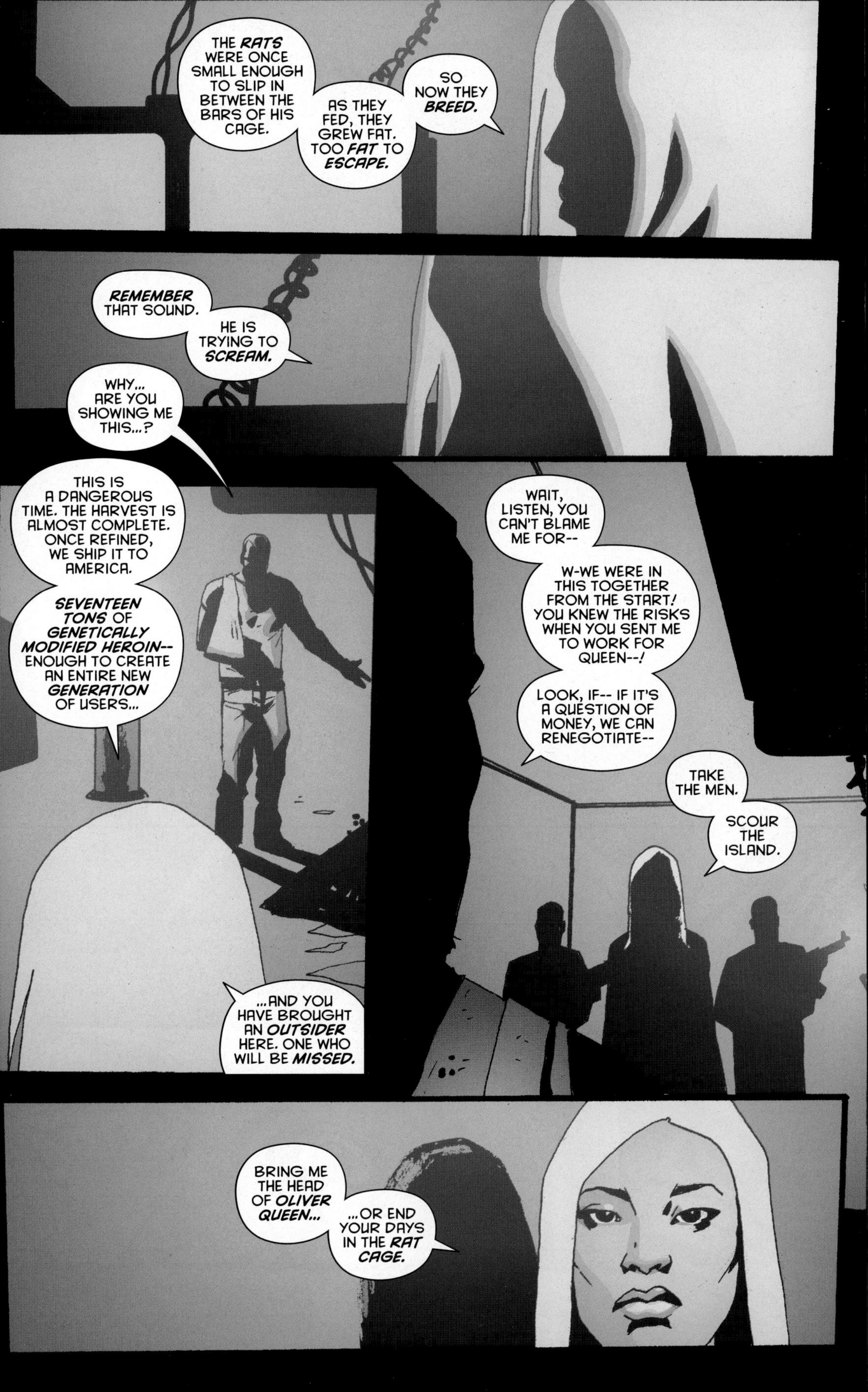
THE RATS WERE ONCE SMALL ENOUGH TO SLIP IN BETWEEN THE BARS OF HIS CAGE.
AS THEY FED, THEY GREW FAT. TOO FAT TO ESCAPE.
SO NOW THEY BREED.
REMEMBER THAT SOUND.
HE IS TRYING TO SCREAM.
WHY... ARE YOU SHOWING ME THIS...?
THIS IS A DANGEROUS TIME. THE HARVEST IS ALMOST COMPLETE. ONCE REFINED, WE SHIP IT TO AMERICA.
SEVENTEEN TONS OF GENETICALLY MODIFIED HEROIN-- ENOUGH TO CREATE AN ENTIRE NEW GENERATION OF USERS...
...AND YOU HAVE BROUGHT AN OUTSIDER HERE. ONE WHO WILL BE MISSED.
WAIT, LISTEN, YOU CAN'T BLAME ME FOR--
W-WE WERE IN THIS TOGETHER FROM THE START! YOU KNEW THE RISKS WHEN YOU SENT ME TO WORK FOR QUEEN--!
LOOK, IF-- IF IT'S A QUESTION OF MONEY, WE CAN RENEGOTIATE--
TAKE THE MEN.
SCOUR THE ISLAND.
BRING ME THE HEAD OF OLIVER QUEEN...
...OR END YOUR DAYS IN THE RAT CAGE.

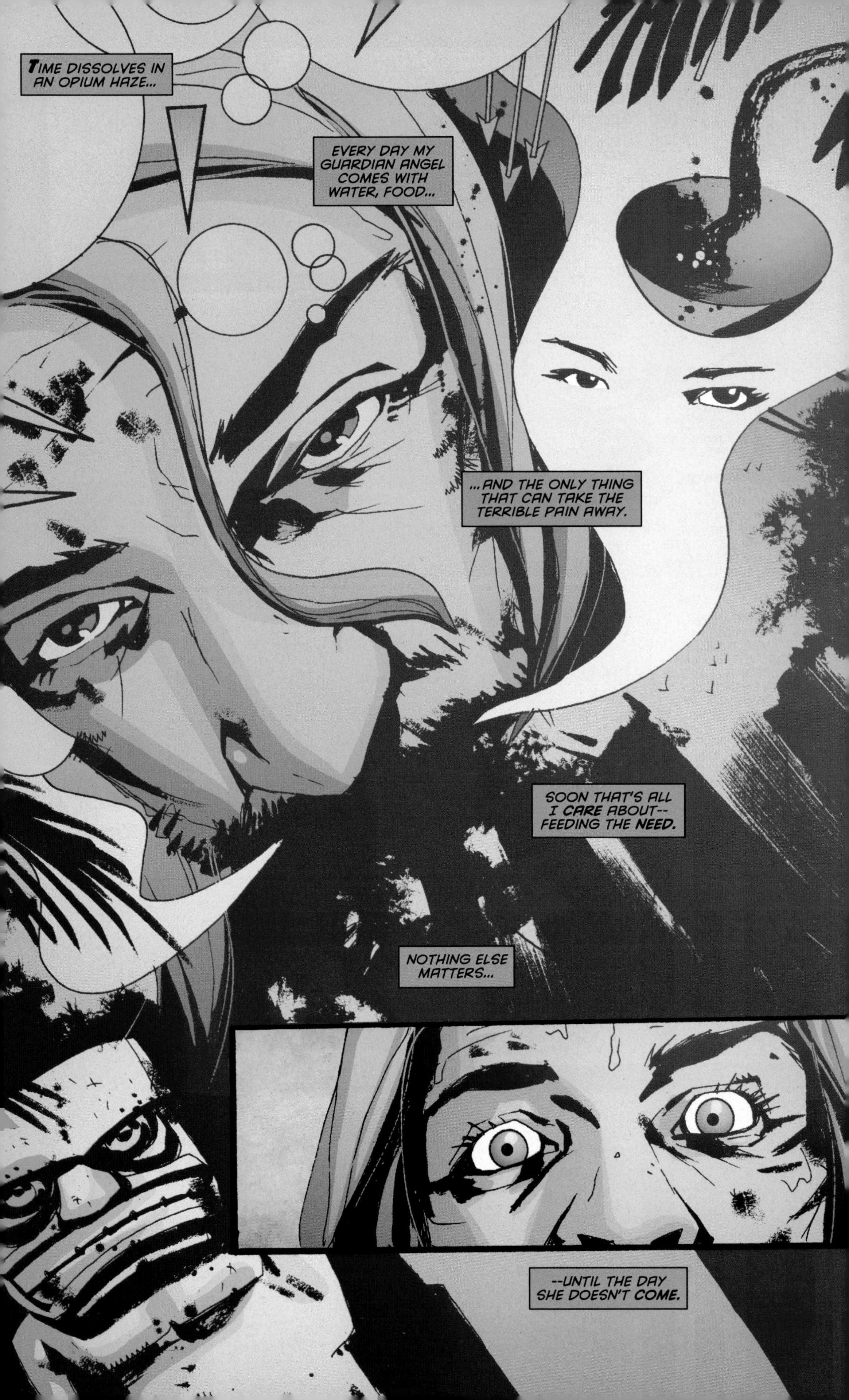
TIME DISSOLVES IN AN OPIUM HAZE...
EVERY DAY MY GUARDIAN ANGEL COMES WITH WATER, FOOD...
...AND THE ONLY THING THAT CAN TAKE THE TERRIBLE PAIN AWAY.
SOON THAT'S ALL I CARE ABOUT-- FEEDING THE NEED.
NOTHING ELSE MATTERS...
--UNTIL THE DAY SHE DOESN'T COME.

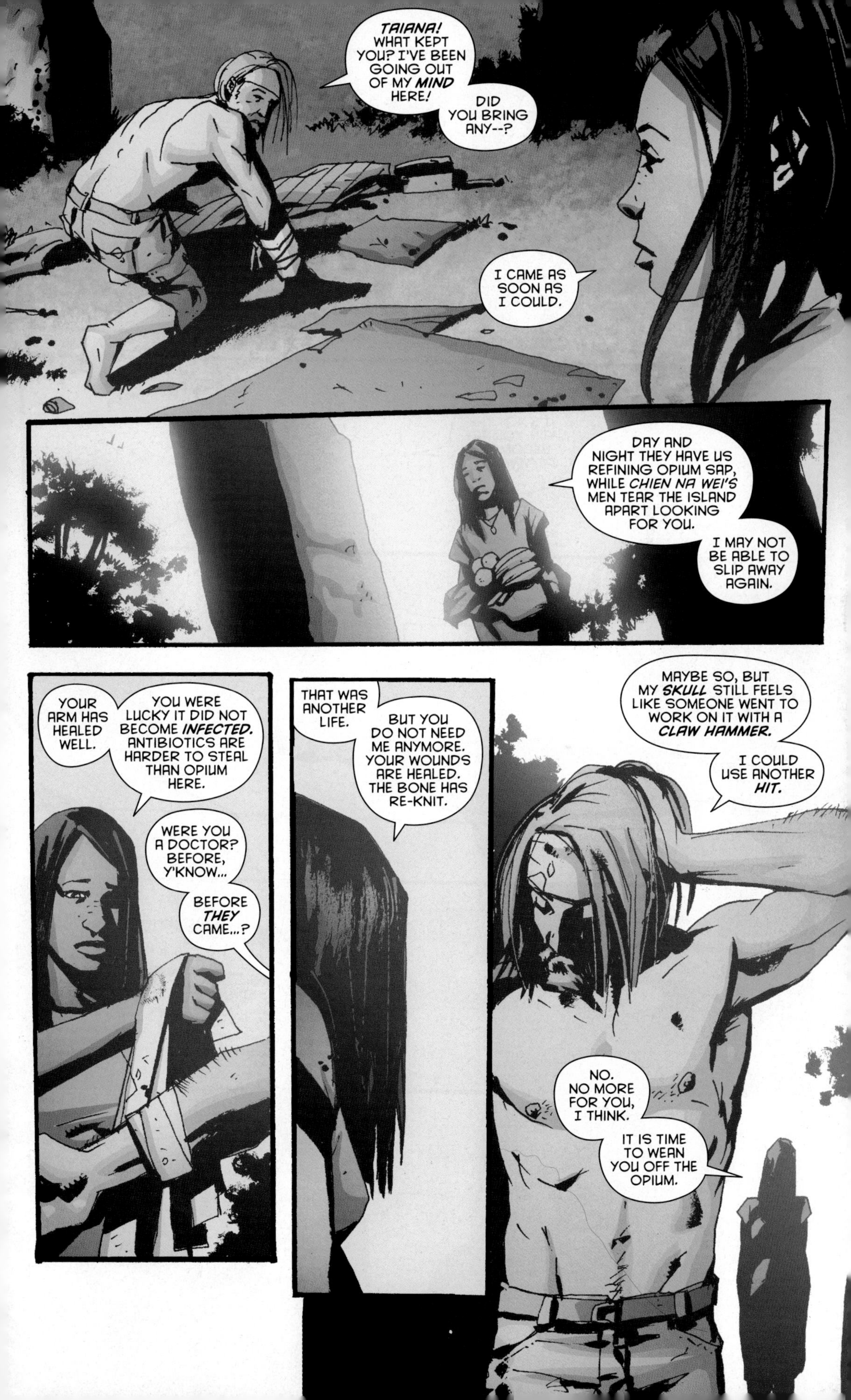

TAIANA! WHAT KEPT YOU? I'VE BEEN GOING OUT OF MY MIND HERE!
DID YOU BRING ANY--?
I CAME AS SOON AS I COULD.
DAY AND NIGHT THEY HAVE US REFINING OPIUM SAP, WHILE CHIEN NA WEI'S MEN TEAR THE ISLAND APART LOOKING FOR YOU.
I MAY NOT BE ABLE TO SLIP AWAY AGAIN.
YOUR ARM HAS HEALED WELL.
YOU WERE LUCKY IT DID NOT BECOME INFECTED. ANTIBIOTICS ARE HARDER TO STEAL THAN OPIUM HERE.
WERE YOU A DOCTOR? BEFORE, Y'KNOW...
BEFORE THEY CAME...?
THAT WAS ANOTHER LIFE.
BUT YOU DO NOT NEED ME ANYMORE. YOUR WOUNDS ARE HEALED. THE BONE HAS RE-KNIT.
MAYBE SO, BUT MY SKULL STILL FEELS LIKE SOMEONE WENT TO WORK ON IT WITH A CLAW HAMMER.
I COULD USE ANOTHER HIT.
NO. NO MORE FOR YOU, I THINK.
IT IS TIME TO WEAN YOU OFF THE OPIUM.

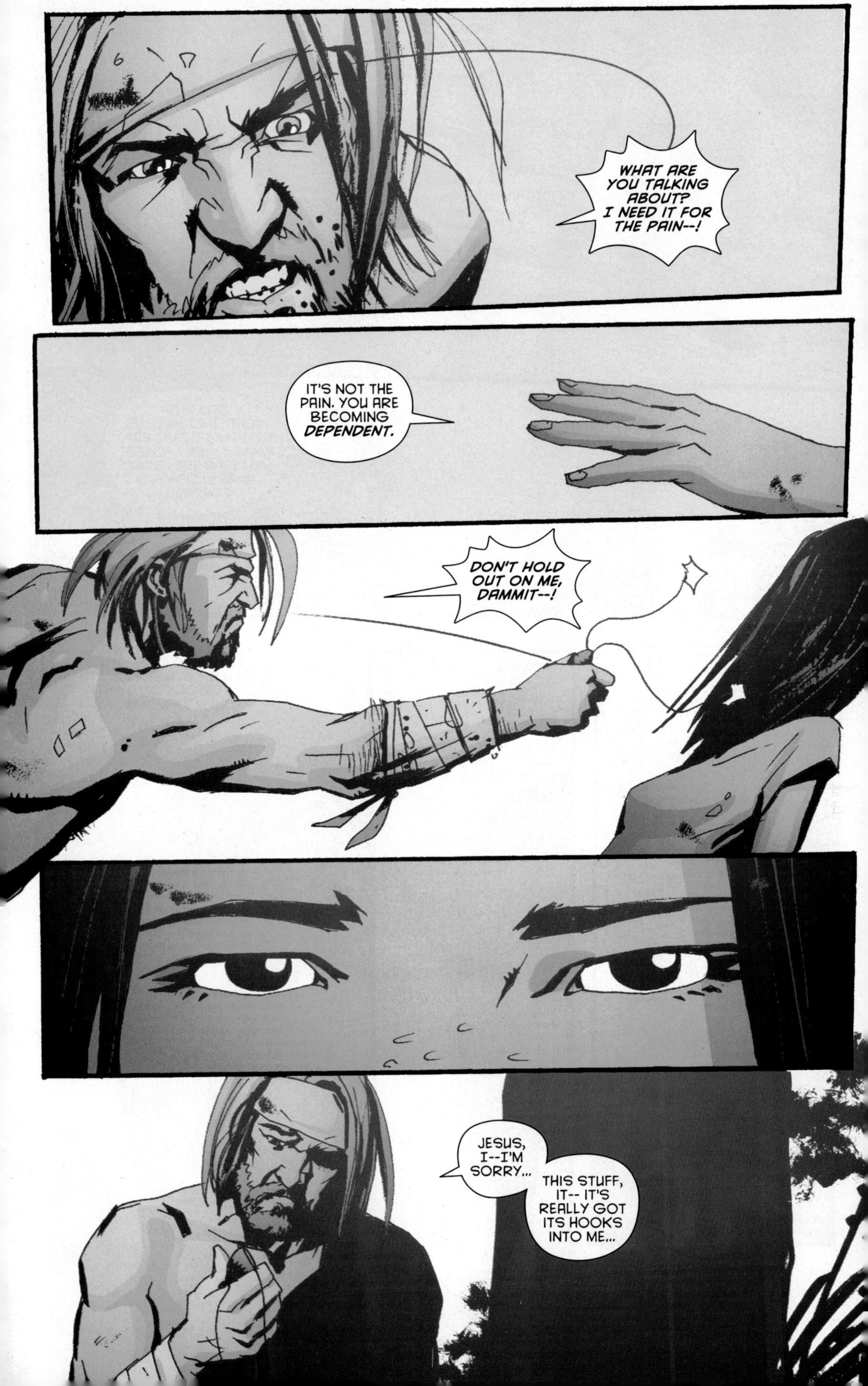
WHAT ARE YOU TALKING ABOUT? I NEED IT FOR THE PAIN--!
IT'S NOT THE PAIN. YOU ARE BECOMING DEPENDENT.
DON'T HOLD OUT ON ME, DAMMIT--!
JESUS, I--I'M SORRY...
THIS STUFF, IT-- IT'S REALLY GOT ITS HOOKS INTO ME...

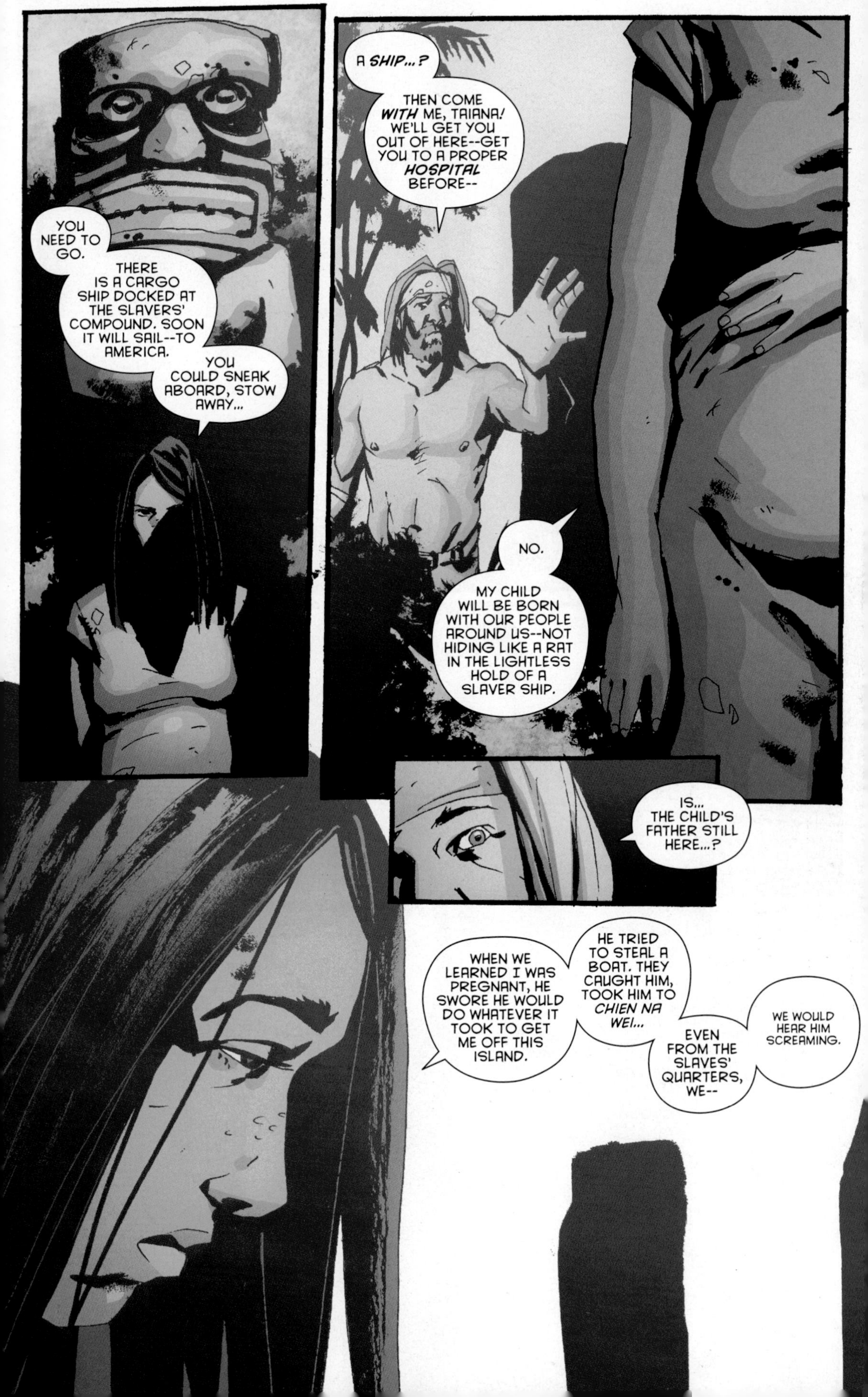
YOU NEED TO GO.
THERE IS A CARGO SHIP DOCKED AT THE SLAVERS' COMPOUND. SOON IT WILL SAIL--TO AMERICA.
YOU COULD SNEAK ABOARD, STOW AWAY...
A *SHIP...?*
THEN COME *WITH* ME, TAIANA! WE'LL GET YOU OUT OF HERE--GET YOU TO A PROPER *HOSPITAL* BEFORE--
NO.
MY CHILD WILL BE BORN WITH OUR PEOPLE AROUND US--NOT HIDING LIKE A RAT IN THE LIGHTLESS HOLD OF A SLAVER SHIP.
IS... THE CHILD'S FATHER STILL HERE...?
WHEN WE LEARNED I WAS PREGNANT, HE SWORE HE WOULD DO WHATEVER IT TOOK TO GET ME OFF THIS ISLAND.
HE TRIED TO STEAL A BOAT. THEY CAUGHT HIM, TOOK HIM TO *CHIEN NA WEI...*
EVEN FROM THE SLAVES' QUARTERS, WE--
WE WOULD HEAR HIM SCREAMING.

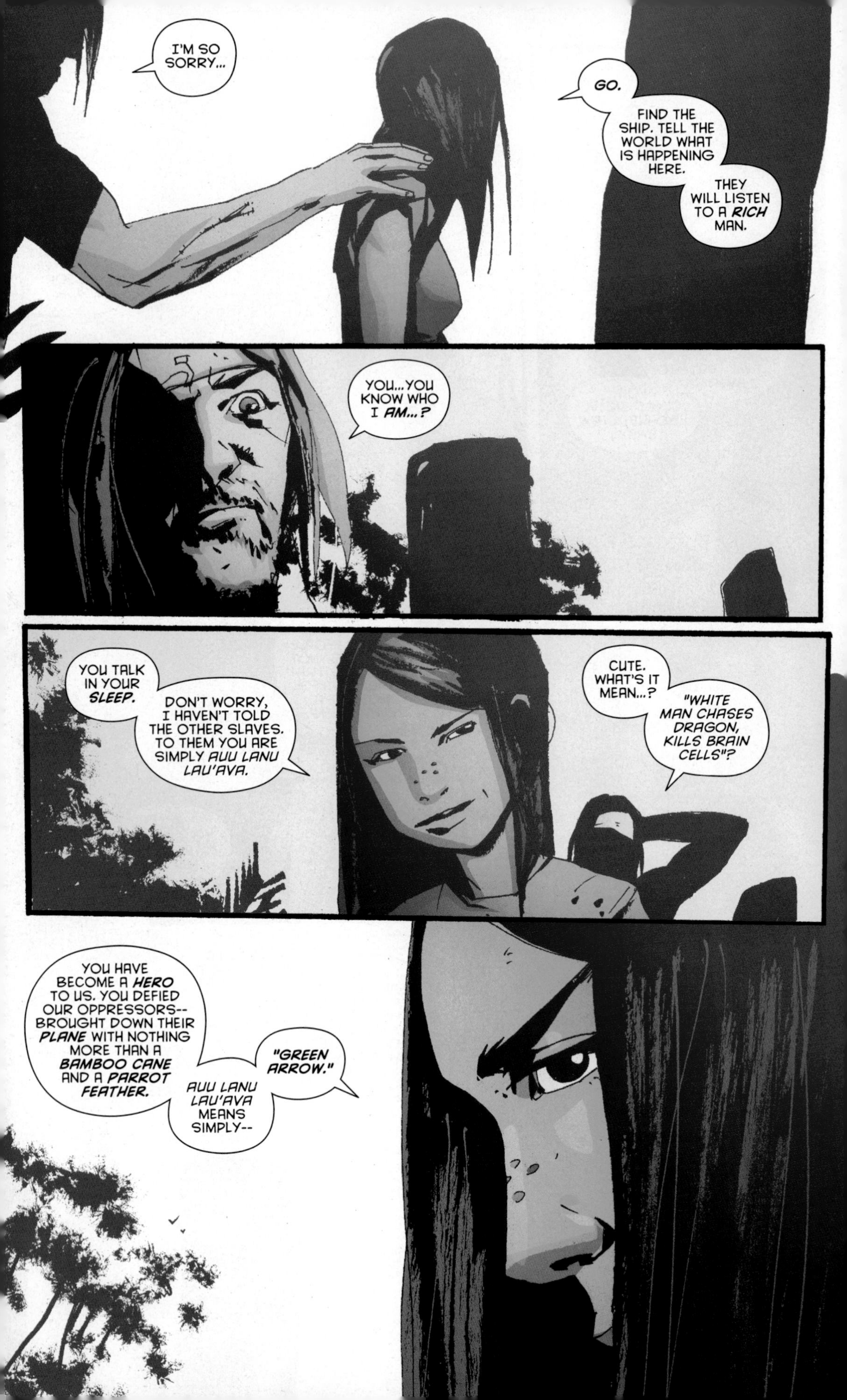
I'M SO SORRY...
GO.
FIND THE SHIP. TELL THE WORLD WHAT IS HAPPENING HERE.
THEY WILL LISTEN TO A *RICH* MAN.
YOU...YOU KNOW WHO I *AM*...?
YOU TALK IN YOUR *SLEEP.*
DON'T WORRY, I HAVEN'T TOLD THE OTHER SLAVES. TO THEM YOU ARE SIMPLY *AUU LANU LAU'AVA.*
CUTE. WHAT'S IT MEAN...?
"WHITE MAN CHASES DRAGON, KILLS BRAIN CELLS"?
YOU HAVE BECOME A *HERO* TO US. YOU DEFIED OUR OPPRESSORS--BROUGHT DOWN THEIR *PLANE* WITH NOTHING MORE THAN A *BAMBOO CANE* AND A *PARROT FEATHER.*
AUU LANU LAU'AVA MEANS SIMPLY--
"GREEN ARROW."

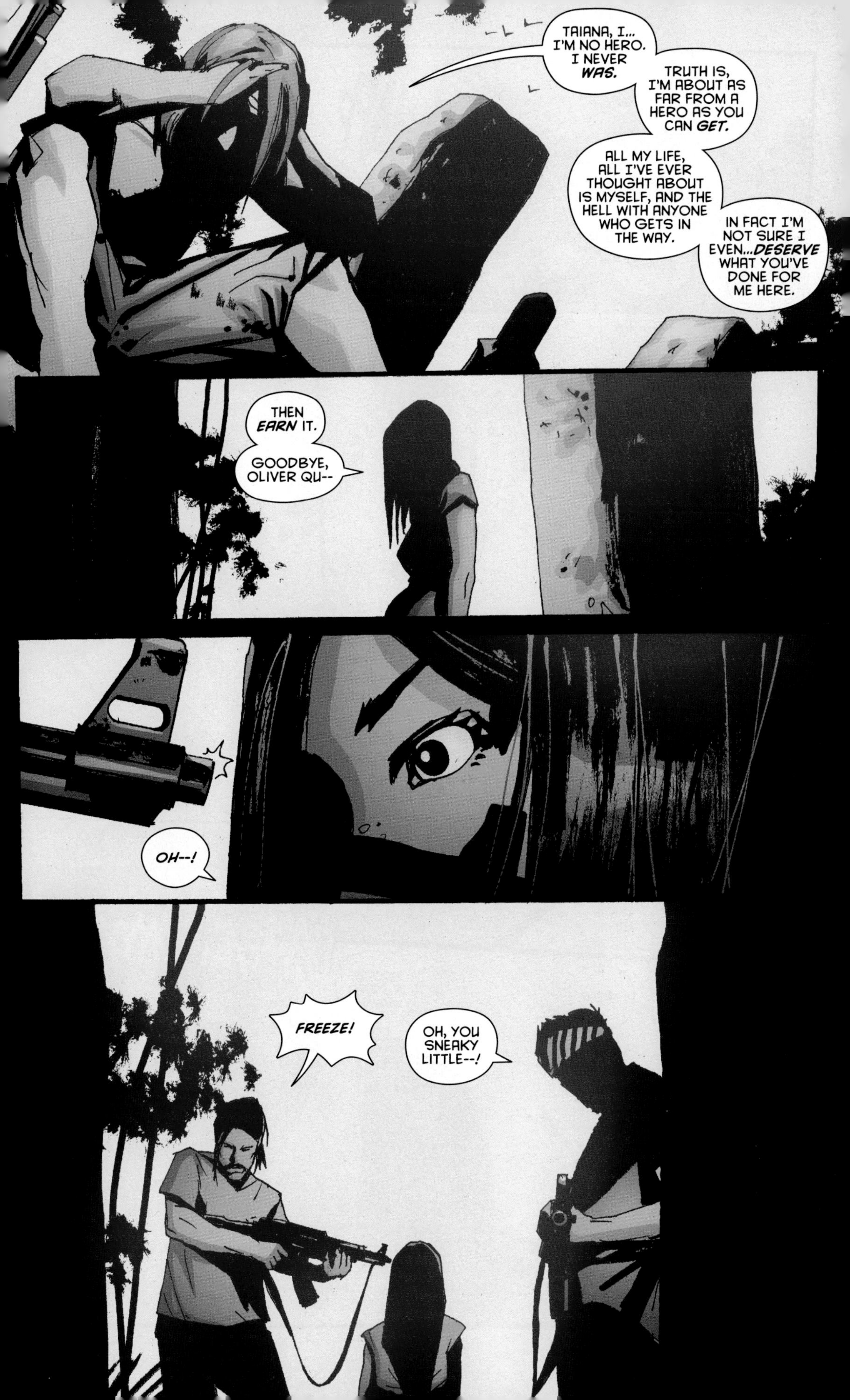
TAIANA, I... I'M NO HERO. I NEVER WAS.
TRUTH IS, I'M ABOUT AS FAR FROM A HERO AS YOU CAN GET.
ALL MY LIFE, ALL I'VE EVER THOUGHT ABOUT IS MYSELF, AND THE HELL WITH ANYONE WHO GETS IN THE WAY.
IN FACT I'M NOT SURE I EVEN...DESERVE WHAT YOU'VE DONE FOR ME HERE.
THEN EARN IT.
GOODBYE, OLIVER QU--
OH--!
FREEZE!
OH, YOU SNEAKY LITTLE--!

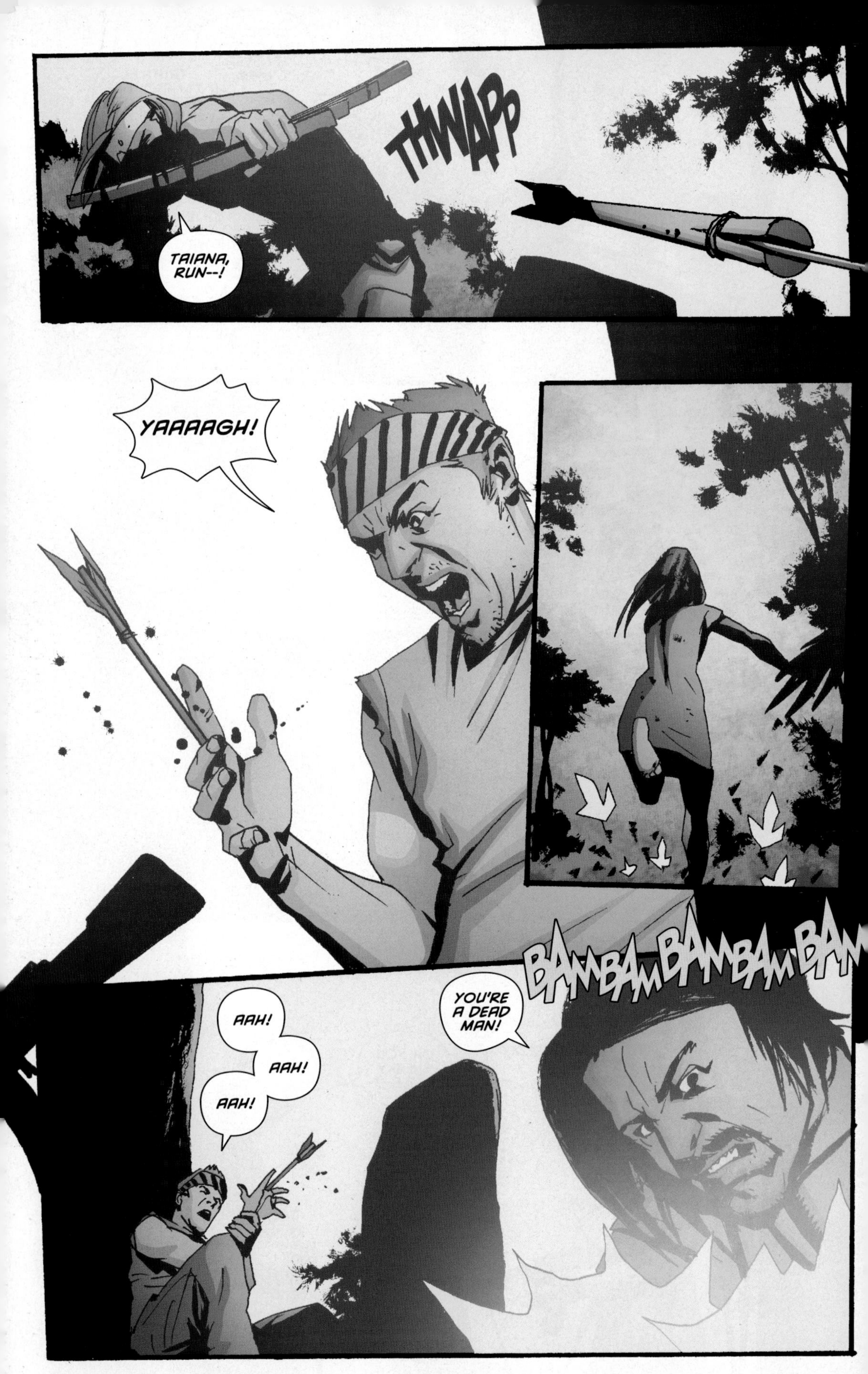
THWAPP
TAIANA, RUN--!
YAAAAGH!
BAMBAMBAMBAMBAM
YOU'RE A DEAD MAN!
AAH!
AAH!
AAH!

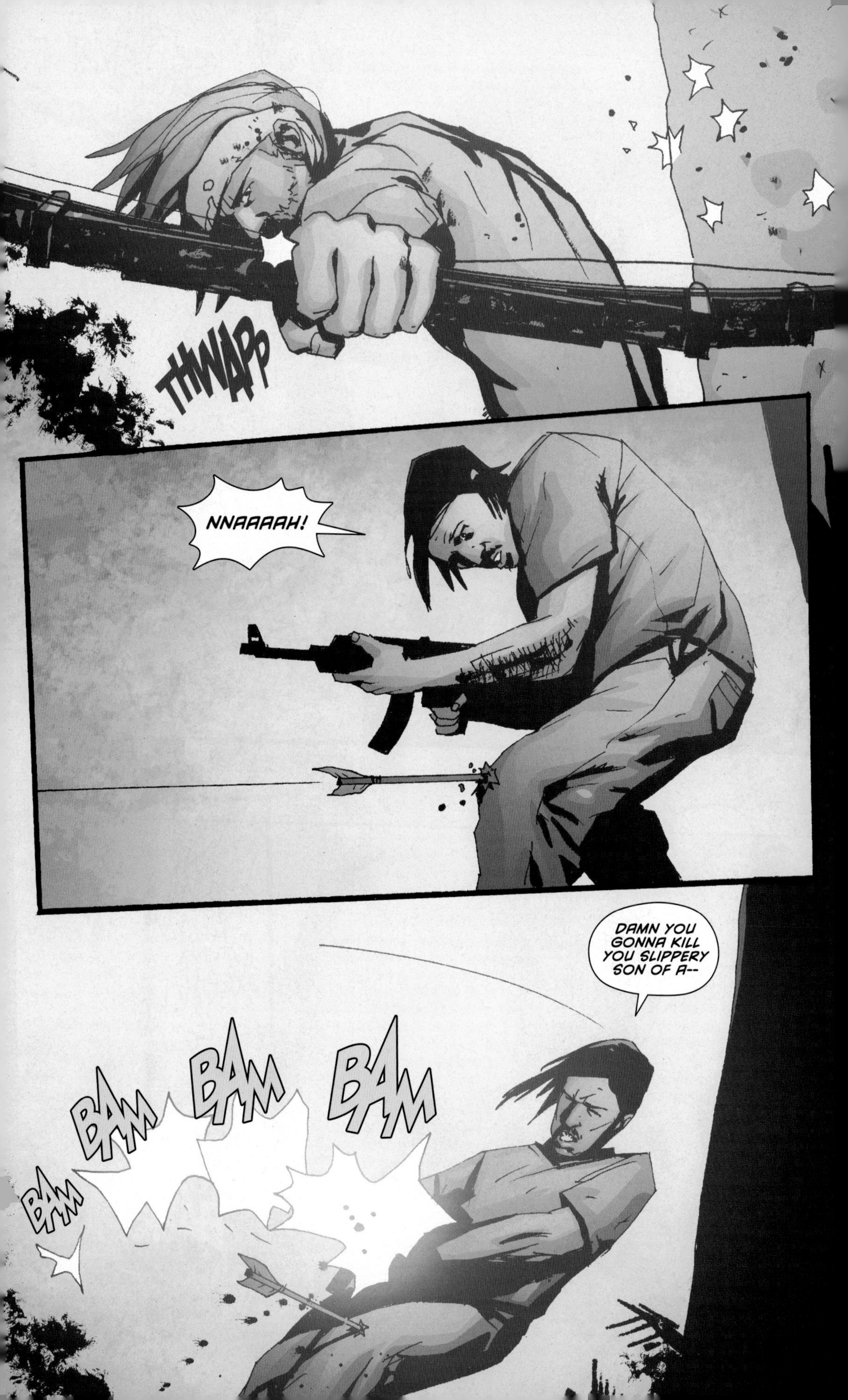
THWAPP
NNAAAAAH!
DAMN YOU GONNA KILL YOU SLIPPERY SON OF A--
BAM
BAM
BAM
BAM

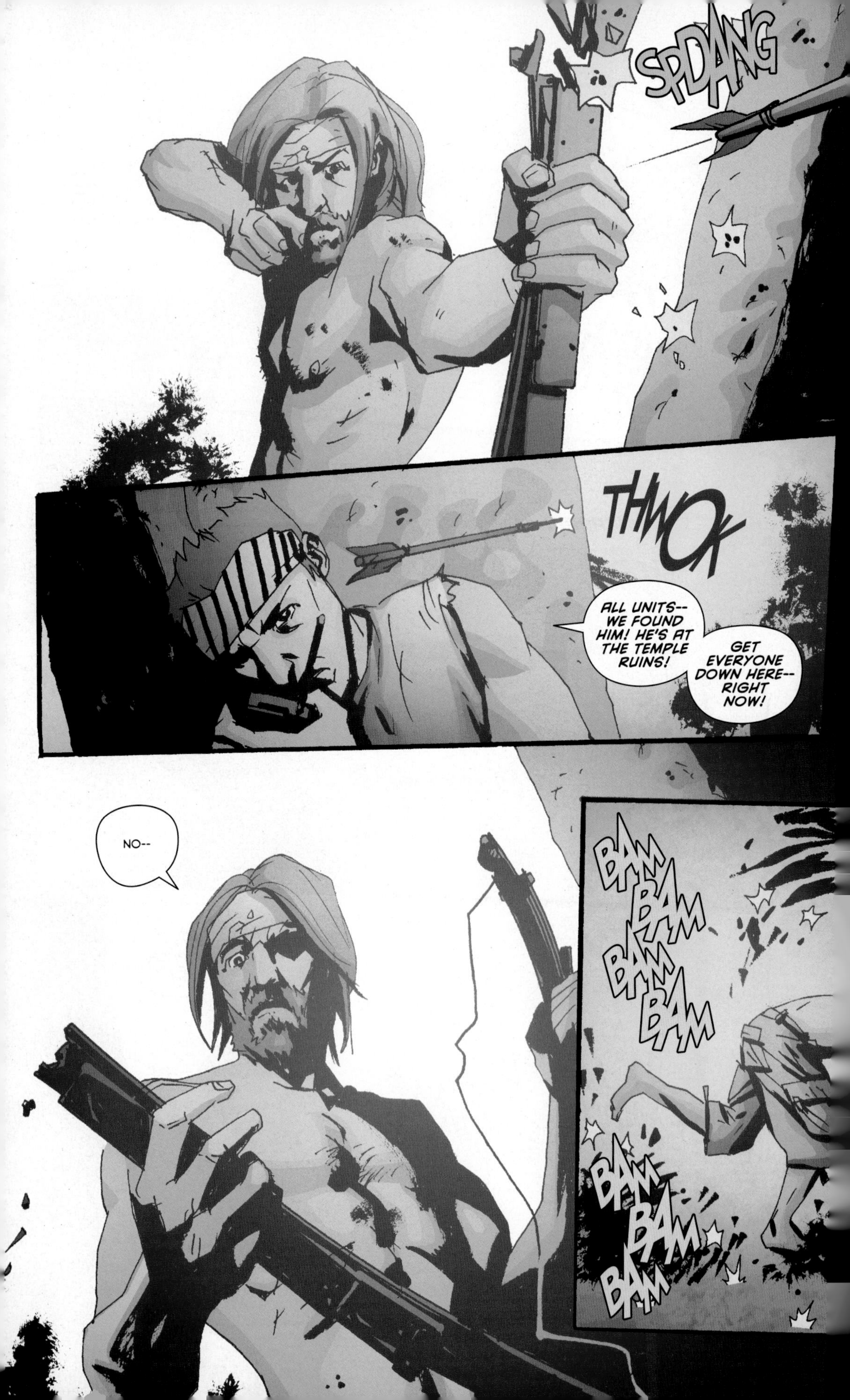
SPDANG
THWOK
ALL UNITS-- WE FOUND HIM! HE'S AT THE TEMPLE RUINS!
GET EVERYONE DOWN HERE-- RIGHT NOW!
NO--
BAM BAM BAM BAM BAM
BAM BAM BAM

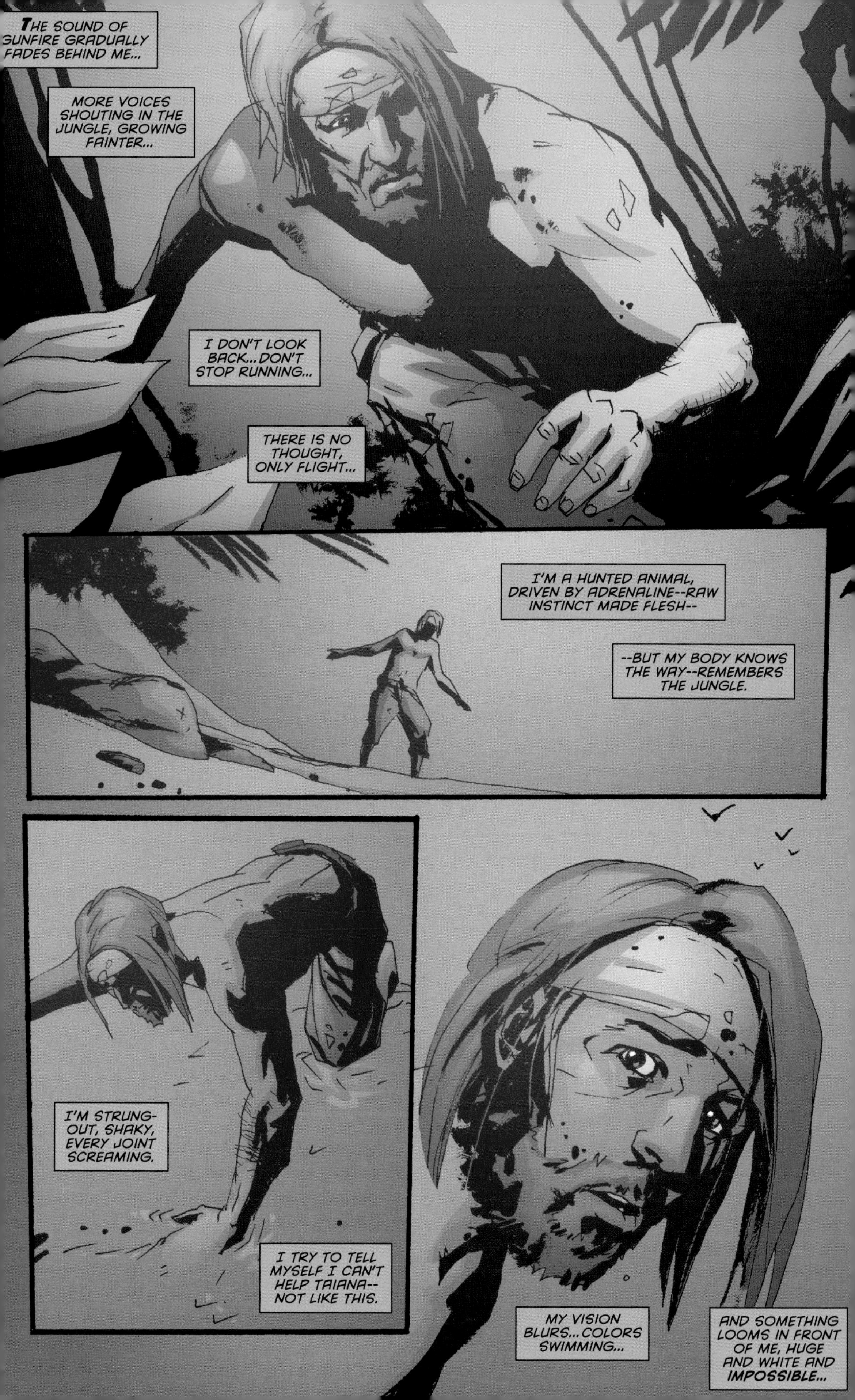
THE SOUND OF GUNFIRE GRADUALLY FADES BEHIND ME...
MORE VOICES SHOUTING IN THE JUNGLE, GROWING FAINTER...
I DON'T LOOK BACK...DON'T STOP RUNNING...
THERE IS NO THOUGHT, ONLY FLIGHT...
I'M A HUNTED ANIMAL, DRIVEN BY ADRENALINE--RAW INSTINCT MADE FLESH--
--BUT MY BODY KNOWS THE WAY--REMEMBERS THE JUNGLE.
I'M STRUNG-OUT, SHAKY, EVERY JOINT SCREAMING.
I TRY TO TELL MYSELF I CAN'T HELP TAIANA--NOT LIKE THIS.
MY VISION BLURS...COLORS SWIMMING...
AND SOMETHING LOOMS IN FRONT OF ME, HUGE AND WHITE AND IMPOSSIBLE...

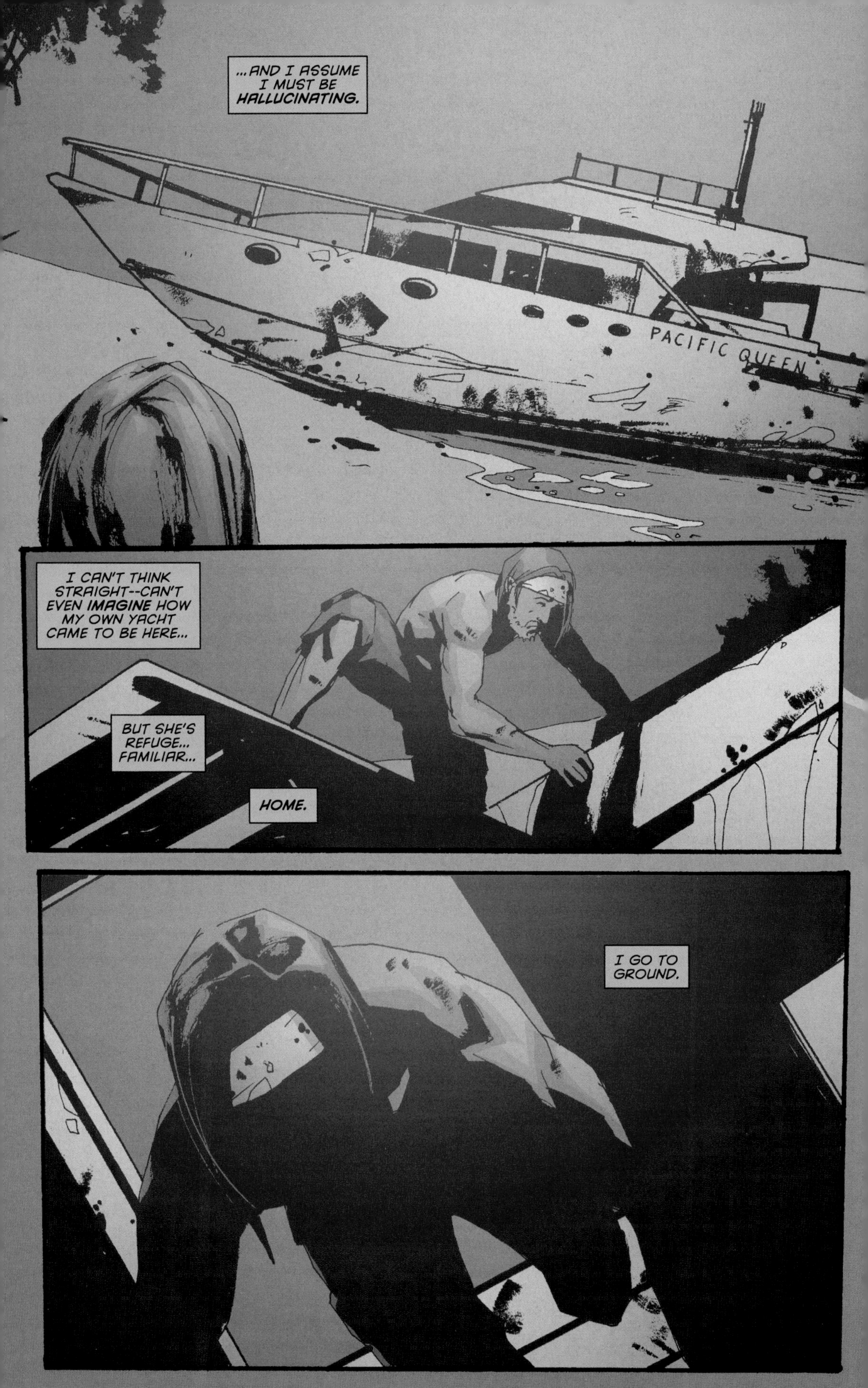
...AND I ASSUME I MUST BE HALLUCINATING.
PACIFIC QUEEN
I CAN'T THINK STRAIGHT--CAN'T EVEN IMAGINE HOW MY OWN YACHT CAME TO BE HERE...
BUT SHE'S REFUGE... FAMILIAR...
HOME.
I GO TO GROUND.

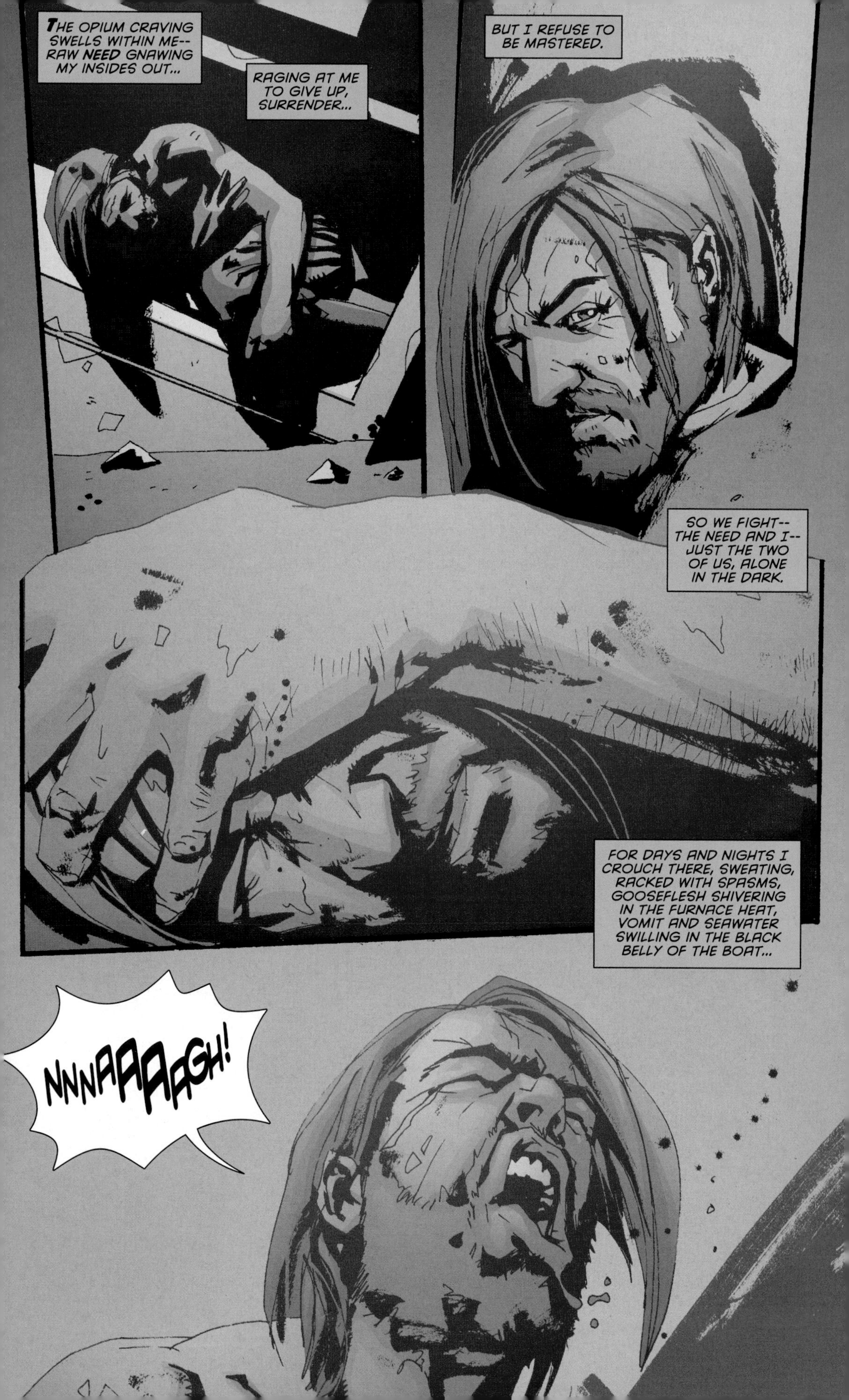
THE OPIUM CRAVING SWELLS WITHIN ME-- RAW NEED GNAWING MY INSIDES OUT...
RAGING AT ME TO GIVE UP, SURRENDER...
BUT I REFUSE TO BE MASTERED.
SO WE FIGHT-- THE NEED AND I-- JUST THE TWO OF US, ALONE IN THE DARK.
FOR DAYS AND NIGHTS I CROUCH THERE, SWEATING, RACKED WITH SPASMS, GOOSEFLESH SHIVERING IN THE FURNACE HEAT, VOMIT AND SEAWATER SWILLING IN THE BLACK BELLY OF THE BOAT...
NNNAAAAAAGH!

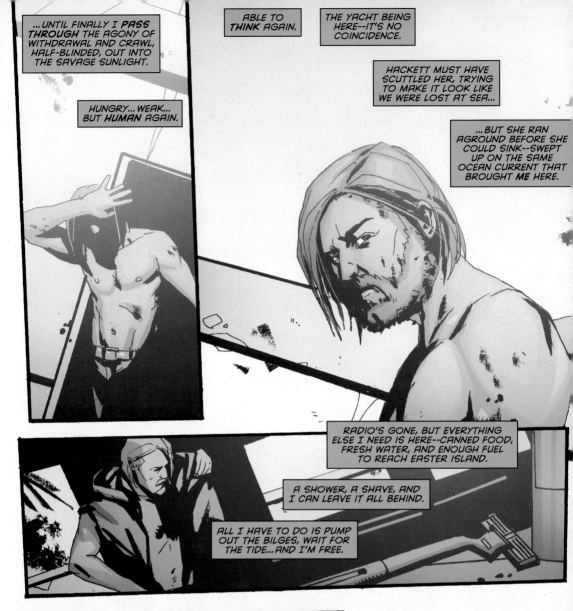

...UNTIL FINALLY I **PASS THROUGH** THE AGONY OF WITHDRAWAL AND CRAWL, HALF-BLINDED, OUT INTO THE SAVAGE SUNLIGHT.

HUNGRY...WEAK... BUT **HUMAN** AGAIN.

ABLE TO **THINK** AGAIN.

THE YACHT BEING HERE--IT'S NO COINCIDENCE.

HACKETT MUST HAVE SCUTTLED HER, TRYING TO MAKE IT LOOK LIKE WE WERE LOST AT SEA...

...BUT SHE RAN AGROUND BEFORE SHE COULD SINK--SWEPT UP ON THE SAME OCEAN CURRENT THAT BROUGHT **ME** HERE.

RADIO'S GONE, BUT EVERYTHING ELSE I NEED IS HERE--CANNED FOOD, FRESH WATER, AND ENOUGH FUEL TO REACH EASTER ISLAND.

A SHOWER, A SHAVE, AND I CAN LEAVE IT ALL BEHIND.

ALL I HAVE TO DO IS PUMP OUT THE BILGES, WAIT FOR THE TIDE...AND I'M FREE.

BUT I **DON'T.** SOMETHING'S HOLDING ME **BACK.**

BECAUSE DEEP INSIDE, IN A PLACE I CAN'T DENY, I KNOW IT'S ONLY DUMB LUCK THAT I WASHED UP ALIVE HERE IN THE FIRST PLACE...

...AND DUMB LUCK THAT'S GIVEN ME THE MEANS TO **ESCAPE** AGAIN.

I NEVER **EARNED** IT.

AND I WON'T BE THE ONE WHO PAYS THE **PRICE.**

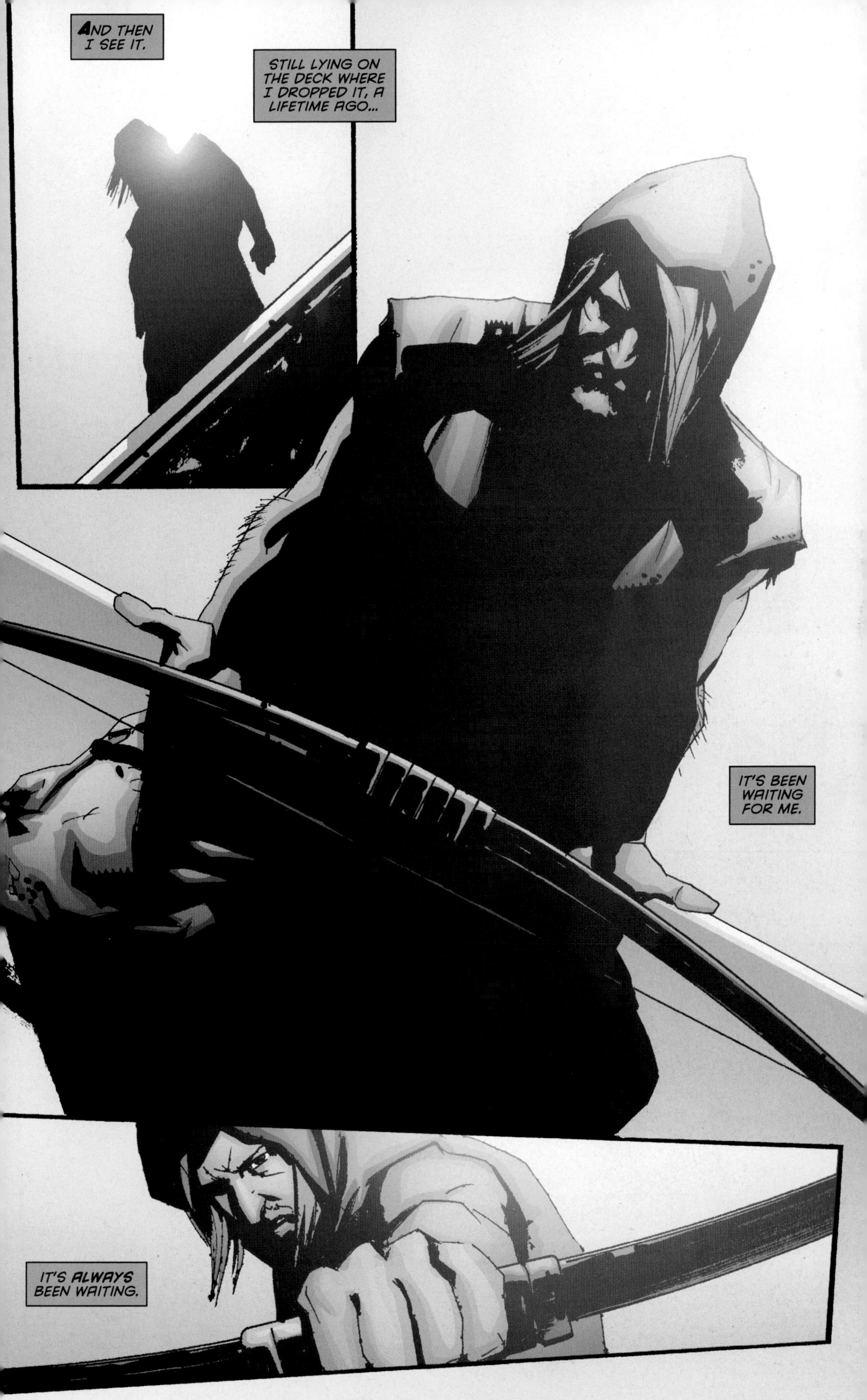
AND THEN I SEE IT.
STILL LYING ON THE DECK WHERE I DROPPED IT, A LIFETIME AGO...
IT'S BEEN WAITING FOR ME.
IT'S ALWAYS BEEN WAITING.

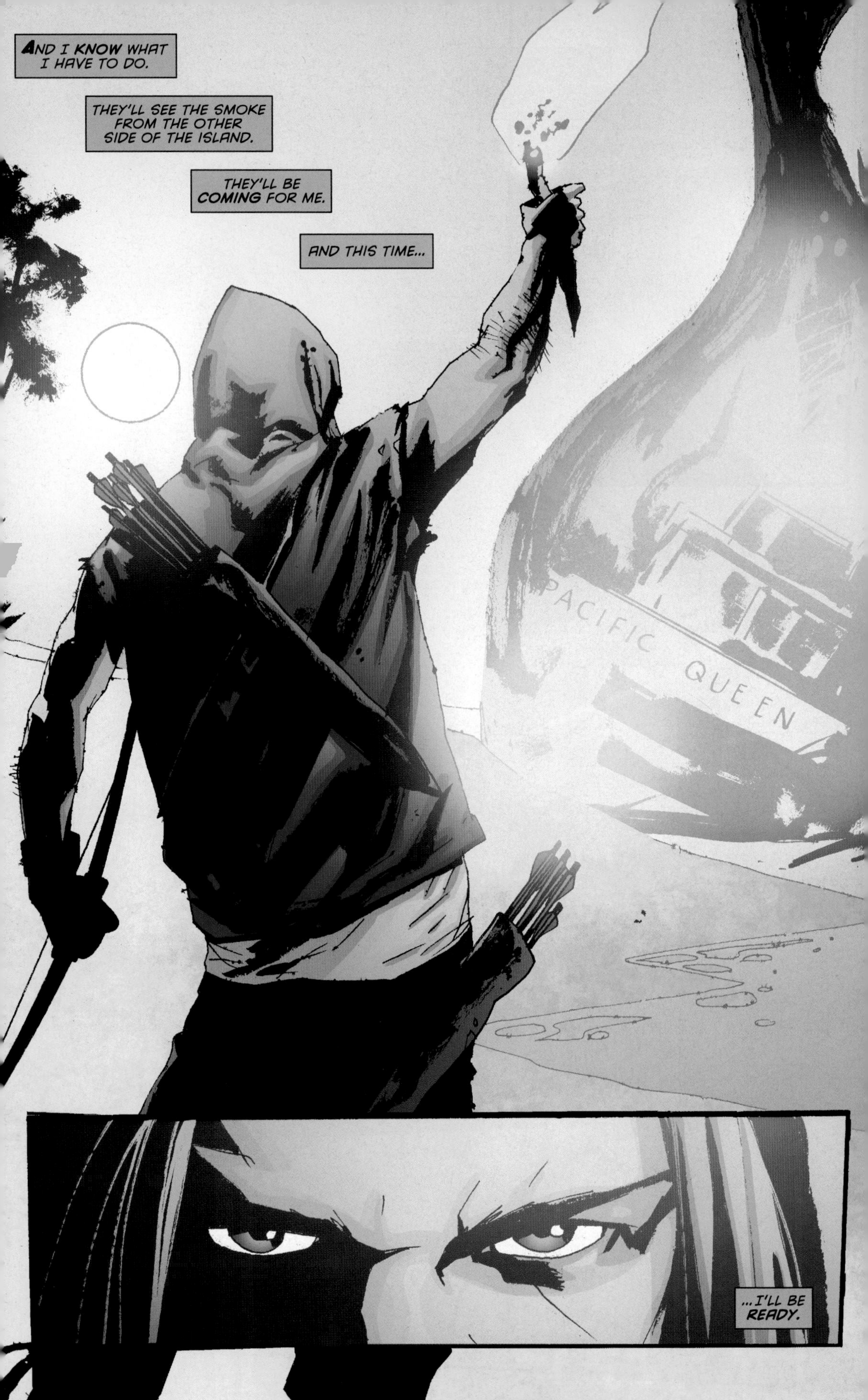
AND I KNOW WHAT I HAVE TO DO.
THEY'LL SEE THE SMOKE FROM THE OTHER SIDE OF THE ISLAND.
THEY'LL BE COMING FOR ME.
AND THIS TIME...
PACIFIC QUEEN
...I'LL BE READY.

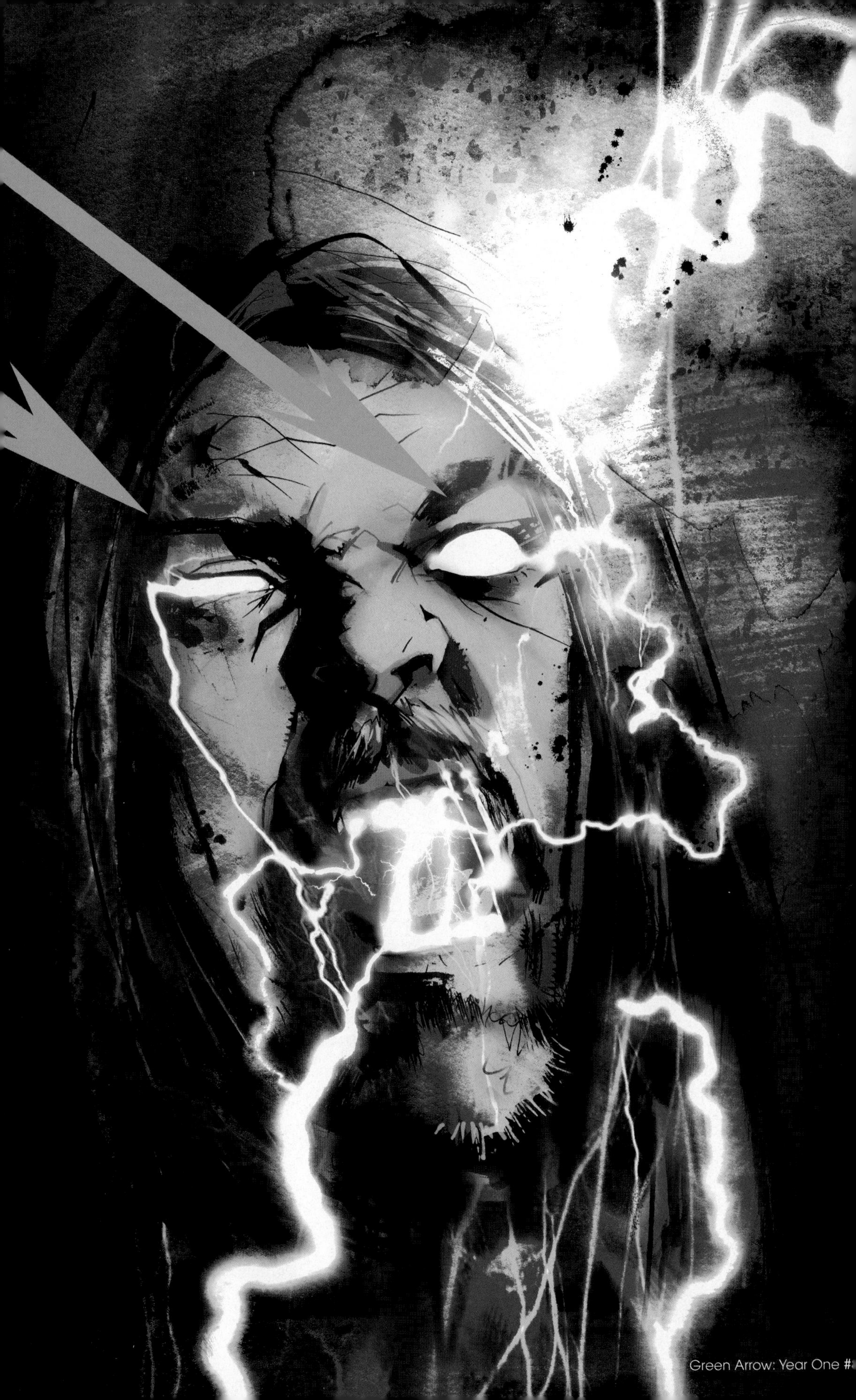

Green Arrow: Year One #

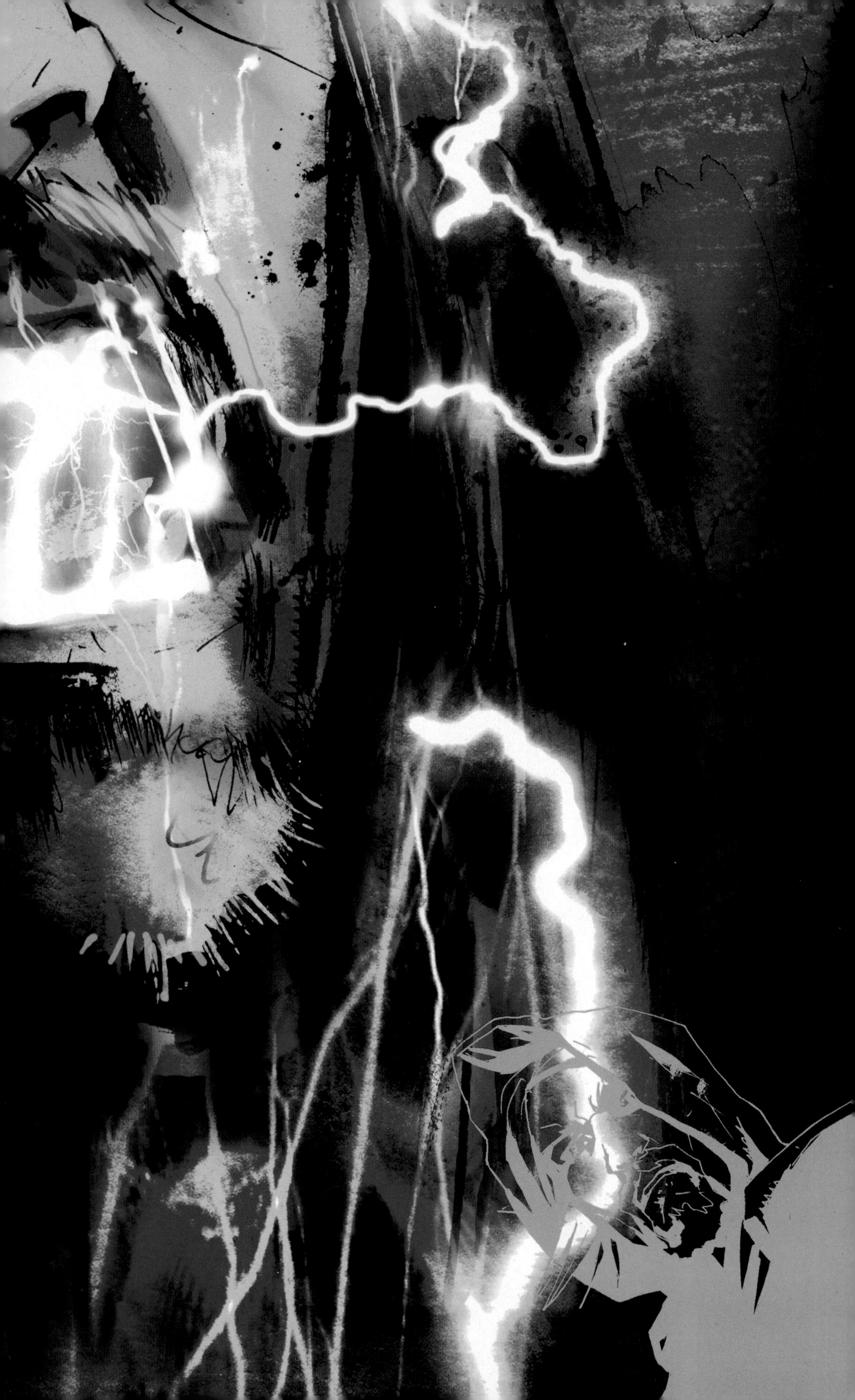

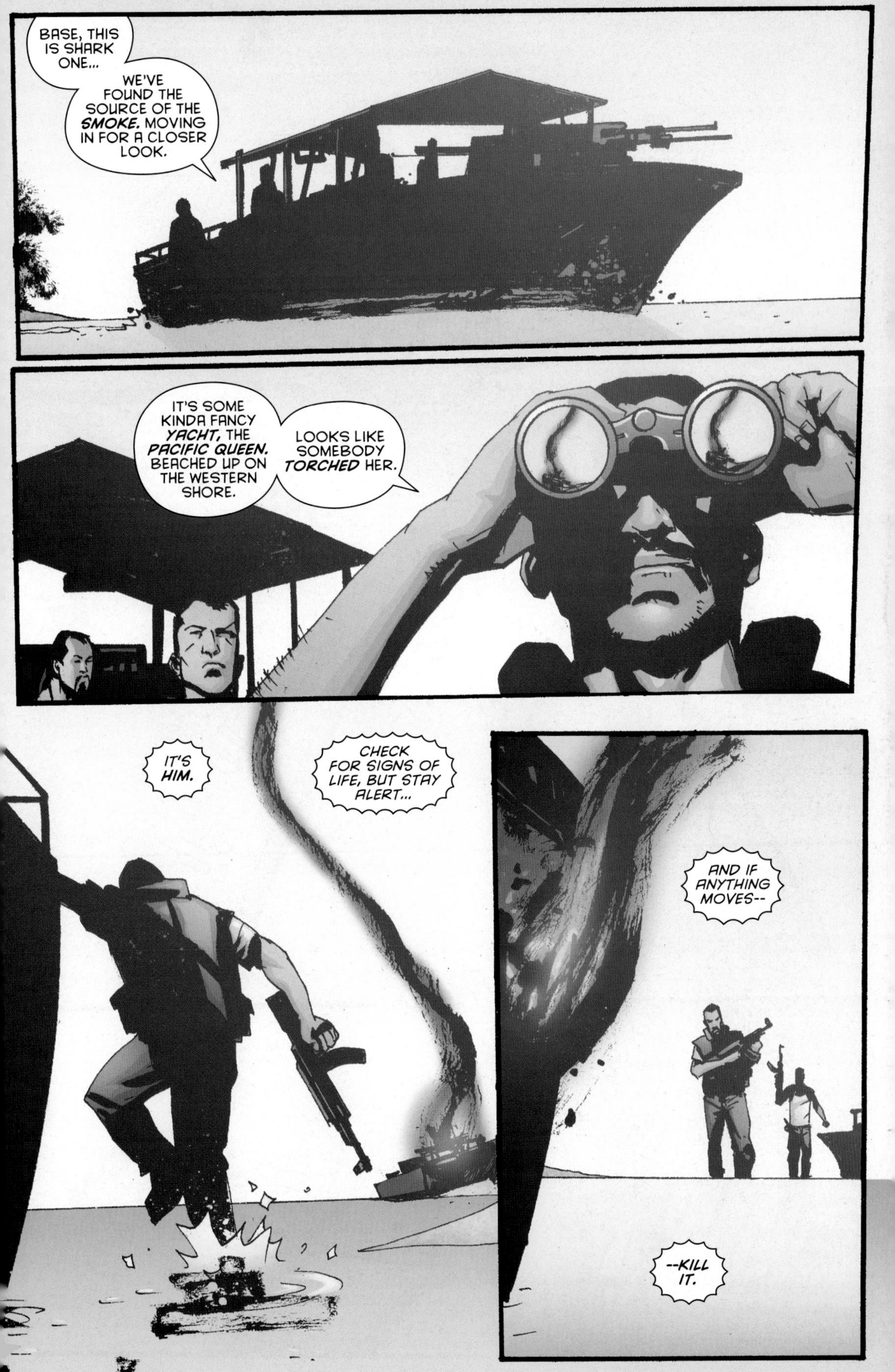
BASE, THIS IS SHARK ONE...
WE'VE FOUND THE SOURCE OF THE SMOKE. MOVING IN FOR A CLOSER LOOK.
IT'S SOME KINDA FANCY YACHT, THE PACIFIC QUEEN. BEACHED UP ON THE WESTERN SHORE.
LOOKS LIKE SOMEBODY TORCHED HER.
IT'S HIM.
CHECK FOR SIGNS OF LIFE, BUT STAY ALERT...
AND IF ANYTHING MOVES--
--KILL IT.

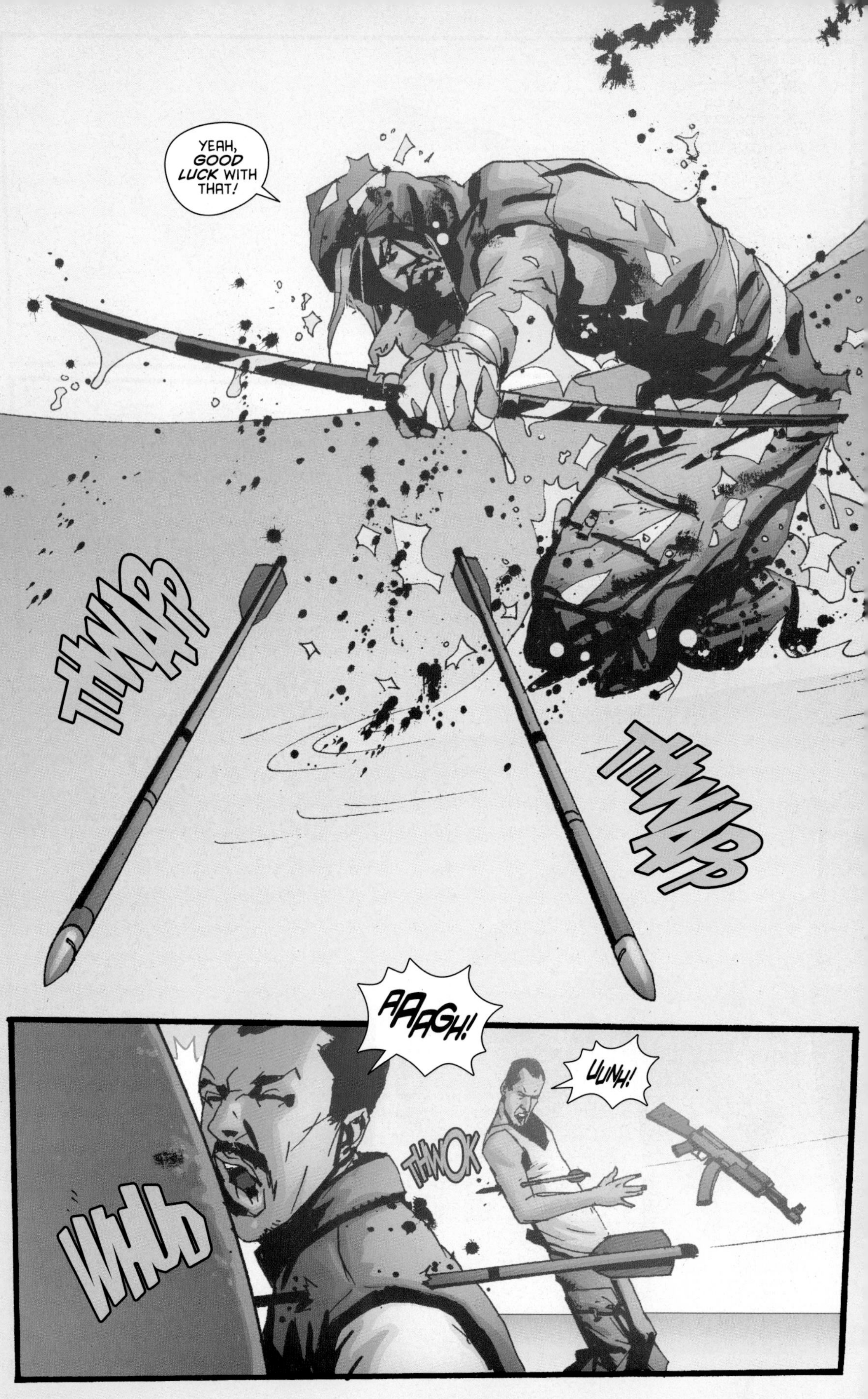
YEAH, GOOD LUCK WITH THAT!
THWAP
THWAP
AAAGH!
UUNH!
THWOK
WHUD

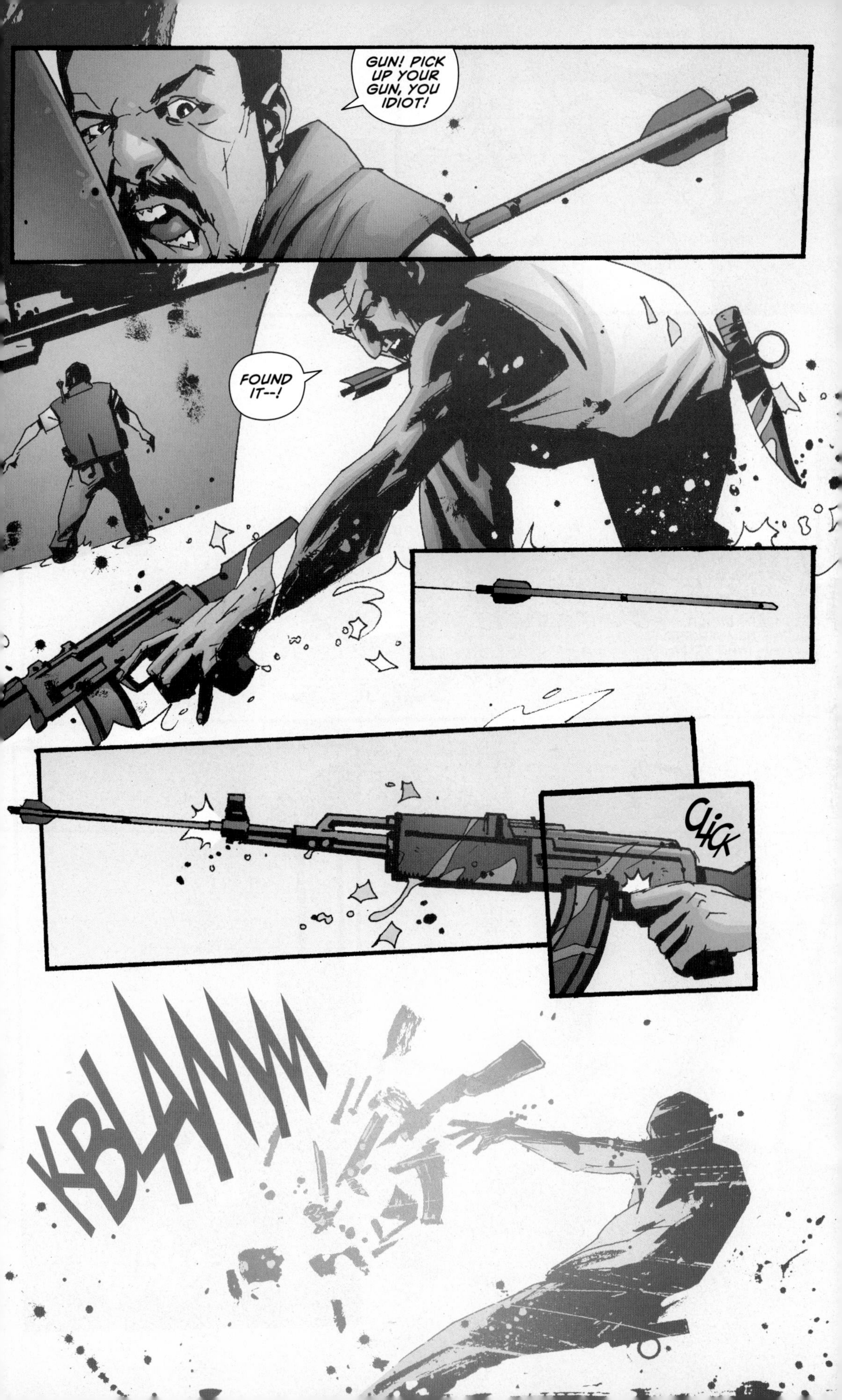
GUN! PICK UP YOUR GUN, YOU IDIOT!
FOUND IT--!
CLICK
KBLAMM

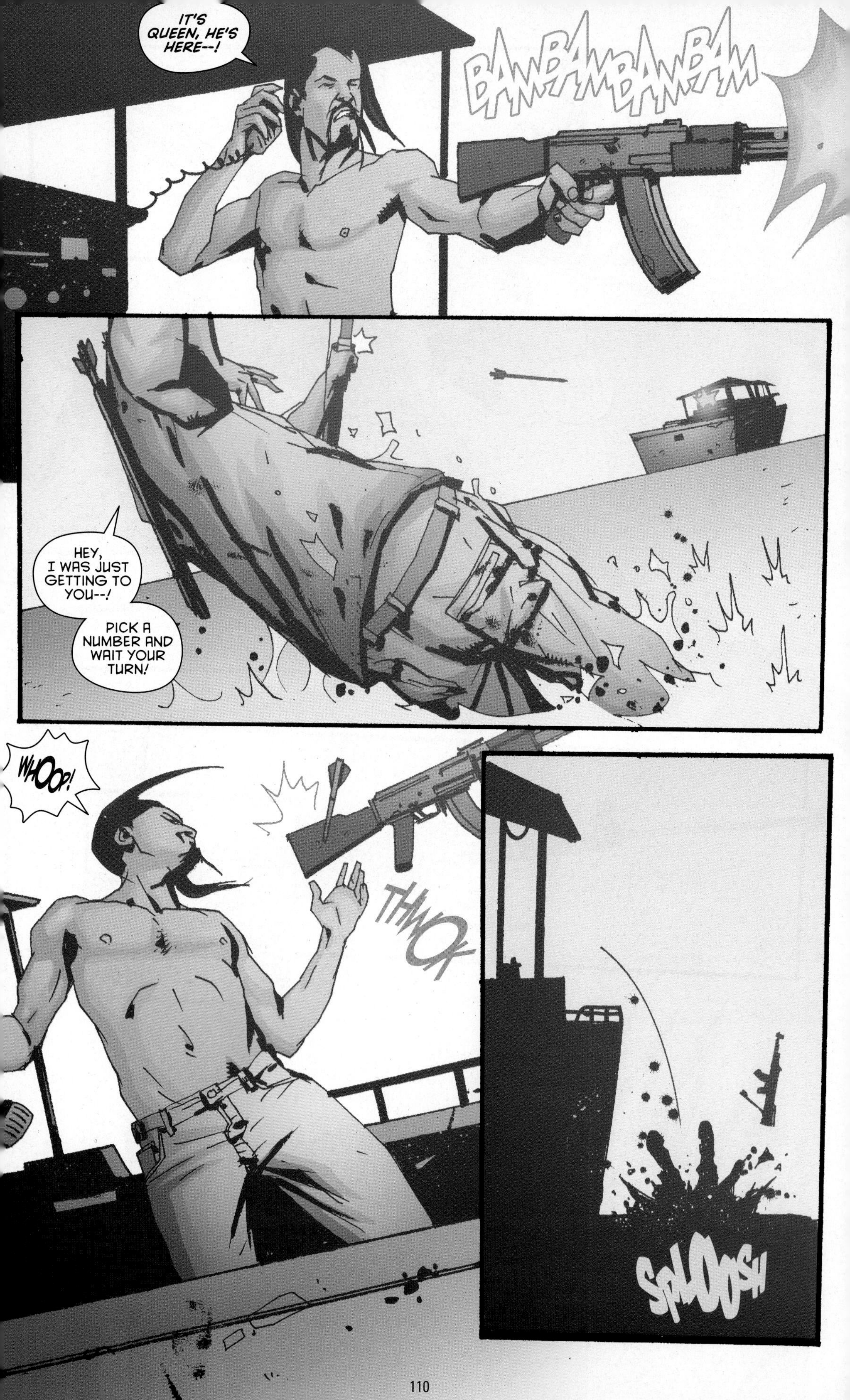
IT'S QUEEN, HE'S HERE--!
BAMBAMBAMBAM
HEY, I WAS JUST GETTING TO YOU--!
PICK A NUMBER AND WAIT YOUR TURN!
WHOOP!
THWOK
SPLOOOSH

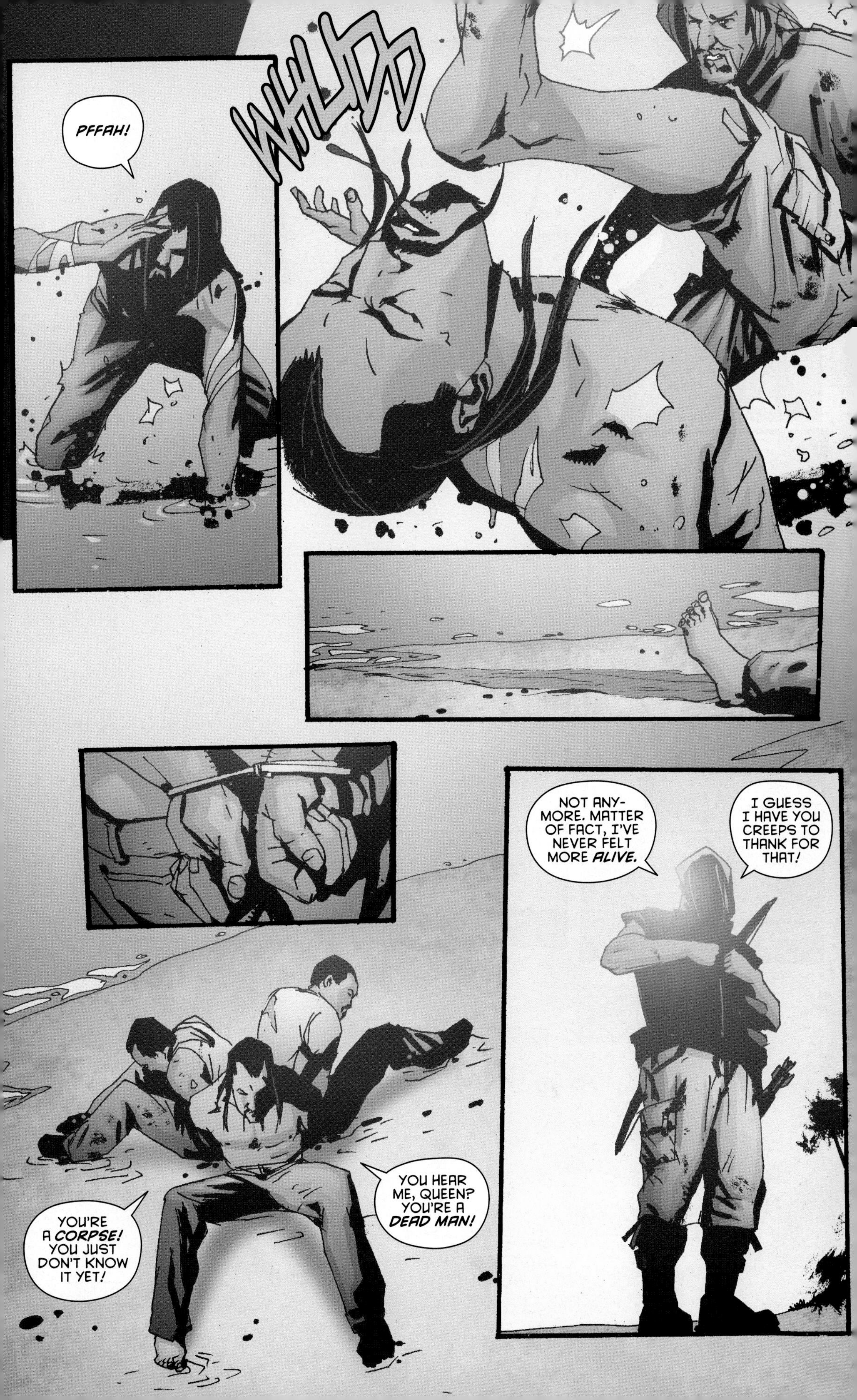
PFFAH!
WHUDD
NOT ANY-MORE. MATTER OF FACT, I'VE NEVER FELT MORE *ALIVE.*
I GUESS I HAVE YOU CREEPS TO THANK FOR THAT!
YOU HEAR ME, QUEEN? YOU'RE A *DEAD MAN*!
YOU'RE A *CORPSE*! YOU JUST DON'T KNOW IT YET!

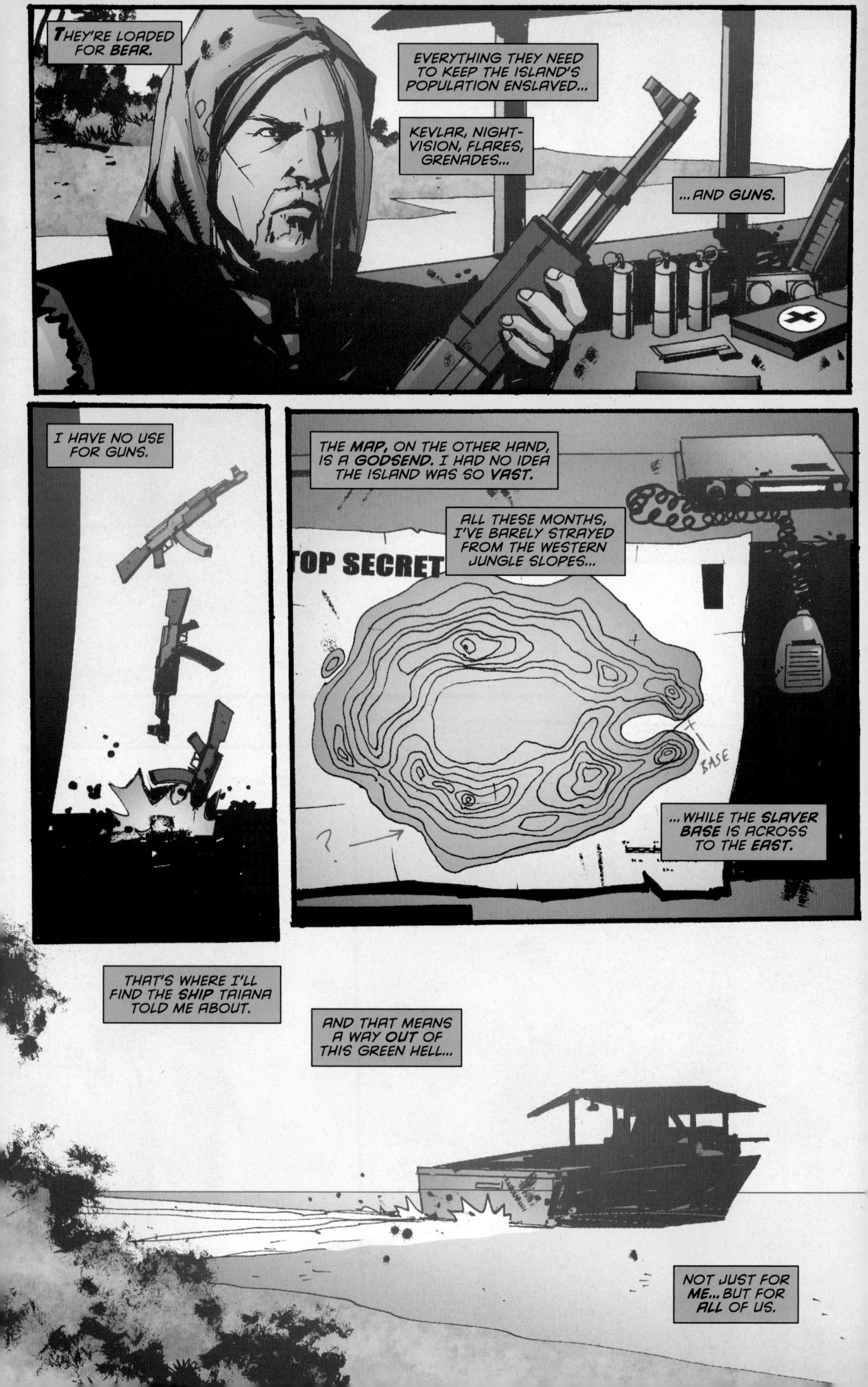
THEY'RE LOADED FOR BEAR.
EVERYTHING THEY NEED TO KEEP THE ISLAND'S POPULATION ENSLAVED...
KEVLAR, NIGHT-VISION, FLARES, GRENADES...
...AND GUNS.
I HAVE NO USE FOR GUNS.
THE MAP, ON THE OTHER HAND, IS A GODSEND. I HAD NO IDEA THE ISLAND WAS SO VAST.
ALL THESE MONTHS, I'VE BARELY STRAYED FROM THE WESTERN JUNGLE SLOPES...
TOP SECRET
BASE
...WHILE THE SLAVER BASE IS ACROSS TO THE EAST.
THAT'S WHERE I'LL FIND THE SHIP TAIANA TOLD ME ABOUT.
AND THAT MEANS A WAY OUT OF THIS GREEN HELL...
NOT JUST FOR ME...BUT FOR ALL OF US.

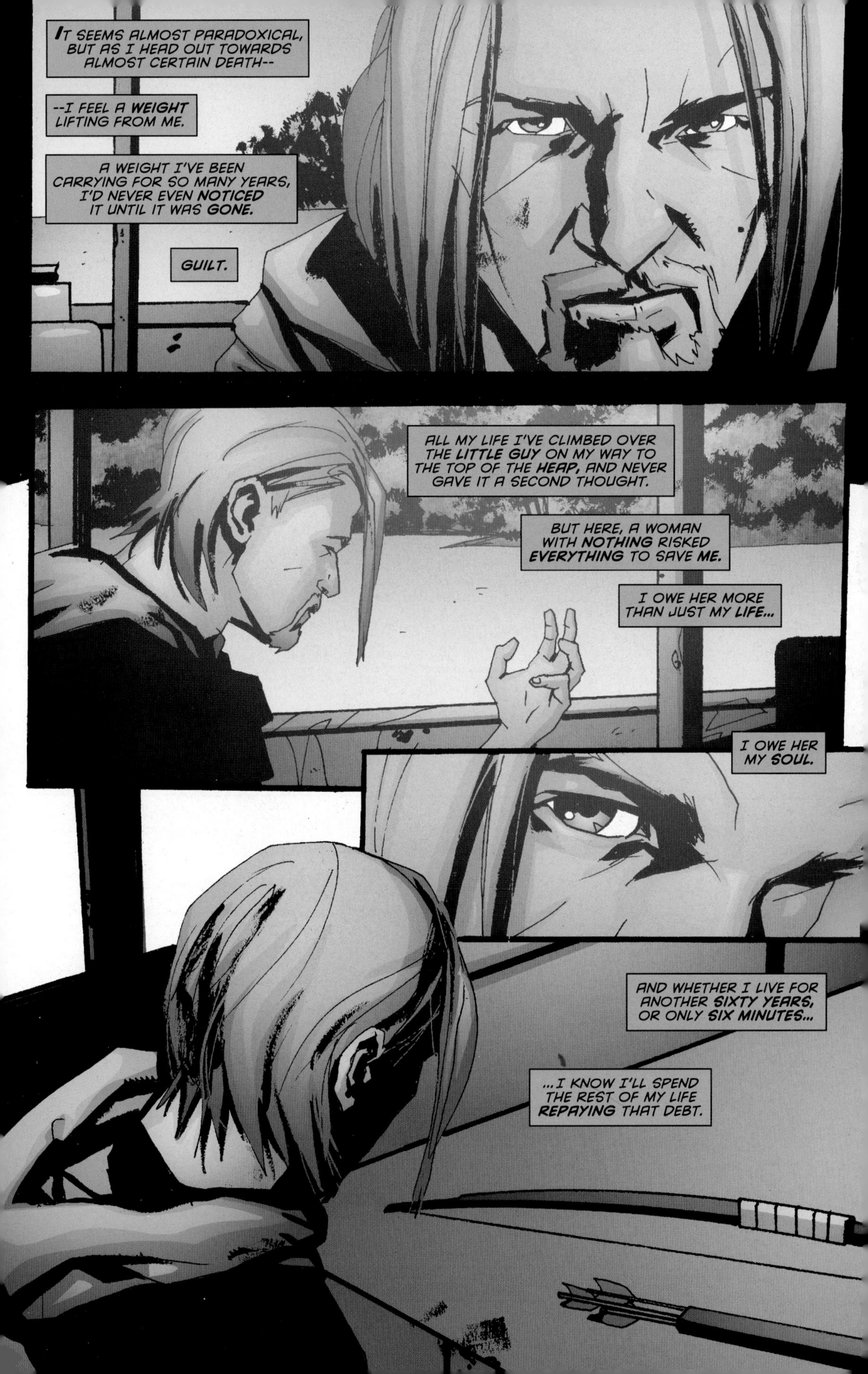
IT SEEMS ALMOST PARADOXICAL, BUT AS I HEAD OUT TOWARDS ALMOST CERTAIN DEATH--
--I FEEL A WEIGHT LIFTING FROM ME.
A WEIGHT I'VE BEEN CARRYING FOR SO MANY YEARS, I'D NEVER EVEN NOTICED IT UNTIL IT WAS GONE.
GUILT.
ALL MY LIFE I'VE CLIMBED OVER THE LITTLE GUY ON MY WAY TO THE TOP OF THE HEAP, AND NEVER GAVE IT A SECOND THOUGHT.
BUT HERE, A WOMAN WITH NOTHING RISKED EVERYTHING TO SAVE ME.
I OWE HER MORE THAN JUST MY LIFE...
I OWE HER MY SOUL.
AND WHETHER I LIVE FOR ANOTHER SIXTY YEARS, OR ONLY SIX MINUTES...
...I KNOW I'LL SPEND THE REST OF MY LIFE REPAYING THAT DEBT.

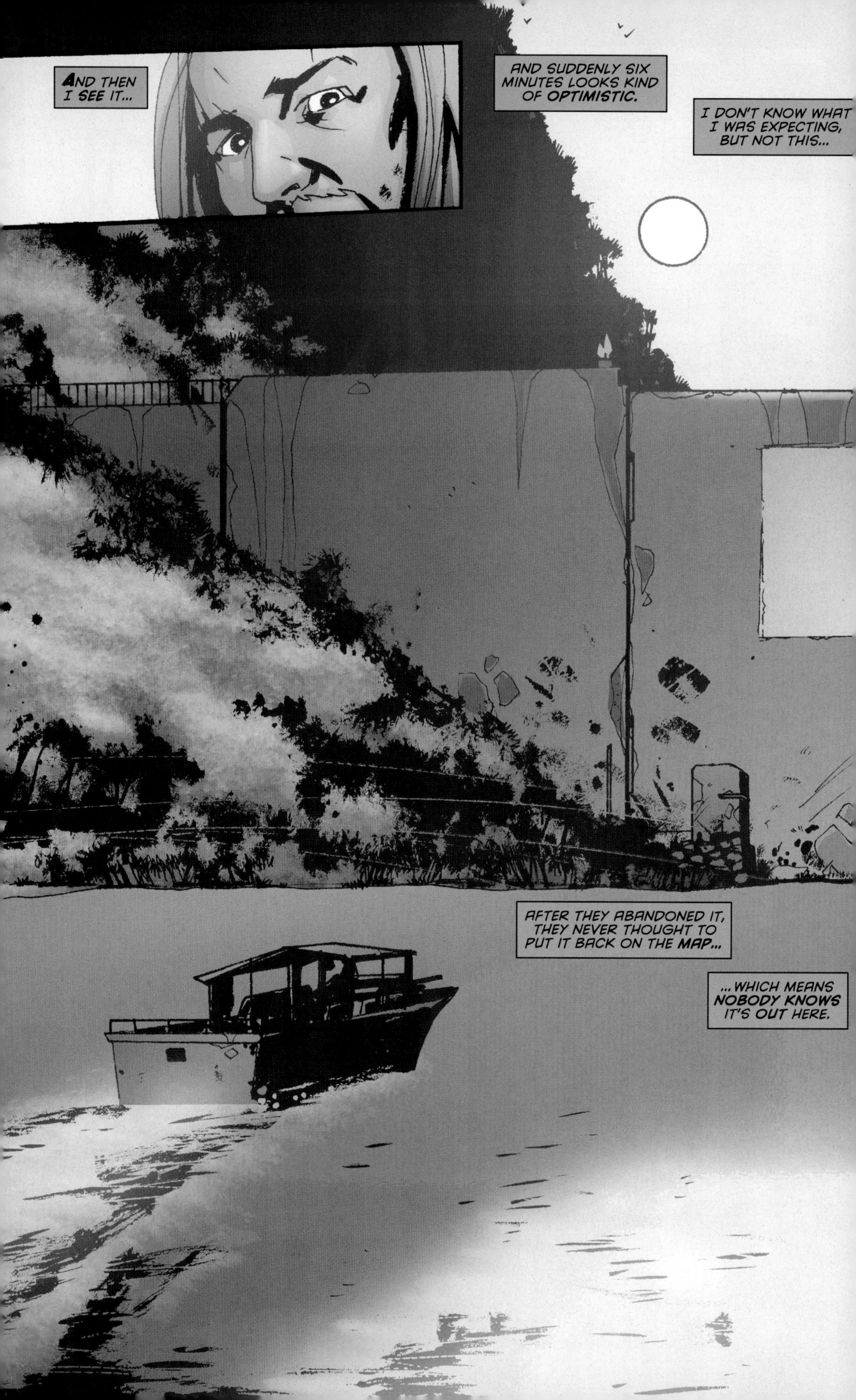
AND THEN I SEE IT...
AND SUDDENLY SIX MINUTES LOOKS KIND OF OPTIMISTIC.
I DON'T KNOW WHAT I WAS EXPECTING, BUT NOT THIS...
AFTER THEY ABANDONED IT, THEY NEVER THOUGHT TO PUT IT BACK ON THE MAP...
...WHICH MEANS NOBODY KNOWS IT'S OUT HERE.

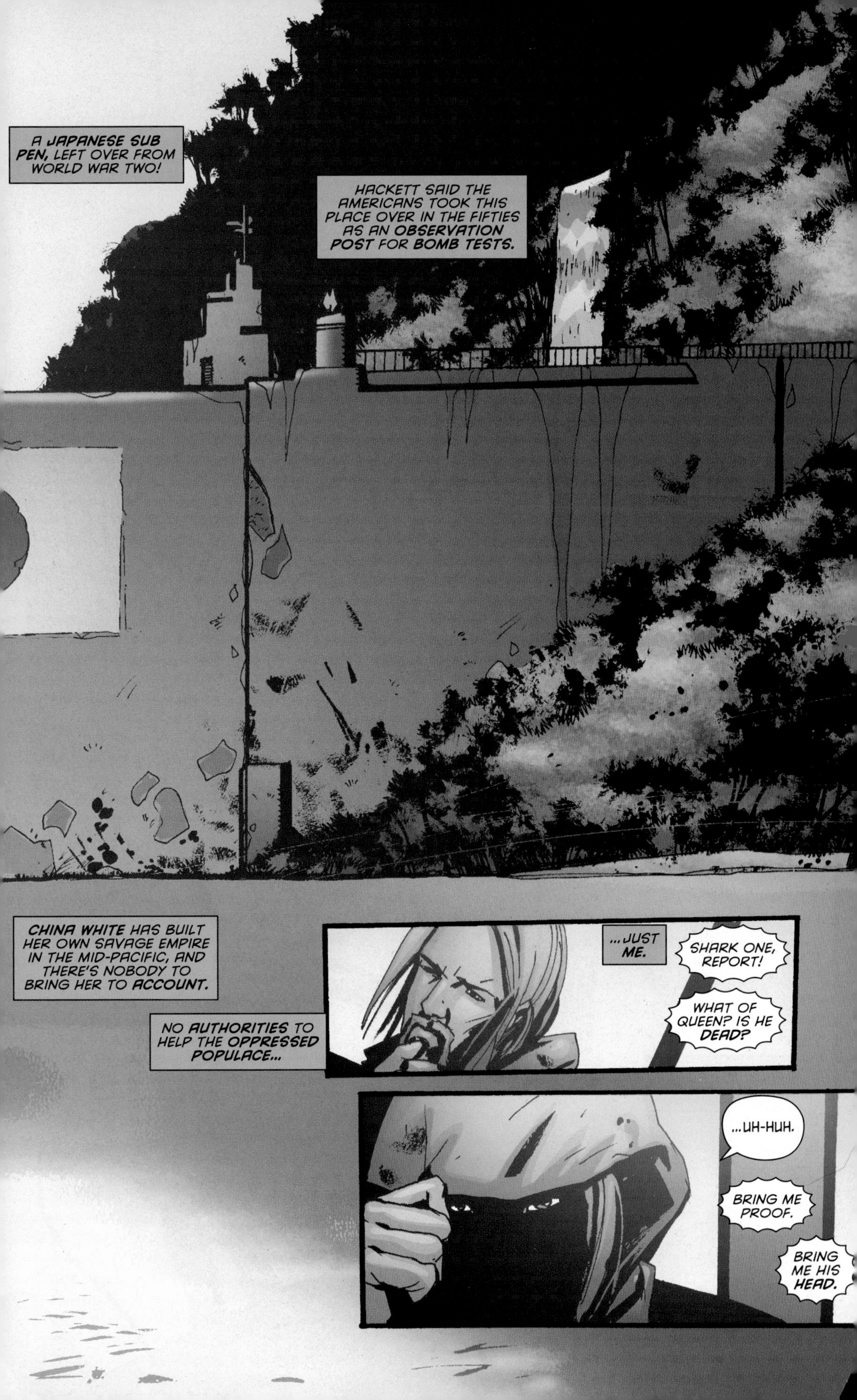
A JAPANESE SUB PEN, LEFT OVER FROM WORLD WAR TWO!
HACKETT SAID THE AMERICANS TOOK THIS PLACE OVER IN THE FIFTIES AS AN OBSERVATION POST FOR BOMB TESTS.
CHINA WHITE HAS BUILT HER OWN SAVAGE EMPIRE IN THE MID-PACIFIC, AND THERE'S NOBODY TO BRING HER TO ACCOUNT.
NO AUTHORITIES TO HELP THE OPPRESSED POPULACE...
...JUST ME.
SHARK ONE, REPORT!
WHAT OF QUEEN? IS HE DEAD?
...UH-HUH.
BRING ME PROOF.
BRING ME HIS HEAD.

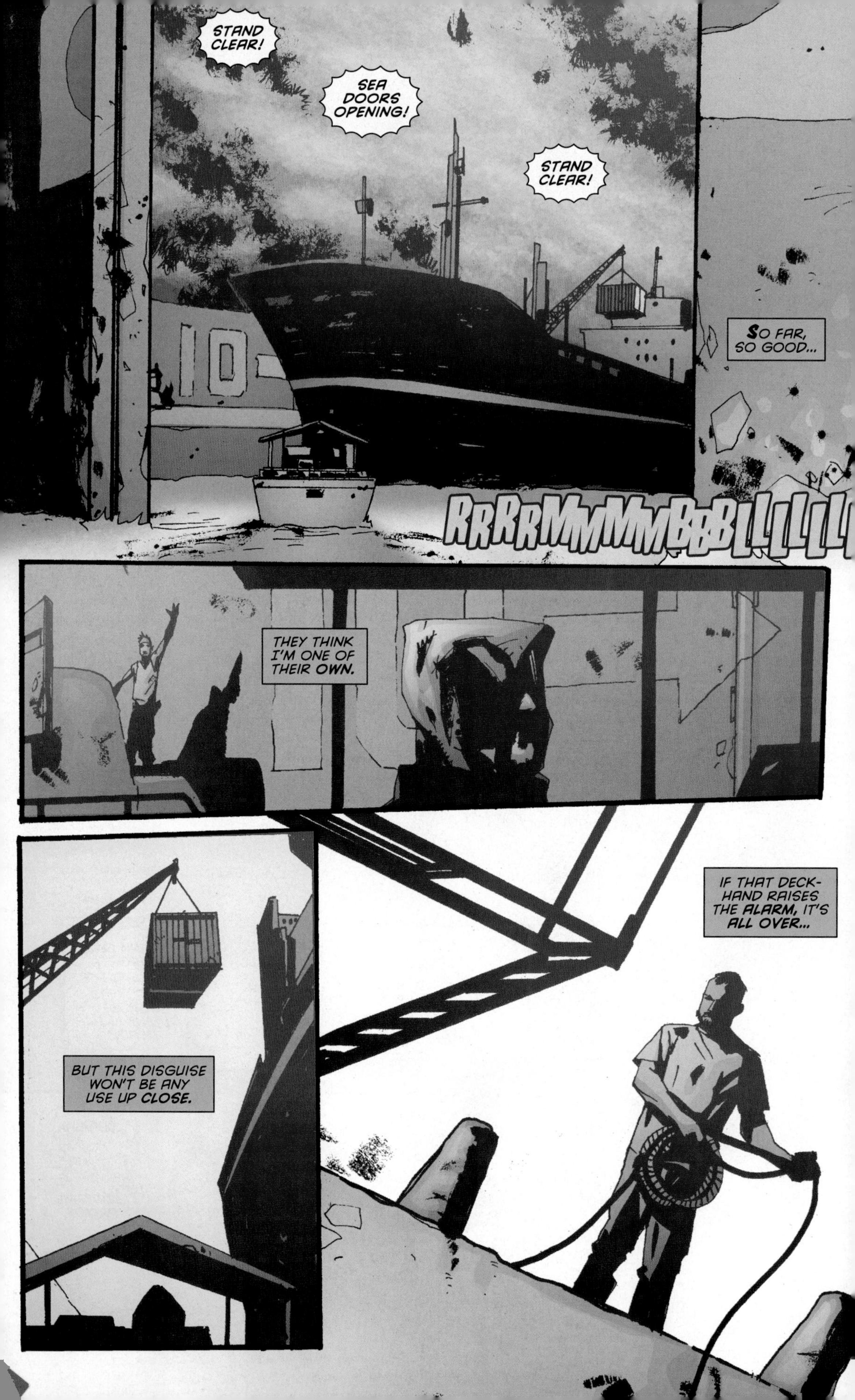
STAND CLEAR!
SEA DOORS OPENING!
STAND CLEAR!
SO FAR, SO GOOD...
RRRRMMMMMBBBLLLLLL
THEY THINK I'M ONE OF THEIR OWN.
BUT THIS DISGUISE WON'T BE ANY USE UP CLOSE.
IF THAT DECK-HAND RAISES THE ALARM, IT'S ALL OVER...

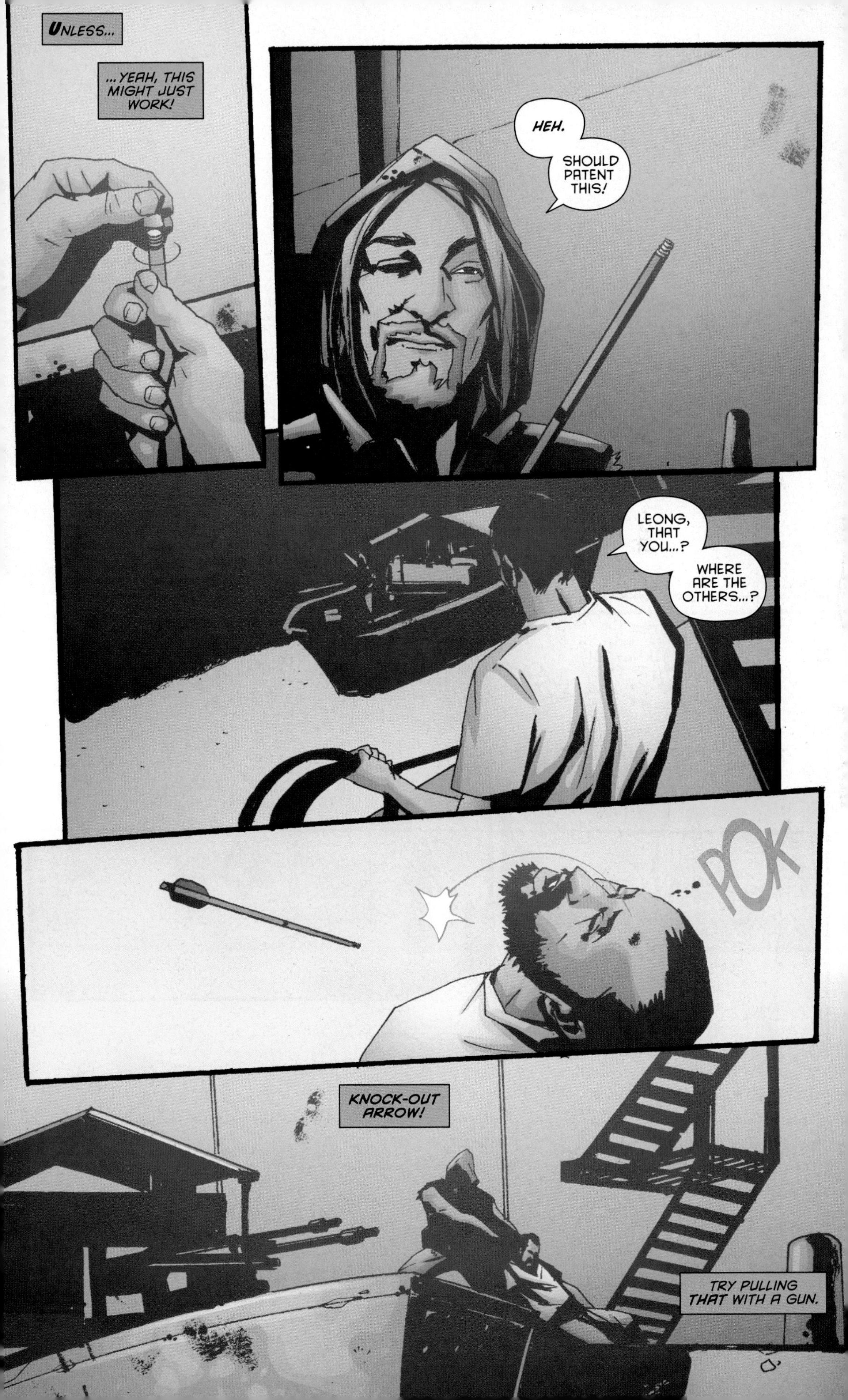
UNLESS...
...YEAH, THIS MIGHT JUST WORK!
HEH.
SHOULD PATENT THIS!
LEONG, THAT YOU...?
WHERE ARE THE OTHERS...?
POK
KNOCK-OUT ARROW!
TRY PULLING THAT WITH A GUN.

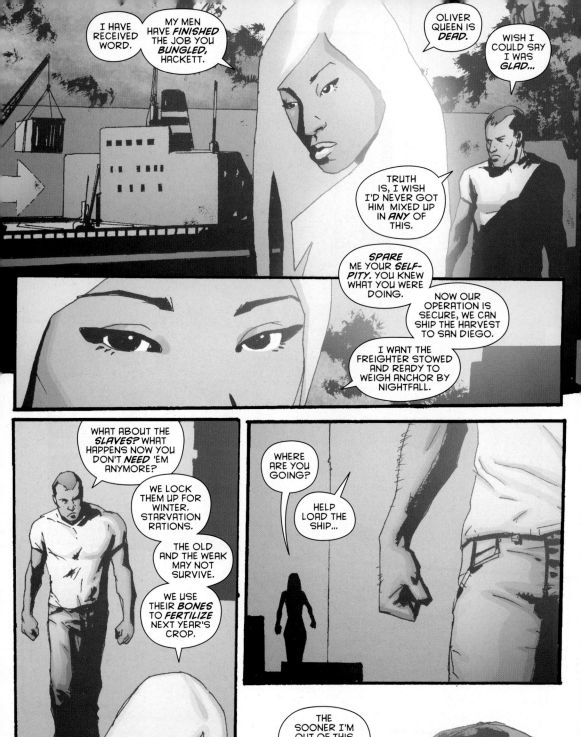

I HAVE RECEIVED WORD.

MY MEN HAVE *FINISHED* THE JOB YOU *BUNGLED,* HACKETT.

OLIVER QUEEN IS *DEAD.*

WISH I COULD SAY I WAS *GLAD...*

TRUTH IS, I WISH I'D NEVER GOT HIM MIXED UP IN *ANY* OF THIS.

SPARE ME YOUR *SELF-PITY.* YOU KNEW WHAT YOU WERE DOING.

NOW OUR OPERATION IS SECURE, WE CAN SHIP THE HARVEST TO SAN DIEGO.

I WANT THE FREIGHTER STOWED AND READY TO WEIGH ANCHOR BY NIGHTFALL.

WHAT ABOUT THE *SLAVES?* WHAT HAPPENS NOW YOU DON'T *NEED* 'EM ANYMORE?

WE LOCK THEM UP FOR WINTER. STARVATION RATIONS.

THE OLD AND THE WEAK MAY NOT SURVIVE.

WE USE THEIR *BONES* TO *FERTILIZE* NEXT YEAR'S CROP.

WHERE ARE YOU GOING?

HELP LOAD THE SHIP...

THE SOONER I'M OUT OF THIS *GODFORSAKEN HELLHOLE,* THE BETTER!

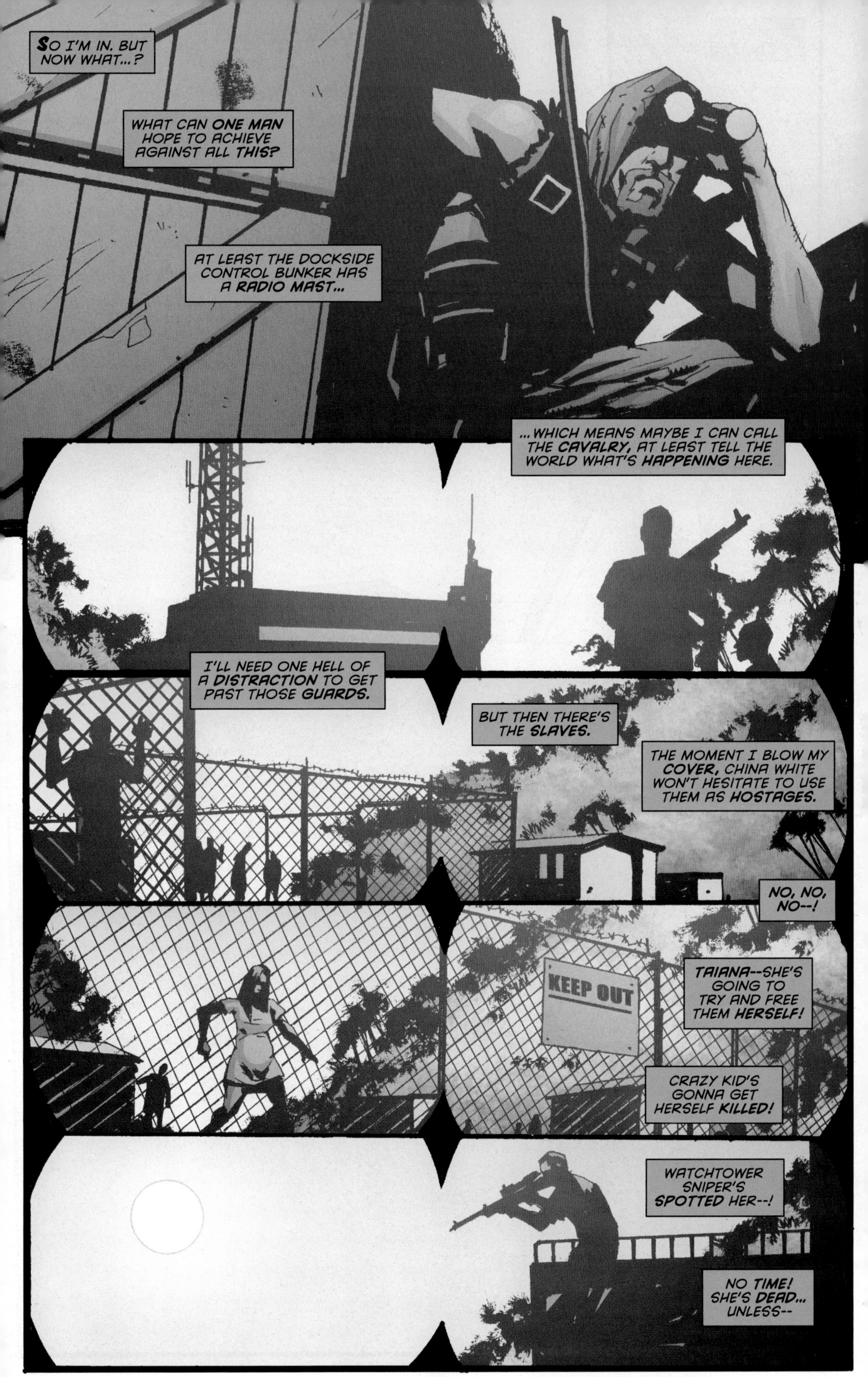
SO I'M IN. BUT NOW WHAT...?
WHAT CAN ONE MAN HOPE TO ACHIEVE AGAINST ALL THIS?
AT LEAST THE DOCKSIDE CONTROL BUNKER HAS A RADIO MAST...
...WHICH MEANS MAYBE I CAN CALL THE CAVALRY, AT LEAST TELL THE WORLD WHAT'S HAPPENING HERE.
I'LL NEED ONE HELL OF A DISTRACTION TO GET PAST THOSE GUARDS.
BUT THEN THERE'S THE SLAVES.
THE MOMENT I BLOW MY COVER, CHINA WHITE WON'T HESITATE TO USE THEM AS HOSTAGES.
NO, NO, NO--!
KEEP OUT
TAIANA--SHE'S GOING TO TRY AND FREE THEM HERSELF!
CRAZY KID'S GONNA GET HERSELF KILLED!
WATCHTOWER SNIPER'S SPOTTED HER--!
NO TIME! SHE'S DEAD... UNLESS--

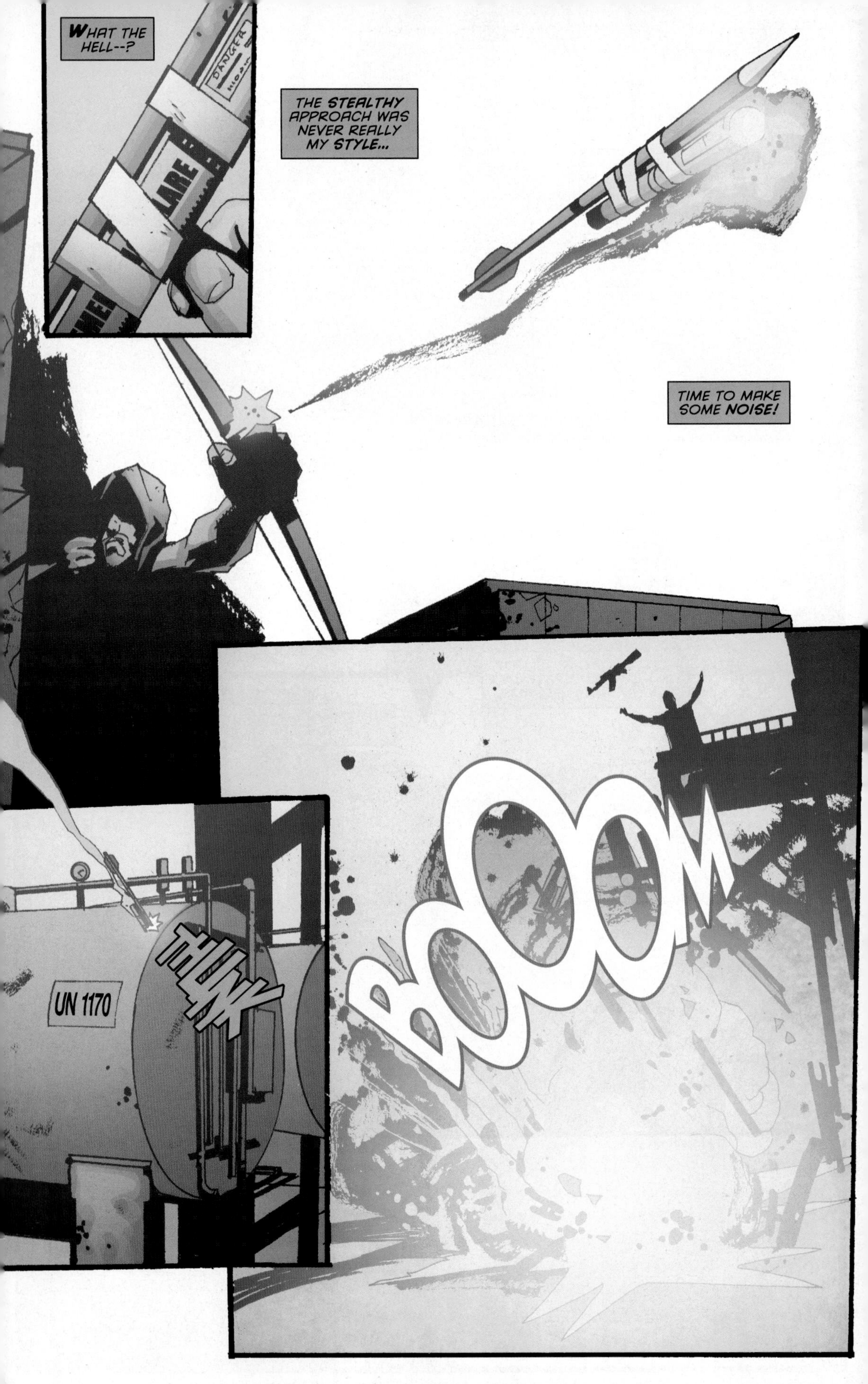
WHAT THE HELL--?
DANGER
FLARE
THE STEALTHY APPROACH WAS NEVER REALLY MY STYLE...
TIME TO MAKE SOME NOISE!
UN 1170
THUNK
BOOOM

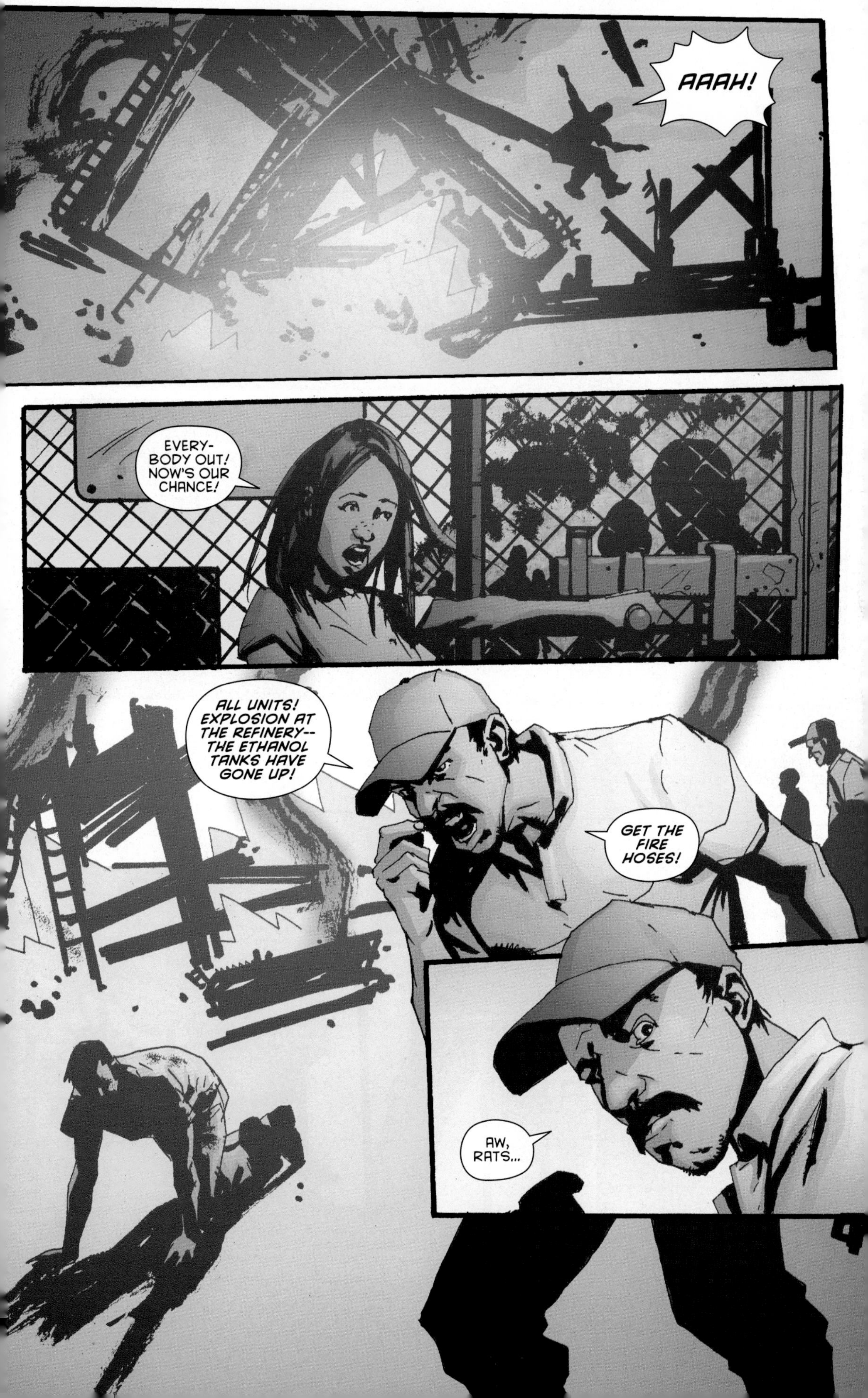
AAAH!
EVERY-BODY OUT! NOW'S OUR CHANCE!
ALL UNITS! EXPLOSION AT THE REFINERY-- THE ETHANOL TANKS HAVE GONE UP!
GET THE FIRE HOSES!
AW, RATS...

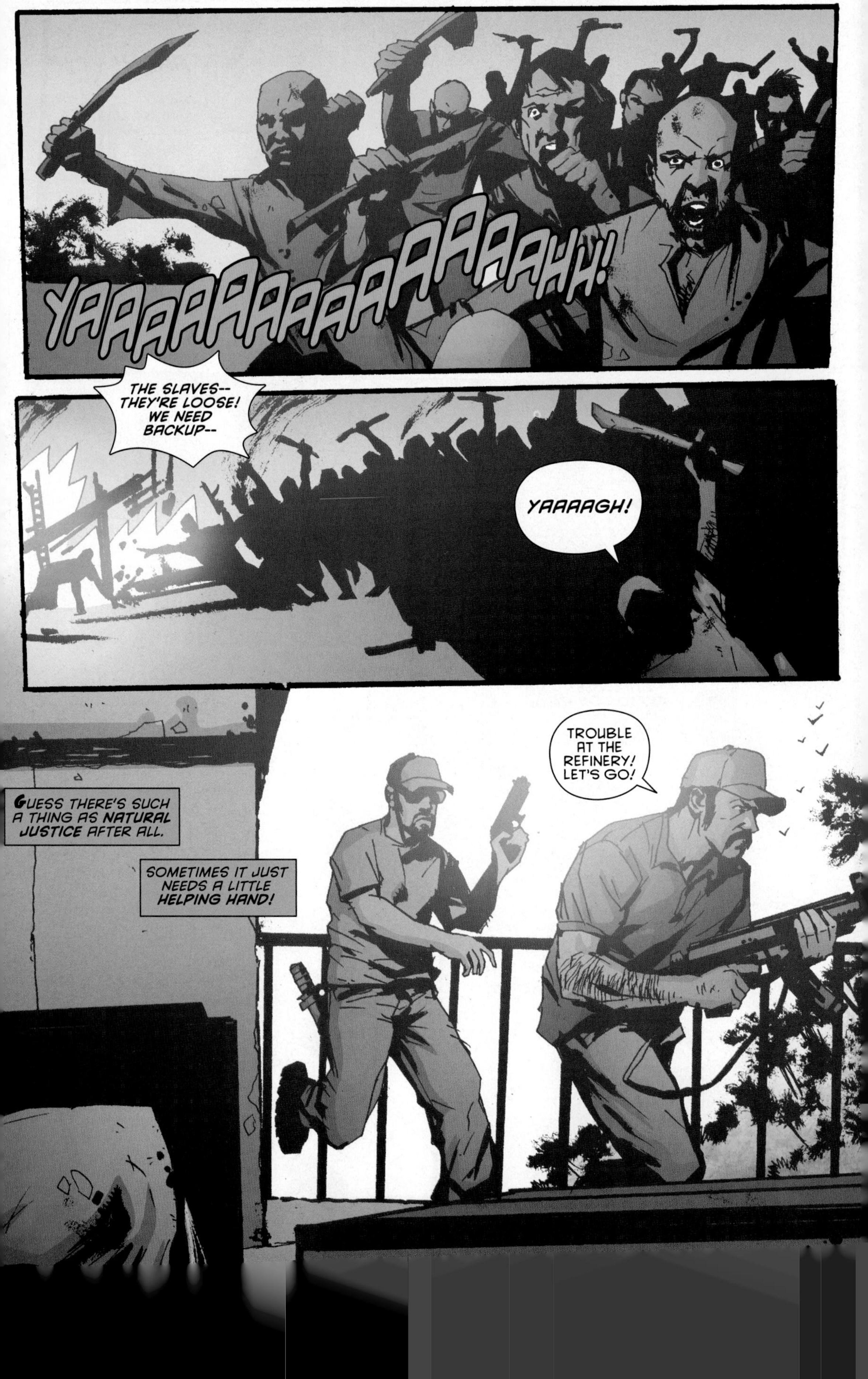
YAAAAAAAAAAAAAAAAAAAAAHH!
THE SLAVES-- THEY'RE LOOSE! WE NEED BACKUP--
YAAAAGH!
GUESS THERE'S SUCH A THING AS NATURAL JUSTICE AFTER ALL.
SOMETIMES IT JUST NEEDS A LITTLE HELPING HAND!
TROUBLE AT THE REFINERY! LET'S GO!

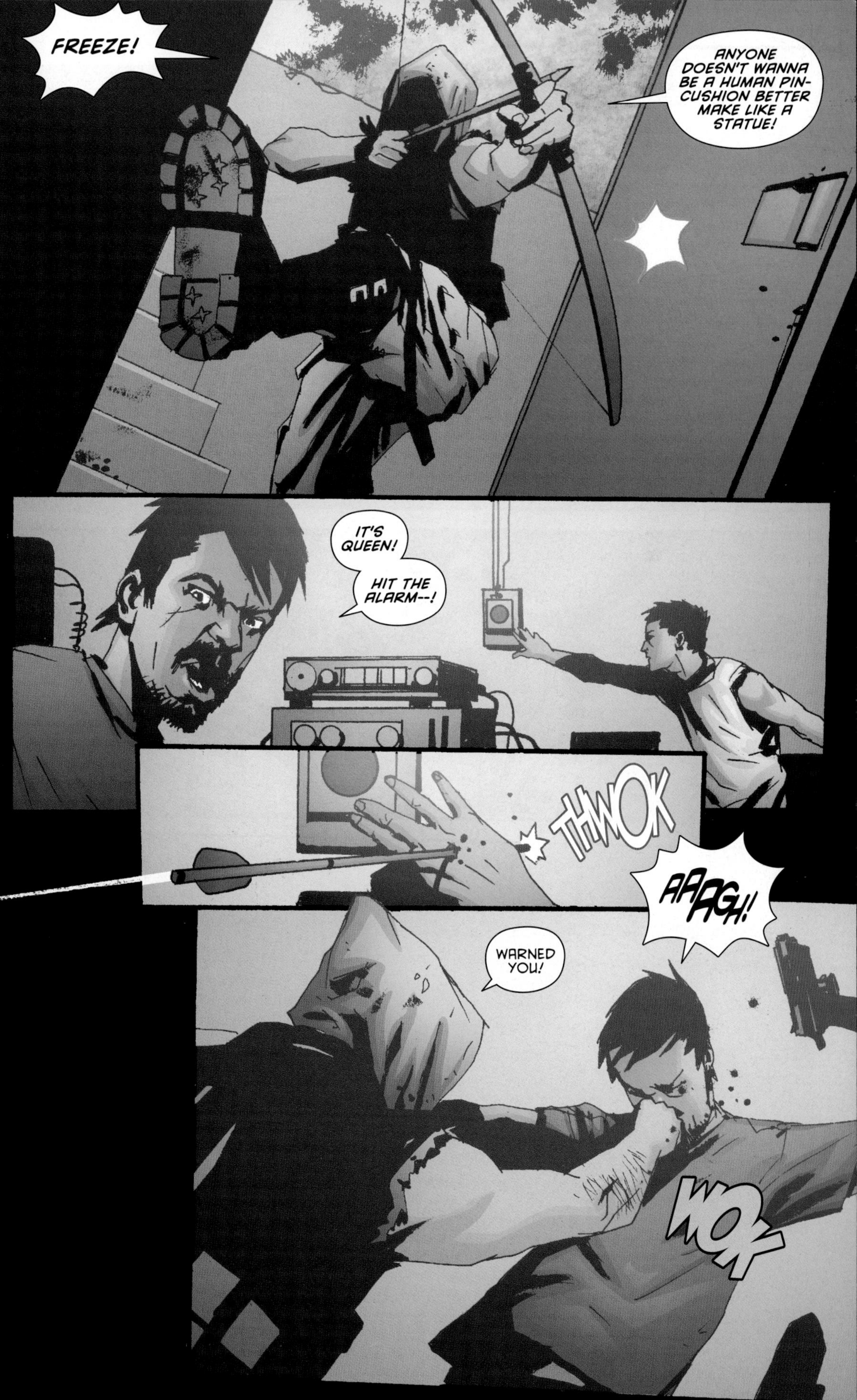
FREEZE!
ANYONE DOESN'T WANNA BE A HUMAN PIN-CUSHION BETTER MAKE LIKE A STATUE!
IT'S QUEEN!
HIT THE ALARM--!
THWOK
AAAGH!
WARNED YOU!
WOK

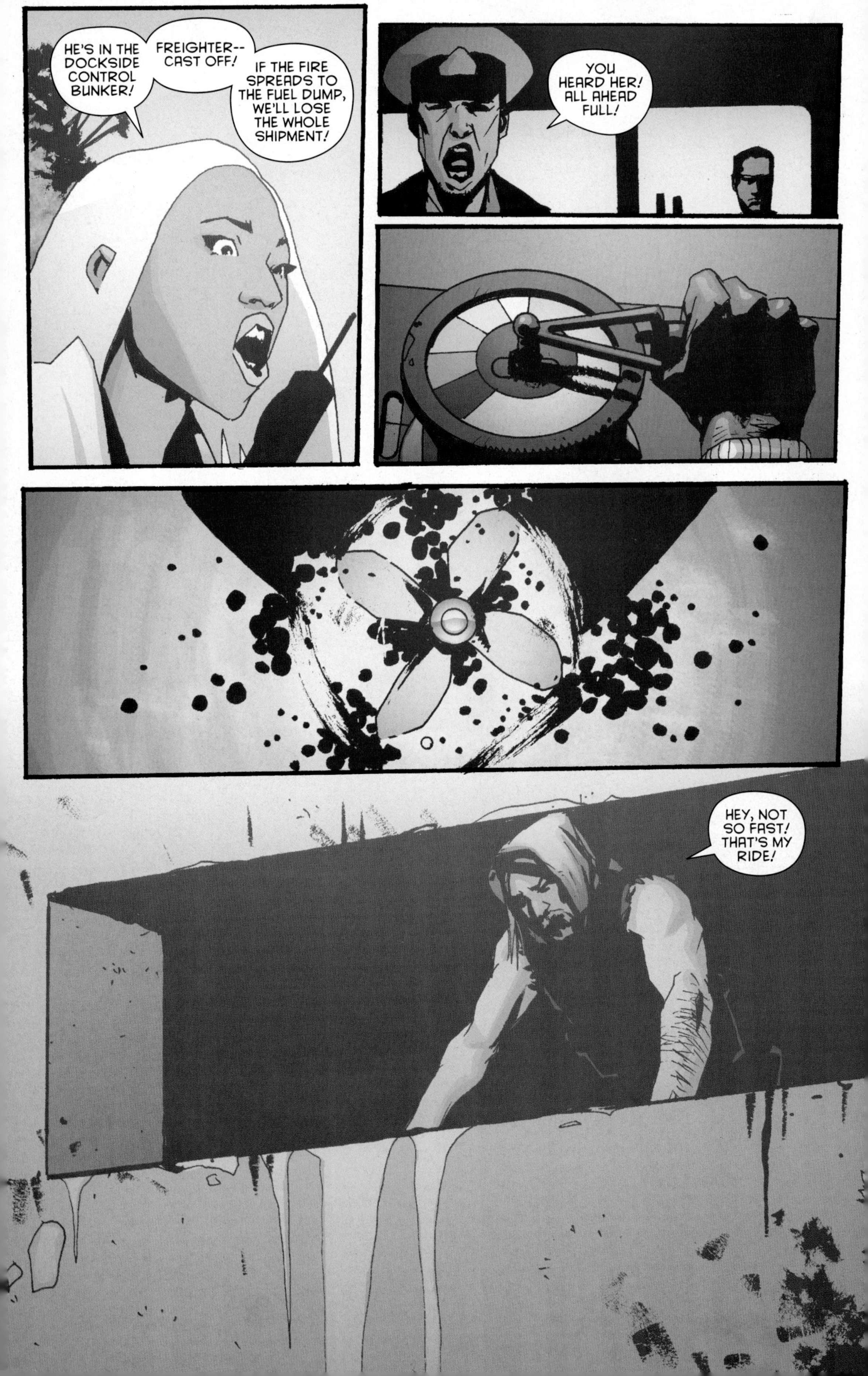
HE'S IN THE DOCKSIDE CONTROL BUNKER!
FREIGHTER-- CAST OFF!
IF THE FIRE SPREADS TO THE FUEL DUMP, WE'LL LOSE THE WHOLE SHIPMENT!
YOU HEARD HER! ALL AHEAD FULL!
HEY, NOT SO FAST! THAT'S MY RIDE!

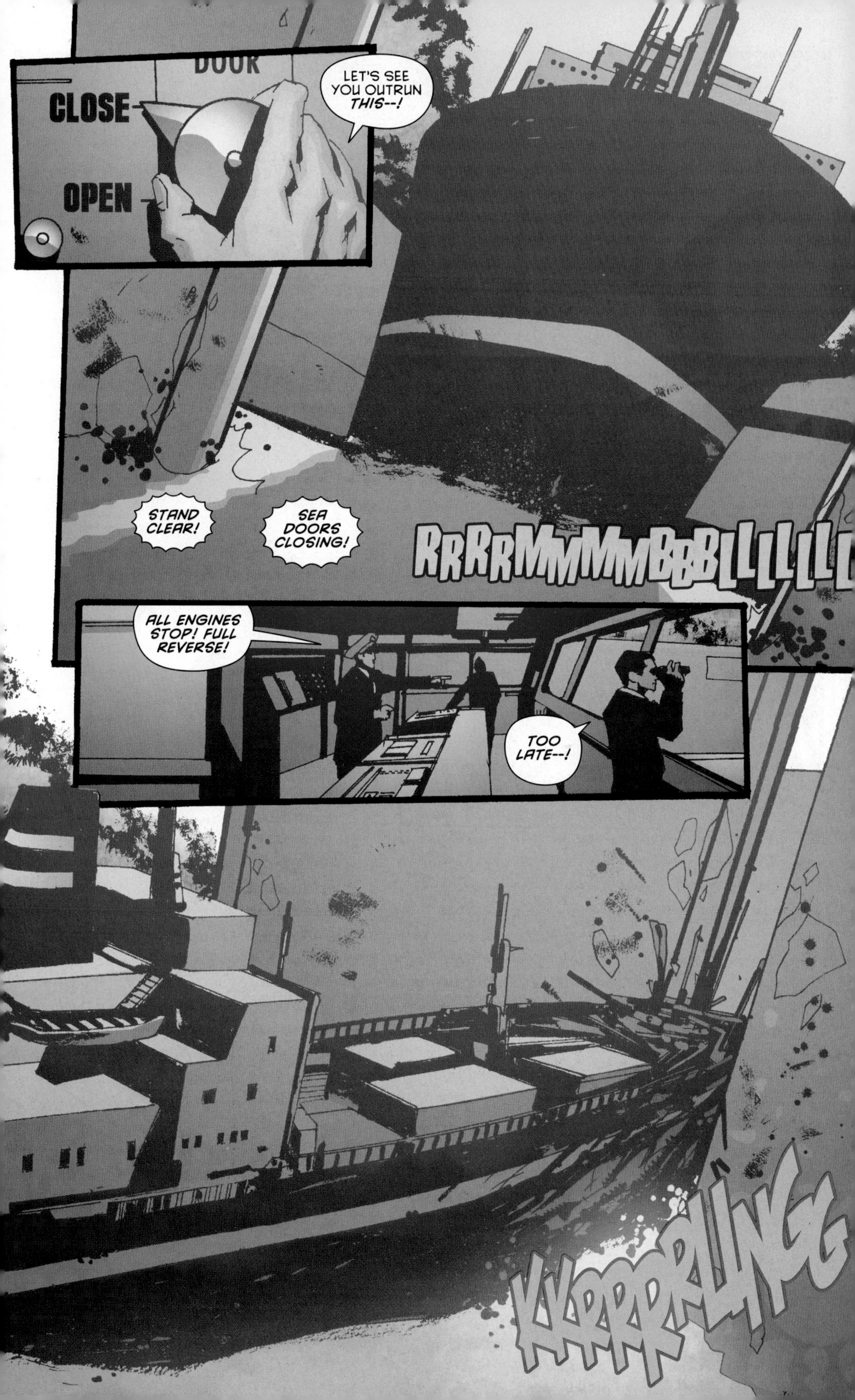

DOOR
CLOSE
OPEN
LET'S SEE YOU OUTRUN *THIS*--!
STAND CLEAR!
SEA DOORS CLOSING!
RRRRMMMMMMBBBLLLLLL
ALL ENGINES STOP! FULL REVERSE!
TOO LATE--!
KKRRRRLLNGG

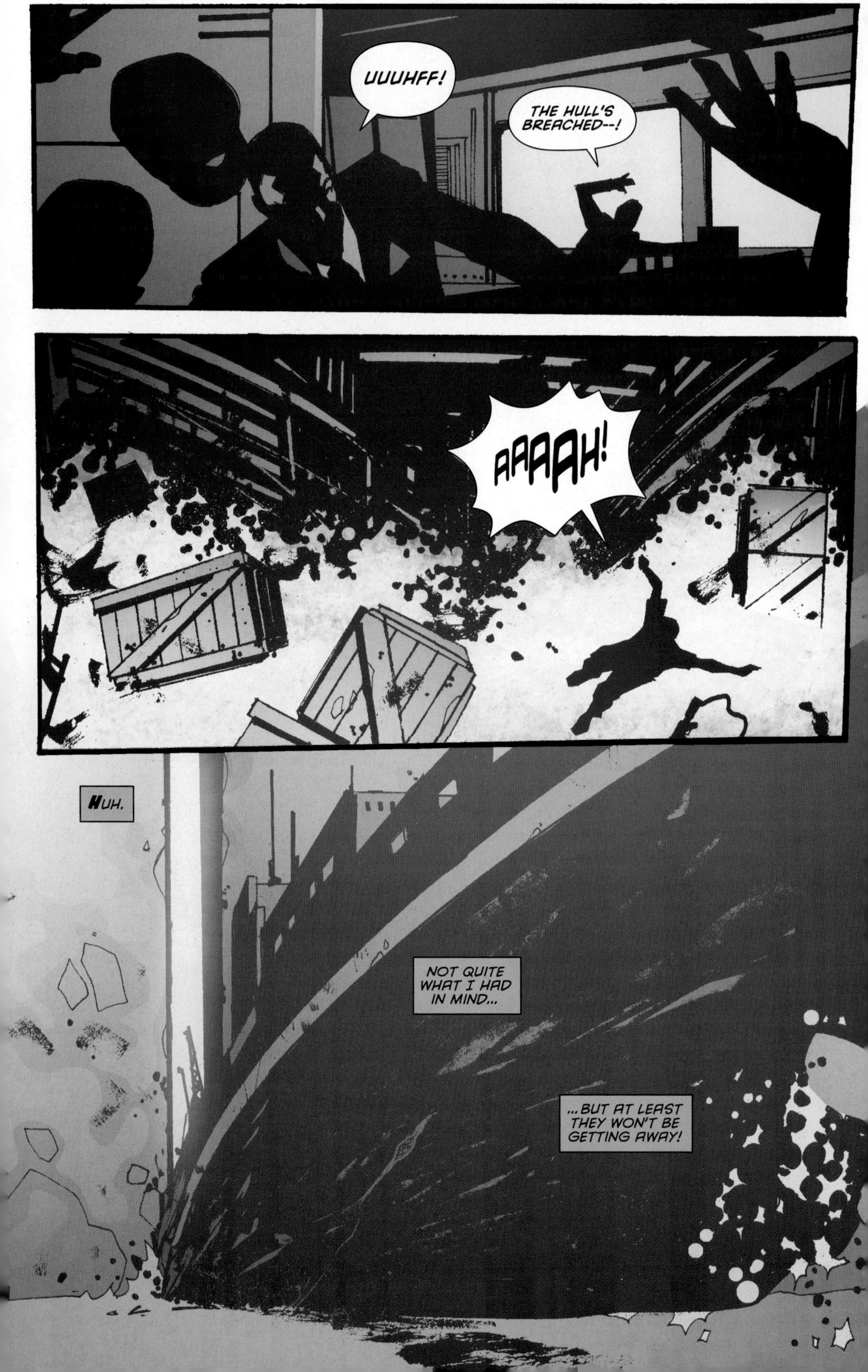
UUUHFF!
THE HULL'S BREACHED--!
AAAAH!
HUH.
NOT QUITE WHAT I HAD IN MIND...
...BUT AT LEAST THEY WON'T BE GETTING AWAY!

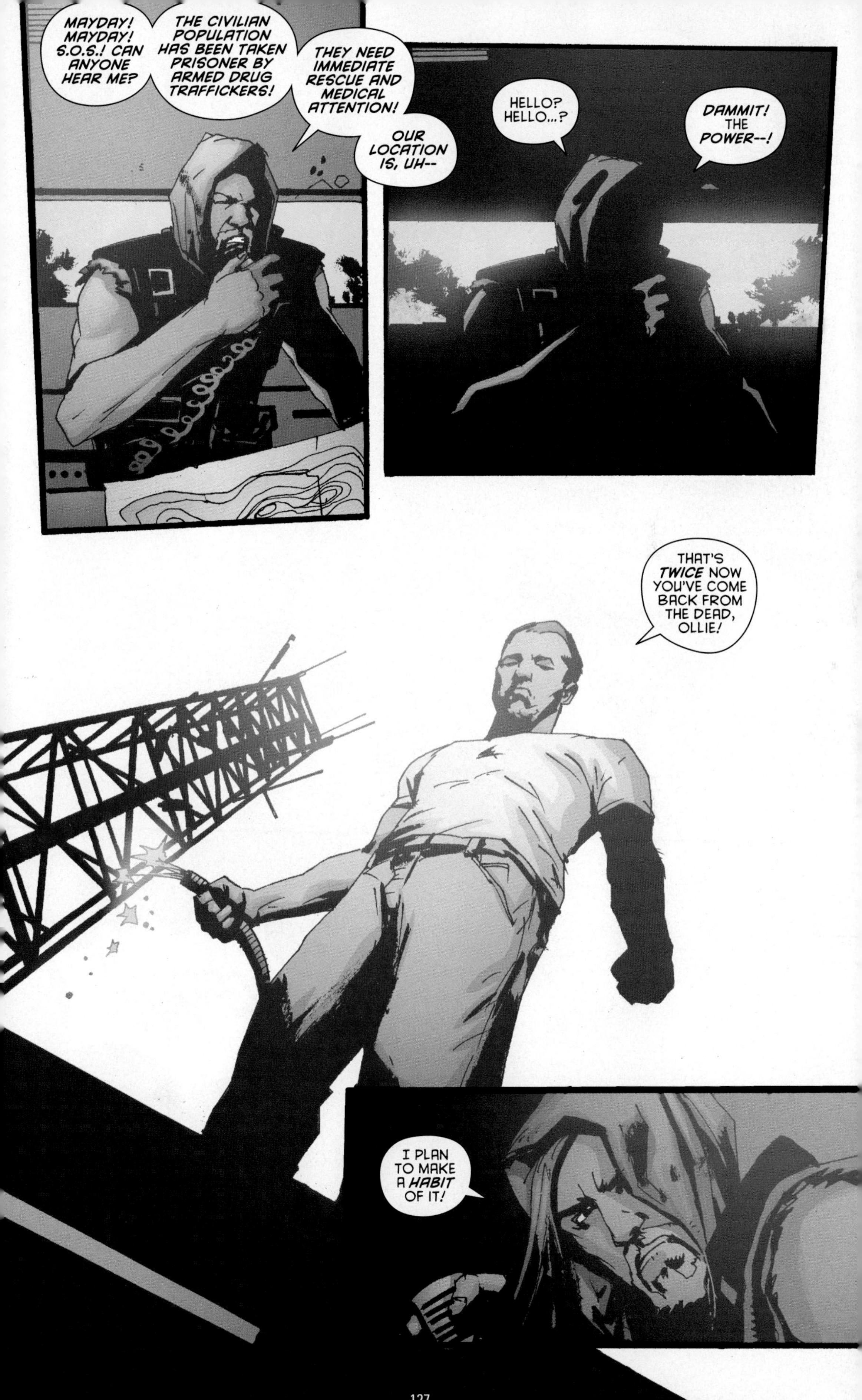
MAYDAY! MAYDAY! S.O.S.! CAN ANYONE HEAR ME?
THE CIVILIAN POPULATION HAS BEEN TAKEN PRISONER BY ARMED DRUG TRAFFICKERS!
THEY NEED IMMEDIATE RESCUE AND MEDICAL ATTENTION!
OUR LOCATION IS, UH--
HELLO? HELLO...?
DAMMIT! THE POWER--!
THAT'S TWICE NOW YOU'VE COME BACK FROM THE DEAD, OLLIE!
I PLAN TO MAKE A HABIT OF IT!

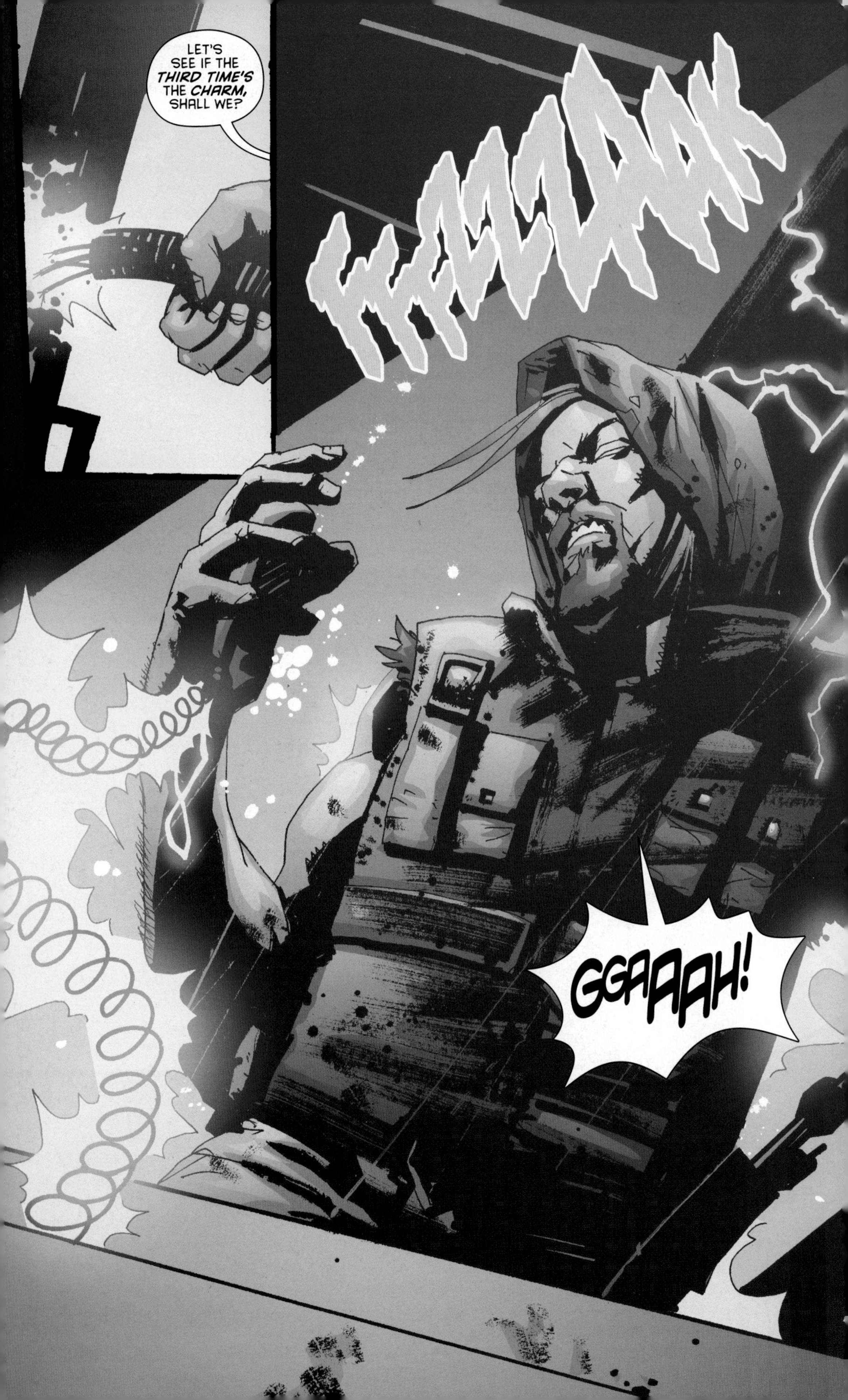
LET'S SEE IF THE *THIRD TIME'S* THE *CHARM,* SHALL WE?
FFZZZAAK
GGAAAH!

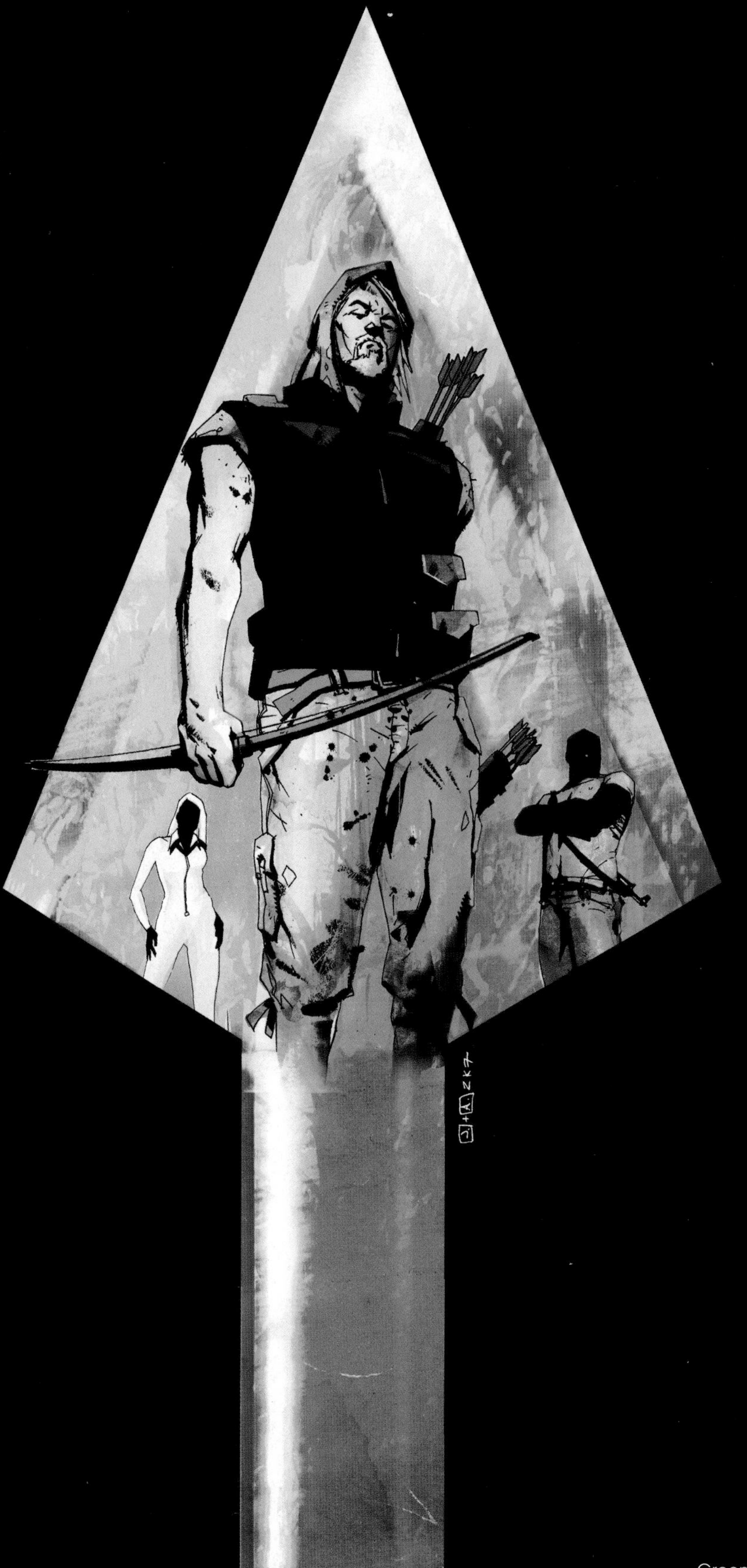

Green Arrow: Year One #6

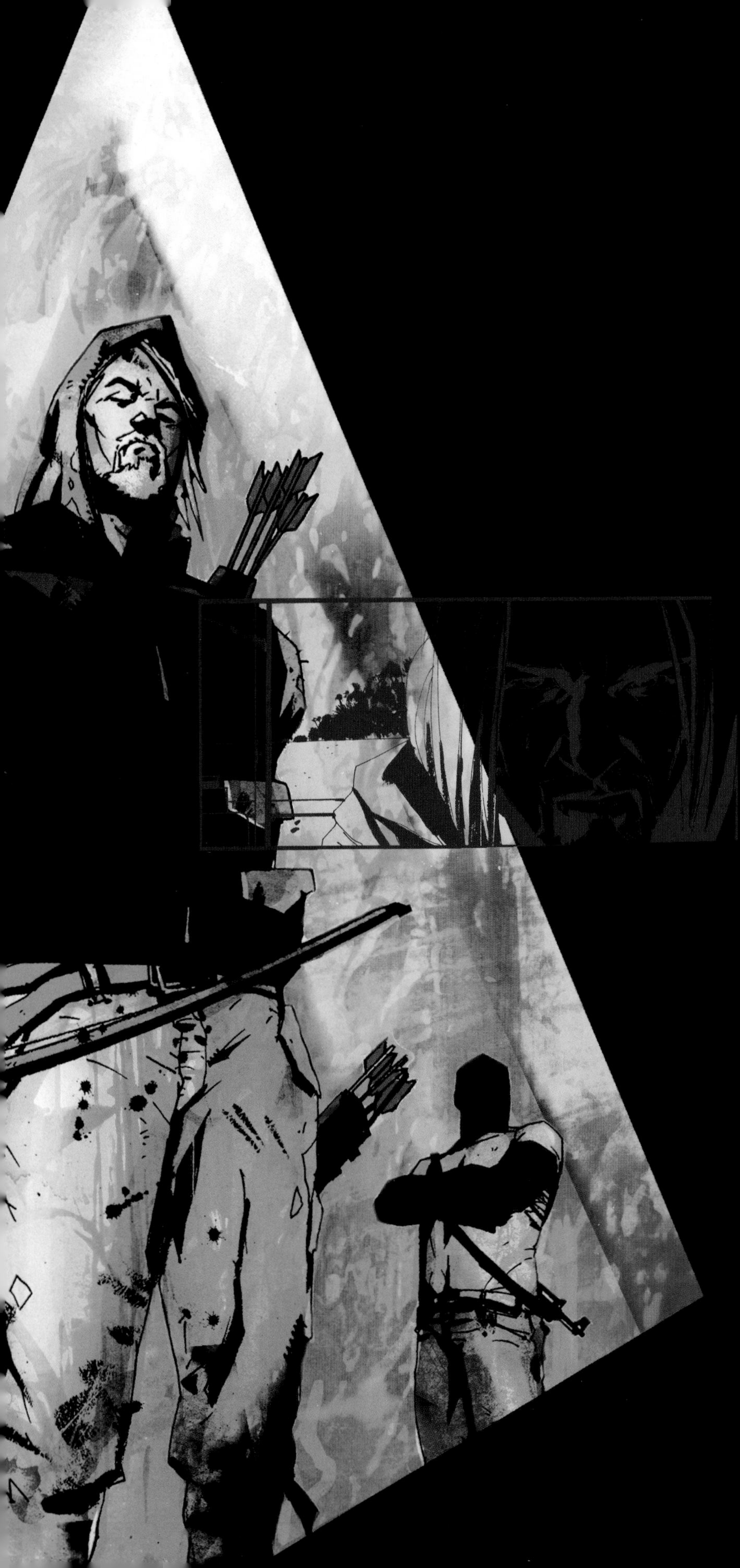

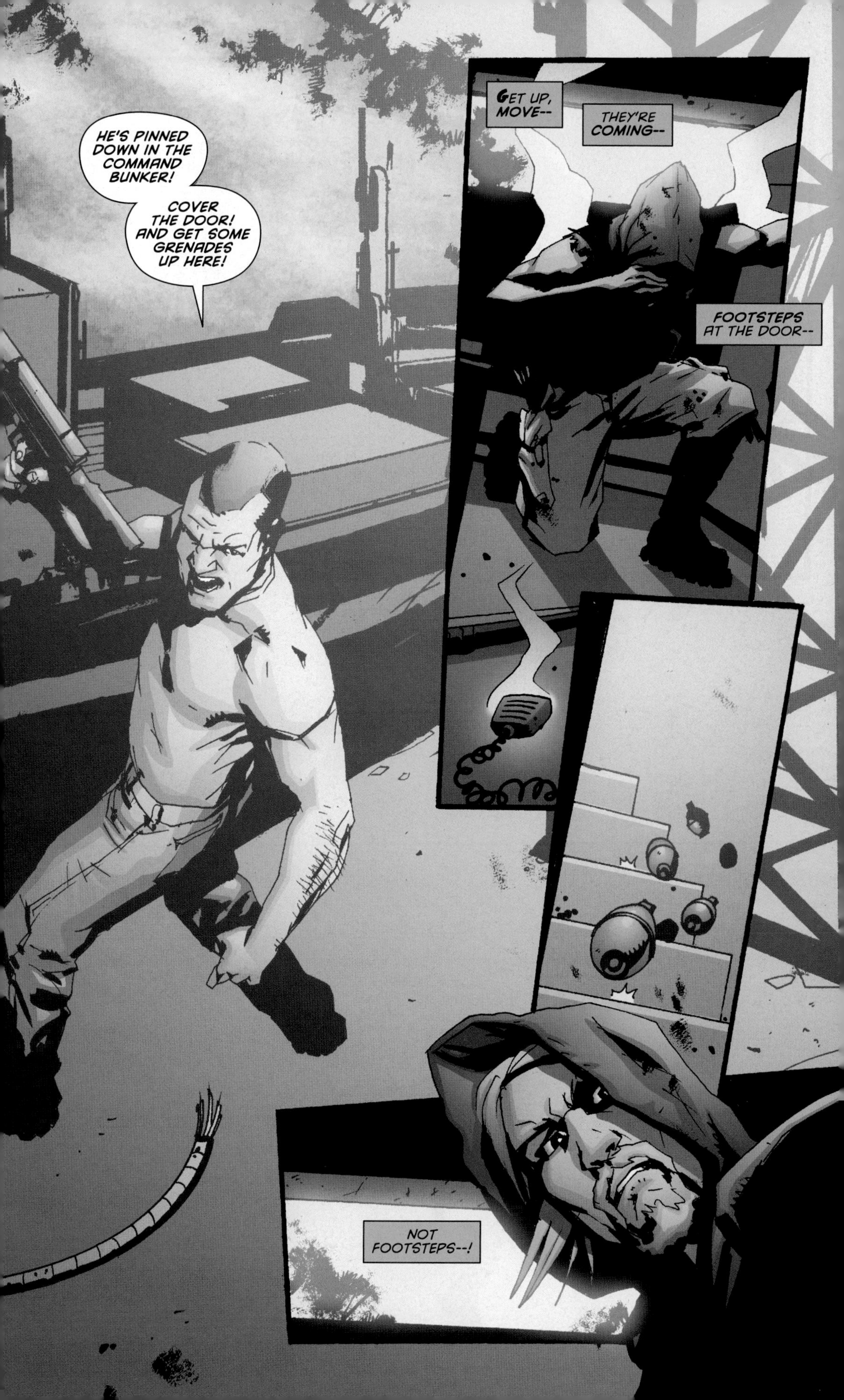
HE'S PINNED DOWN IN THE COMMAND BUNKER!
COVER THE DOOR! AND GET SOME GRENADES UP HERE!
GET UP, MOVE--
THEY'RE COMING--
FOOTSTEPS AT THE DOOR--
NOT FOOTSTEPS--!

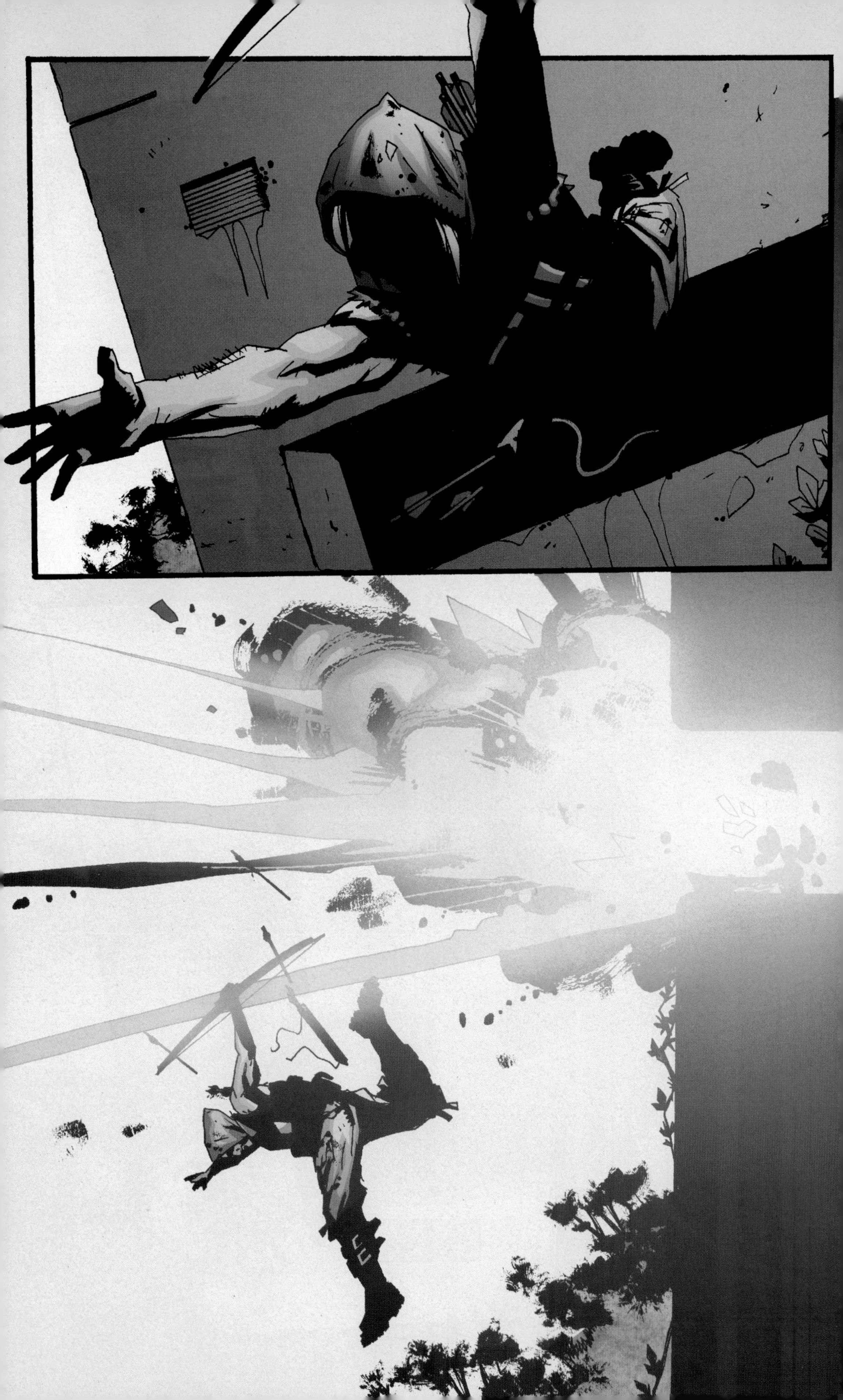

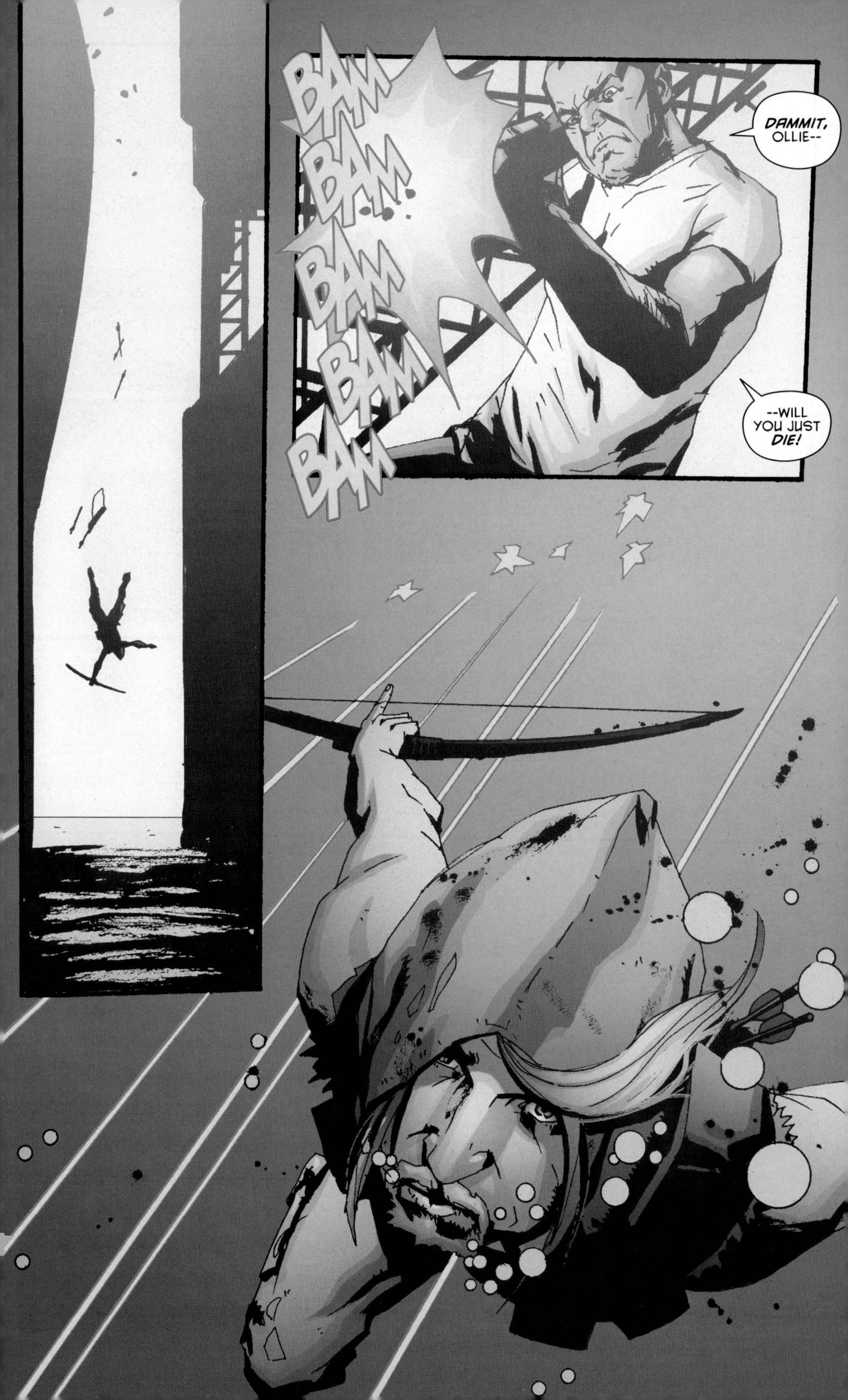
BAM BAM BAM BAM BAM
DAMMIT, OLLIE--
--WILL YOU JUST DIE!

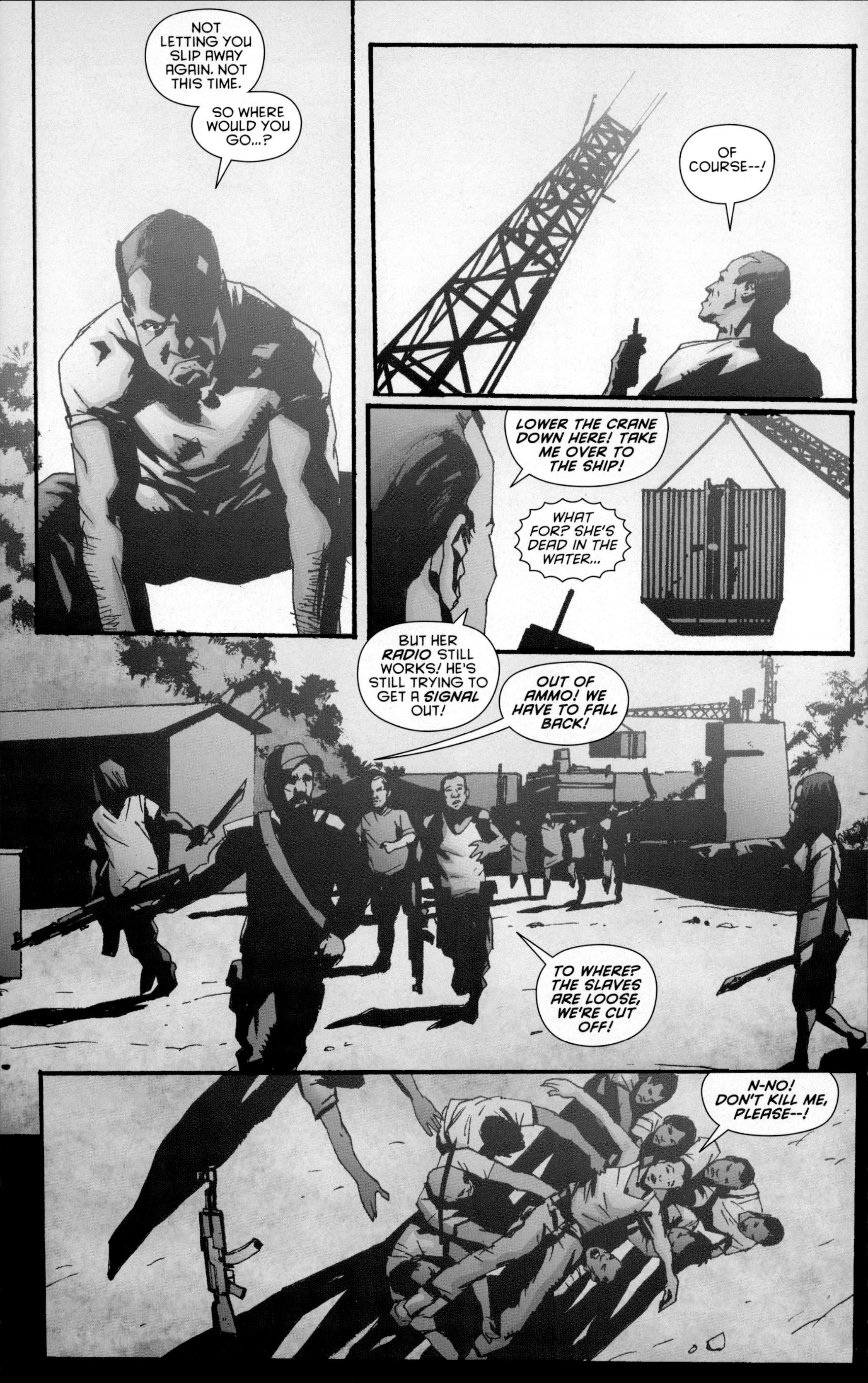
NOT LETTING YOU SLIP AWAY AGAIN. NOT THIS TIME.
SO WHERE WOULD YOU GO...?
OF COURSE--!
LOWER THE CRANE DOWN HERE! TAKE ME OVER TO THE SHIP!
WHAT FOR? SHE'S DEAD IN THE WATER...
BUT HER RADIO STILL WORKS! HE'S STILL TRYING TO GET A SIGNAL OUT!
OUT OF AMMO! WE HAVE TO FALL BACK!
TO WHERE? THE SLAVES ARE LOOSE, WE'RE CUT OFF!
N-NO! DON'T KILL ME, PLEASE--!

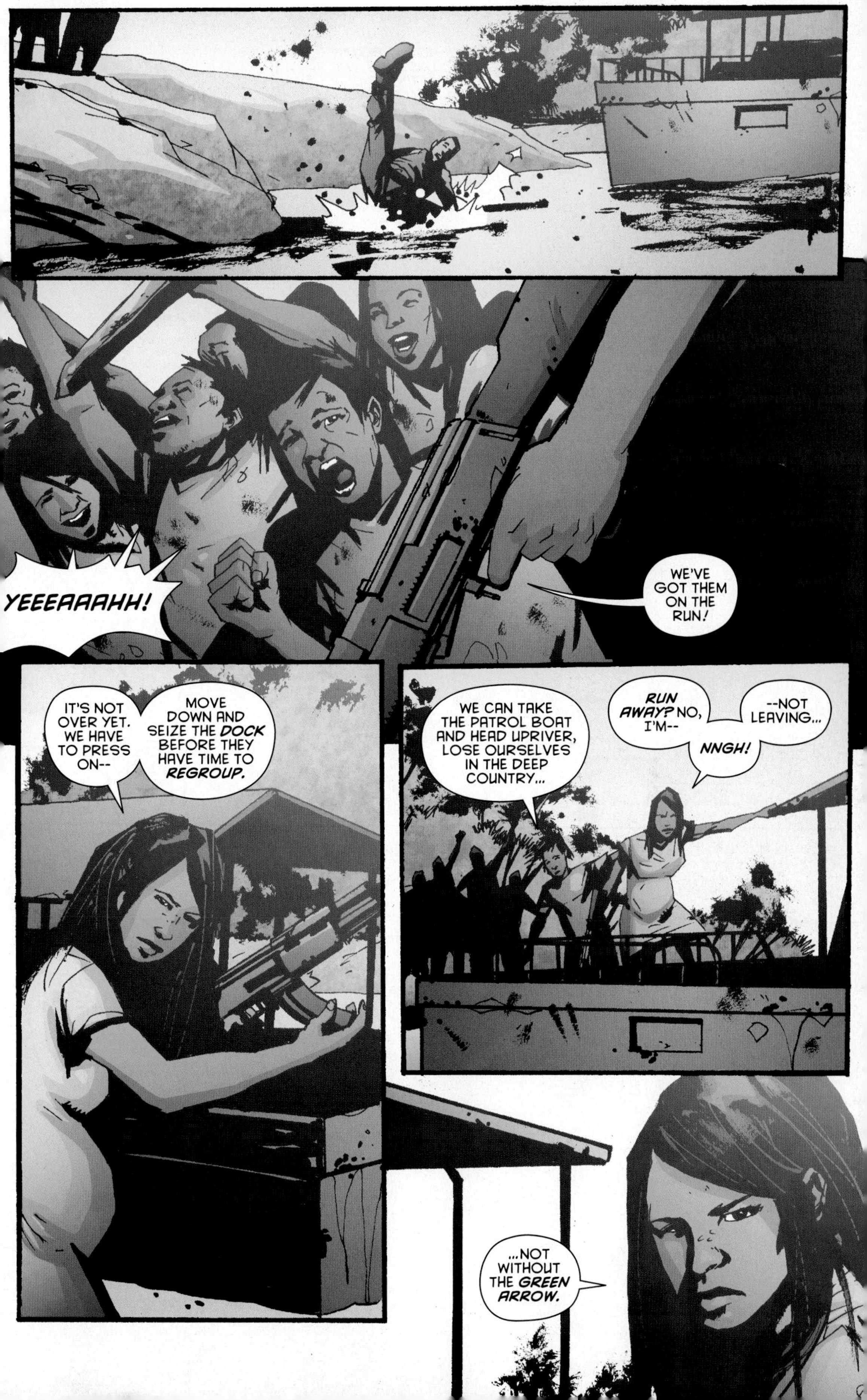
YEEEAAAHH!
WE'VE GOT THEM ON THE RUN!
IT'S NOT OVER YET. WE HAVE TO PRESS ON--
MOVE DOWN AND SEIZE THE DOCK BEFORE THEY HAVE TIME TO REGROUP.
WE CAN TAKE THE PATROL BOAT AND HEAD UPRIVER, LOSE OURSELVES IN THE DEEP COUNTRY...
RUN AWAY? NO, I'M--
NNGH!
--NOT LEAVING...
...NOT WITHOUT THE GREEN ARROW.

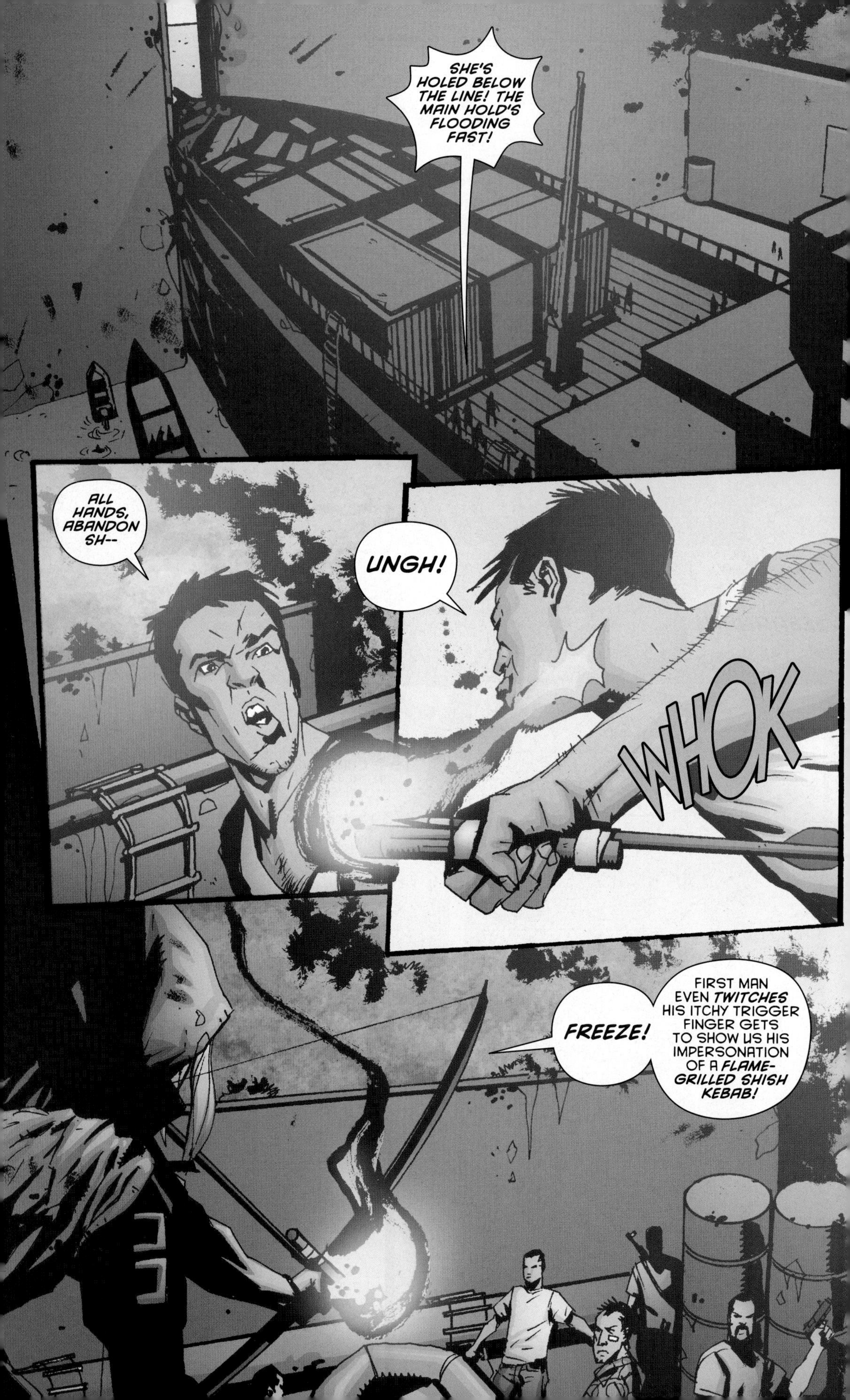
SHE'S HOLED BELOW THE LINE! THE MAIN HOLD'S FLOODING FAST!
ALL HANDS, ABANDON SH--
UNGH!
WHOK
FREEZE!
FIRST MAN EVEN *TWITCHES* HIS ITCHY TRIGGER FINGER GETS TO SHOW US HIS IMPERSONATION OF A *FLAME-GRILLED SHISH KEBAB!*

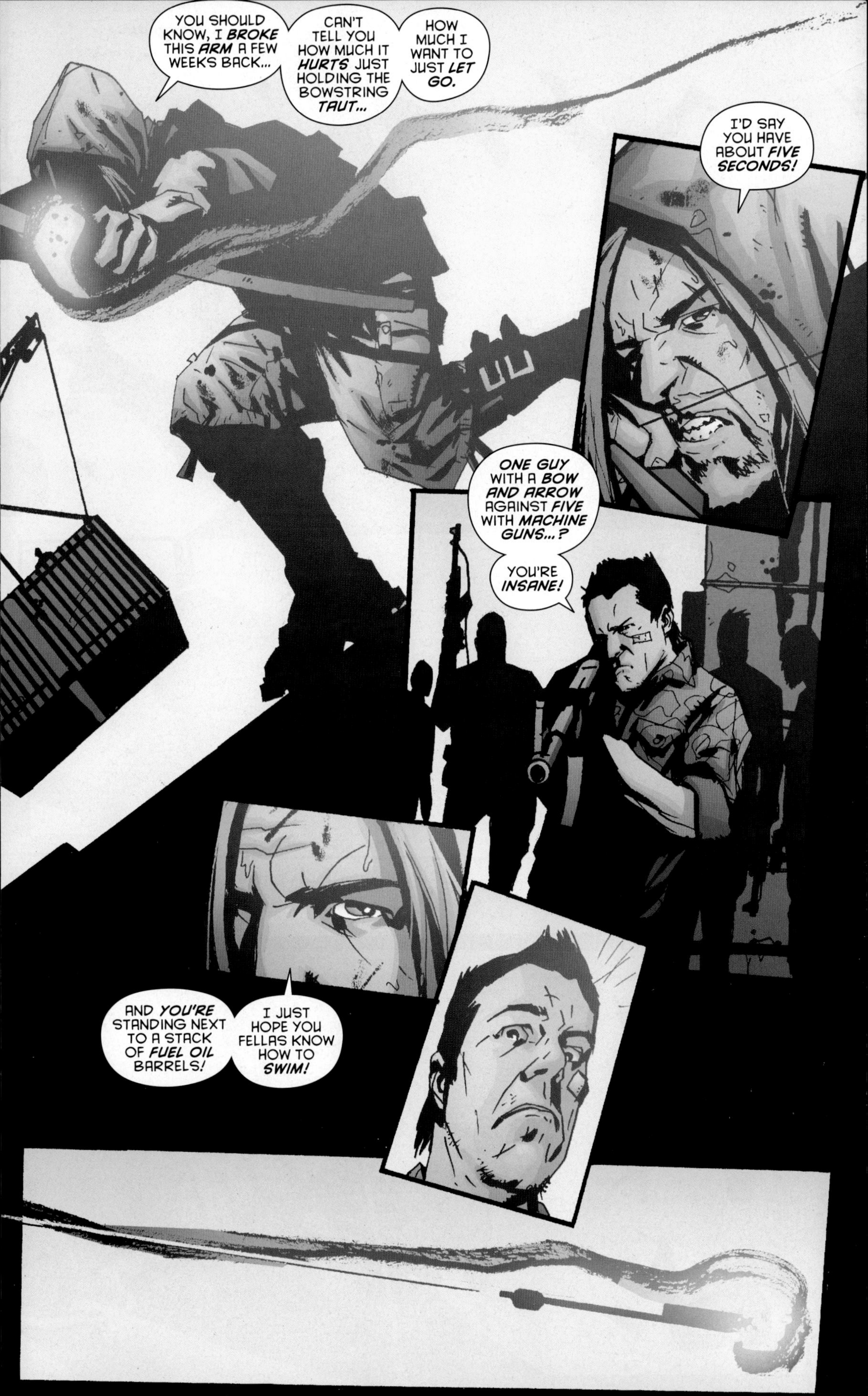
YOU SHOULD KNOW, I BROKE THIS ARM A FEW WEEKS BACK...
CAN'T TELL YOU HOW MUCH IT HURTS JUST HOLDING THE BOWSTRING TAUT...
HOW MUCH I WANT TO JUST LET GO.
I'D SAY YOU HAVE ABOUT FIVE SECONDS!
ONE GUY WITH A BOW AND ARROW AGAINST FIVE WITH MACHINE GUNS...?
YOU'RE INSANE!
AND YOU'RE STANDING NEXT TO A STACK OF FUEL OIL BARRELS!
I JUST HOPE YOU FELLAS KNOW HOW TO SWIM!

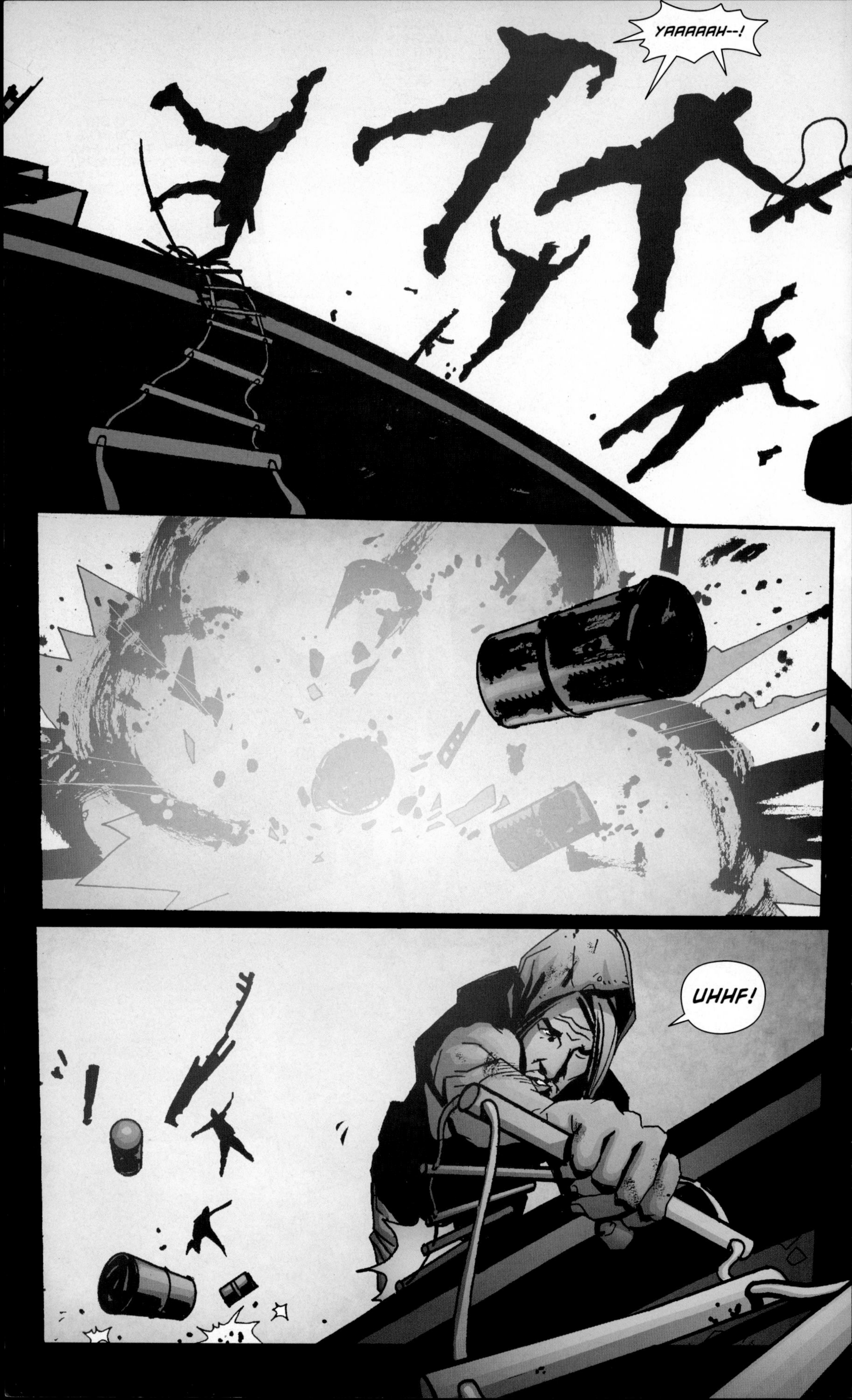
YAAAAAH--!
UHHF!

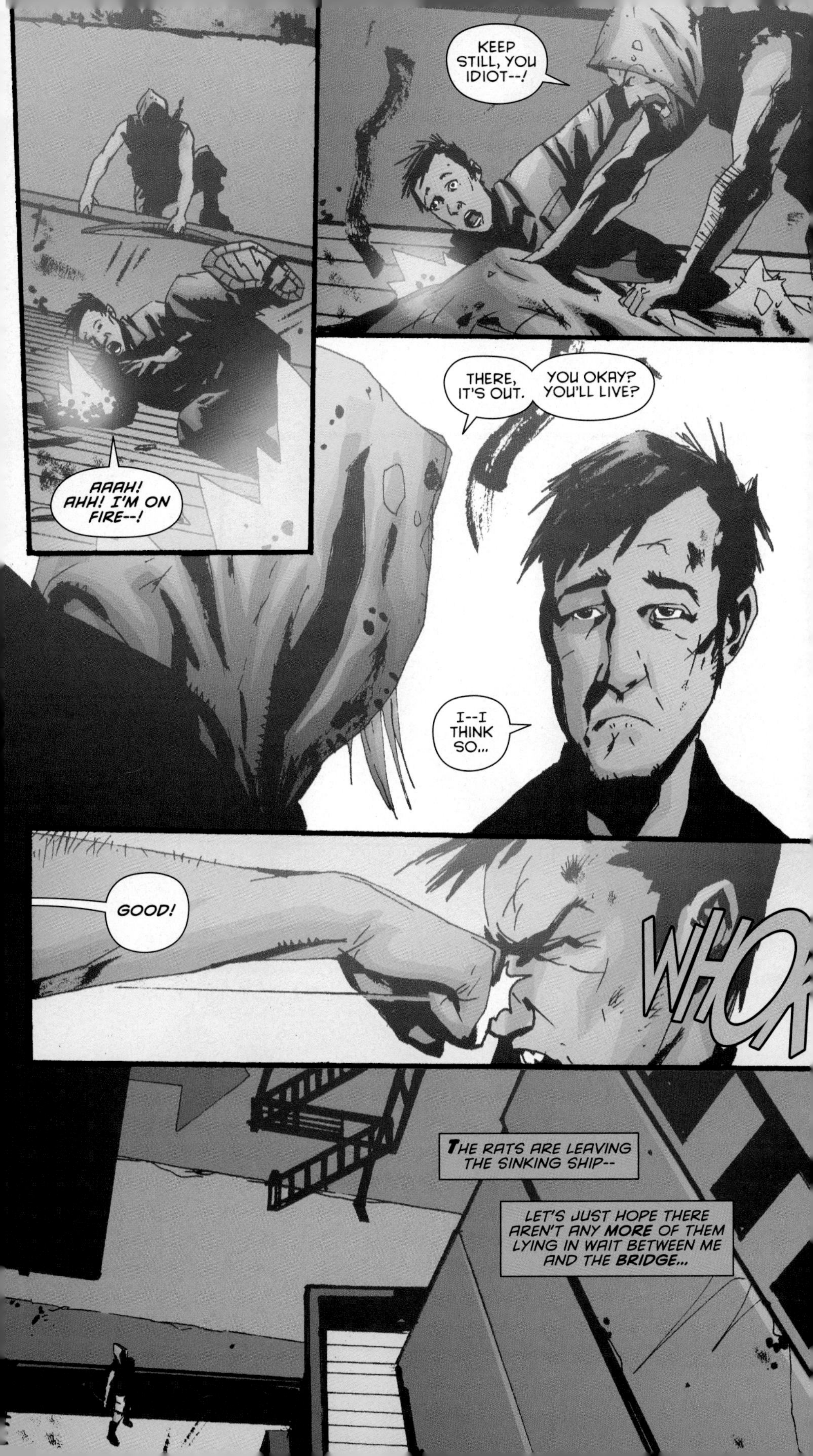
KEEP STILL, YOU IDIOT--!
AAAH! AHH! I'M ON FIRE--!
THERE, IT'S OUT.
YOU OKAY? YOU'LL LIVE?
I--I THINK SO...
GOOD!
WHO
THE RATS ARE LEAVING THE SINKING SHIP--
LET'S JUST HOPE THERE AREN'T ANY MORE OF THEM LYING IN WAIT BETWEEN ME AND THE BRIDGE...

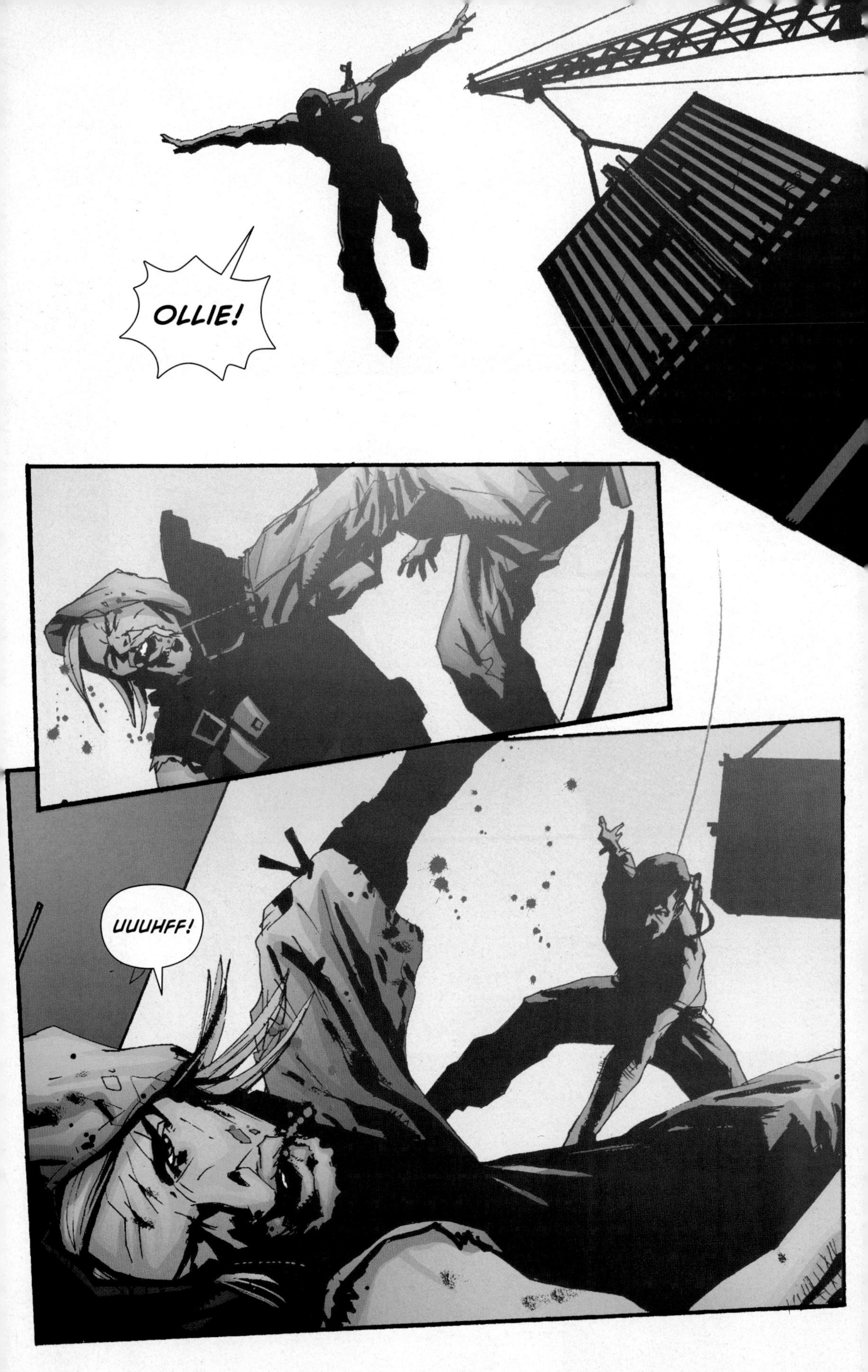
OLLIE!
UUUHFF!

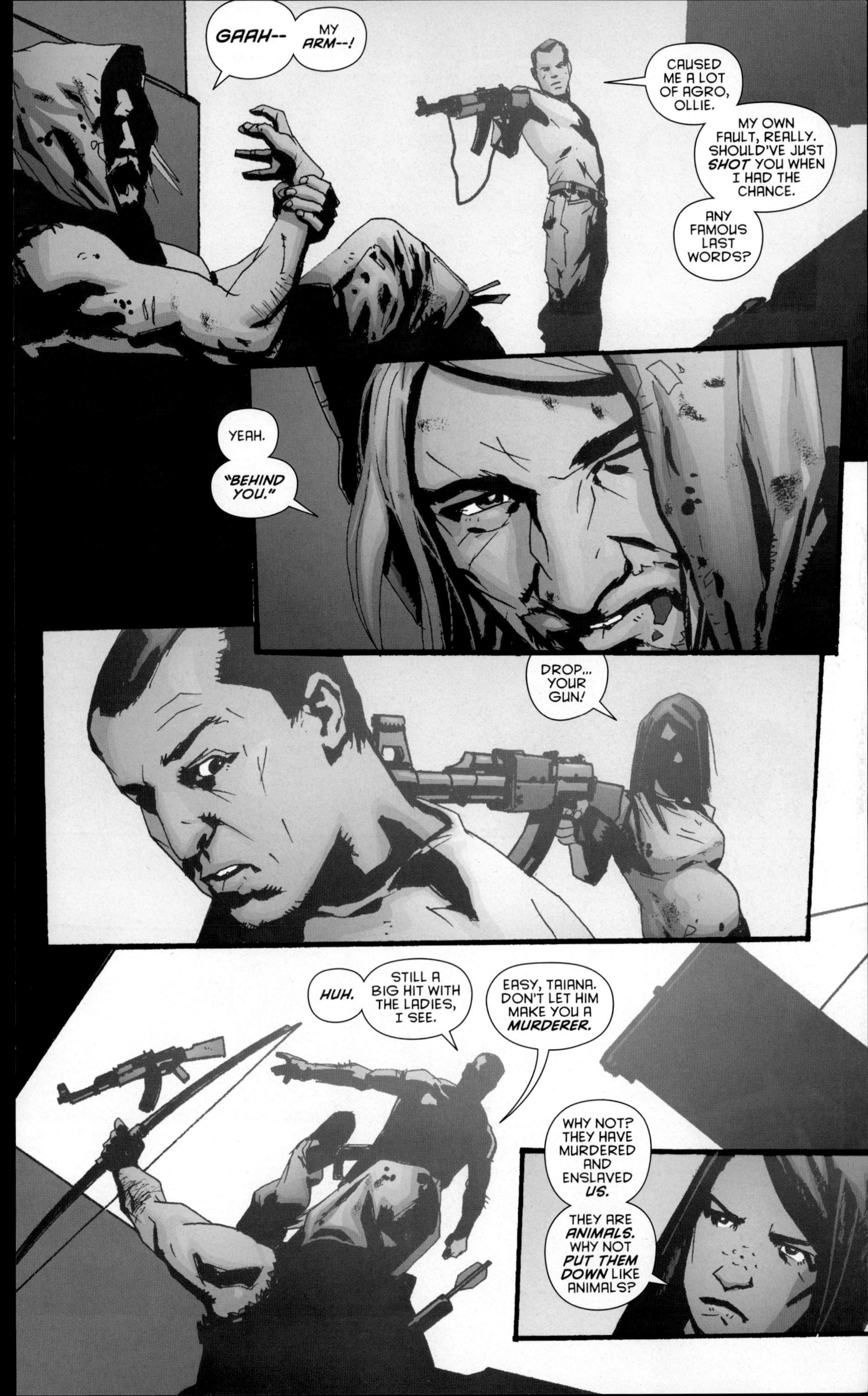
GAAH--
MY ARM--!
CAUSED ME A LOT OF AGRO, OLLIE.
MY OWN FAULT, REALLY. SHOULD'VE JUST SHOT YOU WHEN I HAD THE CHANCE.
ANY FAMOUS LAST WORDS?
YEAH.
"BEHIND YOU."
DROP... YOUR GUN!
HUH.
STILL A BIG HIT WITH THE LADIES, I SEE.
EASY, TAIANA. DON'T LET HIM MAKE YOU A MURDERER.
WHY NOT? THEY HAVE MURDERED AND ENSLAVED US.
THEY ARE ANIMALS. WHY NOT PUT THEM DOWN LIKE ANIMALS?

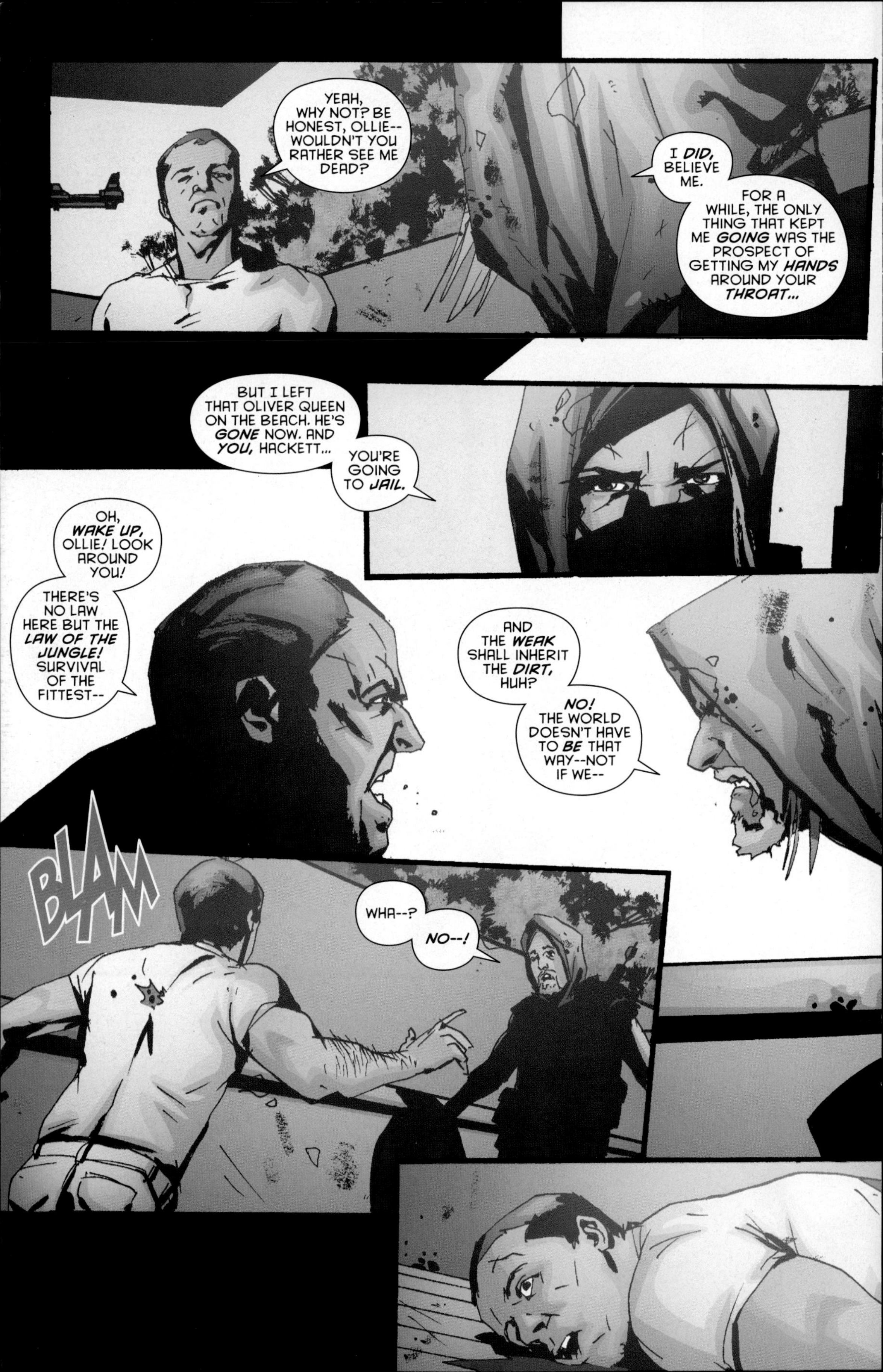
YEAH, WHY NOT? BE HONEST, OLLIE-- WOULDN'T YOU RATHER SEE ME DEAD?
I DID, BELIEVE ME.
FOR A WHILE, THE ONLY THING THAT KEPT ME GOING WAS THE PROSPECT OF GETTING MY HANDS AROUND YOUR THROAT...
BUT I LEFT THAT OLIVER QUEEN ON THE BEACH. HE'S GONE NOW. AND YOU, HACKETT...
YOU'RE GOING TO JAIL.
OH, WAKE UP, OLLIE! LOOK AROUND YOU!
THERE'S NO LAW HERE BUT THE LAW OF THE JUNGLE! SURVIVAL OF THE FITTEST--
AND THE WEAK SHALL INHERIT THE DIRT, HUH?
NO! THE WORLD DOESN'T HAVE TO BE THAT WAY--NOT IF WE--
BLAM
WHA--?
NO--!

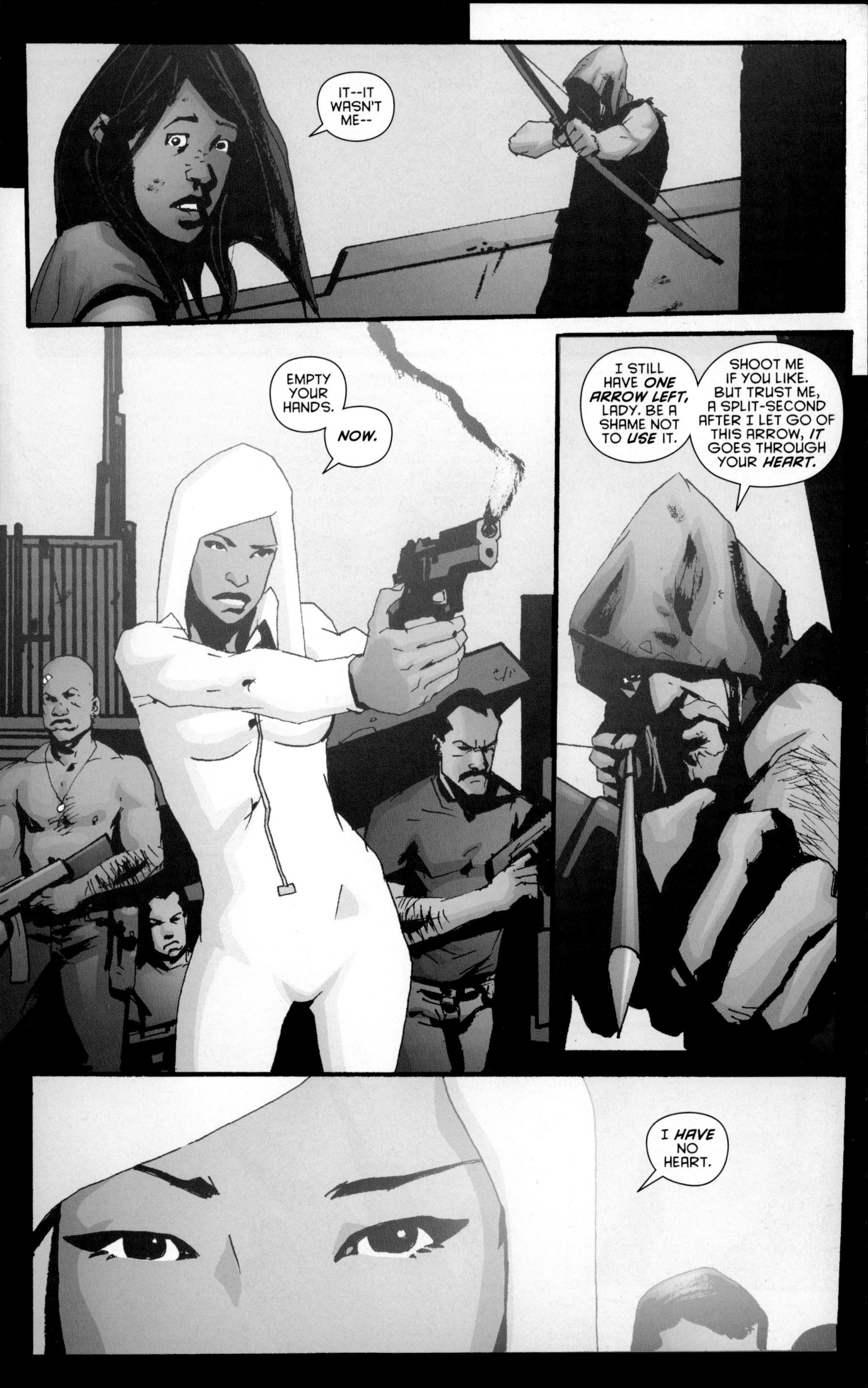
IT--IT WASN'T ME--
EMPTY YOUR HANDS.
NOW.
I STILL HAVE ONE ARROW LEFT, LADY. BE A SHAME NOT TO USE IT.
SHOOT ME IF YOU LIKE. BUT TRUST ME, A SPLIT-SECOND AFTER I LET GO OF THIS ARROW, IT GOES THROUGH YOUR HEART.
I HAVE NO HEART.

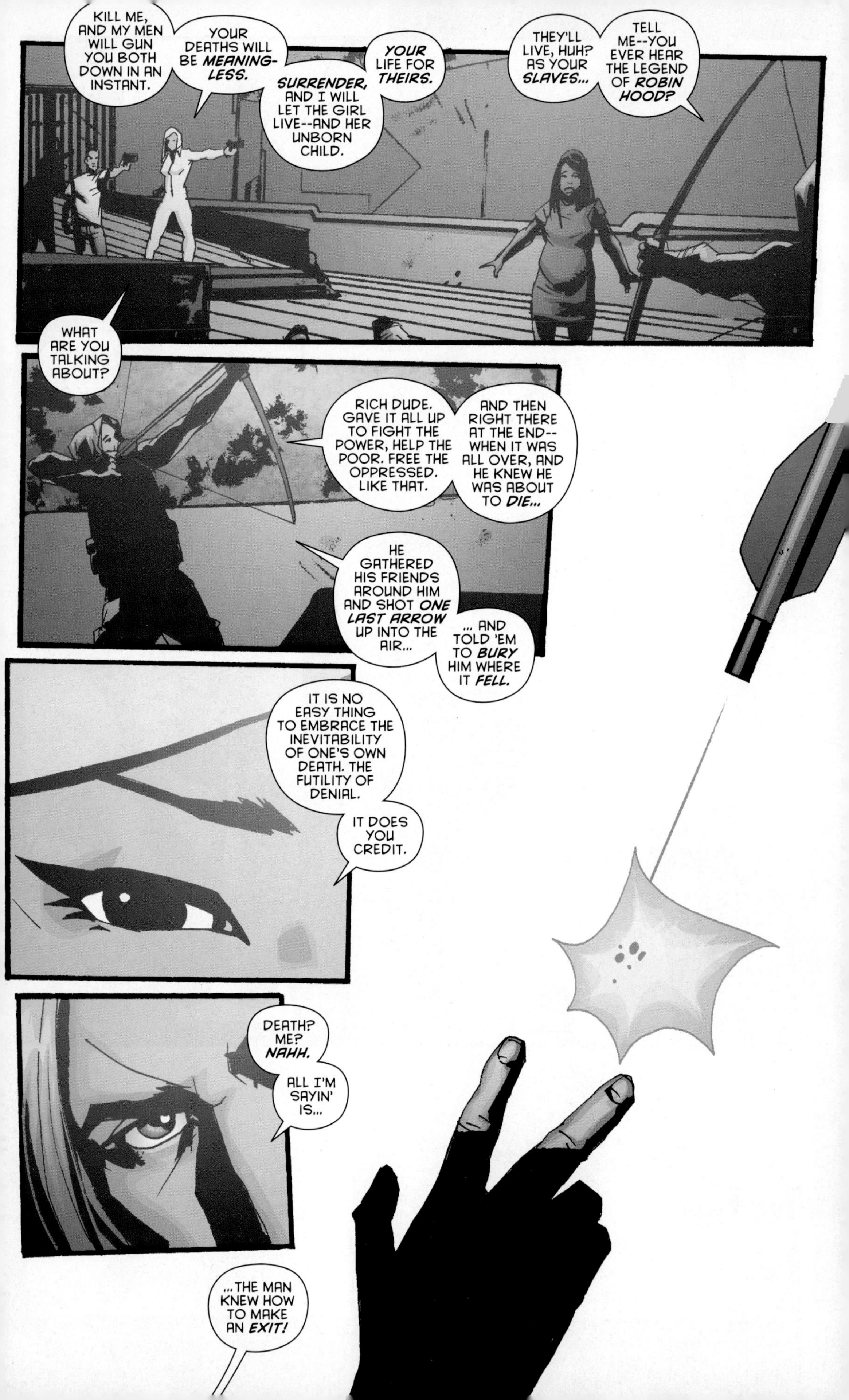
KILL ME, AND MY MEN WILL GUN YOU BOTH DOWN IN AN INSTANT.
YOUR DEATHS WILL BE MEANING-LESS.
SURRENDER, AND I WILL LET THE GIRL LIVE--AND HER UNBORN CHILD.
YOUR LIFE FOR THEIRS.
THEY'LL LIVE, HUH? AS YOUR SLAVES...
TELL ME--YOU EVER HEAR THE LEGEND OF ROBIN HOOD?
WHAT ARE YOU TALKING ABOUT?
RICH DUDE. GAVE IT ALL UP TO FIGHT THE POWER, HELP THE POOR. FREE THE OPPRESSED. LIKE THAT.
AND THEN RIGHT THERE AT THE END--WHEN IT WAS ALL OVER, AND HE KNEW HE WAS ABOUT TO DIE...
HE GATHERED HIS FRIENDS AROUND HIM AND SHOT ONE LAST ARROW UP INTO THE AIR...
... AND TOLD 'EM TO BURY HIM WHERE IT FELL.
IT IS NO EASY THING TO EMBRACE THE INEVITABILITY OF ONE'S OWN DEATH. THE FUTILITY OF DENIAL.
IT DOES YOU CREDIT.
DEATH? ME? NAHH.
ALL I'M SAYIN' IS...
...THE MAN KNEW HOW TO MAKE AN EXIT!

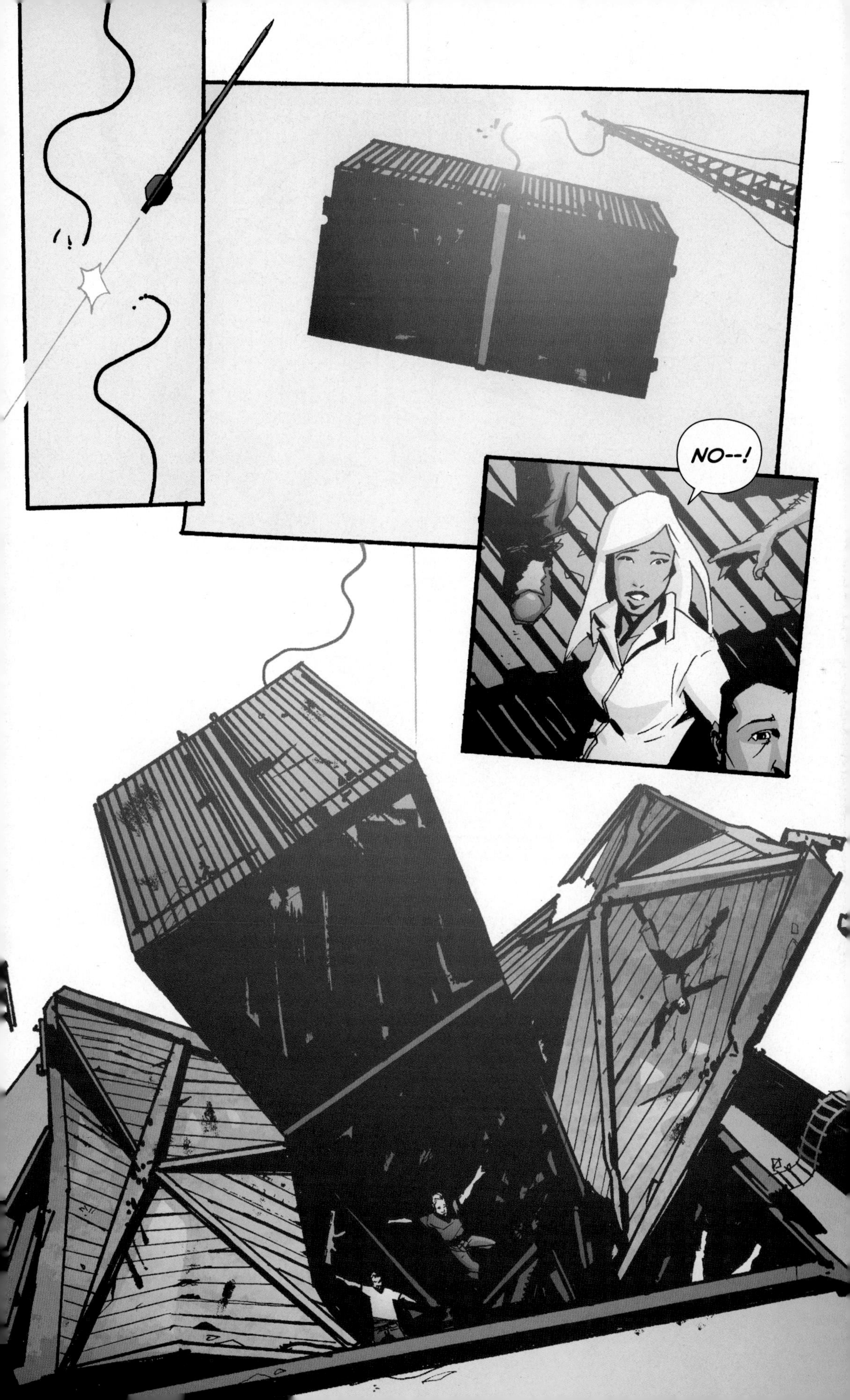
NO--!

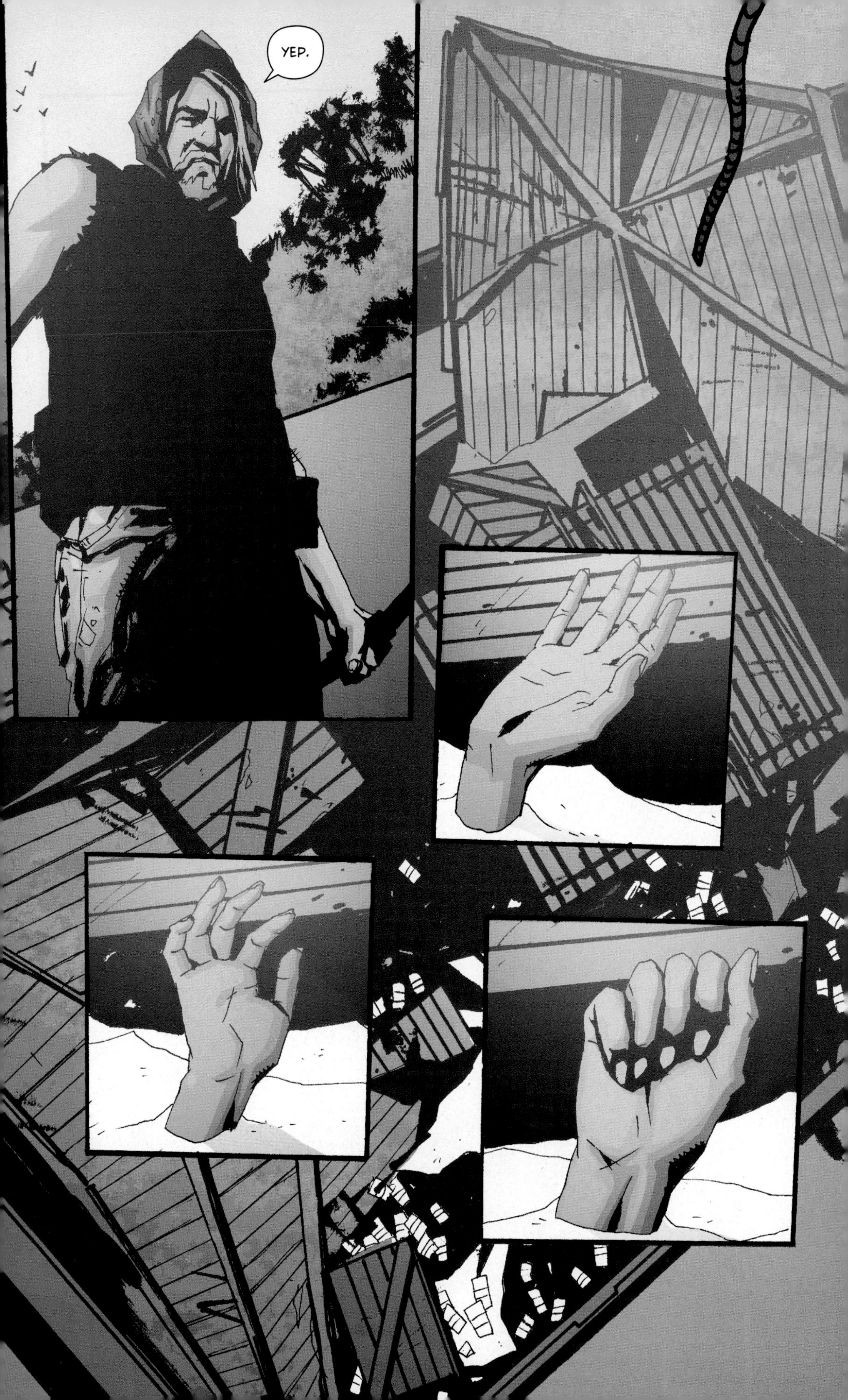
YEP.

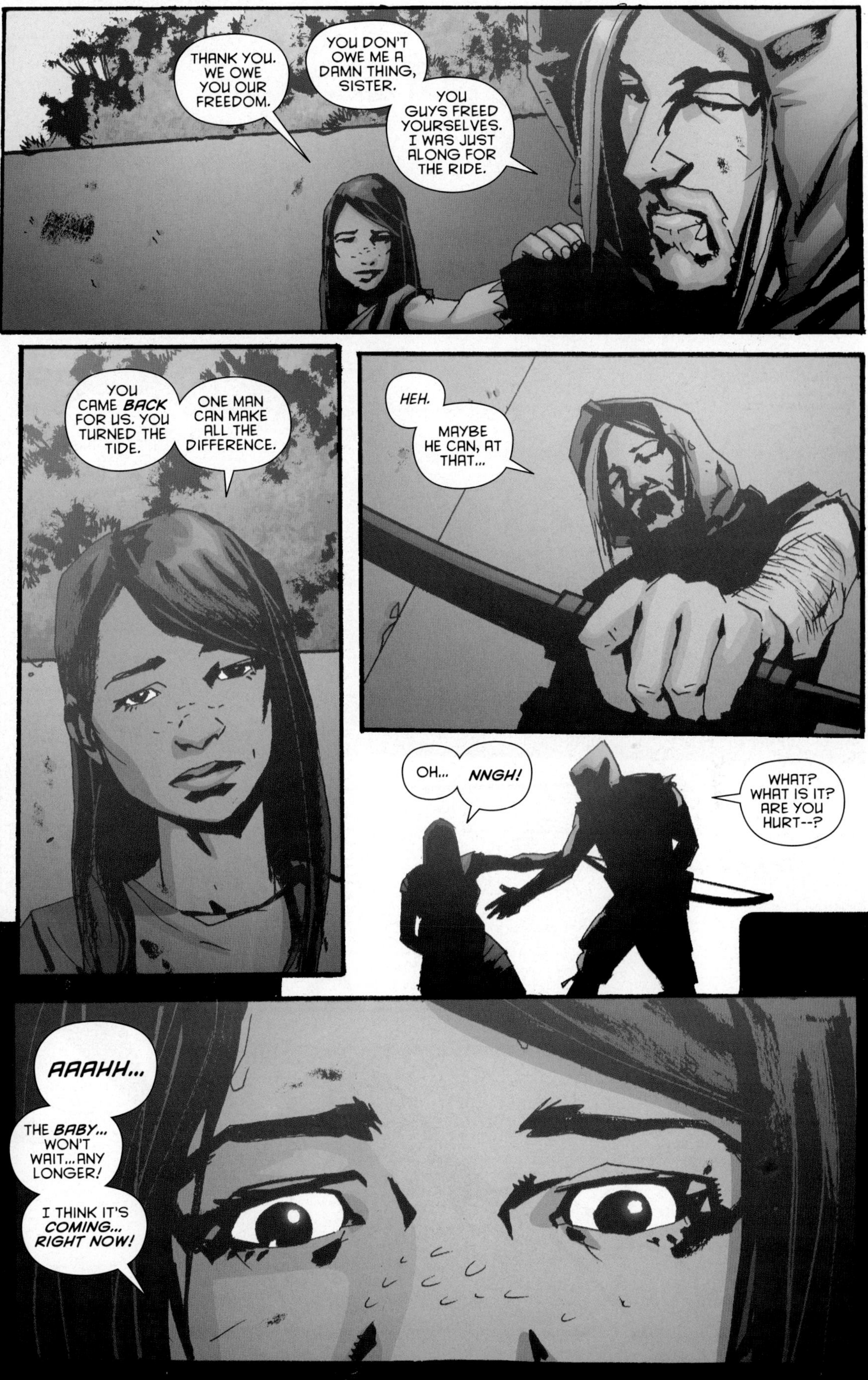
THANK YOU. WE OWE YOU OUR FREEDOM.
YOU DON'T OWE ME A DAMN THING, SISTER.
YOU GUYS FREED YOURSELVES. I WAS JUST ALONG FOR THE RIDE.
YOU CAME *BACK* FOR US. YOU TURNED THE TIDE.
ONE MAN CAN MAKE ALL THE DIFFERENCE.
HEH.
MAYBE HE CAN, AT THAT...
OH... *NNGH!*
WHAT? WHAT IS IT? ARE YOU HURT--?
AAAHH...
THE *BABY...* WON'T WAIT...ANY LONGER!
I THINK IT'S *COMING... RIGHT NOW!*

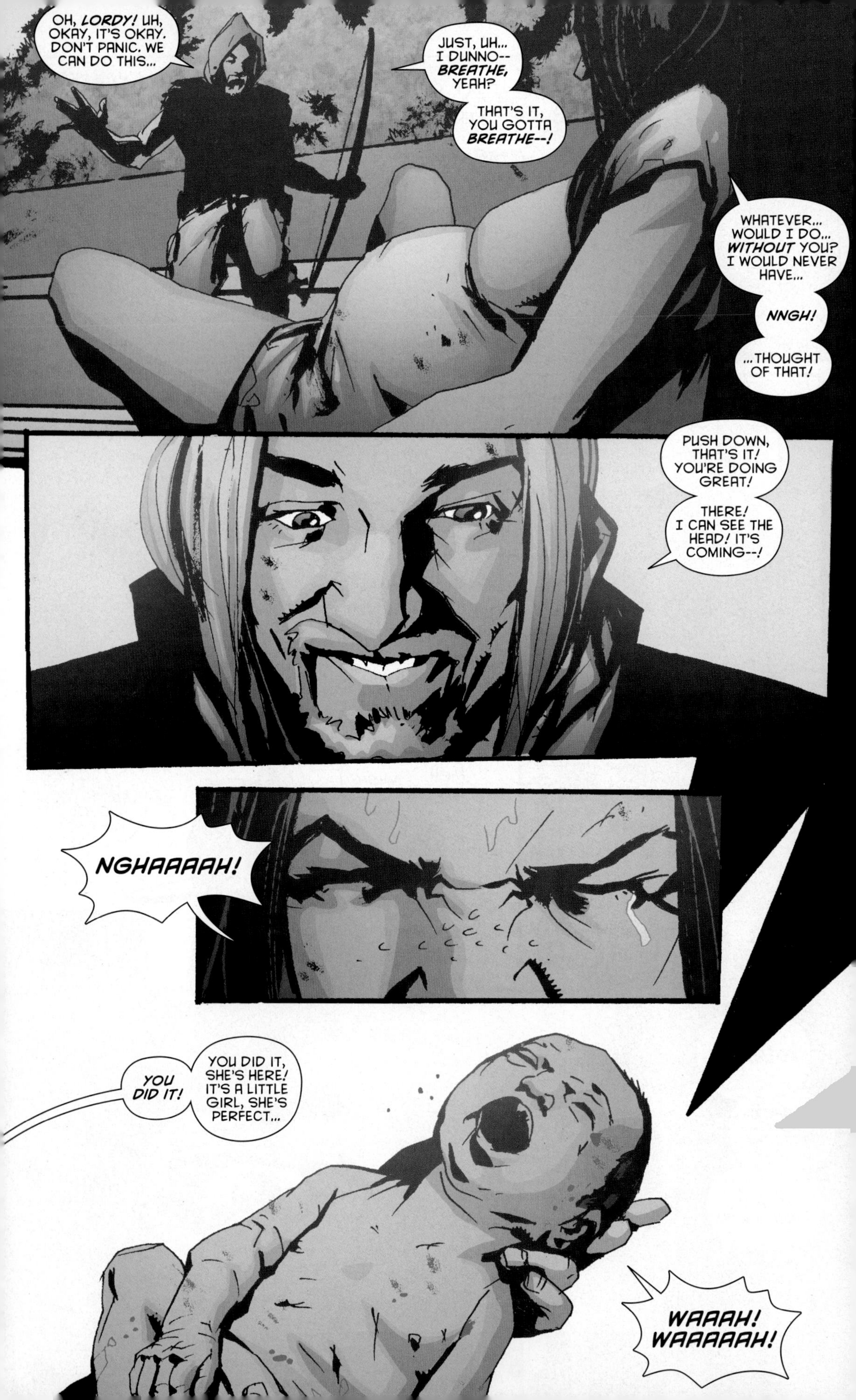
OH, LORDY! UH, OKAY, IT'S OKAY. DON'T PANIC. WE CAN DO THIS...
JUST, UH... I DUNNO-- BREATHE, YEAH?
THAT'S IT, YOU GOTTA BREATHE--!
WHATEVER... WOULD I DO... WITHOUT YOU? I WOULD NEVER HAVE...
NNGH!
...THOUGHT OF THAT!
PUSH DOWN, THAT'S IT! YOU'RE DOING GREAT!
THERE! I CAN SEE THE HEAD! IT'S COMING--!
NGHAAAAH!
YOU DID IT!
YOU DID IT, SHE'S HERE! IT'S A LITTLE GIRL, SHE'S PERFECT...
WAAAH! WAAAAAH!

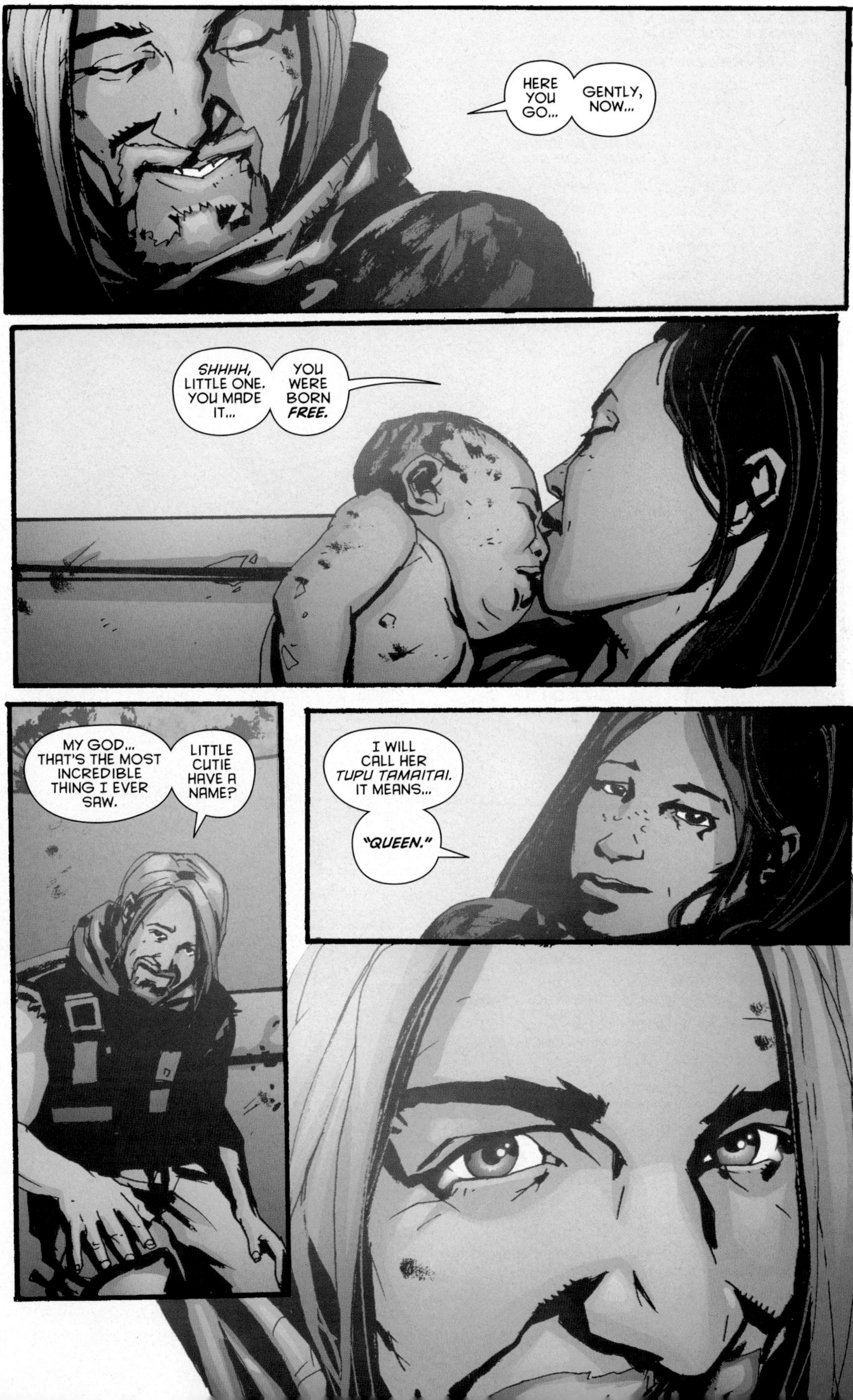
HERE YOU GO...
GENTLY, NOW...
SHHHH, LITTLE ONE. YOU MADE IT...
YOU WERE BORN *FREE.*
MY GOD... THAT'S THE MOST INCREDIBLE THING I EVER SAW.
LITTLE CUTIE HAVE A NAME?
I WILL CALL HER *TUPU TAMAITAI.* IT MEANS...
"QUEEN."

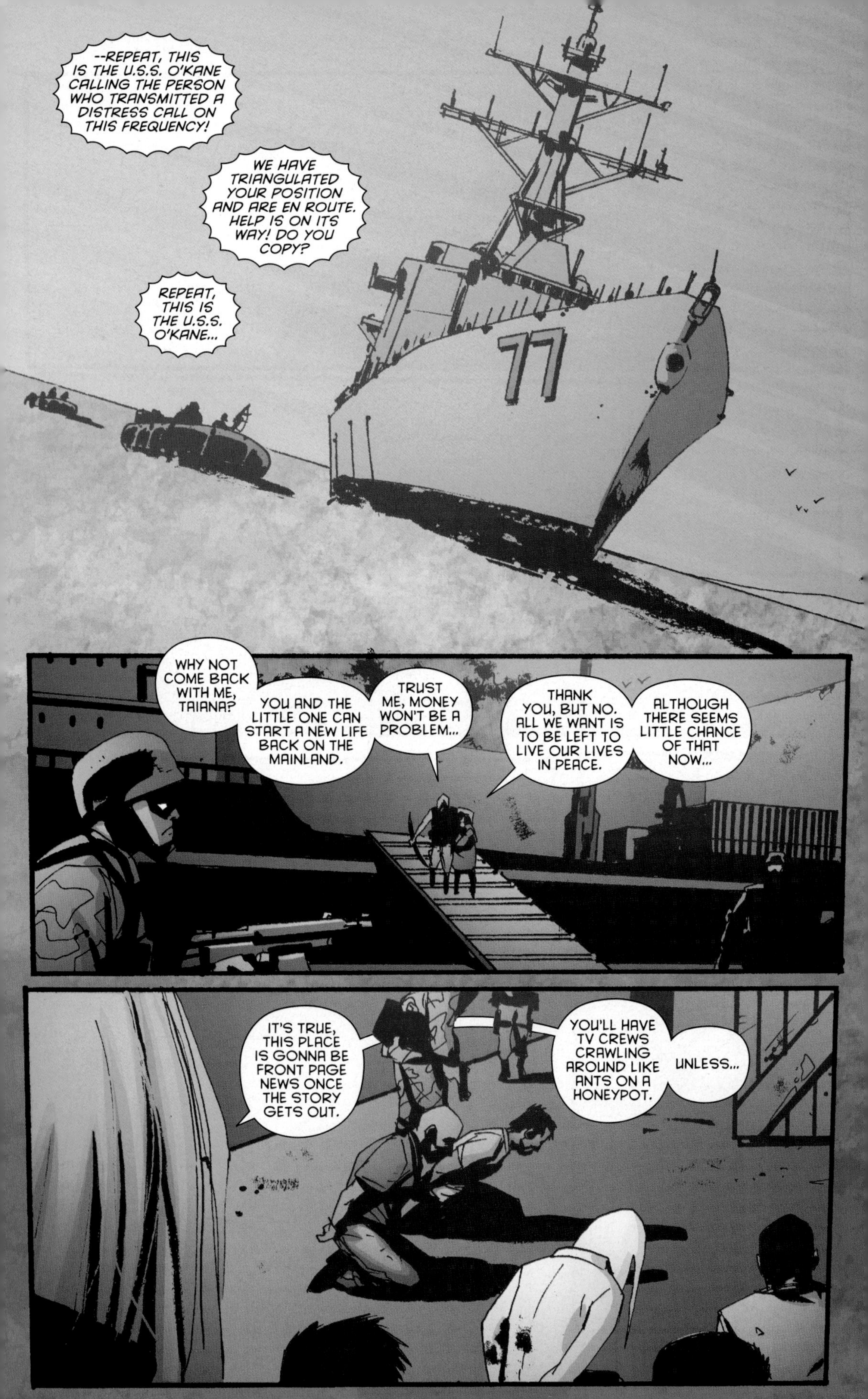
--REPEAT, THIS IS THE U.S.S. O'KANE CALLING THE PERSON WHO TRANSMITTED A DISTRESS CALL ON THIS FREQUENCY!
WE HAVE TRIANGULATED YOUR POSITION AND ARE EN ROUTE. HELP IS ON ITS WAY! DO YOU COPY?
REPEAT, THIS IS THE U.S.S. O'KANE...
77
WHY NOT COME BACK WITH ME, TAIANA?
YOU AND THE LITTLE ONE CAN START A NEW LIFE BACK ON THE MAINLAND.
TRUST ME, MONEY WON'T BE A PROBLEM...
THANK YOU, BUT NO. ALL WE WANT IS TO BE LEFT TO LIVE OUR LIVES IN PEACE.
ALTHOUGH THERE SEEMS LITTLE CHANCE OF THAT NOW...
IT'S TRUE, THIS PLACE IS GONNA BE FRONT PAGE NEWS ONCE THE STORY GETS OUT.
YOU'LL HAVE TV CREWS CRAWLING AROUND LIKE ANTS ON A HONEYPOT.
UNLESS...

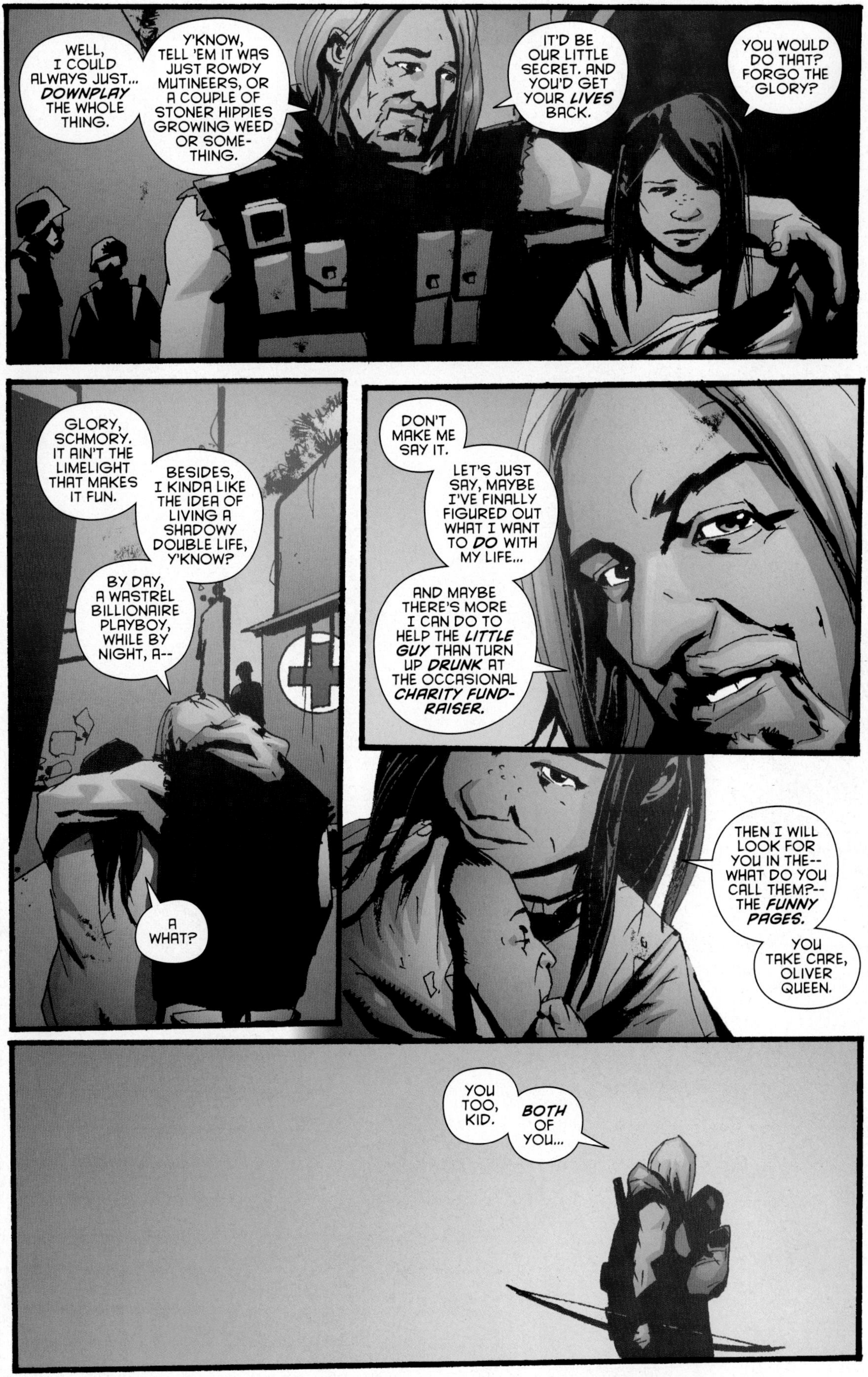
WELL, I COULD ALWAYS JUST... DOWNPLAY THE WHOLE THING.
Y'KNOW, TELL 'EM IT WAS JUST ROWDY MUTINEERS, OR A COUPLE OF STONER HIPPIES GROWING WEED OR SOME-THING.
IT'D BE OUR LITTLE SECRET. AND YOU'D GET YOUR LIVES BACK.
YOU WOULD DO THAT? FORGO THE GLORY?
GLORY, SCHMORY. IT AIN'T THE LIMELIGHT THAT MAKES IT FUN.
BESIDES, I KINDA LIKE THE IDEA OF LIVING A SHADOWY DOUBLE LIFE, Y'KNOW?
BY DAY, A WASTREL BILLIONAIRE PLAYBOY, WHILE BY NIGHT, A--
DON'T MAKE ME SAY IT.
LET'S JUST SAY, MAYBE I'VE FINALLY FIGURED OUT WHAT I WANT TO DO WITH MY LIFE...
AND MAYBE THERE'S MORE I CAN DO TO HELP THE LITTLE GUY THAN TURN UP DRUNK AT THE OCCASIONAL CHARITY FUND-RAISER.
A WHAT?
THEN I WILL LOOK FOR YOU IN THE--WHAT DO YOU CALL THEM?--THE FUNNY PAGES.
YOU TAKE CARE, OLIVER QUEEN.
YOU TOO, KID.
BOTH OF YOU...

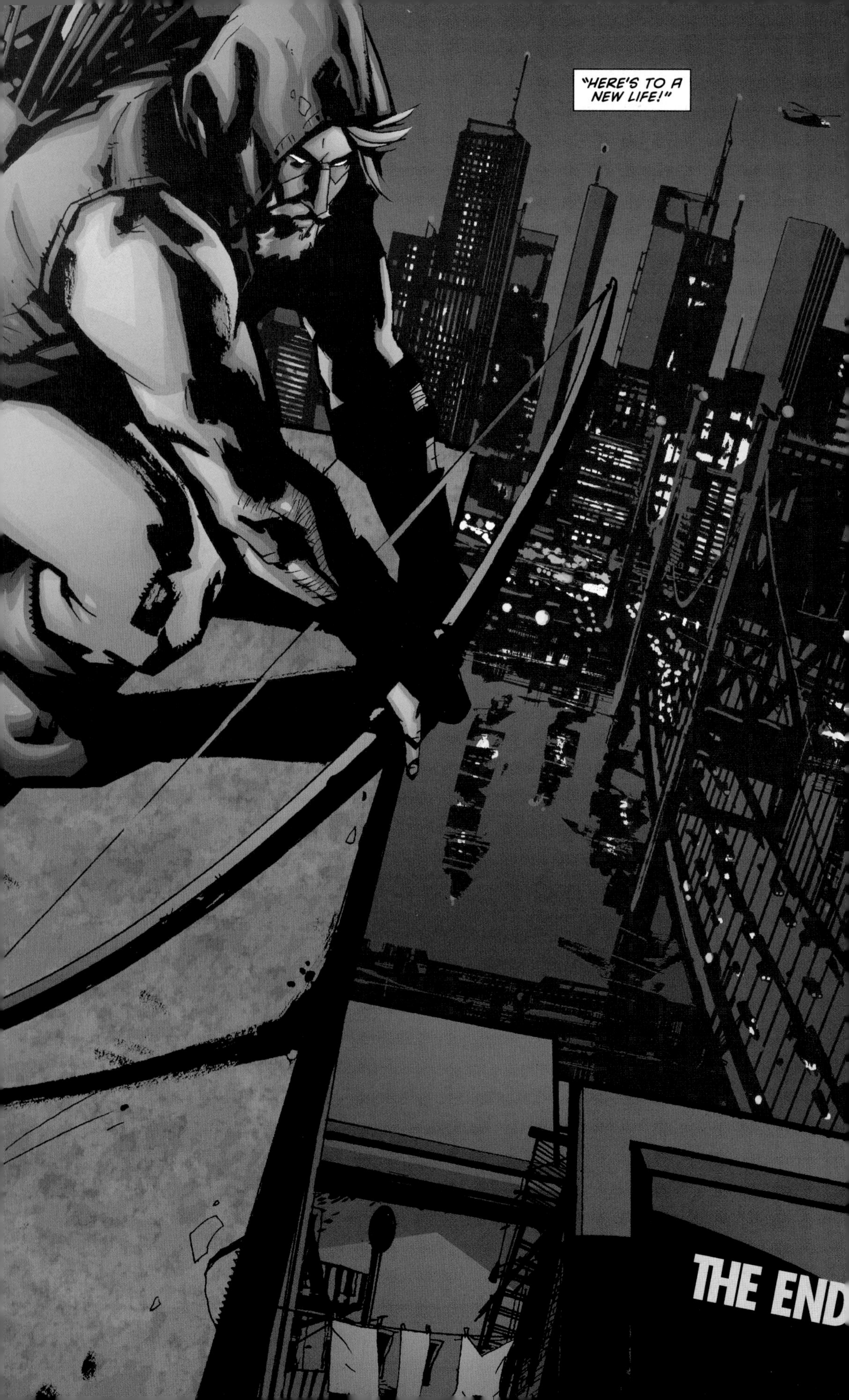
"HERE'S TO A NEW LIFE!"
THE END

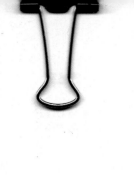

GREEN ARROW: YEAR ONE

Part 1 of 6

by

Andy Diggle

First Draft

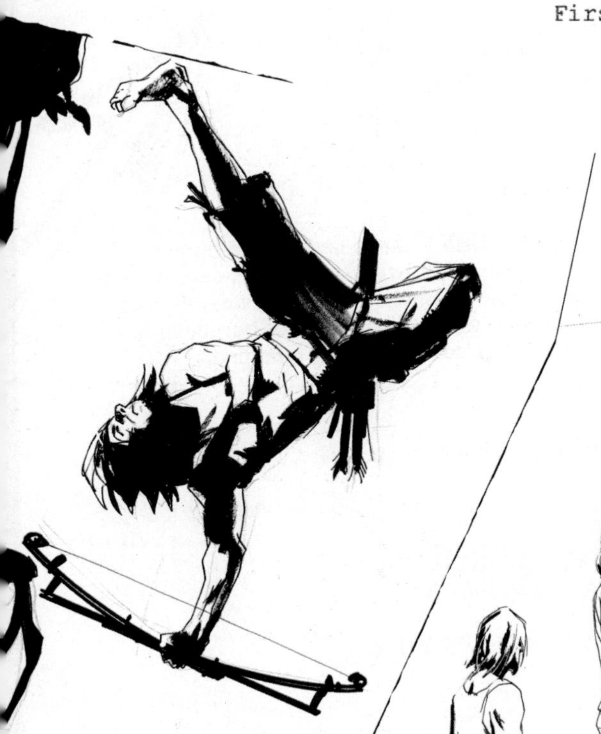

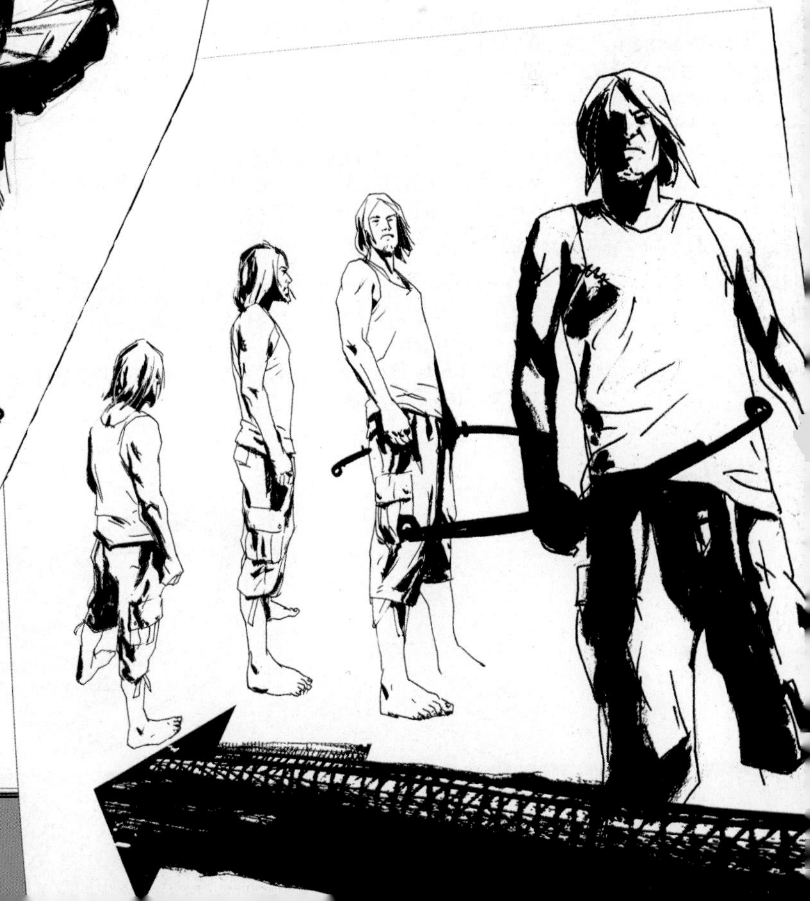

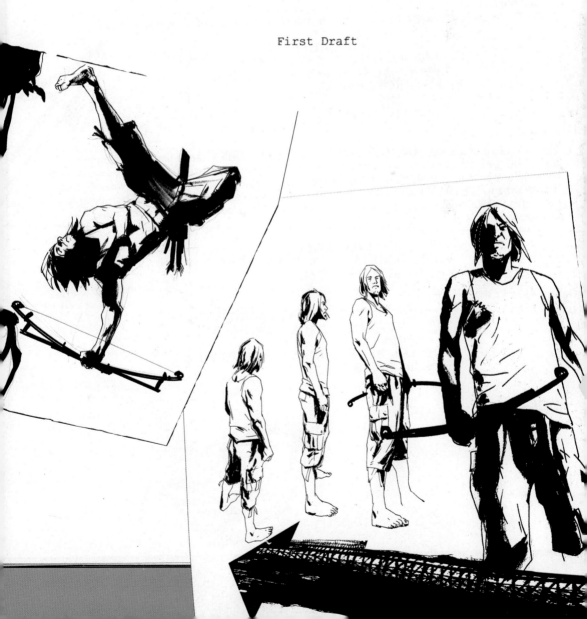

PAGE 1

This opening sequence should be dominated by bland, desaturated color in an ocean of WHITE. We start with a series of FULL-WIDTH PANELS, slowly pulling back in a smooth, continuous reverse-zoom:

1) A blank, featureless WHITE space...

2) Pull back to reveal the tip of a GREEN ARROW tilting into the panel, floating on the blank white space...

3) Pull back to reveal that the green arrow is actually the luminous tip of a COMPASS NEEDLE in massive close-up. The big capital N sits a skewed angle near the top of the panel, with degree-lines radiating around the outer edge of the compass face...

4) Pull back to reveal the compass is held in a thickly-gloved hand. The needle has moved around the face, *never settling*. *The compass is held* by a MAN (HACKETT) bundled up in heavy Arctic gear, his back to us, his features hidden by the hood of his massive parka.

> **HACKETT**
> NEEDLE DOESN'T KNOW WHICH WAY TO
> *POINT. WE'RE ALMOST ON TOP OF IT* -
> MAGNETIC NORTH.
> (link)
> UNFORTUNATELY...

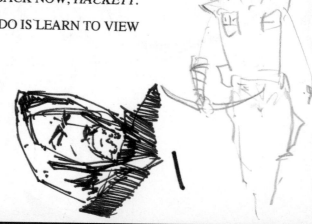

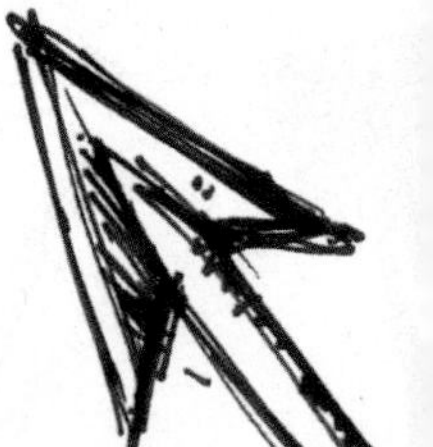

5) Pull back to reveal that ANOTHER MAN (OLIVER QUEEN) stands next to him on panel right. Both men dressed in heavy Arctic gear, peppered gray-white with snow. Pale, desaturated colors. They both have their backs to us, the compass visible in Hackett's hand as we pull back between them. We're still too close in on the two of them to get any real sense of our location - nothing is visible around them except blank white space. The composition is cramped, claustrophobic...

> **HACKETT**
> ... IT LOOKS LIKE THIS IS ABOUT AS CLOSE
> AS WE'RE GOING TO GET.

> **OLLIE**
> I DIDN'T TREK THREE DAYS ACROSS THE
> *ICE JUST TO TURN BACK NOW, HACKETT.*
> (link)
> ALL YOU HAVE TO DO IS LEARN TO VIEW
> AN OBSTACLE...

PAGE 2

FULL-PAGE SPLASH! Now we pull way, WAY back, high and wide, to reveal Hackett and Ollie as two tiny figures dwarfed by the blank immensity of the Arctic wasteland - and slashing across the featureless white desert right in front of them is a 30-foot wide CREVASSE! A yawning, bottomless gulf, stretching as fast as the eye can see in either direction, too long to walk around and too wide to jump across. This is the end of the road... except there's a narrow ice bridge across the middle of the crevasse, barely thick enough to walk on. The flat, featureless white desert stretches to the horizon in every direction, utterly devoid of color or features of any kind, beneath a dull gray sky. Hackett has been hauling a lightweight sled with their camping equipment. Twin rows of footprints lead up to them, tracking across the featureless snow...

OLLIE
... AS A *CHALLENGE*.

TITLE AND CREDITS
GREEN ARROW: YEAR ONE (CHAPTER 1)

<u>NOTE TO LETTERER</u>: Please try to keep the title and credits as unobtrusive as possible, so as not to detract too much from the "blank whiteness" of this image. The main title could be white on white, with just a thin gray outline to pick it out against the snow.

<u>PAGE 3</u>

1) Low angle, view from down in the crevasse looking up at the ice bridge as Ollie strides fearlessly out onto it, linked to Hackett by a red safety line. Hackett stands back on the solid ice, gesturing to Ollie to stop --

OLLIE
COME ON! LAST ONE ACROSS BUYS THE DRINKS!

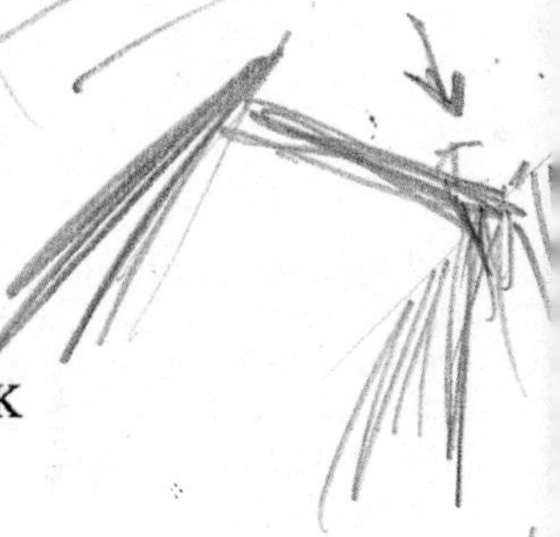

HACKETT
WAIT, YOU'VE GOTTA BE--
(link)
OLLIE, NO! THE ICE BRIDGE DOESN'T LOOK STRONG ENOUGH TO--

2) The ice-bridge suddenly CRACKS beneath Ollie's boots --

3) Hackett GRABS Ollie by the shoulders and YANKS him back to safety, even as the ice bridge COLLAPSES down into the chasm in front of them --

4) High angle, looking down on the two men as they lie flat on their backs, staring up at the sky, panting with exhaustion. Split this panel into two if you like.

HACKETT
YOU STUPID, RECKLESS, IRRESPONSIBLE --

OLLIE

... RICH EMPLOYER WHO KEEPS YOU IN THE
LIFESTYLE TO WHICH YOU WOULD LIKE TO
BECOME ACCUSTOMED?

PAGE 4

1) Hackett sits up in the snow and pulls off his goggles, his snow-crusted face-scarf already
pulled down around his neck. There's a Union Jack name-patch saying "HACKETT" sewn onto
his parka, over his heart. He's a tough-looking British ex-soldier, his hair shaved back to a
stubble to hide his receding hairline. He's rugged and professional, but easygoing, enjoys a good
laugh, smiles easily - although right now he's pissed off. Picture JASON STATHAM.

> **HACKETT**
> SO YOU PAY ME TO TAKE YOU TO
> *EXTREMES - BUT YOU ALSO PAY ME TO*
> KEEP YOU *ALIVE*, OLLIE.
> (link)
> I MEAN, WHAT'S THE MATTER WITH YOU?
> LIFE MIGHT NOT MEAN MUCH TO YOU, BUT
> IT DOES TO ME!

2) Hackett scowls down at the COMPASS held in his hand. Wistful, as if the compass somehow
symbolizes all his life's regrets...

> **HACKETT**
> IN THE PAST SIX MONTHS YOU'VE PULLED
> BARREL ROLLS IN A STEALTH FIGHTER,
> BASE-JUMPED THE GRAND CANYON, DIVED
> THE TITANIC AND BAGGED MORE
> SUPERMODELS THAN HELMUT NEWTON...
> (link)
> YOU'VE GOT ENOUGH MONEY TO DO
> *WHATEVER YOU WANT WITH YOUR LIFE* -
> BUT INSTEAD YOU'RE JUST SPINNING
> AROUND, LOOKING FOR A DIRECTION...

3) Close on Hackett's gloved hand as he gently jabs a finger into Ollie's chest. There's an
American flag name-patch saying "QUEEN" sewn over the heart of Ollie's parka. Ollie is pulling
back his hood, but his face and eyes are still hidden by his goggles and scarf.

> **HACKETT**
> (off-panel above)
> THERE'S SOMETHING MISSING IN YOU,
> OLLIE. AND UNTIL YOU FIGURE OUT WHAT
> IT IS, NOTHING --
> (link)
> THE BOOZE, THE WOMEN, ALL OF THIS
> POINTLESS ADRENALINE-JUNKIE CRAP...
> (link)

-- NONE OF IT'S NEVER GOING TO BE
ENOUGH TO FILL THE HOLE.

4) EXTREME *CLOSE* on *Oliver Queen* as he pushes his snow goggles up onto his forehead, his brilliant GREEN eyes making direct eye-contact with the reader for the first time. In fact, these striking green eyes are the only green we've seen since the compass needle on page 1. Ollie is in his early 20s and doesn't yet have the trademark goatee beard - although he is sporting a three day stubble. He's a spoilt, thrill-seeking rich kid, looking for something to fill the pointless emptiness of his extravagant playboy lifestyle. He GRINS mischievously.

OLLIE
WOW, THAT'S TOTALLY ZEN. "WHEREVER
YOU GO, THERE YOU ARE..."
(link)
THEY TEACH YOU THAT STUFF IN THE
ROYAL MARINES?

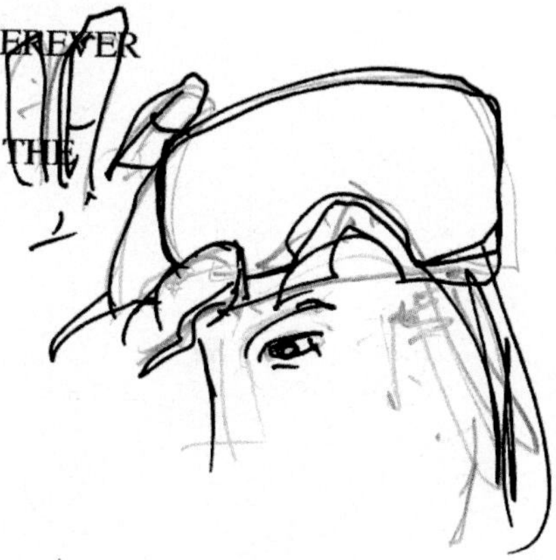

PAGE 5

Another page of full-width panels, pulling back and away.

1) Hackett grins right back at us, his anger passed now.

HACKETT
NAH. MOSTLY THEY TRIED TO TEACH ME
TO TAKE ORDERS. DIDN'T WORK OUT.
(link)
THAT'S ALRIGHT. THIS PAYS BETTER.

2) Pull back wider. Ollie slumps down onto his ass in the snow beside Hackett, rubbing a snowy hand through *his own hair, tousling it like a carefree* child. *Friends again.*

OLLIE
PLUS, Y'KNOW. SUPERMODELS.

HACKETT
THERE'S THAT.
(link)
SO NOW WHAT? IT'S A THREE-DAY TREK
BACK TO THE ICEBREAKER...

3) Pull back wider. Ollie offers Hackett a metal hip-flask, the hinged lid unscrewed and hanging open...

OLLIE
HELL WITH THAT. I'VE HAD MY NEAR-
DEATH EXPERIENCE FOR THE WEEK, I'M
CALLING IN THE CHOPPER.

HACKETT
LIGHTWEIGHT. I THOUGHT WE WERE
SUPPOSED TO BE KEEPING IT REAL... ?

4) Pull back wider, leaving the two of them dwarfed by the immensity of the snow desert. Most of the panel is a featureless white blank...

OLLIE
REAL'S JUST FOR PEOPLE WHO CAN'T
AFFORD TO FAKE IT.

5) Fade to white.

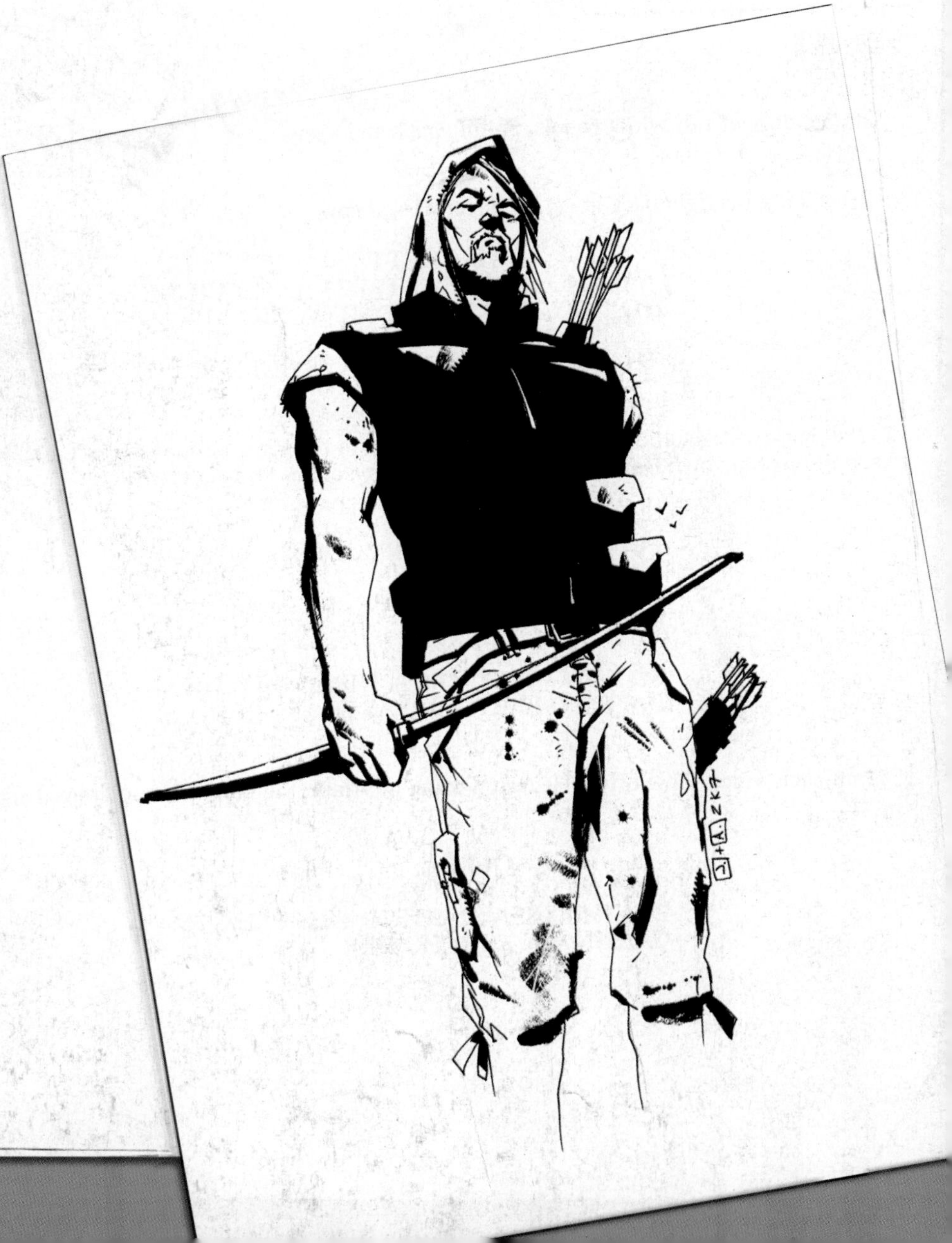

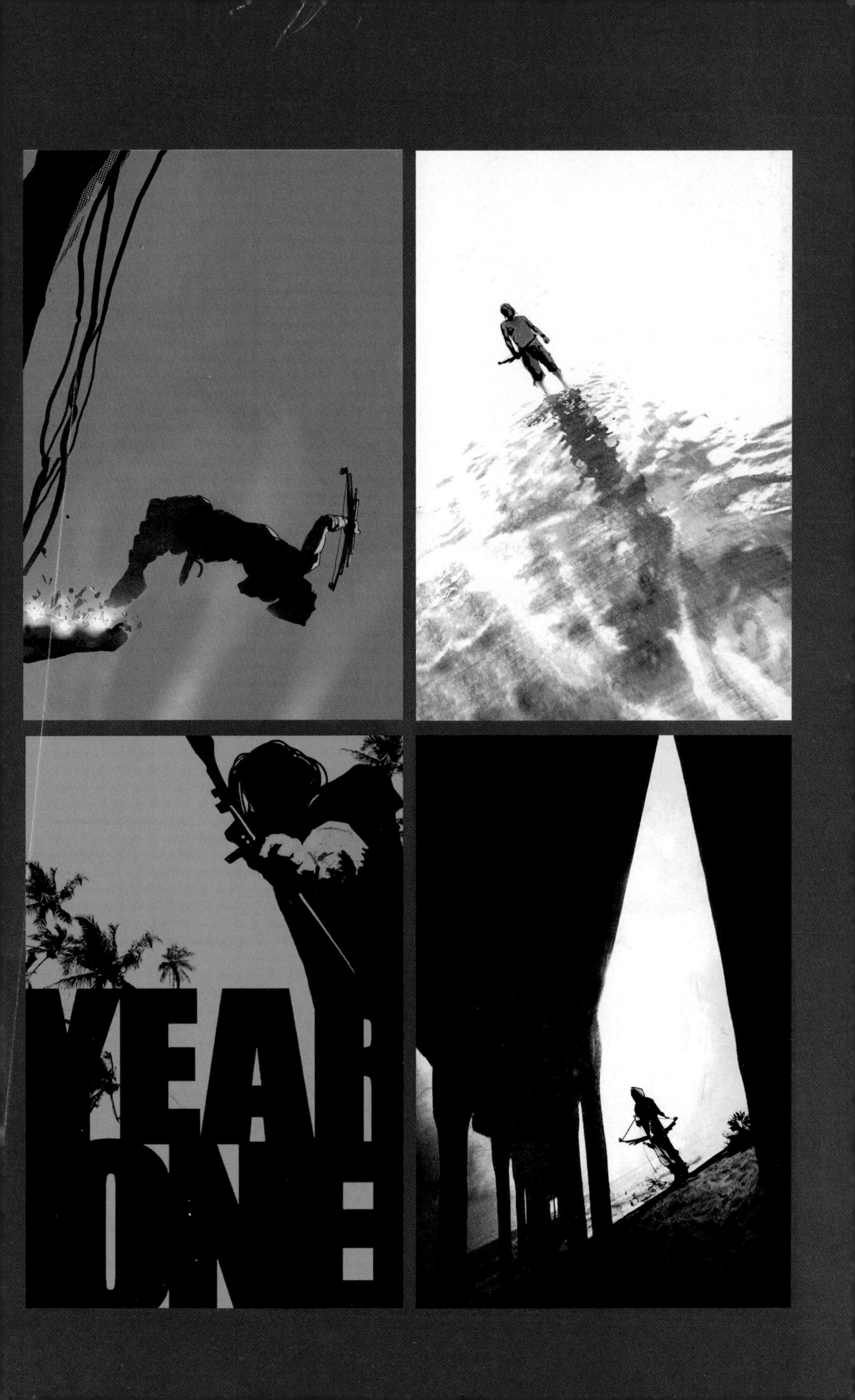
YEAR ONE:

SMALLER
GREEN ARROW
PUT EXTRA PANEL HERE
LARGER
SMALLER
QUEEN

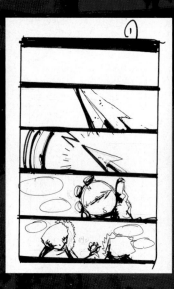

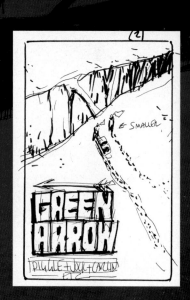